AN INTRODUCTION TO THE THEORY OF GROUPS OF FINITE ORDER

BY

HAROLD HILTON, M.A.

LECTURER IN MATHEMATICS AT BEDFORD COLLEGE
FORMERLY FELLOW OF MAGDALEN COLLEGE, OXFORD
AND ASSISTANT MATHEMATICAL LECTURER AT
THE UNIVERSITY COLLEGE, BANGOR

OXFORD
AT THE CLARENDON PRESS
1908

This scarce antiquarian book is included in our special *Legacy Reprint Series*. In the interest of creating a more extensive selection of rare historical book reprints, we have chosen to reproduce this title even though it may possibly have occasional imperfections such as missing and blurred pages, missing text, poor pictures, markings, dark backgrounds and other reproduction issues beyond our control. Because this work is culturally important, we have made it available as a part of our commitment to protecting, preserving and promoting the world's literature.

PREFACE

THIS book aims at introducing the reader to more advanced treatises and original papers on Groups of finite order. The subject requires for its study only an elementary knowledge of Algebra (especially Theory of Numbers), but the average student may nevertheless find the many excellent existing treatises rather stiff reading. I have tried to lighten for him the initial difficulties, and to show that even the most recent developments of pure Mathematics are not necessarily beyond the reach of the ordinary mathematical reader.

I have omitted as far as possible lengthy and difficult investigations; their place is taken by an unusually numerous selection of examples. Students who have had no previous acquaintance with the subject should work a few of these examples after reading each section. Many of them can be solved at sight, and are inserted merely to make the reader familiar with the definitions and theorems of the text. Hints for the solution of the rest will be found at the end of the book.

In an elementary treatise references would be out

of place; for complete lists the reader may consult Easton's *Constructive Development of Group-Theory* (Philadelphia University, 1902), and Miller's 'Reports on Group-Theory' in *Bulletin Amer. Math. Soc.*, v (1899), p. 227; vii (1900), p. 121; ix (1902), p. 106; xiv (1907), pp. 78, 124.

I have derived much help from Burnside's *Theory of Groups* (Cambridge Univ. Press, 1897), Weber's *Algebra* (Vieweg und Sohn, 1898), Séguier's *Groupes Abstraits* (Gauthier-Villars, 1904), Bianchi's *Gruppi di Sostituzioni* (Spoerri, 1900), Dickson's *Linear Groups* (Teubner, 1901), &c.: to these treatises I hope to introduce the reader. In addition I have consulted a very large number of papers in *Proc. London Math. Soc., Berliner Sitzungsberichte, Bulletin Amer. Math. Soc., Amer. Journal Math., Math. Annalen, Crelle's Journal, Messenger of Math.*, and other periodicals. Most of the examples are taken from these books and papers, but I have added others of my own when I could not otherwise find a suitable illustration of any theorem.

The theory of Group-characteristics seemed to be too advanced for an introductory treatise, but I have devoted one short chapter to the subject to assist the reader in understanding Frobenius' and Burnside's recent contributions to group-theory.

I have omitted the theory of Algebraic equations; partly from considerations of space, and partly because the necessary information is already accessible to English readers, e.g. in Dickson's *Theory of Algebraic Equations* (Chapman, 1903) and in Mathews' *Alge-*

braic Equations (Cambridge Math. Tracts, No. 6, 1907).

The nomenclature of the subject is by no means settled. I have tried to select definitions which have the advantage of being either self-explanatory (e.g. 'greatest common subgroup') or concise ('normal'); but the task was not at all easy.

I have treated the pure group-theory with greater thoroughness than the applications. The aim of chapters II, III, IV, VI, VII, VIII is to stimulate interest, rather than to give a complete or rigid investigation of the subjects there dealt with. On a first reading the student may omit, if he chooses, chapters III, IV, VII, VIII, XIV, XV, and the last section of Chapter V.

The following conventions are adopted:—(1) p denotes a positive *prime* integer throughout; (2) a reference such as V 10 means 'the tenth section of the fifth chapter', while V 10_3 means 'the third example in the tenth section of the fifth chapter'.

Lastly, it is my pleasant duty to express my warmest thanks to three mathematicians who have given me most valuable assistance. Prof. E. B. Elliott, F.R.S., at whose suggestion the book was undertaken, kindly read through the MS. of the earlier chapters and indicated several improvements; Mr. J. E. Campbell, F.R.S., generously devoted much time to the reading of the proofs, and pointed out many obscurities; Prof. W. Burnside, F.R.S., kindly helped me throughout with much useful advice on questions of nomenclature, &c., and has supplied me with material for the Appendix. My best thanks are also due to the Delegates of the Oxford University Press for undertaking the publication of the book, and to the staff of the Press for the care and skill with which the printing has been done.

H. H.

April, 1908.

CONTENTS

CHAPTER I
ELEMENTS

	PAGE
§ 1. Definition of an element	1
2. Order of an element	2
3. Transforms	3
4. Commutators	4

CHAPTER II
PERMUTATIONS

§ 1. Definition of a permutation	6
2. Circular permutations	7
3. Cycles	7
4. Order of a permutation	9
5. Transform of a permutation	9
6. Product of transpositions	10

CHAPTER III
SUBSTITUTIONS

§ 1, 2. Definition of a substitution	12
3. Transform of a substitution	14
4. Homogeneous linear substitutions	15
5. Hermitian forms	18
6. Poles and characteristic equations	20
7. Multiplications and similarity-substitutions	23
8. Substitutions of finite order	24
9. Fractional linear substitutions	26
10. Galois Fields	28
11. Primitive roots of a Field	31

CHAPTER IV

GEOMETRICAL ELEMENTS

		PAGE
§ 1.	Definition of a geometrical movement	33
2.	Euler's construction	35
3, 4.	Rotatory-inversions	37
5.	Screws	38
6.	Congruence and enantiomorphy	39
7.	Movements considered as elements	39
8.	Geometrical representations of movements	40
9.	Transform of a movement	41
10.	Symmetry	42
11.	Successive inversions	43
12.	Collineations	44
13.	Collineations of order two	46

CHAPTER V

GROUPS

§ 1.	Groups and semi-groups	51
2.	Sets of elements	54
3.	Generators	55
4.	Subgroups	57
5.	Cyclic groups	60
6.	Conjugate elements and subgroups	60
7.	Normal elements and subgroups	62
8.	Normaliser of an element	64
9.	Normaliser of a subgroup	65
10, 11, 12.	Greatest common subgroup	66
13.	Permutable groups	67
14.	Subgroup whose order is prime to its index	68
15.	Direct product	69
16.	Isomorphic groups	70
17, 18.	Factor-groups	72
19, 20.	Abelian groups	75
21.	Frobenius' theorem	75

CONTENTS

CHAPTER VI

PERMUTATION-GROUPS

		PAGE
§ 1.	Alternating and symmetric groups	79
2, 3.	Permutation-group isomorphic with a given group	81
4.	Cayley's colour-groups	85
5, 6.	Transitive groups	90
7, 8.	Intransitive groups	91
9.	Primitive and imprimitive groups	93
10, 11.	Normal subgroups of transitive groups	94
12.	Groups containing a transposition	95
13.	Groups containing all circular permutations of degree r	96
14.	The alternating group is simple	96
15.	Normal subgroups of the symmetric group	97

CHAPTER VII

SUBSTITUTION-GROUPS

§ 1.	Definition of a substitution-group	98
2.	Transform of a substitution-group	98
3.	Invariants	99
4.	Reducible and irreducible groups	100
5.	Homogeneous linear groups	101
6.	Hermitian invariants	102
7.	Reducibility of a finite homogeneous group	102
8.	Finite Abelian substitution-groups	104
9.	General homogeneous linear group	105
10.	Fractional linear group	107

CHAPTER VIII

GROUPS OF MOVEMENTS

§ 1.	Definition of a group of movements	108
2.	The screws form a normal subgroup	108
3.	Equivalent points and lines	109
4.	Translation-groups	109

CONTENTS

	PAGE
§ 5. n-al rotations and rotatory-inversions.	110
6, 7. Holoaxial point-groups	111
8. Extended point-groups	114
9. Nets and lattices	115
10. Groups containing no infinitesimal translation	118
11. Isomorphic groups of substitutions and movements	119
12. Example of isomorphic groups	121

CHAPTER IX

GENERATORS OF GROUPS

§ 1, 2. Generators	124
3. Generators of an Abelian group	126
4, 5, 6. Invariants of an Abelian group	127
7. Prime-power Abelian groups	130
8. Abelian groups of the type (1, 1, ..., 1)	131

CHAPTER X

THE COMMUTANT AND GROUP OF AUTOMORPHISMS

§ 1. Definition of the commutant	133
2. The commutant is normal	133
3. The commutant of a factor-group	134
4. The group of inner automorphisms	135
5. Metabelian groups	135
6. The groups of automorphisms	136
7. Holomorphs and characteristic subgroups	139
8. Permutation-groups isomorphic with the holomorph and group of automorphisms	140

CHAPTER XI

PRIME-POWER GROUPS

§ 1. The central of a prime-power group	142
2. The series of normal subgroups	143

CONTENTS

	PAGE
§ 3. A subgroup of order p^s is contained normally in a subgroup of order p^{s+1}	144
4. The G. C. S. of the subgroups of index p	145
5. The number of subgroups of given order	146
6. Groups with only one subgroup of given order . . .	147
7, 8. The groups with a cyclic subgroup of index p . . .	148
9. Groups with one subgroup of order 2	150

CHAPTER XII

SYLOW'S THEOREM

§ 1. Sylow subgroups	152
2. Frobenius' extension of Sylow's theorem	156

CHAPTER XIII

SERIES OF GROUPS

§ 1. Series of groups	158
2. The composition-series	158
3. Composition-factor-groups	159
4. Composition-series containing a given normal subgroup .	161
5. Soluble groups	161
6. Composition-series of a minimum normal subgroup . .	162
7. The chief-series	164
8. Chief-factor-groups	164
9. The characteristic-series	165
10, 11. The series of derived groups	166
12, 13. The series of adjoined groups	167

CHAPTER XIV

SOME WELL-KNOWN GROUPS

§ 1. The group $\{a, b\}$ in which $\{a\}$ is normal . . .	169
2. Dihedral, dicyclic, &c., groups	170
3. Metacyclic groups	171
4, 5. Groups with cyclic Sylow subgroups	172
6. Definition of Hamiltonian and quaternion groups . .	175
7, 8, 9. The determination of all Hamiltonian groups . .	176

CHAPTER XV

CHARACTERISTICS

	PAGE
§ 1. Representations and characteristics	179
2. Sets of characteristics	180
3. Characteristics of an Abelian group	181
4. Reciprocal subgroups of an Abelian group	182
5. Characteristics of a non-Abelian group	183
6. No simple group contains a conjugate set of p^s elements	186
HINTS FOR SOLUTION OF THE EXAMPLES	189
APPENDIX. Problems awaiting solution	233
INDEX	234

CHAPTER I

ELEMENTS

§ 1. THINGS represented by the symbols $a, b, c, \ldots$ (which may be quantities, operations, &c.) will be called *elements* or *operations* if they satisfy the following conditions :—

(1) Elements possess a *law of combination*; i.e. any element b can be combined in one way only with any element a to form a third element g, which is called the *product* or *resultant* of a and b and is denoted by ab, $a \cdot b$, or $a \times b$. The equivalence of ab and g is denoted by the equation $ab = g$.

The result of combining b with a is not in general the same as the result of combining a with b; i.e. ab is not in general the same as ba. If $ab = ba$, a and b are called *permutable* or *commutative* elements.

(2) Elements obey the *associative law*; i.e. if $ab = g$ and $bc = h$, $gc = ah$; or, as it may be otherwise expressed, $(ab)c = a(bc)$.

We write abc for $(ab)c = a(bc)$; $abcd$ for $(abc)d = (ab)(cd) = a(bcd) = a(bc)d$, and so on.

(3) A fixed element e exists such that $ae = ea = a$, whatever element a may be. We call e the *identical element* or *identity*. It is denoted by the symbol 1, if no confusion can be caused thereby.

(4) An element a always exists such that $aa = e$, whatever element a may be. We call a the *inverse* of a or 'the element inverse to a'. It follows that if $ag = ah$, $aag = aah$; and hence $eg = eh$ or $g = h$.

We denote for convenience aa by a^2, a^2a by a^3, a^3a by a^4, and so on. The inverses of a, $a^2, a^3, \ldots$ are denoted by $a^{-1}, a^{-2}, a^{-3}, \ldots$. We define a^1, a^0 by the equations $a^1 = a$, $a^0 = 1$.

Ex. 1. If O is any fixed point, it is shown in IV 2 that the result of rotating any body first through an angle θ about a line OA and then through ϕ about OB is the same as that of rotating the body about a certain line OC. Hence any rotation about a line through O may be considered as an 'element' according to the definition given above. The 'identical element' is the act of leaving the body unmoved. The element 'inverse' to the rotation about OA is a rotation about OA through the same angle but in the opposite direction. In general the result of first rotating the body through θ about OA and then through ϕ about OB is not the same as that of first rotating through ϕ about OB and then through θ about OA; i.e. the two rotations are not in general permutable.

Ex. 2. (i) Prove $aa = e$; (ii) deduce that $g = h$ if $ga = ha$.

Ex. 3. The inverse of $ab \ldots kl$ is $l^{-1}k^{-1} \ldots b^{-1}a^{-1}$.

Ex. 4. $(a^{-1})^n = a^{-n}$, n being a positive or negative integer.

Ex. 5. $a^m \cdot a^n = a^n \cdot a^m = a^{m+n}$ and $(a^m)^n = (a^n)^m = a^{mn}$, m and n being any positive or negative integers.

Ex. 6. If $ab = ba$, $a^m b^n = b^n a^m$.

Ex. 7. If each pair of the elements $a, b, c, \ldots$ is permutable, (i) $(abc\ldots)^n = a^n b^n c^n \ldots$; (ii) $a^{x_1} b^{y_1} c^{z_1} \ldots \times a^{x_2} b^{y_2} c^{z_2} \ldots \times \ldots = a^{x_1+x_2+\cdots} b^{y_1+y_2+\cdots} c^{z_1+z_2+\cdots} \ldots$.

Ex. 8. If $ba = a^2 b^2$, (i) $ba^2 = a^{2n}(ba^2)b^{2n}$, (ii) $b^2 a^3 = a^{2n}(b^2 a^3)(b^2 a)^{2n}$, (iii) $bab^2 a = (a^2 b)^{2n}(bab^2 a)b^{2n}$, (iv) $(ba)^2 = (a^4 b)^n (ba)^2 (ab^4)^n$.

Ex. 9. If $ba = a^r b^s$, (i) $b^2 a^t = (a^r b^{s-2})^n (b^2 a^t)(a^{r-t-1} b^s a^{t-1})^n$, (ii) $b^t a^2 = (b^{t-1} a^r b^{s-t-1})^n (b^t a^2)(a^{r-2} b^s)^n$.

Ex. 10. When the law of combination is ordinary addition, (i) all positive and negative integers (including zero), (ii) all rational quantities (including 0 and ∞), (iii) all real quantities, (iv) all complex quantities, may be considered as elements any two of which are permutable.

Ex. 11. When the law of combination is ordinary multiplication, (i) all rational quantities, (ii) all real quantities, (iii) all complex quantities, may be considered as elements any two of which are permutable.

§ 2. It may happen that the powers $a, a^2, a^3, \ldots$ are not all distinct. Suppose $a^r = a^s (r > s)$. Then $a^{r-s} = a^r \cdot a^{-s} = a^s \cdot a^{-s} = 1$. Let a^n be the first of the powers $a, a^2, a^3, \ldots$ which $= 1$. Then n is called the *order* of a.

Ex. 1. A rotation of a body through $2\pi \div n$ about any line may be considered as an element of order n. For the body is brought back to its original position when the rotation is performed n times.

Ex. 2. The identical element is the only element of order 1.

Ex. 3. If an element is equivalent to its inverse, its order is 2; and conversely.

Ex. 4. If a is of order n, (i) $a^{kn} = 1$ and $a^{m+kn} = a^m$, k being a positive or negative integer; (ii) conversely if $a^x = 1$, $x = kn$.

Ex. 5. If $n = qr$, the order of a^q is r.

Ex. 6. If d is the H.C.F. of n and x, the order of a^x is $n \div d$.

Ex. 7. If each pair of the elements $a, b, c, \ldots$ is permutable, the order of $abc \ldots$ is a factor of the L.C.M. of the orders of $a, b, c, \ldots$.

Ex. 8. If a, b are elements of orders n, m, prove that (i) if a^x is the lowest power of a which is permutable with b, $n \div x$ is integral; (ii) if a^x is the lowest power of a which is also a power of b, $n \div x$ is integral; (iii) if $a^r b^s = b^s a^r$, where r is prime to n and s to m, $ab = ba$.

Ex. 9. If $a^2 = b^2 = 1$, ab is the inverse of ba.

Ex. 10. If $a^2 = b^2 = (ab)^2 = 1$, $ab = ba$.

Ex. 11. The order of a is qr, where q is prime to r. Prove that (i) integers α and β can be chosen so that $a = a^\alpha \cdot a^\beta$, where the order of a^α is q and of a^β is r; (ii) conversely if $a = bc$, where b and c are permutable elements of orders q and r, $b = a^\alpha$ and $c = a^\beta$.

Ex. 12. If a, b are elements of orders n, m and $ba = a^2b^2$, prove that (i) $(m-n)(m-2n)(2m-n) = 0$; (ii) a^4b and ab^4 are of the same order.

Ex. 13. If $ba = a^r b^s$, $a^r b^{s-2}$ and $a^{r-2} b^s$ are of the same order.

§ 3. The element $b^{-1}ab$ is called the *transform* of a by b or the *result of transforming* a by b.

The t-th power of the transform of a by b = the transform of the t-th power of a by b, t being a positive or negative integer.

For since $b^{-1}a^{t-1}b \cdot b^{-1}ab = b^{-1}a^t b$, it follows at once by induction that $(b^{-1}ab)^t = b^{-1}a^t b$, when t is positive. Again, since $b^{-1}a^t b \cdot b^{-1}a^{-t}b = 1, (b^{-1}a^t b)^{-1} = b^{-1}a^{-t}b = (b^{-1}ab)^{-t}$ when t is negative; and therefore $(b^{-1}ab)^t = b^{-1}a^t b$ as before.

A case of frequent occurrence is that in which the transform of a by b is a power of a. Suppose $b^{-1}ab = a^k$, then $b^{-y}a^x b^y = a^{xk^y}$, y being a positive integer. For this is evidently true when $y = 1$: and since $b^{-1}a^{xk^y}b = (a^{xk^y})^k = a^{xk^{y+1}}$, by induction the result is true in general.

Again, $(b^y a^x)^t = b^{yt} a^{x(k^{yt}-1) \div (k^y - 1)}$, y and t being positive integers. For this is evidently true when $t = 1$: and since $b^y a^x \cdot b^{yt} a^{x(k^{yt}-1) \div (k^y - 1)} = b^{y(t+1)} \cdot b^{-yt} a^x b^{yt} \cdot a^{x(k^{yt}-1) \div (k^y - 1)} =$
$$b^{y(t+1)} a^{xk^{yt} + x(k^{yt}-1) \div (k^y-1)} = b^{y(t+1)} a^{x(k^{y(t+1)}-1) \div (k^y - 1)},$$
by induction the result is true in general.

Ex. 1. $b^{-1}ab$ and a have the same order.

Ex. 2. If $b^{-1}ab = a$, a and b are permutable.

Ex. 3. ab and ba have the same order.

Ex. 4. The transform of ab by c is the product of the transforms of a and b by c.

Ex. 5. If the transforms of c by a and b are the same, ba^{-1} and ab^{-1} are permutable with c.

Ex. 6. If $b^{-1}ab = a^k$, (i) $(a^xb^y)^t = b^{yt}a^{xk^y(k^{yt}-1)\div(k^y-1)}$, (ii) the transform of b^ya^x by b^sa^r is $b^ya^{xk^s+r-rk^s}$.

Ex. 7. If in Ex. 6 a and b are of orders n and m, $k^m \equiv 1$ (mod. n).

Ex. 8. If $b^5 = 1$ and $b^{-1}ab = a^2$, find the order of a.

Ex. 9. If a, b are of orders p, $p-1$ (p prime*), the relation $ab = ba^k$ is possible for all values of k not divisible by p.

Ex. 10. If b transforms a into its inverse and a transforms b into its inverse, $a^4 = b^4 = 1$.

Ex. 11. If a and b both transform c into one of its powers, ab and ba transform c into the same power of c.

§ 4. The element $c = a^{-1}b^{-1}ab$ is called the *commutator* of a and b.

Of course c is not in general permutable with either a or b. If c is permutable with a, c^α is the commutator of a^α and b. For since $b^{-1}ab = ac$, $b^{-1}a^\alpha b = (ac)^\alpha = a^\alpha c^\alpha$ when $ac = ca$. Hence $a^{-\alpha}b^{-1}a^\alpha b = c^\alpha$. Similarly if $bc = cb$, c^β is the commutator of a and b^β.

If c is permutable with both a and b, $c^{\alpha\beta} = (c^\alpha)^\beta$ is the commutator of a^α and b^β, since c^α is the commutator of a^α and b. Moreover from $ab^\beta = b^\beta ac^\beta$ we deduce $(ba)^2 = baba = b \cdot bac \cdot a = b^2a^2c$, $(ba)^3 = bab^2a^2c = b \cdot b^2ac^2 \cdot a^2c = b^3a^3c^3$, and by induction in general $(ba)^t = b^ta^tc^{\frac{1}{2}t(t-1)}$. Similarly $(ab)^t = b^ta^tc^{\frac{1}{2}t(t+1)}$. Again, since c^{xy} is the commutator of a^x and b^y, $(b^ya^x)^t = b^{yt}a^{xt}c^{\frac{1}{2}xy\,t(t-1)}$, and so on.

Ex. 1. If $c = 1$, a and b are permutable; and conversely.

Ex. 2. The commutator of a and b is the inverse of the commutator of b and a.

Ex. 3. Any transform of a commutator is a commutator.

Ex. 4. Identity is the only element which is the commutator of another element and itself.

Ex. 5. If the commutators of g and a and of g and b are identical, g is permutable with ba^{-1} and ab^{-1}.

Ex. 6. Every commutator is the product of two elements of equal order.

Ex. 7. The commutators of a and b, a^{-1} and b^{-1} have the same order.

Ex. 8. If $a^2 = b^2 = 1$, $(ab)^2$ is the commutator of a and b.

Ex. 9. If a and b transform g into powers of g, their commutator c is permutable with g.

Ex. 10. If c is permutable with a, its order is a factor of the order of a.

* See Preface, p. v.

Ex. 11. If c is permutable with a and b, (i) $(ba)^t = a^t b^t c^{-\frac{1}{2}t(t+1)}$, (ii) $(ab)^t = a^t b^t c^{-\frac{1}{2}t(t-1)}$, (iii) $c^{xs-yr} =$ the commutator of $b^y a^x$ and $b^s a^r =$ the commutator of $a^x b^y$ and $a^r b^s =$ the commutator of $a^x b^y c^s$ and $a^r b^s c^t$.

Ex. 12. If the commutator c_{ij} of g_i and g_j is permutable with $g_1, g_2, \ldots, g_x$ for each value of i and j, $(g_x g_{x-1} \cdots g_1)^t = g^t_x g^t_{x-1} \cdots g^t_1 \times (c_{12} c_{13} \cdots c_{1x} c_{23} \cdots c_{2x} c_{34} \cdots c_{3x} \cdots)^{\frac{1}{2}t(t-1)}$.

Ex. 13. If $ab = ba^k$, find the commutator (i) of $b^y a^x$ and $b^s a^r$, (ii) of $a^x b^y$ and $a^r b^s$.

§ 5. In the following chapters we shall illustrate the abstract idea of an element by applying it to certain concrete cases. Chapter II is devoted to permutations, Chapter III to substitutions, Chapter IV to various geometrical examples. The corresponding groups of elements are discussed in Chapters VI, VII, and VIII respectively.

CHAPTER II

PERMUTATIONS

§ 1. Suppose we are given any m letters or other symbols (in this section we take the numbers $1, 2, \ldots, m$) arranged in a definite order. If we rearrange them so that α takes the place of 1, β of 2, γ of 3, ..., μ of m (where $\alpha, \beta, \gamma, \ldots, \mu$ are all distinct and all included among the symbols $1, 2, \ldots, m$), the operation (S) performed is called a *permutation* or *substitution**
of *degree* m, and is denoted by the symbol $\begin{pmatrix} 1 & 2 & 3 & \ldots & m \\ \alpha & \beta & \gamma & \ldots & \mu \end{pmatrix}$.

If a second permutation $T \equiv \begin{pmatrix} \alpha & \beta & \gamma & \ldots & \mu \\ A & B & C & \ldots & M \end{pmatrix}$ replaces α by A, β by B, γ by C, ..., μ by M, the law of combination of permutations is defined by $ST = U$, where $U \equiv \begin{pmatrix} 1 & 2 & 3 & \ldots & m \\ A & B & C & \ldots & M \end{pmatrix}$. This is denoted symbolically by $\begin{pmatrix} 1 & 2 & 3 & \ldots & m \\ \alpha & \beta & \gamma & \ldots & \mu \end{pmatrix} \begin{pmatrix} \alpha & \beta & \gamma & \ldots & \mu \\ A & B & C & \ldots & M \end{pmatrix} = \begin{pmatrix} 1 & 2 & 3 & \ldots & m \\ A & B & C & \ldots & M \end{pmatrix}$. We notice that U gives the result of performing first the rearrangement defined by S and then that defined by T.

It is obvious that, when the law of combination is defined in this way, permutations obey the associative law and satisfy the conditions by which 'elements' were defined (I 1). The permutation $\begin{pmatrix} 1 & 2 & 3 & \ldots & m \\ 1 & 2 & 3 & \ldots & m \end{pmatrix}$ not displacing any symbol is the identical element, and $\begin{pmatrix} \alpha & \beta & \gamma & \ldots & \mu \\ 1 & 2 & 3 & \ldots & m \end{pmatrix}$ is the element inverse to S.

Ex. 1. Every permutation (except identity) displaces at least two symbols.

Ex. 2. Find the order of $\begin{pmatrix} 1 & 2 & 3 & 4 & 5 \\ 3 & 5 & 4 & 1 & 2 \end{pmatrix}$.

Ex. 3. If $S \equiv \begin{pmatrix} 1 & 2 & 3 & 4 \\ 4 & 3 & 1 & 2 \end{pmatrix}$, $T \equiv \begin{pmatrix} 1 & 2 & 3 & 4 \\ 3 & 4 & 1 & 2 \end{pmatrix}$, prove that T, ST, TS, S^2, and S^2T are of order 2.

---

* 'Substitution' is perhaps more frequently used than 'permutation'. We shall, however, always use 'permutation' in this book, in order to avoid confusion with the operations defined in III 1.

Ex. 4. The numbers of ways in which m queens can be placed on a chessboard of m^2 squares so that no two can take each other is the number of permutations S such that the distance between any pair of symbols in the upper line $\neq$ the distance between the same pair in the lower line.

§ 2. A permutation such as $\begin{pmatrix} 1 & 2 & 3 & \ldots & m-1 & m \\ 2 & 3 & 4 & \ldots & m & 1 \end{pmatrix}$ is called a *circular* permutation and is denoted for the sake of brevity by $(1\ 2\ 3\ \ldots\ m)$. Each symbol in $(1\ 2\ 3\ \ldots\ m)$ is replaced by the one that follows it.

The order of a circular permutation is equal to its degree.

Take, for example, the permutation $S \equiv (1\ 2\ 3\ 4)$
$\equiv \begin{pmatrix} 1 & 2 & 3 & 4 \\ 2 & 3 & 4 & 1 \end{pmatrix}$ of degree 4. Then $S^2 \equiv \begin{pmatrix} 1 & 2 & 3 & 4 \\ 3 & 4 & 1 & 2 \end{pmatrix}$, $S^3 \equiv \begin{pmatrix} 1 & 2 & 3 & 4 \\ 4 & 1 & 2 & 3 \end{pmatrix}$,
$S^4 \equiv \begin{pmatrix} 1 & 2 & 3 & 4 \\ 1 & 2 & 3 & 4 \end{pmatrix} = 1$; and the reasoning is general.

A circular permutation of degree and order 2, such as $(1\ 2)$, is called a *transposition*.

Ex. 1. A circular permutation of degree 1 is identity.
Ex. 2. $(2\ 1) \equiv (1\ 2)$.
Ex. 3. $(1\ 2\ 3\ \ldots\ m) \equiv (2\ 3\ \ldots\ m\ 1) \equiv (3\ \ldots\ m\ 1\ 2) \equiv \ldots$.
Ex. 4. $(m\ m-1\ \ldots\ 2\ 1)$ is inverse to $(1\ 2\ \ldots\ m-1\ m)$.
Ex. 5. Two circular permutations with no symbol in common are permutable.
Ex. 6. $(b\ c) = (a\ b)(a\ c)(a\ b)$.
Ex. 7. $(a\ b\ c)$ is the commutator of two transpositions.
Ex. 8. Prove (i) $(1\ 3\ 4) = (1\ 2\ 3)(2\ 1\ 4)(2\ 1\ 3)$, (ii) $(2\ 4\ 5) = (2\ 1\ 4)(1\ 2\ 5)(1\ 2\ 4)$, (iii) $(3\ 4\ 5) = (2\ 1\ 3)(2\ 4\ 5)(1\ 2\ 3)$.
Ex. 9. If $S \equiv (1\ 2\ 3\ 4\ \ldots)$, $S^t \equiv \begin{pmatrix} 1 & 2 & 3 & 4 & \ldots \\ t+1 & t+2 & t+3 & t+4 & \ldots \end{pmatrix}$.

§ 3. *Every permutation is the product of circular permutations no two of which have a symbol in common.*

Consider, for example, the permutation
$$S \equiv \begin{pmatrix} 1 & 2 & 3 & 4 & 5 & 6 & 7 & 8 & 9 & 10 & 11 \\ 5 & 8 & 3 & 4 & 2 & 11 & 10 & 1 & 6 & 7 & 9 \end{pmatrix}.$$

It replaces 1 by 5, 5 by 2, 2 by 8, 8 by 1. Take any symbol not already involved, such as 6; then S replaces 6 by 11, 11 by 9, 9 by 6. Take another symbol not already involved, such as 7; then S replaces 7 by 10 and 10 by 7. Finally, S does not displace 3 and 4. Hence S is the product of $(1\ 5\ 2\ 8)$, $(6\ 11\ 9)$, $(7\ 10)$, (3), and (4); or $S \equiv (1\ 5\ 2\ 8)(6\ 11\ 9)$

(7 10) (3) (4). We call (1 5 2 8), (6 11 9), (7 10), (3), (4) the *cycles* of S. The *degree* of a cycle is the number of symbols it contains. Since (3) and (4) are each identity, we write $S \equiv (1\ 5\ 2\ 8)\ (6\ 11\ 9)\ (7\ 10)$, unless we wish to call attention to the fact that S involved originally all the eleven symbols and was of degree 11.* Two permutations containing the same number of cycles of the same degrees—such as (1 2 5 8) (6 4 9) (3 10) (7 11) and (1 9 7 3) (5 4 8) (2 6) (10 11)—are called *similar*. A permutation with the same number of symbols in each cycle—such as (1 4 3) (2 5 7) (9 6 8)—is called *regular*.

Ex. 1. Resolve $\begin{pmatrix} 1 & 2 & 3 & 4 & 5 & 6 & 7 & 8 & 9 & 10 \\ 3 & 8 & 6 & 9 & 2 & 4 & 10 & 5 & 1 & 7 \end{pmatrix}$,

$\begin{pmatrix} 1 & 2 & 3 & 4 & 5 & 6 & 7 & 8 & 9 & 10 & 11 & 12 & 13 & 14 & 15 \\ 11 & 7 & 5 & 12 & 1 & 2 & 8 & 4 & 6 & 9 & 10 & 8 & 14 & 13 & 15 \end{pmatrix}$,

and $\begin{pmatrix} a & b & c & d & e & f & g \\ e & g & f & d & a & b & c \end{pmatrix}$ into cycles.

Ex. 2. The inverse of $(a\ b\ ...\ g\ h)\ (i\ j\ ...\ q\ r)\ (s\ t\ ...\ w\ x)\ ...$ is $(h\ g\ ...\ b\ a)\ (r\ q\ ...\ j\ i)\ (x\ w\ ...\ t\ s)\ ...$.

Ex. 3. $(a\ b)(c\ d)$ and $(a\ c)(bd)$ are permutable.

Ex. 4. $(a\ b\ c\ ...\ k)(a\ l) = (a\ b\ c\ ...\ k\ l)$.

Ex. 5. Find the product of (i) $(a\ b\ ...\ l\ m\ n\ ...\ x)$ and $(a\ m)$, (ii) $(a\ b\ c\ ...)\ (x\ y\ s\ ...)$ and $(a\ x)$.

Ex. 6. The number of cycles into which the permutation S of § 1 is resolved is increased or diminished by 1 when two of the symbols $\alpha, \beta, \gamma, ..., \mu$ are interchanged, according as these symbols occur in the same or in different cycles of S.

Ex. 7. Prove (i) $(a\ b\ ...\ l\ m\ \mu\ \lambda\ ...\ \beta\ \alpha) = (a\ \alpha)(b\ \beta)\ ...\ (l\ \lambda)\ (m\ \mu)$ $.(ab)(\beta c)...(\kappa l)(\lambda m) = (a\ \beta)(b\ \gamma)...(k\ \lambda)(l\ \mu).(a\ \alpha)(b\ \beta)...(l\ \lambda)(m\ \mu);$ (ii) $(a\ b\ ...\ k\ l\ m\ \lambda\ \kappa\ ...\ \beta\ \alpha) = (a\ \alpha)(b\ \beta)...(l\ \lambda).(a\ b)(\beta c)...(\kappa\ l)(\lambda\ m)$ $= (a\ \beta)(b\ \gamma)\ ...\ (k\ \lambda)(l\ m)\ .\ (a\ \alpha)(b\ \beta)\ ...\ (l\ \lambda)$.

Ex. 8. Find the product of (i) $(a\ b\ ...\ g\ h\ i\ j\ x\ y\ s\ ...)$ and $(h\ g\ ...\ b\ a\ i\ j\ \xi\ \eta\ \zeta\ ...)$; (ii) $(a\ b\ ...\ g\ h\ i\ j\ k\ x\ y\ s\ ...)$ and $(h\ g\ ...\ b\ a\ i\ j\ k\ \xi\ \eta\ \zeta\ ...)$.

Ex. 9. If $S \equiv (a_1\ a_2\ ...\ a_m)$, (i) one cycle of S^t is $(a_1\ a_{t+1}\ a_{2t+1}\ a_{3t+1}\ ...)$, where a_x and a_y are identical when $x \equiv y$ (mod. m); (ii) S^t is circular, when t is prime to m; (iii) S^t is a regular permutation containing t cycles of degree q, when $m = qt$; (iv) S^t is a regular permutation containing d cycles, when d is the H.C.F. of m and t.

---

* The reader should notice the distinction between the 'degree of S' and the 'degree of a cycle of S'.

Ex. 10. Every regular permutation is a power of a circular permutation.

Ex. 11. Express $(1\ 8\ 5\ 12)(2\ 7\ 6\ 11)(4\ 8\ 10\ 9)$ as a power of a circular permutation.

§ 4. *The order of a permutation S is the L. C. M. of the degrees of its cycles.*

Let $S = ABC\ldots$, where $A, B, C,\ldots$ are circular permutations no two of which have a symbol in common. Then $A, B, C,\ldots$ are evidently permutable elements. Hence we have $S^n = A^n B^n C^n \ldots$; so that $S^n = 1$, if and only if $A^n = B^n = C^n = \ldots = 1$. Therefore the order of S is the L. C. M. of the orders of $A, B, C, \ldots$. But the order of a circular permutation = its degree, and hence the theorem follows.

Ex. 1. The order of a regular permutation = the degree of each cycle.

Ex. 2. Find the order of $\begin{pmatrix} 1\ 2\ 3\ 4\ 5\ 6\ 7 \\ 8\ 5\ 6\ 7\ 2\ 1\ 4 \end{pmatrix}$,

$\begin{pmatrix} 1\ 2\ 3\ 4\ 5\ 6\ 7\ 8\ 9\ 10\ 11 \\ 5\ 11\ 6\ 8\ 4\ 3\ 10\ 9\ 1\ 2\ 7 \end{pmatrix}$ and $\begin{pmatrix} a\ b\ c\ d\ e\ f \\ d\ f\ e\ a\ c\ b \end{pmatrix}$.

Ex. 3. Every permutation can be expressed as the product of two permutations of order 2 in the same symbols.

Ex. 4. The order of a permutation of degree m is a factor of $m!$.

§ 5. *The transform of a permutation S by a permutation T is found by performing the permutation T on the cycles of S.*

Suppose $\quad S \equiv (a\ b\ c\ \ldots)(k\ l\ m\ \ldots)\ldots,$

and $\quad\quad T \equiv \begin{pmatrix} a\ b\ c\ \ldots\ k\ l\ m\ \ldots\ \ldots \\ \alpha\ \beta\ \gamma\ \ldots\ \kappa\ \lambda\ \mu\ \ldots\ \ldots \end{pmatrix}.$

Then $T^{-1}(a\ b\ c\ \ldots)T = \begin{pmatrix} \alpha\ \beta\ \gamma\ \ldots \\ a\ b\ c\ \ldots \end{pmatrix}(a\ b\ c\ \ldots)\begin{pmatrix} a\ b\ c\ \ldots \\ \alpha\ \beta\ \gamma\ \ldots \end{pmatrix}$

$= \begin{pmatrix} \alpha\ \beta\ \gamma\ \ldots \\ b\ c\ d\ \ldots \end{pmatrix}\begin{pmatrix} a\ b\ c\ \ldots \\ \alpha\ \beta\ \gamma\ \ldots \end{pmatrix} = \begin{pmatrix} \alpha\ \beta\ \gamma\ \ldots \\ \beta\ \gamma\ \delta\ \ldots \end{pmatrix} = (\alpha\ \beta\ \gamma\ \ldots).$

Similarly $\quad T^{-1}(k\ l\ m\ \ldots)T = (\kappa\ \lambda\ \mu\ \ldots)$, &c.

Hence $\quad T^{-1}ST = T^{-1}(a\ b\ c)T \cdot T^{-1}(k\ l\ m\ \ldots)T \ldots$
$\quad\quad\quad\quad\quad = (\alpha\ \beta\ \gamma\ \ldots)(\kappa\ \lambda\ \mu\ \ldots)\ldots.$

Ex. 1. Transform $(1\ 3\ 6\ 4)(9\ 5\ 2)(7\ 8)$ by $(1\ 5\ 8\ 7\ 2)(8\ 6)$, and $\begin{pmatrix} 1\ 2\ 3\ 4\ 5\ 6\ 7\ 8 \\ 8\ 4\ 1\ 2\ 6\ 5\ 7\ 3 \end{pmatrix}$ by $\begin{pmatrix} 1\ 2\ 3\ 4\ 5\ 6\ 7\ 8 \\ 4\ 7\ 8\ 8\ 6\ 2\ 5\ 1 \end{pmatrix}$.

Ex. 2. A permutation is similar to every transform.

Ex. 3. A permutation can be transformed into any similar permutation on the same symbols by some permutation on these symbols.

Ex. 4. If A, B are two similar permutations and $B = AC$, C is a commutator.

Ex. 5. If two permutations have only one symbol in common, their commutator is of order 3.

Ex. 6. If two permutations have just two symbols in common, their commutator is of order 2, 3, or 5.

Ex. 7. The only permutations on m given symbols which are permutable with a circular permutation S on the m symbols are the powers of S.

Ex. 8. Find all the permutations on the 10 symbols involved in $S \equiv (a\ b\ c\ d\ e)(1\ 2\ 3\ 4\ 5)$ which are permutable with S.

Ex. 9. The permutation $(1\ 2\ \ldots\ m)\ (m+1\quad m+2\ \ldots\ 2m)$ is permutable with $(1\quad m+1)(2\quad m+2)\ldots(m\quad 2m)$.

§ 6. *Any permutation can be expressed as the product of transpositions.*

Since any permutation is the product of circular permutations, it is sufficient to prove this theorem for a circular permutation.

Now we have at once $(a\ b\ c\ldots k)\ (a\ l) = \begin{pmatrix} a\ b\ \ldots\ k \\ b\ c\ \ldots\ a \end{pmatrix} \cdot \begin{pmatrix} a\ l \\ l\ a \end{pmatrix}$
$= \begin{pmatrix} a\ b\ \ldots\ k\ l \\ b\ c\ \ldots\ l\ a \end{pmatrix} = (a\ b\ \ldots\ k\ l)$. Hence by induction $(a\ b\ c\ \ldots\ l)$
$= (a\ b)\ (a\ c)\ \ldots\ (a\ l)$.

Ex. 1. The number of ways in which a permutation can be expressed as a product of transpositions is unlimited.

Ex. 2. Express

$$\begin{pmatrix} 1\ 2\ 3\ 4\ 5\ 6\ 7\ 8\ 9\ 10 \\ 3\ 8\ 6\ 9\ 2\ 4\ 10\ 5\ 1\ 7 \end{pmatrix} \text{ and } \begin{pmatrix} a\ b\ c\ d\ e\ f\ g\ h\ i \\ c\ h\ e\ b\ f\ a\ g\ i\ d \end{pmatrix}$$

as products of transpositions.

Ex. 3. Any permutation on $1, 2, \ldots, m$ can be expressed as the product of transpositions of the form $(1\ 2), (1\ 3), \ldots, (1\ m)$.

Ex. 4. If the product of k transpositions is of degree m with s cycles (including cycles of degree 1), $k \geq m - s$.

Ex. 5. A circular permutation of degree m can be expressed as the product of $m - 1$ transpositions, but of no smaller number.

Ex. 6. m volumes of a book disarranged on a shelf in the order $\alpha, \beta, \gamma, \ldots, \mu$ are brought into numerical order by repeated interchanging of two volumes. Prove that $m - s$ interchanges are

necessary, where s is the number of cycles (including cycles of degree 1) in
$$\begin{pmatrix} 1 & 2 & 3 & \dots & m \\ \alpha & \beta & \gamma & \dots & \mu \end{pmatrix}.$$

§ 7. *In whatever way a given permutation is expressed as a product of transpositions, the number of the transpositions is always odd or always even.*

Consider the expression
$$D = (a-b)(a-c)(a-d)(a-e)\dots(b-c)(b-d)(b-e)$$
$$\dots(c-d)(c-e)\dots(d-e)\dots$$
which is the product of the differences of all possible pairs of the symbols $a, b, c, d, e, \dots$. A transposition of two symbols changes D into $-D$; and therefore a permutation expressed as a product of an odd number of transpositions changes D into $-D$, while a permutation expressed as the product of an even number of transpositions leaves D unaltered.

Hence if a given permutation is expressed as a product of transpositions, the number of such transpositions is always odd or always even. The permutation is called an *odd* or *even* ('negative' or 'positive') permutation in the two cases respectively.

Ex. 1. The product of r odd and s even permutations is odd or even according as r is odd or even.

Ex. 2. A circular permutation is odd or even according as its order is even or odd.

Ex. 3. A permutation of degree m containing s cycles (including cycles of degree 1) is odd or even as $m-s$ is odd or even.

Ex. 4. A commutator is always even.

Ex. 5. Every even permutation can be expressed as the product of circular permutations of order 3.

Ex. 6. Every even permutation on $1, 2, 3, \dots, m$ can be expressed as the product of circular permutations of the form (1 2 3), (1 2 4), (1 2 5), $\dots$, (1 2 m).

Ex. 7. If a_{ij} is the element in the i-th row and j-th column of a determinant, the coefficient of $a_{1\alpha} a_{2\beta} a_{3\gamma} \dots$ in the expansion of the determinant is $+1$ or -1 according as the permutation $\begin{pmatrix} 1 & 2 & 3 & \dots \\ \alpha & \beta & \gamma & \dots \end{pmatrix}$ is even or odd.

Ex. 8. A permutation is always permutable with some odd permutation on the same symbols unless the degrees of its cycles are all odd and all distinct.

CHAPTER III

SUBSTITUTIONS

§ 1. SUPPOSE we are given m independent quantities $x_1, x_2, \ldots, x_m$ which we shall call the 'variables'. If we change them respectively into the m independent quantities $x_1', x_2', \ldots, x_m'$, where x_i' is a function $f_i(x_1, x_2, \ldots, x_m)$ of $x_1, x_2, \ldots, x_m$, the operation performed is called a *substitution of degree* m. This substitution is denoted by the notation $x_i' = f_i(x_1, x_2, \ldots, x_m)$, $(i = 1, 2, \ldots, m)$, or, if no ambiguity is thereby introduced, by $(f_1, f_2, \ldots, f_m)$, or even by $x' = f(x)$.

Solving the equations $x_i' = f_i(x_1, x_2, \ldots, x_m)$ we obtain m equations of the form $x_i = F_i(x_1', x_2', \ldots, x_m')$. We shall only consider the case of a 'birational' substitution in which the functions f_i, F_i are one-valued. The simplest and most important example of such a birational substitution is the 'homogeneous linear' substitution

$$x_i' = a_{i1}x_1 + a_{i2}x_2 + \ldots + a_{im}x_m.$$

If $S \equiv (f_1, f_2, \ldots, f_m)$ and $T \equiv (\phi_1, \phi_2, \ldots, \phi_m)$, the law of combination of substitutions is defined by $ST = U$, where

$$U \equiv (\phi_1(f_1, f_2, \ldots, f_m), \phi_2(f_1, f_2, \ldots, f_m), \ldots, \phi_m(f_1, f_2, \ldots, f_m)),$$

which may be written $x' = \phi[f(x)]$. It should be noticed that ST is obtained by first changing x_i into $x_i' = f_i(x_1, x_2, \ldots, x_m)$ and then changing x_i' into $\phi_i(x_1', x_2', \ldots, x_m')$; or by eliminating $x_1', x_2', \ldots, x_m'$ from the $2m$ equations

$$x_i' = f_i(x_1, x_2, \ldots, x_m), \quad x_i'' = \phi_i(x_1', x_2', \ldots, x_m'),$$

and then putting x_i' for x_i''.

It is obvious that, when the law of combination of substitutions is defined in this way, substitutions obey the associative law and satisfy the conditions by which 'elements' were defined. The substitution $(x_1, x_2, \ldots, x_m)$ is the identical element. The element inverse to S is $(F_1, F_2, \ldots, F_m)$, since $F_i(f_1, f_2, \ldots, f_m) = F_i(x_1', x_2', \ldots, x_m') = x_i$.

A permutation may be considered as that special type of

substitution in which $x_1', x_2', \ldots, x_m'$ are the quantities $x_1, x_2, \ldots, x_m$ in some order or other.

§ 2. Some authors define ST as the result of first substituting $f_i(x_1, x_2, \ldots, x_m)$ for x_i and then substituting $\phi_i(x_1, x_2, \ldots, x_m)$ for x_i; which is the same as substituting $f_i(\phi_1, \phi_2, \ldots, \phi_m)$ for x_i. From this point of view ST is the substitution $x_i' = f[\phi(x)]$, not $x_i' = \phi[f(x)]$ as in § 1. Though this is in some ways the more natural convention, we have adopted the definition of § 1 as being that used by the majority of writers, and as being more readily adaptable to the geometrical applications. We pass from one definition to the other by interchanging ST and TS.

Ex. 1. The coordinates (x, y) of any point in a plane are changed into $\cos\theta\, x + \sin\theta\, y - h$, $-\sin\theta\, x + \cos\theta\, y - k$ by rotating the rectangular Cartesian axes of reference through an angle θ and transferring the origin to the point (h, k). Hence the changing of the axes is equivalent to performing the substitution
$$(\cos\theta\, x + \sin\theta\, y - h,\ -\sin\theta\, x + \cos\theta\, y - k).$$

Ex. 2. The product of two birational substitutions is birational.

Ex. 3. If S is $x' = f(x)$, T is $x' = \phi(x)$, and V is $x' = \psi(x)$, STV is $x' = \psi\{\phi[f(x)]\}$.

Ex. 4. Find the inverses of $x' = (ax+b) \div (cx+d)$,
$(13x-8y, -8x+5y)$, and $(8x+8y+2z, x-y+z, 2x+3y+z)$.

Ex. 5. $(ax+by, cx+dy)$ and $(Ax+By, Cx+Dy)$ are permutable if $a-d:b:c = A-D:B:C$.

Ex. 6. Find the orders of
$$x' = b \div x,\ x' = a - x,\ x' = (x-1) \div x,$$
$$x' = \sqrt{-1}\,(x+1) \div (x-1),\ x' = \tfrac{1}{2}(\sqrt{3}+\sqrt{-1})x,\ (x-y, x),$$
$$(8x-13y, 5x-8y),\ (5x+6y, -4x-5y, 8x+8y-z),$$
$$(8x-3y+4z, 2x-3y+4z, -y+z).$$

Ex. 7. Find the condition that $x' = ax + b$ should be of finite order.

Ex. 8. Find the n-th power of $(ax, bx+ay, cx+az)$, and show that it cannot be of finite order unless $b = c = 0$.

Ex. 9. Find the n-th power of $(ax, cx+dy)$, and find the conditions that its order should be finite.

Ex. 10. If $S \equiv (3x+y+2z,\ x-y+z,\ 2x+3y+z)$, $T \equiv (-4x+3y+5z,\ x-y-z,\ 5x-3y-6z)$ find TS and T^2STS^3.

Ex. 11. The product of $x' = \dfrac{x-2}{x-1},\ \dfrac{-1}{x},\ \dfrac{x+2}{-x-1}$ is $x' = x - 3$.

Ex. 12. (i) If $\cos \phi = (a+d) \div 2\sqrt{ad-bc}$,

the n-th power of $x' = \dfrac{ax+b}{cx+d}$ is

$$x' = \frac{(ax+b)\sin(n+1)\phi - (dx-b)\sin(n-1)\phi}{(cx+d)\sin(n+1)\phi + (cx-a)\sin(n-1)\phi}$$

when $\sin\phi \neq 0$;

and is $x' = \dfrac{[(1+n)a + (1-n)d]x + 2nb}{2ncx + [(1+n)d + (1-n)a]}$ when $\sin\phi = 0$.

(ii) Find the condition that the substitution should be of finite order.

Ex. 13. Express the n-th power of $x' = (ax+b) \div (cx+d)$ as a continued fraction.

Ex. 14. The n-th power of
$$x' = -[ab(k-1) + (a-bk)x] \div [(b-ak) + (k-1)x]$$
is found by putting k^n for k.

Ex. 15. If $S \equiv (a_1x + b_1y + c_1z + d_1w,\ a_2x + b_2y + c_2z + d_2w,$
$$a_3x + b_3y + c_3z + d_3w,\ a_4x + b_4y + c_4z + d_4w)$$
is of finite order, so is
$$T \equiv (a_1x + b_1y + c_1z,\ a_2x + b_2y + c_2z,\ a_3x + b_3y + c_3z).$$

Ex. 16. (i) If $y_i = -(x_i - x_{i+1})(x_{i+2} - x_{i+3})$
$$\div (x_i - x_{i+2})(x_{i+1} - x_{i+3}),\ (i = 1, 2, \ldots, m-3),$$
find the substitutions effected on $y_1, y_2, \ldots, y_{m-3}$ by performing the permutations (x_1x_2) and $(x_1x_2 \ldots x_m)$ on $x_1, x_2, \ldots, x_m$. (ii) Show that the substitutions so obtained are birational.

Ex. 17. The substitution $x' = ax + by,\ y' = cx + dy$ is represented geometrically by making (x, y) and (x', y') corresponding points on the conic $acx^2 + bdy^2 + 2bcxy = k$ and its polar reciprocal with respect to $cx^2 + by^2 = k$; or on the conic
$$\{a(a-d) + c(b-c)\}x^2 + \{d(a-d) + b(b-c)\}y^2 + 2\{ab-cd\}xy = k$$
and its polar reciprocal with respect to
$$(a-d)(x^2+y^2) + 2(b-c)xy = k.$$

Ex. 18. The substitution
$$x' = ax + hy + gz,\ y' = hx + by + fz,\ z' = gx + fy + cz$$
is represented geometrically by making (x, y, z) and (x', y', z') corresponding points on the conicoid
$$ax^2 + by^2 + cz^2 + 2fyz + 2gzx + 2hxy = 1$$
and its polar reciprocal with respect to $x^2 + y^2 + z^2 = 1$.

§ 3. *The transform of a substitution S by a substitution T is found by expressing S in terms of new variables defined by T.*

III 4] HOMOGENEOUS LINEAR SUBSTITUTIONS

Let S, T, T^{-1} be respectively the substitutions
$$x_i' = f_i(x_1, x_2, \ldots, x_m), \quad x_i' = \phi_i(x_1, x_2, \ldots, x_m),$$
$$x_i' = \Phi_i(x_1, x_2, \ldots, x_m), \quad (i = 1, 2, \ldots, m).$$
Consider new variables $y_1', y_2', \ldots, y_m', y_1, y_2, \ldots, y_m$ defined by $y_i' = \phi_i(x_1', x_2', \ldots, x_m')$, $y_i = \phi_i(x_1, x_2, \ldots, x_m)$. Then S is expressed in terms of these new variables by eliminating $x_1', x_2', \ldots, x_m', x_1, x_2, \ldots, x_m$ between the $3m$ equations
$$y_i' = \phi_i(x_1', x_2', \ldots, x_m'), \quad x_i' = f_i(x_1, x_2, \ldots, x_m),$$
$$y_i = \phi_i(x_1, x_2, \ldots, x_m), \ldots\ldots\ldots(i)$$
and solving the resulting m equations for $y_1', y_2', \ldots, y_m'$ in terms of $y_1, y_2, \ldots, y_m$. Suppose we obtain thus
$$y_i' = \psi_i(y_1, y_2, \ldots, y_m).$$
Then $x_i' = \psi_i(x_1, x_2, \ldots, x_m)$ is the substitution $T^{-1}ST$.

For by § 1 $T^{-1}ST$ is obtained by eliminating
$$x_1', x_2', \ldots, x_m', x_1, x_2, \ldots, x_m$$
between the $3m$ equations
$$y_i' = \phi_i(x_1', x_2', \ldots, x_m'), \quad x_i' = f_i(x_1, x_2, \ldots, x_m),$$
$$x_i = \Phi_i(y_1, y_2, \ldots, y_m) \ldots\ldots\ldots(ii)$$
and then replacing y_i' by x_i', y_i by x_i. But equations (ii) are immediately deducible from equations (i).

Ex. 1. If we put $\phi_i(x_1', x_2', \ldots, x_m')$ for x_i' and $\phi_i(x_1, x_2, \ldots, x_m)$ for x in the equations $x_i' = f_i(x_1, x_2, \ldots, x_m)$, and then solve for x_i' in terms of $x_1, x_2, \ldots, x_m$, we obtain the substitution TST^{-1}.

Ex. 2. Find the transform of (i) $x' = (\alpha x + \beta) \div (\gamma x + \delta)$ by $x' = ax + b$; (ii) $(\omega_1 x_1 + \epsilon_2 x_2 + \ldots + \epsilon_m x_m, \omega_2 x_2, \ldots, \omega_m x_m)$ by
$$\left(x_1 + \frac{\epsilon_2}{\omega_1 - \omega_2} x_2 + \ldots + \frac{\epsilon_m}{\omega_1 - \omega_m} x_m, x_2, \ldots, x_m\right);$$
(iii) $(\omega_1 x_1, \epsilon_2 x_1 + \omega_2 x_2, \ldots, \epsilon_m x_1 + \omega_m x_m)$ by
$$\left(x_1, \frac{\epsilon_2}{\omega_2 - \omega_1} x_1 + x_2, \ldots, \frac{\epsilon_m}{\omega_m - \omega_1} x_1 + x_m\right);$$
(iv) $(y + 3z, -x + 2y + z, -x + y + 4z)$ by
$$(x - z, x - y - z, -x + y + 2z);$$
(v) $\quad(8x - 13y, 5x - 8y)$ by $(2x - y, -3x + 2y)$.

§ 4. The most important type of substitution is the *homogeneous linear substitution*.
$$A \equiv (a_{11}x_1 + a_{12}x_2 + \ldots + a_{1m}x_m, \; a_{21}x_1 + a_{22}x_2 + \ldots + a_{2m}x_m,$$
$$\ldots, \; a_{m1}x_1 + a_{m2}x_2 + \ldots + a_{mm}x_m),$$
where the 'coefficients' (a_{ij}) and 'variables' (x_i) are any real or complex quantities.

The square matrix

$$\begin{vmatrix} a_{11} & a_{12} & \cdots & a_{1m} \\ a_{21} & a_{22} & \cdots & a_{2m} \\ \cdot & \cdot & & \cdot \\ \cdot & \cdot & & \cdot \\ a_{m1} & a_{m2} & \cdots & a_{mm} \end{vmatrix}$$

is denoted by $|a|$, if no ambiguity is introduced thereby. When $|a|$ is considered as a determinant, it is called the 'determinant of the substitution A'. Since A possesses an inverse A^{-1}, $|a| \neq 0$.

If
$$B \equiv (b_{11}x_1 + b_{12}x_2 + \ldots + b_{1m}x_m, \ b_{21}x_1 + b_{22}x_2 + \ldots + b_{2m}x_m,$$
$$\ldots, b_{m1}x_1 + b_{m2}x_2 + \ldots + b_{mm}x_m),$$
we verify at once that
$$AB \equiv (c_{11}x_1 + c_{12}x_2 + \ldots + c_{1m}x_m, \ c_{21}x_1 + c_{22}x_2 + \ldots + c_{2m}x_m,$$
$$\ldots, c_{m1}x_1 + c_{m2}x_2 + \ldots + c_{mm}c_m)$$
where $\qquad c_{ij} = b_{i1}a_{1j} + b_{i2}a_{2j} + \ldots + b_{im}a_{mj}.$

Employing the usual rule for the multiplication of determinants we at once prove that $|a| \cdot |b| = |c|$; i.e. the determinant of the product of two substitutions is equal to the product of their determinants.

We may associate with each substitution such as A (or with the matrix $|a|$) a corresponding *bilinear form*

$$a(x, y) \equiv \Sigma a_{ij} y_i x_j, \ (i, j = 1, 2, \ldots, m).$$

The substitution A' derived from A by interchanging a_{ij} and a_{ji} (for all values of i and j) is called the *transposed* substitution of A. The substitution $\bar{A}$ derived from A by replacing a_{ij} by the conjugate complex quantity $\bar{a}_{ij}$ is called the substitution *conjugate* to A. Similarly $\bar{A}'$ denotes the substitution conjugate to A'.

The substitution A is called *real* if $\bar{A} \equiv A$ (i.e. a_{ij} is real for all values of i and j), *symmetric* if $A' \equiv A$ (i.e. $a_{ij} = a_{ji}$), *Hermitian* if $\bar{A}' \equiv A$ (i.e. $\bar{a}_{ij} = a_{ji}$) and the bilinear form $a(x, \bar{x})$ is a positive Hermitian form (§ 5), *orthogonal* if $AA' = 1$, *unitary* if $A\bar{A}' = 1$.

If the substitution A changing x_i into
$$x_i' = a_{i1}x_1 + a_{i2}x_2 + \ldots + a_{im}x_m$$
is orthogonal, we prove at once by forming the product AA' that $a_{1i}a_{1j} + a_{2i}a_{2j} + \ldots + a_{mi}a_{mj} = 1$ if $i = j$, and $= 0$ if $i \neq j$.

III 4]   ORTHOGONAL SUBSTITUTIONS, ETC.   17

Therefore
$$x_1'^2 + x_2'^2 + \ldots + x_m'^2 \equiv (a_{11}x_1 + a_{12}x_2 + \ldots + a_{1m}x_m)^2$$
$$+ (a_{21}x_1 + a_{22}x_2 + \ldots + a_{2m}x_m)^2 + \ldots + (a_{m1}x_1 + a_{m2}x_2$$
$$+ \ldots + a_{mm}x_m)^2 \equiv x_1^2 + x_2^2 + \ldots + x_m^2.$$

Conversely, if $x_1'^2 + x_2'^2 + \ldots + x_m'^2 \equiv x_1^2 + x_2^2 + \ldots + x_m^2$ for all values of $x_1, x_2, \ldots, x_m$, $AA' = 1$ and hence A is orthogonal.

Similarly if A is unitary,
$$x_1'\bar{x}_1' + x_2'\bar{x}_2' + \ldots + x_m'\bar{x}_m' \equiv x_1\bar{x}_1 + x_2\bar{x}_2 + \ldots + x_m\bar{x}_m;$$
and conversely, if this relation holds, A is unitary.*

Ex. 1. What are the conditions that $AB = BA$?

Ex. 2. The determinant of A^{-1} is $\{|a|\}^{-1}$.

Ex. 3. The determinant of a substitution = the determinant of any transform.

Ex. 4. The determinant of a substitution of order n is an n-th root of unity.

Ex. 5. If $C = KLM \ldots RST$, $c_{ij} = \Sigma t_{i\tau} s_{\tau\sigma} r_{\sigma\rho} \ldots m_{\mu\nu} l_{\nu\lambda} k_{\lambda j}$ ($\tau, \sigma, \rho, \ldots, \nu, \mu, \lambda = 1, 2, \ldots, m$).

Ex. 6. Matrices may be considered as elements defined by the law of combination $|a| \cdot |b| = |c|$.

Ex. 7. The determinants of A and A' are equal, and the determinants of A and $\bar{A}$ are conjugate complex quantities.

Ex. 8. If $AB = C$; $\bar{A}\bar{B} = \bar{C}$, $B'A' = C'$, and $\bar{B}'\bar{A}' = \bar{C}'$.

Ex. 9. The transposed substitution of $B^{-1}AB$ is $B'A'B'^{-1}$.

Ex. 10. If A and B are (i) real, (ii) orthogonal, (iii) unitary, so is C.

Ex. 11. (i) A real orthogonal substitution is unitary, (ii) a unitary orthogonal substitution is real, (iii) a real unitary substitution is orthogonal.

Ex. 12. If A is (i) real, (ii) symmetric, (iii) Hermitian, (iv) orthogonal, (v) unitary, (vi) of order n, so are A^{-1}, A', $\bar{A}$, and $\bar{A}'$.

Ex. 13. The substitutions A, A' may be defined as the operations of changing x_i into $\dfrac{\partial a(x, y)}{\partial y_i}$, $\dfrac{\partial a(y, x)}{\partial y_i}$ respectively.

Ex. 14. If A changes x_i into x_i',
(i) $a(x, y) = y_1 x_1' + y_2 x_2' + \ldots + y_m x_m'$; (ii) $c(x, y) = b(x', y)$.

Ex. 15. (i) AA' is symmetric, (ii) $A\bar{A}'$ and $A\bar{A}$ are Hermitian.

Ex. 16. (i) The determinant of an orthogonal substitution is ± 1, (ii) the determinant of a unitary substitution has unit modulus, (iii) the determinant of a Hermitian substitution is real and positive.

* $\bar{x}_i'$ denotes $\bar{a}_{i1}\bar{x}_1 + \bar{a}_{i2}\bar{x}_2 + \ldots + \bar{a}_{im}\bar{x}_m$.

Ex. 17. From the $\tfrac{1}{2}m(m+1)$ relations
$$a_{1i}a_{1j}+a_{2i}a_{2j}+\ldots+a_{mi}a_{mj}=1 \text{ if } i=j, =0 \text{ if } i\neq j$$
we can deduce the $\tfrac{1}{2}m(m+1)$ relations
$$a_{i1}a_{j1}+a_{i2}a_{j2}+\ldots+a_{im}a_{jm}=1 \text{ if } i=j, =0 \text{ if } i\neq j;$$
and conversely.

Ex. 18. Every orthogonal substitution of degree 2 can be put in the shape $(\cos\theta\, x - \sin\theta\, y,\ \pm\sin\theta\, x \pm \cos\theta\, y)$.

Ex. 19. An orthogonal substitution of order 2 is symmetric, and conversely.

Ex. 20. If l_1, m_1, n_1; l_2, m_2, n_2; l_3, m_3, n_3 are the direction-cosines of three mutually perpendicular straight lines,
$$(l_1 x + m_1 y + n_1 z,\ l_2 x + m_2 y + n_2 z,\ l_3 x + m_3 y + n_3 z)$$
is an orthogonal substitution.

Ex. 21. (i) The transform of a real substitution by a real substitution is real. (ii) The transform of a symmetric substitution by an orthogonal substitution is symmetric. (iii) The transform of a Hermitian substitution by a unitary substitution is Hermitian.

Ex. 22. Find an orthogonal substitution of order 2 changing x_1 into $a_1 x_1 + a_2 x_2 + \ldots + a_m x_m$, where $a_1, a_2, \ldots, a_m$ are any quantities such that $a_1^2 + a_2^2 + \ldots + a_m^2 = 1$.

Ex. 23. (i) If $B^{-1}AB = D$ and B is orthogonal, $a(x, y) \equiv d(\xi, \eta)$ where
$$\xi_i = b_{i1}x_1 + b_{i2}x_2 + \ldots + b_{im}x_m,\quad \eta_i = b_{i1}y_1 + b_{i2}y_2 + \ldots + b_{im}y_m.$$
(ii) If B is unitary $a(x, \bar{y}) \equiv d(\xi, \bar{\eta})$.

§ 5. The bilinear form
$$a(x, \bar{x}) \equiv \Sigma a_{ij}\bar{x}_i x_j\ (i, j = 1, 2, \ldots, m)$$
is called *Hermitian* when $\bar{a}_{ij} = a_{ji}$ (a_{ij} is real if $i = j$).*
If we express $a(x, \bar{x})$ in terms of other variables
$$X_1, X_2, \ldots, X_m$$
(homogeneous linear functions of $x_1, x_2, \ldots, x_m$), the new bilinear form is still Hermitian. For if
$$x_i = \epsilon_{i1}X_1 + \epsilon_{i2}X_2 + \ldots + \epsilon_{im}X_m,$$
$$a(x, \bar{x}) \equiv \Sigma\{a_{ij}(\bar{\epsilon}_{i1}\bar{X}_1 + \ldots + \bar{\epsilon}_{im}\bar{X}_m)(\epsilon_{j1}X_1 + \ldots + \epsilon_{jm}X_m)$$
$$+ a_{ji}(\bar{\epsilon}_{j1}\bar{X}_1 + \ldots + \bar{\epsilon}_{jm}\bar{X}_m)(\epsilon_{i1}X_1 + \ldots + \epsilon_{im}X_m)\}$$
$$\equiv \Sigma\{\Sigma(a_{ij}\bar{\epsilon}_{is}\epsilon_{jt}\bar{X}_s X_t + \bar{a}_{ij}\epsilon_{is}\bar{\epsilon}_{jt}X_s\bar{X}_t)\},$$
which is Hermitian.

We shall show that by choosing X_k as a suitable linear function of $x_k, x_{k+1}, \ldots, x_m$ we may bring a Hermitian form of non-zero determinant into the canonical shape
$$a_1 X_1 \bar{X}_1 + a_2 X_2 \bar{X}_2 + \ldots + a_m X_m \bar{X}_m,$$

* As in § 4 $\bar{x}_i, \bar{a}_{ij}$ are complex quantities conjugate to x_i, a_{ij}.

where
$$a_1 a_2 \ldots a_k \equiv \begin{vmatrix} a_{11} & a_{12} & \cdots & a_{1k} \\ a_{21} & a_{22} & \cdots & a_{2k} \\ \cdot & \cdot & & \cdot \\ \cdot & \cdot & & \cdot \\ \cdot & \cdot & & \cdot \\ a_{k1} & a_{k2} & \cdots & a_{kk} \end{vmatrix}.$$

This is obvious if $m = 1$. Assume it true for every value of m less than the one considered. Then we shall prove the result true in general by induction.

Choose $\quad a_{11} X_1 = a_{11} x_1 + a_{12} x_2 + \ldots + a_{1m} x_m,$
so that $\quad a_{11} \bar{X}_1 = a_{11} \bar{x}_1 + a_{21} \bar{x}_2 + \ldots + a_{m1} \bar{x}_m.$
Then
$a_{11} \cdot a(x, \bar{x}) \equiv a_{11}^2 X_1 \bar{X}_1 + \Sigma (a_{11} a_{ij} - a_{i1} a_{1j}) \bar{x}_i x_j \, (i, j = 2, 3, \ldots, m)$
$\equiv$ (by our assumption) $a_{11}^2 X_1 \bar{X}_1 + b_2 X_2 \bar{X}_2 + b_3 X_3 \bar{X}_3 + \ldots + b_m X_m \bar{X}_m,$

where $b_2 b_3 \ldots b_k$

$$\equiv \begin{vmatrix} a_{11} a_{22} - a_{21} a_{12} & a_{11} a_{23} - a_{21} a_{13} & \cdots & a_{11} a_{2k} - a_{21} a_{1k} \\ a_{11} a_{32} - a_{31} a_{12} & a_{11} a_{33} - a_{31} a_{13} & \cdots & a_{11} a_{3k} - a_{31} a_{1k} \\ \cdot & \cdot & & \cdot \\ \cdot & \cdot & & \cdot \\ \cdot & \cdot & & \cdot \\ a_{11} a_{k2} - a_{k1} a_{12} & a_{11} a_{k3} - a_{k1} a_{13} & \cdots & a_{11} a_{kk} - a_{k1} a_{1k} \end{vmatrix}$$

$$\equiv \frac{1}{a_{11}} \begin{vmatrix} a_{11} & 0 & 0 & \cdots & 0 \\ a_{21} & a_{11} a_{22} - a_{21} a_{12} & a_{11} a_{23} - a_{21} a_{13} & \cdots & a_{11} a_{2k} - a_{21} a_{1k} \\ a_{31} & a_{11} a_{32} - a_{31} a_{12} & a_{11} a_{33} - a_{31} a_{13} & \cdots & a_{11} a_{3k} - a_{31} a_{1k} \\ \cdot & \cdot & \cdot & & \cdot \\ \cdot & \cdot & \cdot & & \cdot \\ \cdot & \cdot & \cdot & & \cdot \\ a_{k1} & a_{11} a_{k2} - a_{k1} a_{12} & a_{11} a_{k3} - a_{k1} a_{13} & \cdots & a_{11} a_{kk} - a_{k1} a_{1k} \end{vmatrix}$$

$\equiv a_{11}^{k-2} a_1 a_2 \ldots a_k$ (multiplying the 1st column by a_{1t} and adding to the t-th column).

Hence $b_k = a_{11} a_k$, and therefore
$$a(x, \bar{x}) \equiv a_1 X_1 \bar{X}_1 + a_2 X_2 \bar{X}_2 + \ldots + a_m X_m \bar{X}_m.$$

Since $a_1 X_1 \bar{X}_1 + \ldots + a_m X_m \bar{X}_m$ is Hermitian, $a_1, a_2, \ldots, a_m$ are real.

Again, since $X \bar{X}_1, X \bar{X}_2, \ldots, X_m \bar{X}_m$ are real and positive, $a(x, \bar{x})$ is real and is always > 0 if $a_1, a_2, \ldots, a_m$ are all > 0,

whatever values (not all zero) are given to $x_1, x_2, \ldots, x_m$. In this case $a(x, \bar{x})$ is called a *positive* or *definite* Hermitian form. If we write y_i for $\sqrt{a_i} X_i$ when a_i is positive
$$(i = 1, 2, \ldots, m),$$
$a(x, \bar{x})$ becomes $y_1 \bar{y}_1 + y_2 \bar{y}_2 + \ldots + y_m \bar{y}_m$. This is the canonical shape of a positive Hermitian form.

In the above argument we have assumed that no one of the quantities $a_1, a_2, \ldots, a_m$ vanishes. This is legitimate; for since the determinant of the form $\neq 0$, at least one of the $(m-k)$-th minor determinants (with k rows and columns) of $|a|$ does not vanish. We can therefore by a suitable arrangement of the m variables always ensure that $a_k \neq 0$.

Ex. 1. A homogeneous function of the second degree in m variables with non-zero determinant can be expressed in the shape $X_1^2 + X_2^2 + \ldots + X_m^2$.

Ex. 2. A real symmetric substitution A is Hermitian if the bilinear form $a(x, x)$ can be expressed as the sum of m real squares.

Ex. 3. In whatever way $a(x, \bar{x})$ is reduced to canonical shape the number of positive coefficients in the canonical form is always the same.

Ex. 4. The sum of any number of Hermitian forms is Hermitian; and the sum of any number of positive Hermitian forms is positive.

Ex. 5. If $A(x, \bar{x})$ is a form of zero determinant such that $\bar{a}_{ij} = a_{ji}$, while all the $(m-t-1)$-th minors of the determinant vanish but not all the $(m-t)$-th minors, $a(x, \bar{x})$ can be brought to the shape $a_1 X_1 \bar{X}_1 + a_2 X_2 \bar{X}_2 + \ldots + a_{m-t} X_{m-t} \bar{X}_{m-t}$.*

Ex. 6. The bilinear form $a(x, y)$ with non-zero determinant can be reduced to the form $u_1 v_1 + u_2 v_2 + \ldots + u_m v_m$ where $u_1, u_2, \ldots, u_m$ are linear functions of $x_1, x_2, \ldots, x_m$ and $v_1, v_2, \ldots, v_m$ of $y_1, y_2, \ldots, y_m$.

§ 6. Quantities $X_1, X_2, \ldots, X_m$ not all zero such that
$$\lambda X_i = a_{i1} X_1 + a_{i2} X_2 + \ldots + a_{im} X_m, \quad (i = 1, 2, \ldots, m) \ldots \ldots (\text{i})$$
are said to define a *pole* $(X_1, X_2, \ldots, X_m)$ of the substitution A of § 4. Two poles $(X_1, X_2, \ldots, X_m)$ and $(Z_1, Z_2, \ldots, Z_m)$ are not considered distinct if $\dfrac{X_1}{Z_1} = \dfrac{X_2}{Z_2} = \ldots = \dfrac{X_m}{Z_m}$. Eliminating

---

* If $a_1, a_2, \ldots, a_{m-t}$ are all positive, the form is called 'hypohermitian of rank t'.

$X_1, X_2, ..., X_m$ from the m equations (i) we get

$$\theta(\lambda) \equiv \begin{vmatrix} a_{11}-\lambda & a_{12} & \cdots & a_{1m} \\ a_{21} & a_{22}-\lambda & \cdots & a_{2m} \\ \cdot & \cdot & & \cdot \\ \cdot & \cdot & & \cdot \\ \cdot & \cdot & & \cdot \\ a_{m1} & a_{m2} & \cdots & a_{mm}-\lambda \end{vmatrix} = 0.$$

This is called the *characteristic equation* of A.

By § 3 the characteristic equation of $B^{-1}AB$ is obtained by eliminating Y_i, x_i', x_i from the $3m$ equations

$$\lambda Y_i = b_{i1}x_1' + b_{i2}x_2' + ... + b_{im}x_m',$$
$$Y_i = b_{i1}x_1 + b_{i2}x_2 + ... + b_{im}x_m,$$
$$x_i' = a_{i1}x_1 + a_{i2}x_2 + ... + a_{im}x_m, \quad (i = 1, 2, ..., m)\ldots\ldots\ldots(ii),$$

where $(Y_1, Y_2, ..., Y_m)$ is a pole of $B^{-1}AB$.

From (ii) we deduce $x_i' = \lambda x_i$. Therefore the characteristic equation of $B^{-1}AB$ is obtained by eliminating $x_1, x_2, ..., x_m$ from $\lambda x_i = a_{i1}x_1 + a_{i2}x_2 + ... + a_{im}x_m$, and is $\theta(\lambda) = 0$.

Hence the characteristic equation of A is identical with the characteristic equation of any transform of A. Obviously $X_1, X_2, ..., X_m$ are values of $x_1, x_2, ..., x_m$ satisfying equations (ii). Therefore

$$Y_i = b_{i1}X_1 + b_{i2}X_2 + ... + b_{im}X_m\ldots\ldots\ldots\ldots(iii)$$

Hence any pole of $B^{-1}AB$ is obtained by applying the substitution B to a pole of A corresponding to the same root of the common characteristic equation.

Ex. 1. The product of the roots of $\theta(\lambda) = 0$ is $|a|$, and their sum is $a_{11} + a_{22} + ... + a_{mm}$.

Ex. 2. No root of $\theta(\lambda) = 0$ is zero.

Ex. 3. If $a_{ij} = 0$ when $j < i$, the roots of $\theta(\lambda) = 0$ are $a_{11}, a_{22}, ..., a_{mm}$.

Ex. 4. If the equations (i) of § 6 are equivalent to only $m-2$ independent equations for a certain value of λ, A has an infinite number of poles.

Ex. 5. If A has more than m poles, it has an infinite number.

Ex. 6. If $(1, 0, 0, ..., 0)$ is a pole of A, $a_{21} = a_{31} = ... = a_{m1} = 0$.

Ex. 7. Every substitution has at least one pole and can be transformed into a substitution with a given pole.

Ex. 8. If A, B have a common pole, so have $T^{-1}AT$ and $T^{-1}BT$.

Ex. 9. (i) A pole common to A and B is a pole of AB. (ii) The corresponding root of the characteristic equation of AB is the product of the corresponding roots of the characteristic equations of A and B.

Ex. 10. The poles of A corresponding to the roots $\lambda_1, \lambda_2, \lambda_3, ...$ of $\theta(\lambda) = 0$ are poles of A^n corresponding to the roots $\lambda_1{}^n, \lambda_2{}^n, \lambda_3{}^n, ...$ of the characteristic equation of A^n.

Ex. 11. If A is Hermitian, the coefficients in $\theta(\lambda)$ are real.

Ex. 12. Prove (i) $a(X, y) = \lambda(X_1 y_1 + X_2 y_2 + ... + X_m y_m)$; (ii) $c(X, y) = \lambda \cdot b(X, y)$, if $AB = C$.

Ex. 13. A and A' have the same characteristic equation.

Ex. 14. If $(X_1, X_2, ..., X_m)$, $(Z_1, Z_2, ..., Z_m)$ are poles of A, A' respectively corresponding to unequal roots λ, μ of their common characteristic equation,
$$a(X, Z) = X_1 Z_1 + X_2 Z_2 + ... + X_m Z_m = 0.$$

Ex. 15. If $AB = C$, the characteristic equation of A is
$$\begin{vmatrix} \lambda b_{11} - c_{11} & \lambda b_{12} - c_{12} & \cdots & \lambda b_{1m} - c_{1m} \\ \lambda b_{21} - c_{21} & \lambda b_{22} - c_{22} & \cdots & \lambda b_{2m} - c_{2m} \\ \cdots & \cdots & \cdots & \cdots \\ \cdots & \cdots & \cdots & \cdots \\ \lambda b_{m1} - c_{m1} & \lambda b_{m2} - c_{m2} & \cdots & \lambda b_{mm} - c_{mm} \end{vmatrix} = 0.$$

Ex. 16. If A is orthogonal

(i) $\theta(\lambda) \equiv \pm \lambda^m \cdot \theta\left(\frac{1}{\lambda}\right)$, (ii) $X_1^2 + X_2^2 + ... + X_m^2 = 0$

unless the corresponding root of $\theta(\lambda) = 0$ is ± 1.

Ex. 17. If A is unitary (or leaves unchanged a positive Hermitian form), the roots of $\theta(\lambda) = 0$ have unit modulus.

Ex. 18. If A is (i) real and symmetric, (ii) the product of two real symmetric substitutions C and D, the roots of $\theta(\lambda) = 0$ are real, provided the bilinear form corresponding to C or D is the sum of m real squares.

Ex. 19. If A is (i) Hermitian, (ii) the product of two Hermitian substitutions C and D, the roots of $\theta(\lambda) = 0$ are real and positive.

Ex. 20. The characteristic equation of a hypohermitian substitution of rank t (defined in the same way as when $|a| \neq 0$) has t zero roots and $(m-t)$ real positive roots.

Ex. 21. Show that the determinant of $S \equiv (X_k x_k, X_2 x_k - X_k x_2, ..., X_{k-1} x_k - X_k x_{k-1}, X_1 x_k - X_k x_1, X_{k+1} x_k - X_k x_{k+1}, ..., X_m x_k - X_k x_m)$ is $(-X_k)^m$; and that if $X_k \neq 0$, $S^{-1}AS$ has $(1, 0, 0, ..., 0)$ as a pole.

Ex. 22. Show that if $T \equiv (X_1 x_1 + t_{12} x_2 + ... + t_{1m} x_m,$
$X_2 x_1 + t_{22} x_2 + ... + t_{2m} x_m, ..., X_m x_1 + t_{m2} x_2 + ... + t_{mm} x_m)$,
TAT^{-1} has $(1, 0, 0, ..., 0)$ as a pole.

Ex. 23. Show that if $T \equiv (X_1 x_1 + X_2 x_2 + ... + X_m x_m,$
$t_{21} x_1 + t_{22} x_2 + ... + t_{2m} x_m, ..., t_{m1} x_1 + t_{m2} x_2 + ... + t_{mm} x_m)$
is orthogonal, $T^{-1}AT$ has $(1, 0, 0, ..., 0)$ as a pole; and conversely

if $T^{-1}AT$ has $(1, 0, 0, ..., 0)$ as the pole corresponding to the pole $(X_1, X_2, ..., X_m)$ of A and T is orthogonal, T changes x_1 into a multiple of $X_1 x_1 + X_2 x_2 + ... + X_m x_m$.

Ex. 24. A symmetric substitution can be transformed into a symmetric substitution with $(1, 0, 0, ..., 0)$ as pole by an orthogonal substitution of order 2.

Ex. 25. Find the roots of the characteristic equation and the poles of
  (i) $(\cos\theta\, x - \sin\theta\, y,\ \sin\theta\, x + \cos\theta\, y)$,
  (ii) $(ix + (1-i)y,\ -iy)$, where $i = \sqrt{-1}$,
  (iii) $(ix + (1-i)y,\ (1+i)x - iy)$,
  (iv) $(y + 8z,\ -x + 2y + z,\ -x + y + 4z)$,
  (v) $(5x + 6y,\ -4x - 5y,\ 8x + 8y - z)$,
  (vi) $(20x - 15y - 24z,\ -18x + 6y + 16z,\ 24x - 16y - 29z)$.

§ 7. The homogeneous linear substitution
$$(a_1 x_1,\ a_2 x_2,\ ...,\ a_m x_m)$$
is called a *multiplication*; the multiplication
$$(ax_1,\ ax_2,\ ...,\ ax_m)$$
whose coefficients are all equal is called a *similarity-substitution*.

The substitution $(a_1 x_\alpha,\ a_2 x_\beta,\ ...,\ a_m x_\mu)$, where $\alpha, \beta, ..., \mu$ are the symbols $1, 2, ..., m$ in some order or other, is called a *monomial* substitution.

Ex. 1. (i) A permutation and a multiplication are special types of monomial substitution. (ii) A multiplication is symmetric and is Hermitian if its coefficients are real and positive.

Ex. 2. The product of two multiplications, similarities, or monomial substitutions is respectively a multiplication, similarity, or monomial.

Ex. 3. Any two multiplications are permutable.

Ex. 4. A similarity is permutable with every substitution; and a substitution permutable with every substitution on the same variables is a similarity.

Ex. 5. Every substitution on $x_1, x_2, ..., x_m$ permutable with $(a_1 x_1,\ a_2 x_2,\ ...,\ a_m x_m)$ is a multiplication if no two of the coefficients $a_1, a_2, ..., a_m$ are equal; and is of the form
$$(b_{11} x_1 + ... + b_{1k} x_k,\ ...,\ b_{k1} x_1 + ... + b_{kk} x_k,\ b_{k+1} x_{k+1},\ ...,\ b_m x_m)$$
if $a_1 = a_2 = ... = a_k$ and no two of $a_k, a_{k+1}, a_{k+2}, ..., a_m$ are equal.

Ex. 6. The coefficients of a multiplication of order n are n-th roots of 1.

Ex. 7. A multiplication of finite order is unitary.

Ex. 8. The product of the coefficients of a monomial substitution of order n is an n-th root of 1.

Ex. 9. A substitution with $(1, 0, 0, \ldots, 0)$, $(0, 1, 0, \ldots, 0)$, $\ldots$, $(0, 0, 0, \ldots, 1)$ as poles is a multiplication; and conversely.

Ex. 10. If two coefficients of a multiplication are equal, the substitution has an infinite number of poles.

Ex. 11. The coefficients of a multiplication are the roots of its characteristic equation.

Ex. 12. If $a_1 \neq a_2, a_3, \ldots, a_m$, every substitution permutable with $S \equiv (a_1 x_1, a_2 x_2, \ldots, a_m x_m)$ has $(1, 0, 0, \ldots, 0)$ as a pole.

Ex. 13. If any substitution is multiplied by a similarity, its poles are unaltered and the roots of its characteristic equation are all multiplied by the same quantity.

§ 8. *Any homogeneous linear substitution of finite order n and degree m can be transformed into a multiplication.*

The result is obviously true when $m = 1$. We shall assume it true for every substitution of degree $m-1$, and then prove it true by induction for a substitution of degree m.

Let the substitution be the substitution A of § 4, and let $(X_1, X_2, \ldots, X_m)$ be any pole of A. It is obviously possible to choose the m^2 quantities b_{ij} of § 6 in an infinite number of ways so that their determinant $|b|$ is $\neq 0$ and
$$Y_1 = 1, \ Y_2 = Y_3 = \ldots = Y_m = 0.$$
Then $B^{-1}AB$ has $(1, 0, 0, \ldots, 0)$ as a pole.*

Suppose $B^{-1}AB \equiv (a_{11}x_1 + a_{12}x_2 + \ldots + a_{1m}x_m,\ a_{21}x_1 + a_{22}x_2 + \ldots + a_{2m}x_m, \ldots, a_{m1}x_1 + a_{m2}x_2 + \ldots + a_{mm}x_m).$

Since $(1, 0, 0, \ldots, 0)$ is a pole of $B^{-1}AB$, we see at once that
$$a_{21} = a_{31} = \ldots = a_{m1} = 0.$$

Because $B^{-1}AB$ is of finite order and changes $x_2, x_3, \ldots, x_m$ into linear functions of $x_2, x_3, \ldots, x_m$, we can by our assumption find linear functions $z_2, z_3, \ldots, z_m$ of $x_2, x_3, \ldots, x_m$ such that $B^{-1}AB$ changes z_2 into $\omega_2 z_2$, z_3 into $\omega_3 z_3, \ldots, z_m$ into $\omega_m z_m$. Expressing $B^{-1}AB$ in terms of $x_1, z_2, z_3, \ldots, z_m$ it becomes
$$(\omega_1 x_1 + \epsilon_2 z_2 + \epsilon_3 z_3 + \ldots + \epsilon_m z_m,\ \omega_2 z_2, \ldots, \omega_m z_m).$$

The r-th power of $B^{-1}AB$ is at once proved by induction to be
$$\left(\omega_1^r x_1 + \epsilon_2 \frac{\omega_1^r - \omega_2^r}{\omega_1 - \omega_2} z_2 + \ldots + \epsilon_m \frac{\omega_1^r - \omega_m^r}{\omega_1 - \omega_m} z_m,\ \omega_2^r z_2, \ldots, \omega_m^r z_m\right).$$

---

* See also § 6, Ex. 21, 22, 23.

III 8]   SUBSTITUTIONS OF FINITE ORDER   25

Now if $\omega_1 = \omega_i$, $(\omega_1{}^r - \omega_i{}^r) \div (\omega_1 - \omega_i) = r\omega_i{}^{r-1}$; and therefore in this case $\epsilon_i = 0$, since $B^{-1}AB$ is of finite order.

Express $B^{-1}AB$ in terms of the variables
$$z_1 = x_1 + c_2 z_2 + \ldots + c_m z_m,\ z_2,\ z_3,\ \ldots,\ z_m;$$
where $c_i = \epsilon_i \div (\omega_1 - \omega_i)$ if $\omega_1 \neq \omega_i$ and $c_i = 0$ if $\omega_1 = \omega_i$. Then we readily see that $B^{-1}AB$ takes the form
$$(\omega_1 z_1,\ \omega_2 z_2,\ \ldots,\ \omega_m z_m).$$
Therefore A is transformed into a multiplication by BD, where D is the substitution $x_i' = z_i$.

Since the n-th power of $B^{-1}AB$ is
$$(\omega_1{}^n z_1,\ \omega_2{}^n z_2,\ \ldots,\ \omega_m{}^n z_m),\ \omega_1{}^n = \omega_2{}^n = \ldots = \omega_m{}^n = 1.$$

A practical method of transforming any given substitution A into a multiplication is as follows. Find if possible m poles
$$(Z_1',\ Z_2',\ \ldots,\ Z_m'), (Z_1'',\ Z_2'',\ \ldots,\ Z_m''),\ \ldots,\ (Z_1^{(m)},\ Z_2^{(m)},\ \ldots,\ Z_m^{(m)})$$
of A', corresponding respectively to the roots $\lambda_1, \lambda_2, \ldots, \lambda_m$ (not necessarily all unequal) of the characteristic equation of A', such that the determinant of the substitution
$$T \equiv (Z_1' x_1 + Z_2' x_2 + \ldots + Z_m' x_m,\ Z_1'' x_1 + Z_2'' x_2 + \ldots + Z_m'' x_m,$$
$$\ldots,\ Z_1^{(m)} x_1 + Z_2^{(m)} x_2 + \ldots + Z_m^{(m)} x_m)$$
is not zero. Then if $M \equiv (\lambda_1 x_1,\ \lambda_2 x_2,\ \ldots,\ \lambda_m x_m)$, we verify at once by using the equations corresponding to (i) of § 6 that $AT = TM$. Therefore T transforms A into a multiplication.*

Ex. 1. Every substitution of degree m and finite order has at least m distinct poles.

Ex. 2. If all the roots of the characteristic equation of a substitution of finite order are equal, the substitution is a similarity.

Ex. 3. If $(a_1 x_1, a_2 x_2, \ldots, a_m x_m)$ is transformed into $(e_1 x_1, e_2 x_2, \ldots, e_m x_m)$, (i) the a's are the same as the e's in some order or other; (ii) if no two of the a's are equal, the transforming substitution is monomial.

Ex. 4. A substitution of degree 2 with 2 distinct poles can be transformed into a multiplication.

Ex. 5. If the commutator of two substitutions of degree 2 with a common pole is of finite order, they have both poles in common.

Ex. 6. Transform
   (i) $(8x - 13y,\ 5x - 8y)$,   (ii) $(ix + (1-i)y,\ -iy)$,
   (iii) $(ix + (1-i)y,\ (1+i)x - iy)$,
   (iv) $(y + 3z,\ -x + 2y + z,\ -x + y + 4z)$,
   (v) $(5x + 6y,\ -4x - 5y,\ 8x + 8y - z)$,
   (vi) $(\omega_1 x_1,\ \epsilon_2 x_1 + \omega_2 x_2,\ \ldots,\ \epsilon_m x_1 + \omega_m x_m)$
into multiplications.

* See also Ex. 7.

Ex. 7. (i) If $(X_1', X_2', ..., X_m')$, $(X_1'', X_2'', ..., X_m'')$, ..., $(X_1^{(m)}, X_2^{(m)}, ..., X_m^{(m)})$ are m poles of A such that the determinant of $T \equiv (X_1'x_1 + X_1''x_2 + ... + X_1^{(m)}x_m, \ X_2'x_1 + X_2''x_2 + ... + X_2^{(m)}x_m, \ ..., \ X_m'x_1 + X_m''x_2 + ... + X_m^{(m)}x_m)$ is not zero, TAT^{-1} is a multiplication. (ii) If A can be transformed into a multiplication, such poles always exist.

Ex. 8. (i) If a substitution
$$x' = a_1x + b_1y + c_1z, \ y' = a_2x + b_2y + c_2z, \ z' = a_3x + b_3y + c_3z$$
is transformed by $x' = X$, $y' = Y$, $z' = Z$ into the multiplication $(\lambda x, \mu y, \nu z)$, (x, y, z) and (x', y', z') are corresponding points on the conicoid $\lambda X^2 + \mu Y^2 + \nu Z^2 = 1$ and its polar reciprocal with respect to $X^2 + Y^2 + Z^2 = 1$. (ii) If the lines joining three poles of the substitution to the origin are mutually perpendicular and the same is true of the axes of reference, the substitution is symmetric. (iii) Conversely, if the axes of reference are rectangular, non-coplanar lines joining the origin to three poles of a symmetric substitution are mutually perpendicular in general.

Ex. 9. If any power of a substitution is a similarity, it can be transformed into a multiplication.

Ex. 10. If no two roots of the characteristic equation of a substitution are equal, it can be transformed into a multiplication.

Ex. 11. If A is a symmetric substitution whose characteristic equation has the roots $\lambda_1, \lambda_2, ..., \lambda_m$, (i) A can be transformed into a multiplication by means of an orthogonal substitution; (ii) $a(x, y)$ can be put in the form $\lambda_1 \xi_1 \eta_1 + \lambda_2 \xi_2 \eta_2 + ... + \lambda_m \xi_m \eta_m$, where ξ_i is a homogeneous linear function of $x_1, x_2, ..., x_m$ and η_i is the same function of $y_1, y_2, ..., y_m$.

Ex. 12. Prove that every substitution can be transformed into the *normal* form $(a_{11}x_1 + a_{12}x_2 + ... + a_{1m}x_m, \ a_{22}x_2 + ... + a_{2m}x_m, \ ..., \ a_{mm}x_m)$, in which $a_{ij} = 0$ if $i > j$.

Ex. 13. (i) The product of two substitutions in normal form is in normal form. (ii) The inverse of a substitution in normal form is in normal form.

Ex. 14. Transform into normal form
  (i) $(-10x - 9y, \ 16x + 14y)$,
  (ii) $(20x - 15y - 24z, \ -13x + 6y + 16z, \ 24x - 16y - 29z)$.

§ 9. By writing x_i' for $x_i' \div x_m'$, x_i for $x_i \div x_m$ in the homogeneous linear substitution A of degree m (see § 4) we may derive the *fractional linear substitution* $\mathfrak{a}$ of degree $m-1$ defined by

$$x_i' = \frac{a_{i1}x_1 + a_{i2}x_2 + ... + a_{i\,m-1}x_{m-1} + a_{im}}{a_{m1}x_1 + a_{m2}x_2 + ... + a_{m\,m-1}x_{m-1} + a_{mm}}, \ (i = 1, 2, ..., m-1).$$

Evidently $\mathfrak{a}$ is not altered if we multiply each coefficient
$$a_{ij} \ (i, j = 1, 2, ..., m)$$

III 9] FRACTIONAL LINEAR SUBSTITUTIONS

by the same quantity. Therefore in dealing with fractional substitutions we may always suppose the determinant formed by the coefficients (in this case $|a|$) to be 1.

We call $(X_1, X_2, ..., X_{m-1})$ a *pole* of a, if $(X_1, X_2, ..., X_{m-1}, 1)$ is a pole of A. The poles
$$(X_1, X_2, ..., X_{m-1}) \text{ and } (Z_1, Z_2, ..., Z_{m-1})$$
of a are considered distinct unless
$$X_1 = Z_1, X_2 = Z_2, ..., X_{m-1} = Z_{m-1};$$
i. e. we are concerned with the actual magnitudes of
$$X_1, X_2, ..., X_{m-1},$$
not with their ratios only as in § 6.

Ex. 1. The product of two fractional linear substitutions is a fractional linear substitution.

Ex. 2. a is not altered if we replace A by AM, where M is any similarity.

Ex. 3. Let a, b, c be the fractional substitutions derived from the homogeneous substitutions A, B, C. Then (i) if $AB = C$, $ab = c$; (ii) if $ab = c$, $AB = CM$; where M is a similarity.

Ex. 4. (i) If A is of finite order, so is a. (ii) If A is a multiplication, so is a.

Ex. 5. A fractional linear substitution of finite order can be transformed into a multiplication.

Ex. 6. If $(X_1, X_2, ..., X_{m-1})$ is a pole of a,
$$X_i = (a_{i1}X_1 + a_{i2}X_2 + ... + a_{im}) \div (a_{m1}X_1 + a_{m2}X_2 + ... + a_{mm}).$$

Ex. 7. Prove that the poles of $b^{-1}ab$ are obtained by applying b to the poles of a.

Ex. 8. The substitution $S \equiv \left(x' = \dfrac{ax+b}{cx+d}\right)$, where $ad-bc = 1$ and $2\cos\phi = a+d$, is called *parabolic, elliptic, hyperbolic*, or *loxodromic* according as $\tan\phi$ is zero, real ($\neq 0$), a pure imaginary, or complex. The poles of S are denoted by α and β. Prove that:

(i) α, β have the values $\dfrac{1}{2c}(a - d \mp 2i \sin\phi)$, where $i = \sqrt{-1}$.

(ii) $(x'-\alpha) = (x-\alpha) \div (cx+d)(ca+d) = e^{\phi i}(x-\alpha) \div (cx+d)$.

(iii) If $\alpha = \beta$, S is parabolic; and conversely.

(iv) If S is parabolic, it can be put in the form
$$\frac{1}{x'-\alpha} = \frac{1}{x-\alpha} + c.$$

(v) If S is parabolic, it is a transform of $x' = x+c$.

(vi) If S is non-parabolic, it can be put in the form
$$\frac{x'-\alpha}{x'-\beta} = e^{2\phi i}\frac{x-\alpha}{x-\beta}.$$

(vii) If S is non-parabolic, it is a transform of $x' = e^{2\phi i}x$.
(viii) If S is of order 2, it is hyperbolic, and $a+d=0$.
(ix) If S is of finite order (>2), it is elliptic.
(x) If S is loxodromic, it is the product of an elliptic and a hyperbolic substitution.
(xi) ϕ is not altered when we transform S by any substitution.
(xii) The transform of S by $S_1 \equiv \left(x' = \dfrac{a_1 x + b_1}{c_1 x + d_1}\right)$ is

$$\frac{x'-a_1}{x'-\beta_1} = e^{2\phi i}\frac{x-a_1}{x-\beta_1}, \text{ where } a_1 = \frac{a_1 a + b_1}{c_1 a + d_1}, \quad \beta_1 = \frac{a_1\beta + b_1}{c_1\beta + d_1}.$$

(xiii) If S and S_1 have a common pole and their commutator is of finite order, they have a second common pole.

(xiv) The orders of $x' = \dfrac{\sqrt{8}x-1}{x}, \dfrac{1}{\sqrt{2}-x}$, and $\dfrac{x+\sqrt{8}-2}{x+\sqrt{3}}$ are 6, 4, and 12 respectively.

§ 10. In §§ 4 to 9 the symbols used (x_i, a_{ij}, &c.) denoted ordinary real or complex quantities. Much of the preceding is, however, applicable if the symbols denote any quantities with laws of addition, subtraction, multiplication, and division, these operations (additions, &c.) being subject to the laws of ordinary algebra.

Let p be any prime, and let $P(x) \equiv x^r + p_1 x^{r-1} + \ldots + p_r$ be a rational integral function of x with positive integral coefficients less than p and not reducible mod p; i.e. not satisfying any equation of the form

$$P(x) \equiv P_1(x) \cdot P_2(x) + p \cdot P_3(x),$$

where $P_1(x), P_2(x)$, and $P_3(x)$ are integral functions with integral coefficients.

Let $F(x)$ be any integral function of x with integral coefficients. The remainder when $F(x)$ is divided by $P(x)$ is evidently of the form $f(x) + p \cdot \phi(x)$, where $\phi(x)$ is an integral function of degree $r-1$ with integral coefficients and $f(x) \equiv a_0 + a_1 x + a_2 x^2 + \ldots + a_{r-1} x^{r-1}$ in which each coefficient is one of the integers $0, 1, 2, \ldots, p-1$. We call $f(x)$ the *residue* of $F(x)$, mod p and $P(x)$. There are p^r possible residues, for each of the r coefficients $a_0, a_1, \ldots, a_{r-1}$ may be chosen in p ways.

All functions having the same residue are said to form a *class*. If F_1, F_2 are any two functions belonging to two given classes, the classes of $F_1+F_2, F_1-F_2, F_1 F_2$ are evidently definitely and uniquely given, so that the classes obey laws of addition, subtraction, and multiplication. The classes C_0 and C_1 corresponding to the cases $a_0 = a_1 = a_2 = \ldots = a_{r-1} = 0$

and $a_0 = 1$, $a_1 = a_2 = \ldots = a_{r-1} = 0$, are called the *zero* and *unit* classes respectively. If C is any other class, evidently $C + C_0 = C_0 + C = C$ and $CC_1 = C_1 C = C$.

To show that the classes obey a unique law of division (the divisor not being the zero class), we must prove that, C_u and C_v being any two classes, we can always find a single class C_w such that $C_u = C_v C_w$ ($v \neq 0$). Then $C_w = C_u \div C_v$. It is sufficient to show that we can find a single class C_v^{-1} such that $C_v \cdot C_v^{-1} = C_1$; for then $C_w = C_v^{-1} C_u$.

Let $F(x)$ be a function of the class C_v. Then, since C_v is not the zero class and $P(x)$ is not reducible mod p, we can prove that functions $F_1(x)$, $P_1(x)$ exist such that

$$F_1(x) \cdot F(x) - P_1(x) \cdot P(x) \equiv 1 \pmod{p}.$$

The proof is an extension of the method used in showing that if e, f are two integers with no common factor, we can find integers e_1, f_1 such that $e_1 e - f_1 f = 1$ (see Dickson's *Linear Groups*. Teubner, 1901, p. 8). Then $F_1(x)$ belongs to the class C_v^{-1}.

We may represent the classes by the *marks*

$$u_0, u_1, u_2, \ldots, u_{p^r-1},$$

which obey laws of addition, subtraction, multiplication, and division, and form a *Galois Field of order* p^r denoted by $GF[p^r]$. We shall suppose $u_{f(p)}$ the mark of the class to which $f(x)$ belongs. Then u_0 is the zero mark such that $u_e + u_0 = u_0 + u_e = u_e$, and u_1 is the unit mark such that $u_1 u_e = u_e u_1 = u_e$. We may denote the mark $u_{f(p)}$ by the integer $f(p)$ when no ambiguity is introduced thereby. This notation is especially useful when $r = 1$ and in the case of the zero and unit marks of any Field.

The Galois Field contains p *integral marks* $u_0, u_1, u_2, \ldots, u_{p-1}$ corresponding to the cases in which

$$a_1 = a_2 = \ldots = a_{r-1} = 0, \text{ and } a_0 = 0, 1, 2, \ldots, p-1$$

respectively. An important case is that in which $r = 1$. Then $f(x)$ is one of the integers $0, 1, 2, \ldots, p-1$. The Galois Field consists solely of the zero and integral marks which are usually denoted in this case by $0, 1, 2, \ldots, p-1$, and are called 'integers reduced mod p'. All integers leaving the same remainder when divided by p form a class.

Ex. 1. Find $u_{p-1} + u_1$, $u_0 - u_{\lambda p^e}$ ($p > \lambda > 0$), and $u_{p^r-1} - u_t$.

Ex. 2. If $p^r = 2^2$, $P(x)$ is $x^2 + x + 1$.

Ex. 3. If $p^r = 3^2$, $P(x)$ is $x^2 + 1$, $x^2 + x + 2$, or $x^2 + 2x + 2$.

Ex. 4. Find addition and multiplication tables for all marks of the Field (i) when $p^r = 2^2$, (ii) when
$$p^r = 3^2 \text{ and } P(x) \equiv x^2 + 2x + 2.*$$

Ex. 5. In Ex. 4 (ii) find the difference and quotient of u_3 and u_4, u_2 and u_5, u_8 and u_3.

Ex. 6. The substitution $x' = x + b$ is of order p, if b is any non-zero mark of a $GF[p^r]$.

Ex. 7. (i) The substitution (S) $x' = \dfrac{ax+b}{cx+d}$ is of order 2, 3, 4, 6, p if $\dfrac{(a+d)^2}{ad-bc} = u_0$, u_1, $u_1 + u_1$, $u_1 + u_1 + u_1$, $u_1 + u_1 + u_1 + u_1$ respectively; where a, b, c, d are marks of a $GF[p^r]$. (ii) Find the general condition that $S^n = 1$.

Ex. 8. Every linear substitution whose coefficients are marks of a $GF[p^r]$ is of finite order.

Ex. 9. Find the orders of $(y, x+y)$, $(y, x+1)$ in the $GF[2]$.

Ex. 10. Find the orders of $x' = \dfrac{x+3}{x+4}$, $\dfrac{4}{x}$, $x+1$ in the $GF[5]$.

Ex. 11. If S, T, U denote $x' = \dfrac{x+4}{8x+6}$, $\dfrac{4x+1}{4x+8}$, $\dfrac{6}{x}$ in the $GF[7]$, find the orders of S, T, U, TU, ST, STU.

Ex. 12. If S, T, U denote $x' = \dfrac{9x+7}{4x+2}$, $\dfrac{5x+8}{5x+6}$, $\dfrac{4}{8x}$ in the $GF[11]$, find the orders of S, T, U, ST, SU, STU.

Ex. 13. Find the orders of $x' = x+2$, $\dfrac{2x+1}{x}$ in the $GF[2^2]$.

Ex. 14. Find the orders of $x' = \dfrac{2x+4}{4x}$, $\dfrac{7x+1}{6}$ in the $GF[3^2]$ when $P(x) \equiv x^2 + 2x + 2$.

Ex. 15. If u is a solution of an equation of degree k in a $GF[p^r]$ (i.e. an equation of the k-th degree in which the unknown quantity and the coefficients are marks of the Field) but of no equation of degree $< k$, the p^k marks $a_0 + a_1 u + \ldots + a_{k-1} u^{k-1}$ are all distinct; $a_0, a_1, \ldots, a_{k-1}$ being any marks of the Field.

Ex. 16. Every mark of a $GF[p^r]$ is a solution of some equation of degree $\leq r$ in the Field.

Ex. 17. In Ex. 15 every power of u is of the form
$$b_0 + b_1 u + \ldots + b_{k-1} u^{k-1},$$
where $b_0, b_1, \ldots, b_{k-1}$ are marks of the Field.

---

* Unless $r=1$ such tables depend, of course, on the irreducible function chosen as $P(x)$. It may be shown that changing $P(x)$ is merely equivalent to permuting the marks of the Field; i.e. there is only one essentially distinct $GF[p^r]$.

Ex. 18. If $u_1, u_2, \ldots, u_k$ are the roots of the equation
$$F(u) \equiv u^k + a_1 u^{k-1} + \ldots + a_{k-1} u + a_k = 0 \text{ in a } GF[p^r]$$
and S_t denotes $u_1{}^t + u_2{}^t + \ldots + u_k{}^t$, prove that

(i) $F(u)\left(\dfrac{1}{u-u_1} + \dfrac{1}{u-u_2} + \ldots + \dfrac{1}{u-u_k}\right) = ku^{k-1}$
$\qquad\qquad\qquad\qquad\qquad\qquad + (k-1)a_1 u^{k-2} + \ldots + a_{k-1};$

(ii) $S_e + a_1 S_{e-1} + a_2 S_{e-2} + \ldots + a_{e-1} S_1 + e a_e = 0$, $(e = 1, 2, \ldots, k)$;

(iii) $S_e + a_1 S_{e-1} + a_2 S_{e-2} + \ldots + a_k S_{e-k} = 0$, $(e = k+1, k+2, k+3, \ldots)$.

§ 11. If u is any mark of a $GF[p^r]$, the series $u, u^2, u^3, \ldots$ contains at most $p^r - 1$ distinct marks, since the Field only contains $p^r - 1$ marks excluding $0 \ (\equiv u_0)$. Hence for some value of s and t, $u^s = u^t$ and $u^{s-t} = 1 \ (\equiv u_1)$. If u^n is the first mark of the series which $= 1$, n is called the *period* of u. Let u' be a mark not included in the series $S \equiv (u, u^2, \ldots, u^n)$, u'' a mark not included in the series

$$S \text{ or } u'S \equiv (u'u, u'u^2, \ldots, u'u^n),$$

u''' a mark not included in $S, u'S, u''S$, and so on. Then we see at once that no two of the marks included in $S, u'S, u''S, u'''S, \ldots$ are identical. Hence:—

The period of each mark of the $GF[p^r]$ is a divisor of $p^r - 1$.

Just as we prove in ordinary algebra that an equation of the n-th degree has not more than n roots, so we prove that there are not more than n marks u satisfying an equation $c_0 u^n + c_1 u^{n-1} + \ldots + c_n = 0$ whose coefficients are marks of the Galois Field. It follows that, if d is any divisor of $p^r - 1$, there are d marks satisfying $u^d = 1$. For there are $p^r - 1$ marks satisfying $u^{p^r-1} = 1$, and $u^{p^r-1} \equiv (u^d - 1) \cdot \phi(u)$, where $\phi(u)$ is of degree $(p^r - 1) \div d$. But $\phi(u) = 0$ is satisfied by at most $(p^r - 1) \div d$ marks of the Field, and hence there are d marks satisfying $u^d - 1 = 0$.

A mark satisfying $u^k = 1$, but no equation $u^e = 1$ $(e < k)$ is called a *primitive root* of $u^k = 1$.

If $u^k = 1$ and u is a primitive root of $u^x = 1$, x is a factor of k. For if $k = lx + m$ $(x > m \geq 0)$, $u^m = u^{k-lx} = 1$; and therefore $m = 0$.

Let $k = a^\alpha b^\beta c^\gamma \ldots$, where $a, b, c, \ldots$ are primes. Then the numbers of primitive roots of $u^k = 1$ is $k -$ (the number of roots of $u^{k \div a} = 1, u^{k \div b} = 1, u^{k \div c} = 1, \ldots) + $ (the number of roots

of $u^{k+ab}=1$, $u^{k+ac}=1$, ...) — (the number of roots of
$u^{k+abc}=1$, ...) + &c. $= k - \left(\dfrac{k}{a} + \dfrac{k}{b} + \dfrac{k}{c} + ...\right)$
$$+ \left(\dfrac{k}{ab} + \dfrac{k}{ac} + ...\right) - \left(\dfrac{k}{abc} + ...\right) + ...$$
$$= k\left(1 - \dfrac{1}{a}\right)\left(1 - \dfrac{1}{b}\right)\left(1 - \dfrac{1}{c}\right)....*$$

A primitive root of $u^{p^r-1}=1$ is called a *primitive root of the Field*. If u is such a primitive root, the marks of the Field are u_0, u, u^2, u^3, ..., $u^{p^r-1}(\equiv 1)$.

Ex. 1. If a, b, c are marks of a $GF[p^r]$ and the periods of a and c are k and l respectively, the order of $x' = ax+b$ is k, of $(ax, bx+ay)$ is pk, and of $(ax, bx+cy)$ is the L. C. M. of k and l.

Ex. 2. How many primitive roots of the $GF[3^4]$ and $GF[7^3]$ are there?

Ex. 3. Every primitive root of the $GF[p^r]$ satisfies an equation of degree r but no equation of lower degree.

Ex. 4. If u is a primitive root of the $GF[p^r]$ and d is a factor of p^r-1, $u^{(p^r-1)+d}$ is a primitive root of $u^d = 1$.

Ex. 5. No integral mark is a primitive root of a $GF[p^r]$ unless $r = 1$.

Ex. 6. In (i) the $GF[11]$, (ii) the $GF[3^2]$ where $P(x) \equiv x^2 + 2x + 2$, find the primitive roots of the Field and the period of the mark 4.

Ex. 7. (i) Every similarity-substitution on m given variables whose coefficients are marks of a given Field is a power of a given similarity. (ii) The order of a multiplication is the L. C. M. of the periods of the coefficients.

Ex. 8. A mark of a $GF[p^r]$ is called a *square* or a *not-square* according as it is or is not the square of some mark of the Field. Prove that (i) if $p = 2$, every mark is a square; (ii) if $p > 2$, the even powers of any primitive root u are squares and the odd powers are not-squares; (iii) the product and quotient of two squares or of two not-squares are squares; (iv) the product and quotient of a square and a not-square are not-squares.

Ex. 9. If d is the H. C. F. of m and p^r-1, there are exactly $(p^r-1) \div d$ marks ($\neq 0$) of the $GF[p^r]$ which are m-th powers of some mark of the Field.

Ex. 10. By two 'conjugate complex quantities' $\mathbf{a}$ and $\bar{\mathbf{a}}$ we mean two quantities $a_1 + a_2 i$, $a_1 - a_2 i$ where a_1, a_2 are marks of a given $GF[p^r]$ ($p > 2$), and i is defined by $i^2 = $ a given primitive root u of the Field. Prove that (i) $\mathbf{a}\bar{\mathbf{a}} \neq 0$ unless $\mathbf{a} = \bar{\mathbf{a}} = 0$; (ii) $\mathbf{ab} \neq 0$ unless $\mathbf{a}$ or $\mathbf{b} = 0$; (iii) $\mathbf{a}^{p^r} = \bar{\mathbf{a}}$; (iv) $\mathbf{a}^{p^{2r}-1} = 1$.

---

* This number is usually denoted by $\phi(k)$. As the above proof shows, $\phi(k) = $ the number of numbers $\leq k$ and prime to k.

CHAPTER IV

GEOMETRICAL ELEMENTS

§ 1. A GEOMETRICAL *movement* is any displacement of a figure which does not alter the distance between any pair of points. For example, a reflexion in a plane, a rotation about a line, an inversion about a point O,* &c., are 'movements'.

Let a, b be any two planes meeting in a line l (perpendicular to the plane of Fig. 1), and suppose a is brought to coincide with b by a rotation about l through any angle $\frac{1}{2}\alpha$. Then if any point P is brought to Q by reflexion in a, and Q is brought to R by reflexion in b, evidently P is brought to R by a rotation through α about l.† Hence successive reflexions in two planes are in general equivalent to a rotation about the intersection of the planes.

In the particular case in which l is at infinity (Fig. 2) we see that successive reflexions in two parallel planes whose distance apart is $\frac{1}{2}x$ move any point through a distance x in the direction perpendicular to the planes. Such a movement is called a *translation*.

If A, B are two movements such that the effect of applying to any figure first A and then B is the same as that of applying first B and then A, A and B are called *permutable* movements.

In §§ 1 to 6 we shall denote 'successive reflexions in the planes $a, b, c, \ldots$' by $(a).(b).(c)\ldots$

Ex. 1. Reflexions in two given planes are only permutable if the planes are perpendicular.

Ex. 2. The following pairs of movements are permutable:—
(i) a rotation about a line l and a reflexion in a plane perpendicular to l; (ii) rotation about l and inversion about any point of l; (iii) rotation about l and a translation parallel to l; (iv) reflexion

---

* A displacement such that the line joining the initial and final positions of each point of the figure passes through O and is bisected at O.

† Attention must be paid to the sign of α. We consider α positive if it is described in the clockwise direction.

in a plane and a translation parallel to the plane; (v) any two translations.

Ex. 3. A line l meets a plane P at right angles in O. Any two of the three movements (i) reflexion in P, (ii) inversion about O, (iii) rotation through π about l, are permutable; and a combination of any two is equivalent to the third.

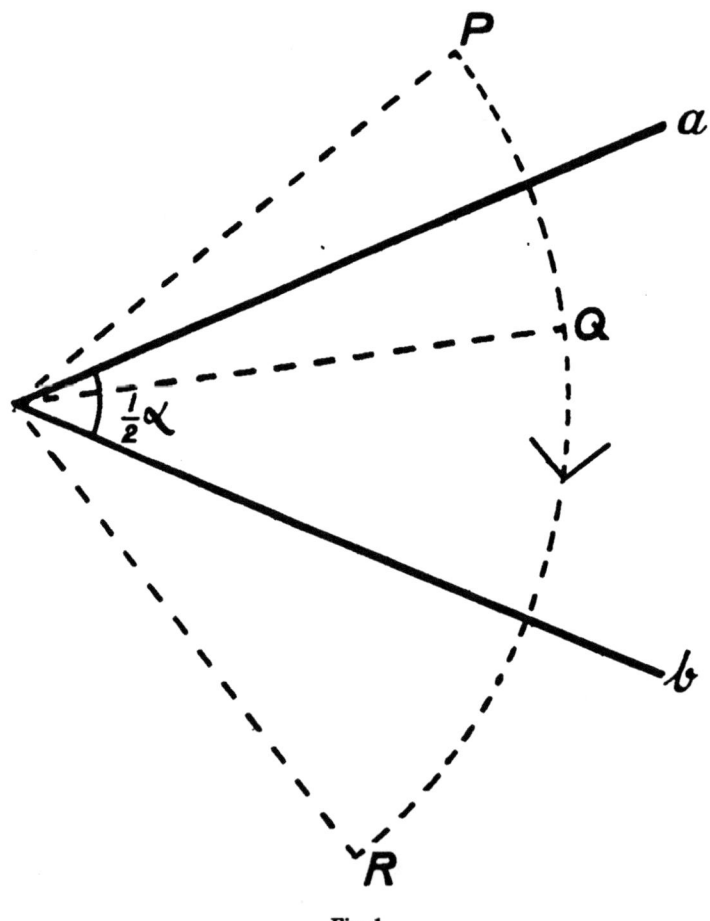

Fig. 1.

Ex. 4. An inversion is equivalent to successive reflexions in three mutually perpendicular planes.

Ex. 5. Any number of successive translations is equivalent to a single translation.

Ex. 6. Translations can be represented by vectors drawn from a fixed point, and combine in accordance with the 'parallelogram law'.

Ex. 7. An inversion followed by a translation is equivalent to an inversion.

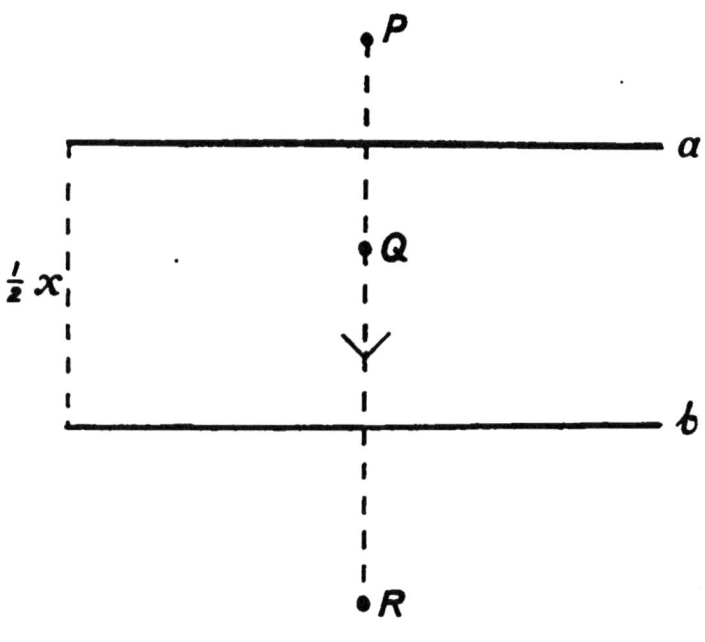

Fig. 2.

Ex. 8. The only movement which leaves three non-collinear points P, Q, R fixed is a reflexion in the plane PQR.

Ex. 9. The only movements which leave two points P, Q fixed are those obtained by combining successive reflexions in planes through PQ.

§ 2. Let OA, OB be two intersecting lines. Take OC such that the angle between the planes OAB, OAC is $\tfrac{1}{2}\alpha$* and the angle between the planes OBC, OBA is $\tfrac{1}{2}\beta$. Let $\tfrac{1}{2}\gamma$ be the angle between the planes OCB, OCA. Then a rotation

* i.e. when the second plane OAC is rotated about OA through an angle $\tfrac{1}{2}\alpha$ it comes into coincidence with the first plane OAB; and so in the other two cases.

through α about OA followed by a rotation through $β$ about $OB \equiv (OAC).(OAB).(OBA).(OBC) \equiv (OCA).(OCB) \equiv$ a rotation through $γ$ about OC. This composition of two rotations is called *Euler's (or Rodrigues') construction*.

Ex. 1. A rotation through $β$ about OB followed by a rotation through α about $OA \equiv$ a rotation through $γ$ about the reflexion of OC in the plane AOB.

Ex. 2. The two rotations of § 2 are permutable only (i) if α, $β$, or AOB is very small, (ii) if $α = β = γ = π$.

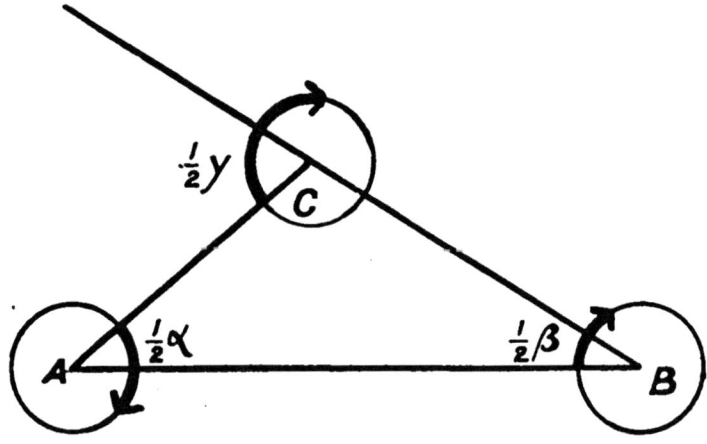

Fig. 3.

Ex. 3. Successive reflexions in any even number of planes through a fixed point are equivalent to a rotation.

Ex. 4. If $α = mβ$ and α, $β$ are small, find $γ$ and the position of OC.

Ex. 5. Successive rotations through angles α, $β$ about parallel lines are equivalent to a rotation through $α+β$ about another parallel line.

Ex. 6. Rotations through α about OA, $β$ about OB, α about OA are equivalent to a rotation about a line in the plane AOB.

Ex. 7. Successive rotations through equal and opposite angles about parallel lines are equivalent to a translation.

Ex. 8. A rotation about l followed by a translation perpendicular to l (or vice versa) is equivalent to a rotation through an equal angle about a line parallel to l. The translation and rotation are never permutable unless one or other is infinitesimal.

IV 4] ROTATORY-INVERSIONS 37

Ex. 9. Successive rotations about three radii of a sphere through twice the angles of the corresponding spherical triangle produce no displacement on any figure.

Ex. 10. AOA', BOB', COC' and aOa', bOb', cOc' are two sets of mutually perpendicular lines. OA, OB, OC are brought into the positions Oa, Ob, Oc; Oa, Ob', Oc'; Oa', Ob, Oc'; Oa', Ob', Oc by rotations about OD, OD_1, OD_2, OD_3. Prove that (i) the planes D_1OA, DOA are perpendicular; (ii) the planes DOD_1, BOC, D_2OD_3 are concurrent; (iii) the planes DOD_1, D_2OD_3 are perpendicular.

Ex. 11. (i) Translations, (ii) rotations about lines through a fixed point may be considered as elements.

§ 3. *Every odd number of successive reflexions is equivalent to three successive reflexions.*

If we prove this for five successive reflexions, we can at once extend it to the case of seven successive reflexions, then to nine, and so on. Take then five successive reflexions in the planes 1, 2, 3, 4, 5. Now by § 1 if the planes 4 and 5 meet in a line l, we can replace the movement (4).(5) by (IV).(V); where IV is any plane through l chosen arbitrarily, and V is a plane through l such that the angle between IV and V is the same as the angle between 4 and 5. Take IV as the plane through l passing through the intersection of 1, 2, 3. Then (1).(2).(3).(IV) is equivalent by § 2 to two successive reflexions, so that the theorem is proved.

Ex. Every even number of successive reflexions is equivalent to four successive reflexions.

§ 4. The movement (1).(2).(3) is reduced to its simplest form as follows. If 2 and 3 meet in a line l, (2).(3) may be replaced as in § 3 by (2').(III); where 2' is perpendicular to 1. Then (1).(2') may be replaced by (I).(II) where I is a plane perpendicular to the planes II and III. Now (II).(III) $\equiv$ a rotation about the intersection h of II and III which is perpendicular to I. Hence (1).(2).(3) $\equiv$ a *rotatory-reflexion*, i.e. a reflexion in a plane followed by a rotation about a line perpendicular to that plane. The reflexion and rotation are obviously permutable.

Since a reflexion in I has evidently the same effect as an inversion about the intersection of I and h followed by a rotation through π about h, the movement is also equivalent to a *rotatory-inversion*, i.e. an inversion about a point followed by a rotation about a line through the point. The inversion and rotation are obviously permutable. Evidently no two rotatory-inversions can be equivalent unless they are identical. Hence :—

Every odd number of successive reflexions is equivalent to a unique rotatory-inversion.

Reflexion, inversion, &c., are particular cases of rotatory-inversion. One case requires special mention; that in which the line h is at infinity. The movement is then called a *gliding-reflexion*, and is equivalent to a reflexion in a plane followed by a translation parallel to that plane.

Ex. 1. (i) An odd number of successive reflexions brings in general one and only one point to its original position. (ii) What are the exceptions?

Ex. 2. Show that a gliding-reflexion S is equivalent to a rotation through π about a line l followed by inversion about a point not lying in l.

§ 5. We shall now show how to reduce an even number of successive reflexions to its simplest form. By § 3 it is sufficient to consider four successive reflexions in the planes 1, 2, 3, 4. As in § 4 we can reduce the movement $(1).(2).(3)$ to $(I).(II).(III)$, where the planes II and III meet in the line h perpendicular to I. Then $(II).(III)$ can be replaced by $(\mathbf{2}).(\mathbf{3})$, where the planes $\mathbf{2}$, $\mathbf{3}$ pass through h and $\mathbf{3}$ is perpendicular to $\mathbf{4}$. Now the planes I and $\mathbf{2}$ are perpendicular, and so are the planes $\mathbf{3}$ and 4. Hence $(1).(2).(3).(4)$ $\equiv$ two successive rotations through π about two lines a, b; where a is the intersection of I and $\mathbf{2}$, and b is the intersection of $\mathbf{3}$ and 4.

Let k be the line meeting a, b at right angles. Let α and β be the planes through k, a and k, b. Let κ_1, κ_2 be the planes through a, b perpendicular to k. Then two successive rotations through π about $a, b \equiv (\alpha) \cdot (\kappa_1) \cdot (\beta) \cdot (\kappa_2)$ $\equiv (\alpha) \cdot (\beta) \cdot (\kappa_1) \cdot (\kappa_2)$, since reflexions in the two perpendicular planes κ_1, β are evidently permutable. But $(\alpha) \cdot (\beta) \equiv$ a rotation about k, and $(\kappa_1) \cdot (\kappa_2) \equiv$ a translation parallel to k.

This combination of a rotation about k followed by a translation parallel to k is called a *screw* about k. The rotation and translation are obviously permutable. Two screws are evidently equivalent only if they coincide. Hence :—

IV 7]   CONGRUENCY AND ENANTIOMORPHY   39

Every even number of successive reflexions is equivalent to a unique screw.

A rotation or translation is a particular case of a screw.

§ **6.** *Every geometrical movement is equivalent to a screw or a rotatory-inversion.*

Let A, B be the initial positions of any two points of a figure, and let A', B' be their final positions after the figure has been subjected to any movement leaving unaltered the distance between every pair of points. Let c be the plane bisecting AA' at right angles; and let B_1 be the reflexion of B in c, so that $A'B_1 = AB$. Let d be the plane bisecting $B'B_1$ at right angles. Since $A'B_1 = AB = A'B'$, d passes through A'. Hence $(c).(d)$ brings A to A' and B to B'. The movement is completed by successive reflexions in planes passing through the line $A'B'$; for evidently every movement keeping both A' and B' fixed is obtained by combining such reflexions. Hence the whole movement is equivalent to a number of successive reflexions; which proves the theorem.

If the movement is equivalent to a screw, the initial and final positions F, G of the figure are *congruent* or 'superposable'. The movement is called a *movement of the first sort*, and is equivalent to an even number of successive reflexions.

If the movement is equivalent to a rotatory-inversion, F and G are *enantiomorphous*; they are related in the same way as a right and left hand, or as an object and its reflexion in a mirror. The movement is called a *movement of the second sort*, and is equivalent to an odd number of successive reflexions.

Ex. 1. AA', BB', CC' are diameters of a sphere. The spherical triangles ABC, $A'B'C'$ have corresponding sides and angles equal and are enantiomorphous.

Ex. 2. A movement is completely determined when we are given the initial and final positions of four non-coplanar points of any figure to which the movement is applied.

Ex. 3. What movements leave a given point O fixed?

§ **7.** If S and T are any two movements, and S brings a figure from the position F to the position G, while T brings it from G to H; the figure is brought from F to H by a unique screw or rotatory-reflexion U which may be considered as the product of S and T $(ST = U)$.

It is obvious that, when the law of combination of movements is defined in this way, elements obey the associative law and satisfy the conditions by which elements were defined. The identical element is the operation of leaving the figure unmoved. The element inverse to S is the unique screw or rotatory-inversion bringing the figure from the position G to F.

Ex. 1. The product of r movements of the first sort and s movements of the second sort is of the first or second sort according as s is even or odd.

Ex. 2. A rotation or rotatory-inversion of angle α is of finite order if and only if $\alpha \div \pi$ is commensurable.

Ex. 3. A screw is not in general of finite order.

Ex. 4. Find the order of a rotatory-inversion of angle $2\pi \div n$ (n integral).

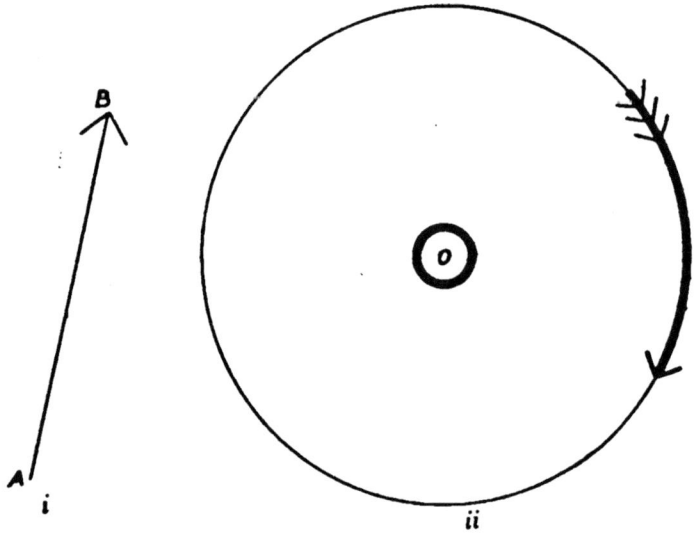

Fig. 4.

§ 8. Any movement may be conveniently represented by a geometrical diagram. Thus Fig. 4 (i) represents a translation parallel to the line AB through a distance AB. Again, Fig. 4 (ii) represents the rotatory-inversion consisting of an inversion about O followed by a rotation about l through α; where l is the line through O perpendicular to the plane of the diagram and α is the angle subtended at O by the arrow there shown.* A rotation may be denoted by omitting the O, and a screw by combining the diagrams representing a translation and a rotation.

Ex. 1. Another convenient representation is as follows:— Denote a screw by a pair of unlimited straight lines, and a rotatory-inversion by a pair of unlimited intersecting straight lines with a O at their point of intersection.

Ex. 2. All equal straight lines drawn in the same direction represent the same translation.

§ 9. *The transform of a movement S by a movement T is found by performing the movement T on the geometrical representation of S.*

Let λ be any geometrical representation of S. Let any point P' be brought to the position P by T^{-1}, let P be brought to Q by S, and let Q be brought to Q' by T. Let λ be brought by T into the position λ'. Then T brings P, Q, λ into the positions P', Q', λ' respectively. Hence the figure $PQ\lambda$ is congruent or enantiomorphous to the figure $P'Q'\lambda'$ according as T is of the first or second sort. Now λ is the representation of the movement S bringing P to Q: hence λ' is the representation of a similar† movement S' bringing P' to Q'. But $T^{-1}ST$ brings P' to Q', and this is true for all positions of the point P'. Hence $S' = T^{-1}ST$.

Ex. 1. If S is a right-handed screw, S' is a similar screw but right- or left-handed according as T is of the first or second sort.

Ex. 2. The transform of a rotation is a rotation, and of a translation is a translation.

Ex. 3. If S is any given screw, T any given translation, we can always find a translation t such that $TS = St$.

Ex. 4. If T, t are given equal translations, we can always find a rotation R such that $TR = Rt$.

Ex. 5. If S, s are two similar screws (both right- or both left-handed) about parallel lines l, l', we can always find translations T, t such that $ST = Ts, S = st$.

Ex. 6. If S is any screw and R any rotation of the same angle about parallel lines l and l', we can find translations T, T' such that $S = RT = T'R$.

---

* The rotatory-inversion may be called 'a rotatory-inversion through α about O and l'.

† For example, if S is a rotatory-inversion, S' is a rotatory-inversion through the same angle; if S is a screw, S' is a screw with the same translation and angle, &c.

Ex. 7. If I, i are any two similar rotatory-inversions about parallel lines, we can find translations T, T' such that $I = iT = T'i$.

Ex. 8. If S is a screw and R a rotation of the same angle about a parallel line, while s is a second screw and r a rotation of the same angle about a parallel line, we can find translations T, T' such that $Ss = Rr \cdot T = T' \cdot Rr$.

Ex. 9. Prove a result similar to that of Ex. 8 for the product of a screw and a rotatory-inversion or of two rotatory-inversions.

Ex. 10. Prove the following practical construction for finding the resultant of screws of angles α, β, ... about lines a, b, ... 'Find the position O to which any convenient point O' is brought by the successive screws. Find the resultant R of rotations through α, β, ... about lines through O parallel to a, b, ... Let M be the screw equivalent to a translation represented by $O'O$ followed by the rotation R. Then M is the required resultant.'

Ex. 11. Obtain a method similar to that of Ex. 10 for finding the resultant of any number of successive screws and rotatory-inversions.

Ex. 12. The resultant of three screws of angle π about three perpendicular non-intersecting sides of a rectangular parallelepipedon whose translations are represented by twice the respective sides is identity. (The resultant of the three translations taken alone is represented by twice that diagonal of the parallelepipedon which meets none of the three sides.)

Ex. 13. If a, b are two lines inclined at an angle θ and at a distance s apart, the resultant of screws through π about a and b whose translations are $2x$ and $2y$ is a screw through 2θ of translation $2z$ about a line whose distances from a and b are $\operatorname{cosec} \theta \, (y + x \cos \theta)$ and $\operatorname{cosec} \theta \, (x + y \cos \theta)$.

Ex. 14. $ABCD$ is the face of a cube; AOA', BOB', COC', DOD' are its diagonals. Find the resultant of a rotatory-inversion through $\dfrac{2\pi}{3}$ about A and AD, a screw of angle π and translation represented by AB about $C'D'$, a screw of angle π and translation $2C'A$ about a line through O parallel to $C'A$, and a gliding-reflexion in the plane $ADB'C'$ of translation AD.

§ 10. If a movement (other than identity) brings every point of a figure F into the position previously occupied either by itself or by some other point of F, F is said to possess *symmetry*. If F is thus brought to self-coincidence by reflexion in a plane s, s is called a *symmetry-plane* of F. If F is brought to self-coincidence by a rotation about a line l through a positive angle α (but through no smaller angle), l is called an *n-al rotation-axis* of F, where $n\alpha = 2\pi$. Similarly we can have an '*n*-al symmetry-axis of rotatory-inversion', a 'centre of symmetry', a 'screw-axis of symmetry', &c.

For example, a cube has its middle point O as a centre of symmetry (i.e. it is its own inverse about O), its diagonal as a 3-al rotation-axis, the plane through two opposite edges as a symmetry-plane, &c.

Ex. 1. Find other symmetry-axes of a cube.

Ex. 2. (i) If l is an n-al rotation-axis or symmetry-axis of rotatory-inversion, n is integral. (ii) Give a case in which $n = \infty$.

Ex. 3. No translation nor screw (unless it reduces to a rotation) can bring a finite figure to self-coincidence.

§ 11. Many other geometrical operations besides 'movements' satisfy the conditions to which elements are subject. As an example we may take successive inversions in any number of circles all of which are orthogonal to a fixed circle.

If we project any figure on a sphere Σ from a point V of Σ on to the plane through the centre O perpendicular to OV (stereographic projection), the projected figure is the inverse of the original with respect to a sphere of centre V and radius $\sqrt{2} \cdot OV$. Hence a circle projects into a circle, and angles are unaltered by projection. If c is any circle on Σ, and P, Q are points on Σ inverse with respect to c (PQ passes through the pole of the plane of c with respect to Σ), all circles on Σ through P and Q are orthogonal to c. Hence, if c', P', Q' are the projections of c, P, Q, all circles through P' and Q' are orthogonal to c', i.e. P' and Q' are inverse with respect to c'. In particular, if c is a great circle, P and Q are reflexions of each other in the plane of c; while c' is orthogonal to the fixed circle which is the projection of the circle at infinity on Σ. Hence from each theorem concerning successive reflexions in planes through a given point, may be deduced a theorem concerning successive inversions in circles orthogonal to a fixed circle.

Ex. 1. Show that in any plane (i) a rotation about a point, (ii) a translation, (iii) a magnification with respect to a point are particular cases of two successive inversions.

Ex. 2. The operation consisting of successive inversions in two given real circles is of finite order only if the circles cut at a real angle commensurable with π. It is equivalent to successive inversions in any two circles cutting at the same angle in the same points.

Ex. 3. Any even number of successive inversions in circles orthogonal to a fixed circle is equivalent to two successive inversions.

Ex. 4. If S is an operation consisting of successive inversions in the circles $j_1, j_2, j_3, \ldots$, and T is a similar operation changing these circles into the circles $i_1, i_2, i_3, \ldots$, $T^{-1}ST$ is the operation consisting of successive inversions in $i_1, i_2, i_3, \ldots$.

Ex. 5. Take rectangular Cartesian axes of reference in a plane. Let any geometrical operation displace a point from the position (x, y) to the position (x', y'). Let $z = x + iy$, $z' = x' + iy'$ ($i = \sqrt{-1}$). Find geometrical operations such that (i) $z' = d - z$, (ii) $z' = b \div z$, b and d being real. Deduce the fact that the product of these substitutions is finite only if ϕ is commensurable with π, where $\cos \phi = d \div 2\sqrt{b}$.

Ex. 6. To successive inversions in any two circles corresponds a substitution of the form $z' = \dfrac{az + b}{cz + d}$.

Ex. 7. If to the substitution $S \equiv \left(z' = \dfrac{az+b}{cz+d}\right)$ corresponds an inversion in a circle j followed by a reflexion in a line l, $\cos \phi \times$ the radius of $j =$ the perpendicular on l from the centre of j (see III 2_{12}).

Ex. 8. If the equations of j and l are real, (i) S is not loxodromic, (ii) A is conjugate to D and B to C with respect to a rectangular hyperbola whose centre is the origin and whose asymptote bisects AD; where A, B, C, D are the points representing the complex quantities a, b, c, d.

Ex. 9. When a, b, c, d are real, to S corresponds an inversion in $c^2x^2 + c^2y^2 + 2cdx + (bc - ad + d^2) = 0$ followed by a reflexion in $2cx = a - d$.

§ 12.
As another example we may take the case of collineation.

If two figures are such that each point P of one figure corresponds to a single point P' of the other, while conversely the single point P' corresponds to P; one figure is said to be derived from the other by a *collinear* or *projective* transformation.

First take the case in which both figures are plane. If (x, y, z), (x', y', z') are the coordinates of P, P' referred to any two triangles of reference (one in each figure), we have evidently relations of the form

$$x' = l_1 x + m_1 y + n_1 z, \quad y' = l_2 x + m_2 y + n_2 z, \quad z' = l_3 x + m_3 y + n_3 z.$$

If we choose the triangles of reference ABC, $A'B'C'$ so that A and A', B and B', C and C' are corresponding points in the two figures, $y' = z' = 0$ when $y = z = 0$, &c. Hence we have obviously $m_1 = n_1 = n_2 = l_2 = l_3 = m_3 = 0$. When we are given

the coordinates of another pair of corresponding points, we can find the ratios $l_1 : m_2 : n_3$. Hence a collinear transformation of one plane figure into another is completely determined by the correspondence between four points of one figure (no three of which lie on a straight line) and four points of the other.

Plane projection evidently establishes a collinear transformation of one plane into another, which is, moreover, the most general possible; for we can always project four given points A, B, C, V into four other arbitrary points a, b, c, v as follows. Let AV, BV meet BC, CA in D and E; and let av, bv meet bc, ca in d and e. Take X on BC such that the cross-ratio of $(BDCX) = bd \div cd$, and take Y on CA such that the cross-ratio of $(CEAY) = ce \div ae$. Then project XY to infinity, the angles BAC, CBA into angles equal to bac, cba, and the line AB into a line of length equal to ab.

Similarly if the figures are three-dimensional, we can show by taking the vertices of the two tetrahedra of reference as corresponding points that the collinear transformation is completely determined by the correspondence between five points of one figure (no four being coplanar) and five points of the other.

It is at once evident that to any number of coplanar points of one figure correspond coplanar points of the other. Similarly to collinear points of one figure correspond collinear points of the other.

Let $\alpha = 0, \beta = 0$ be the equations of two planes in one figure and $\alpha' = 0, \beta' = 0$ the equations of the corresponding planes in the other figure. Then to the planes

$$\alpha = \lambda_1 \beta, \ \alpha = \lambda_2 \beta, \ \alpha = \lambda_3 \beta, \ \alpha = \lambda_4 \beta$$

in one figure correspond the planes

$$\alpha' = \lambda_1 \beta', \ \alpha' = \lambda_2 \beta', \ \alpha' = \lambda_3 \beta', \ \alpha' = \lambda_4 \beta'$$

in the other. Hence the cross-ratios of the corresponding pencils of planes are identical, being both equal to

$$(\lambda_1 - \lambda_2)(\lambda_3 - \lambda_4) \div (\lambda_1 - \lambda_4)(\lambda_3 - \lambda_2).$$

It follows at once that the cross-ratios of corresponding pencils of lines or ranges of points are identical.

The operation of making one figure correspond to another by a collinear transformation is called a *collineation*. A collineation evidently satisfies the conditions by which an element was defined, the identical element being the collineation which makes each point of space correspond to itself.

Ex. 1. Carry out the reasoning of § 12 using Cartesian instead of homogeneous coordinates.

Ex. 2. A collinear transformation of one straight line into another is completely determined when three pairs of corresponding points are given; and the ranges formed by corresponding points are homographic.

Ex. 3. If the coordinates of two corresponding points referred to the same tetrahedron of reference are connected by relations defining a substitution S, the coordinates referred to any other tetrahedron are connected by relations defining a transform of S.

Ex. 4. A geometrical movement is a particular case of collineation.

Ex. 5. A collinear transformation of (i) a line, (ii) a plane, (iii) a three-dimensional figure into itself transforms in general respectively 2, 3, 4 points into themselves. Mention any exceptions.

Ex. 6. Find the self-corresponding points in the collineation defined by (i) a rotation of a plane about a point O, (ii) a screw about a line l, (iii) a rotatory-inversion about O and l.

Ex. 7. When both figures are referred to the same rectangular Cartesian axes of reference a homogeneous linear substitution defines a collineation leaving fixed the origin and the plane at infinity; and an orthogonal substitution defines a rotation or rotatory-inversion.

Ex. 8. A collineation leaving the circle at infinity fixed is equivalent to a magnification with respect to a point followed by a geometrical movement.

§ 13. Suppose now that the two figures derived from each other by collinear transformations are referred to the same tetrahedron of reference. Then the coordinates
$$(x', y', z', w'), (x, y, z, w)$$
of corresponding points P', P are connected by relations of the form
$$x' = l_1 x + m_1 y + n_1 z + p_1 w, \quad y' = l_2 x + m_2 y + n_2 z + p_2 w,$$
$$z' = l_3 x + m_3 y + n_3 z + p_3 w, \quad w' = l_4 x + m_4 y + n_4 z + p_4 w.$$
These equations define a substitution S. If S is of finite order, we can express it in terms of new variables X, Y, Z, W such that
$$X' = \omega_1 X, \quad Y' = \omega_2 Y, \quad Z' = \omega_3 Z, \quad W' = \omega_4 W \dots\dots\dots(\text{III } 8).$$
Taking $X = 0, Y = 0, Z = 0, W = 0$ as the faces of a new tetrahedron of reference, the corresponding points
$$(x', y', z', w'), (x, y, z, w)$$

are connected by the relations

$$x' = \omega_1 x, \quad y' = \omega_2 y, \quad z' = \omega_3 z, \quad w' = \omega_4 z.$$

If S is of order 2, $\omega_1^2 = \omega_2^2 = \omega_3^2 = \omega_4^2 = 1$, and therefore $\omega_1, \omega_2, \omega_3, \omega_4$ each $= \pm 1$.

If in this case $\omega_1 = \omega_2 = \omega_3 = \omega_4$, S is a similarity and the collineation is the identical collineation making each point correspond to itself. If $-\omega_1 = \omega_2 = \omega_3 = \omega_4$, PP' passes through the vertex $(1, 0, 0, 0)$ of the tetrahedron of reference and is divided harmonically by that vertex and the opposite face $x = 0$ of the tetrahedron. If $-\omega_1 = -\omega_2 = \omega_3 = \omega_4$, PP' intersects two opposite edges of the tetrahedron and is divided harmonically by them, as is at once proved.

Hence we see that there are two kinds of collineation of order 2; the 'perspective' in which the line joining two corresponding points passes through a fixed point and is divided harmonically by it and a fixed plane, and the 'non-perspective' in which the line joining two corresponding points intersects two fixed non-intersecting straight lines and is divided harmonically by them.

Just as we deduced from each theorem concerning successive reflexions in planes through a given point a theorem concerning successive inversions in circles orthogonal to a fixed circle, so we may deduce a theorem concerning perspective collineations of a plane whose fixed point and line are pole and polar with respect to a fixed circle (and hence by projection with respect to any fixed conic). For, using the notation of § 11, let c be a great circle of the sphere Σ and let the straight line c' be the ('gnomonic') projection of c from the centre O on to the tangent plane at V. Let the line through O perpendicular to the plane of c meet this tangent plane at C', and let P', Q' be the projections of two points P, Q on Σ which are the reflexions of each other in the plane of c. Then if $C'V$ meets c' in N' (Fig. 5), $C'N'$ is evidently perpendicular to c', and

$$C'V \cdot VN' = OV^2 \text{ since } C'ON' = OVN' = \tfrac{1}{2}\pi.$$

Hence C' is the pole of c' with respect to a fixed circle whose centre is V and radius $\sqrt{-OV^2}$. Moreover, the lines OP, OQ are evidently coplanar with and equally inclined to OC'. Hence if $C'P'Q'$ meets c' in F', $(C'F', P'Q')$ is harmonic since $C'OF' = \tfrac{1}{2}\pi$. Therefore P', Q' are derived from each other by a perspective collineation whose fixed point is C' and fixed line is c'.

48 PERSPECTIVE COLLINEATIONS [IV 13

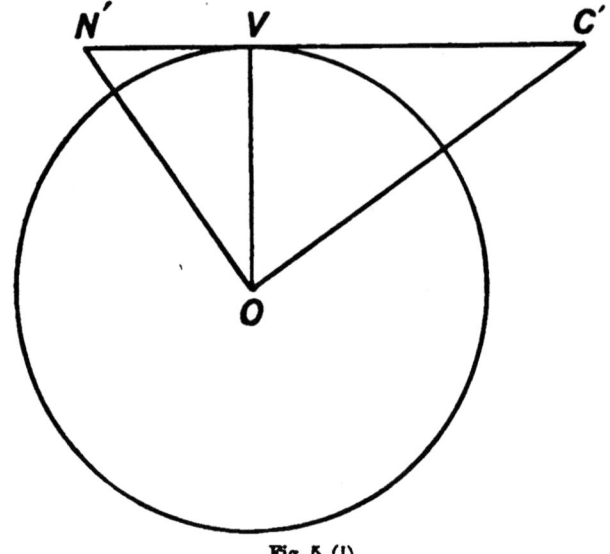

Fig. 5 (i).

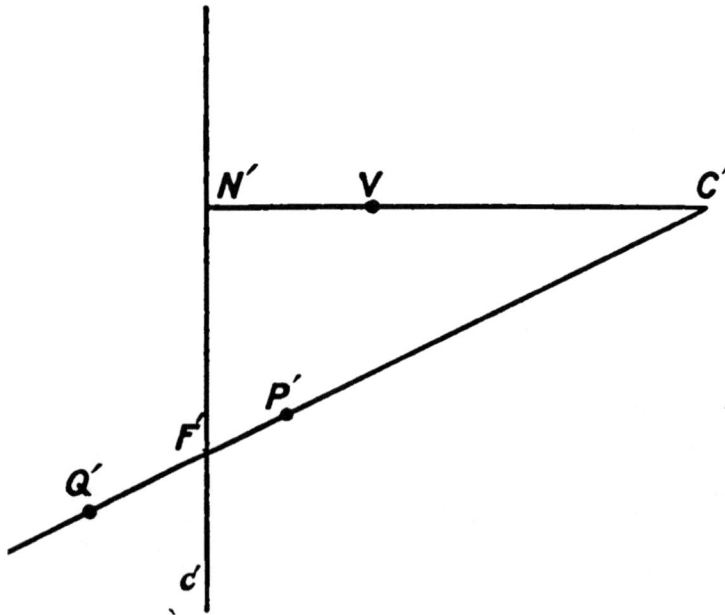

Fig. 5 (ii).

IV 13]   COLLINEATIONS OF ORDER TWO   49

In the above statement, for 'successive reflexions in planes through a given point' we may substitute 'successive rotations through π about lines through a given point'. For if Q_1 is the point diametrically opposite to Q on Σ, Q' is the projection of Q_1 as well as of Q, and P is brought to the position Q_1 by a rotation through π about OC'.

Ex. 1. If a straight line is transformed into itself by a collineation of order 2, corresponding points are the pairs of an involution on the line.

Ex. 2. If a plane is transformed into itself by a collineation of order 2, the line joining corresponding points passes through a fixed point and is divided harmonically by it and a fixed straight line.

Ex. 3. A perspective collineation of order 2 transforms the fixed point and every point of the fixed plane into itself; and a non-perspective collineation of order 2 transforms every point of the two fixed lines into itself.

Ex. 4. A rotation through π about a line l is a particular case of a non-perspective collineation of order 2.

Ex. 5. A reflexion in a plane and inversion about a point are particular cases of a perspective collineation of order 2.

Ex. 6. If a collineation T makes a point P' correspond to a point P and a plane σ' to a plane σ, and S is the perspective collineation whose fixed point and plane are P and σ, $T^{-1}ST$ is the perspective collineation whose fixed point and plane are P' and σ'.

Ex. 7. If T makes lines l', m' correspond to l, m and U is the non-perspective collineation of order 2 whose fixed lines are l, m, $T^{-1}UT$ is the collineation whose fixed lines are l', m'.

Ex. 8. If V is an involutive collineation on a line l whose double points are P, Q and T is a collineation transforming l, P, Q into l', P', Q', $T^{-1}VT$ is an involutive collineation on l' whose double points are P', Q'.

Ex. 9. If two collinear transformations of order 2 on a straight line are permutable, their double points form a harmonic range.

Ex. 10. If O_1, O_2 are the fixed points of two permutable perspective collineations and σ_1, σ_2 are their fixed planes, O_1 lies on σ_2 and O_2 on σ_1. The product of the two collineations is a non-perspective collineation of order 2 whose fixed lines are O_1O_2 and the intersection of σ_1 and σ_2.

Ex. 11. If O_1 and σ_1, O_2 and σ_2 are the fixed points and planes of two perspective collineations S_1, S_2, the fixed points of S_1S_2 are every point on the intersection of σ_1, σ_2 and the double points of the involution determined on O_1O_2 by O_1, σ_1 and O_2, σ_2.

Ex. 12. Any odd number of successive (i) perspective collineations with the same fixed plane, (ii) perspective collineations with the same fixed point and with fixed planes passing through a given straight line, (iii) non-perspective collineations of order 2 with one fixed line in common and the other fixed line passing through a given point, is equivalent to a single such collineation.

Ex. 18. Any odd number of successive perspective collineations whose fixed points all lie in a given plane and which transform a fixed conicoid into itself is equivalent to three such successive collineations.

CHAPTER V

GROUPS

§ 1. A set of elements is said to form a *group*, if (1) the product of any two (or the square of any one) of the elements is an element of the set; (2) the set contains the inverse of each element of the set. If the set satisfies condition (1) but not (2), it is called a *semi-group*.

Any group G contains the identical element; for if a is any element of G, so is a^{-1} and $aa^{-1} = 1$.

If G contains n distinct elements, it is said to be of *order n*. The group is called *finite* or *infinite* according as n is finite or infinite. We shall assume a group finite unless the contrary is stated.

A group or semi-group every two elements of which are permutable is called *Abelian* or *commutative*.

If G is any group and g is any element of finite order m, $g^m = 1$ is in G. If g^r is the first of the elements $g, g^2, g^3, \ldots$ which is contained in G, r is called the order of g *relative* to G. The order r of g relative to G is a factor of the 'absolute' order m. For if $(k+1)r > m \geq kr$ (k being a positive integer), $g^{m-kr} = g^m \cdot g^{-kr} = (g^r)^{-k}$ is in G, and hence $m = kr$.

Similarly we may prove that, if g^l is any positive power of g contained in G, r is a factor of l.

Ex. 1. Suppose we have 6 elements 1, a, b, c, d, e whose laws of combination are given by the 'multiplication table' (see p. 52) in which the product of the element at the left of the i-th row and the element at the top of the j-th column is given at the intersection of the i-th row and the j-th column (e.g. $bc = d$, $cb = e$). Then 1, a, b, c, d, e form a group. Such elements are, for example, the 6 permutations 1, (xyz), (xzy), (yz), (xy), (zx) or the 6 substitutions

$$x' = x, \quad \frac{1}{1-x}, \quad \frac{x-1}{x}, \quad \frac{1}{x}, \quad \frac{x}{x-1}, \quad 1-x.$$

Ex. 2. A group contains every positive and negative power of any element it contains.

Ex. 3. Every element of a finite group is of finite order.

Ex. 4. If a, b are any two elements of a group G, we can always find elements g, h in G such that $ag = b$, $ha = b$.

Ex. 5. The positive powers of any element form a group or semi-group according as the element is of finite or infinite order.

Ex. 6. A finite number of elements satisfying condition (1) of § 1 satisfy condition (2) and form a group.

Ex. 7. Every semi-group contains elements of infinite order.

Ex. 8. If the elements a, b, c, ... form a group, so do $g^{-1}ag$, $g^{-1}bg$, $g^{-1}cg$, ...

1	a	b	c	d	e
1	1	a	b	c	d	e
b	b	1	a	d	e	c
a	a	b	1	e	c	d
c	c	d	e	1	a	b
d	d	e	c	b	1	a
e	e	c	d	a	b	1

Multiplication table of group in Ex. 1.

Ex. 9. Every group of even order contains an odd number of elements of order 2.

Ex. 10. Every group contains an even number of elements of order r ($r > 2$).

Ex. 11. A group whose elements are all of order 1 or 2 is Abelian.

Ex. 12. (i) If g_1, g_2, g_3, ... are the elements of a group, so are $g_1 g_x$, $g_2 g_x$, $g_3 g_x$, ... and so are $g_y g_1$, $g_y g_2$, $g_y g_3$, ... (ii) The permutations $\begin{pmatrix} g_1 & g_2 & g_3 & \cdots \\ g_1 g_x & g_2 g_x & g_3 g_x & \cdots \end{pmatrix}$ and $\begin{pmatrix} g_1 & g_2 & g_3 & \cdots \\ g_y g_1 & g_y g_2 & g_y g_3 & \cdots \end{pmatrix}$ are both regular and are permutable.

Ex. 13. The positive integers form an Abelian semi-group the law of combination being (i) ordinary multiplication, (ii) ordinary addition.

Ex. 14. All positive real quantities form an infinite Abelian group or semi-group according as the law of combination is ordinary multiplication or ordinary addition.

Ex. 15. All positive and negative integers form an infinite Abelian group when the law of combination is ordinary addition.

Ex. 16. (i) The marks of the $GF[p^r]$ form an Abelian group of order p^r, the law of combination being addition. (ii) The marks excluding zero form an Abelian group of order p^r-1, the law of combination being multiplication.

Ex. 17. All the permutations on the symbols $x_1, x_2, \ldots, x_m$ which (i) leave a function $f(x_1, x_2, \ldots, x_m)$ unaltered, (ii) multiply $f(x_1, x_2, \ldots, x_m)$ by some constant independent of $x_1, x_2, \ldots, x_m$ form a group.

Ex. 18. Prove a similar result for substitutions on the variables $x_1, x_2, \ldots, x_m$.

Ex. 19. The movements bringing any geometrical figure to self-coincidence form a group.

Ex. 20. All possible homogeneous linear substitutions of non-zero determinant on m given variables with coefficients in a $GF[p^r]$ form a group.

Ex. 21. The following elements form a group:

(i) The permutations 1, $(xyzw)$, $(xz)(yw)$, $(xwzy)$, (xz), $(xw)(yz)$, (yw), $(xy)(wz)$.

(ii) The permutations 1, $(xyzwu)$, $(xzuyw)$, $(xwyuz)$, $(xuwzy)$, $(uy)(zw)$, $(xu)(yw)$, $(xw)(yz)$, $(xz)(uw)$, $(xy)(zu)$.

(iii) Rotations through $\dfrac{2r\pi}{n}$ about the origin and reflexions in the lines $y = \tan \dfrac{r\pi}{n} \cdot x$ $(r = 1, 2, \ldots, n)$.

(iv) Rotations through $0, \dfrac{2\pi}{3}, \dfrac{4\pi}{3}$ about the diagonals of a cube and rotations through π about lines through its centre perpendicular to its faces.

(v) The substitutions
$x' = \omega^k x,\ x' = \omega^k \div x$ $(k = 1, 2, \ldots, m)$, where $\omega^m = 1$.

(vi) The 12 substitutions
$x' = \pm x,\ \pm \dfrac{1}{x},\ \pm i\dfrac{x+1}{x-1},\ \pm i\dfrac{x-1}{x+1},\ \pm \dfrac{x+i}{x-i},\ \pm \dfrac{x-i}{x+i},\ (i = \sqrt{-1})$.

(vii) The 24 substitutions
$x' = i^k x,\ \dfrac{i^k}{x},\ i^k \dfrac{x \pm 1}{x \mp 1},\ i^k \dfrac{x \pm i}{x \mp i}$ $(k = 0, 1, 2, 3)$.

(viii) The substitutions
$\left(\cos \dfrac{2r\pi}{n} \cdot x - \sin \dfrac{2r\pi}{n} \cdot y,\ \sin \dfrac{2r\pi}{n} \cdot x + \cos \dfrac{2r\pi}{n} \cdot y \right), (r = 1, 2, \ldots, n)$.

(ix) The 8 substitutions $(\pm x, \pm y), (\pm y, \pm x)$.
(x) The 8 substitutions $(\pm x, \pm y, \pm z)$.
(xi) The substitutions
$$x' = x, \frac{3x+4}{4x+1}, \frac{4x+2}{2x+8}, \frac{6x+4}{4x+4}, \frac{6}{x}, \frac{3x+8}{6x+4}, \frac{5x+4}{4x+2}, \frac{8x+6}{3x+4}$$
with coefficients in the $GF[7]$.

(xii) The substitutions $x' = x,\ 4x,\ 2x,\ 8x,\ \dfrac{2}{x},\ \dfrac{8}{x},\ \dfrac{1}{x},\ \dfrac{4}{x}$ with coefficients in the $GF[3^2]$ where $P(x) \equiv x^2 + 2x + 2$.

Ex. 22. Which groups of Ex. 21 are Abelian?

Ex. 23. Find the order of $(xzyw)$ relative to the group (i) of Ex. 21, the order of a rotatory-inversion through $\dfrac{\pi}{6}$ about the centre and diagonal of the cube relative to (iv), the order of $x' = \tfrac{1}{2}(\sqrt{3}+i)x$ relative to (vi), the order of $(-y, -z, -x)$ relative to (x).

Ex. 24. Construct multiplication tables for the groups (i), (iv), (x) of Ex. 21.

§ 2. The set formed by all the elements $a_1, a_2, \ldots, a_r$ is usually denoted by $a_1 + a_2 + \ldots + a_r$. If A denotes this set, so that $A \equiv a_1 + a_2 + \ldots + a_r$, and b is any element; then the set
$$a_1 b + a_2 b + \ldots + a_r b$$
is denoted by Ab, and the set
$$ba_1 + ba_2 + \ldots + ba_r$$
by bA. If B denotes the set $b_1 + b_2 + \ldots + b_s$, AB denotes the set of rs elements $a_i b_j$ ($i = 1, 2, \ldots, r$; $j = 1, 2, \ldots, s$), and BA denotes the set of rs elements $b_j a_i$.

If $a, b, c, \ldots$ are any elements, $\{a, b, c, \ldots\}$ denotes the group or semi-group composed of all distinct elements obtained by combining in every possible way all products and powers of $a, b, c, \ldots$.

More generally, if $A, B, \ldots$ denote sets of elements, and $g, h, \ldots$ denote elements, $\{A, B, \ldots, g, h, \ldots\}$ denotes the group or semi-group composed of all distinct elements obtained by combining in every possible way all products and powers of $g, h, \ldots$ and every element of $A, B, \ldots$.

Ex. 1. Let a, b, c be elements of orders 4, 2, 2 respectively such that $ab = ba^3$, $ac = ca$, $bc = cb$. Combining all possible powers of b and c we get only the 4 elements $1, b, c, bc$; for example, $b^6 c^7 b^5 c^4 b^2 = cb$. Hence $\{b, c\}$ is a group H of order 4.

Again, combining all possible powers of a, b, c we get only the 16 elements $1, a, a^2, a^3, b, ba, ba^2, ba^3, c, ca, ca^2, ca^3, cb, cba, cba^2, cba^3$;

for example, $a^6c^7b^3abc^9b^5 = a^2ba = ba^3$. Hence $\{a, b, c\}$ is a group G of order 16 identical with $\{H, a\}$.

Ex. 2. If a is of order n, $\{a\}$ contains n elements.

Ex. 3. $\{a, b, c, ...\}$ is identical with $\{\{a\}, \{b\}, \{c\}, ...\}$, $\{\{a, b\}, c, ...\}$, $\{\{a, c\}, b, ...\}$, ...

Ex. 4. If $a^5 = b^3 = 1$ and $ab = ba$, $\{a, b\}$ contains 15 elements.

Ex. 5. If $ab = ba^k$, every element of $\{a, b\}$ is of the form $b^y a^x$.

Ex. 6. If in §2 r is finite and $A^2 \equiv A + A + A + ...$, A is a group.

Ex. 7. If A and B are groups and
$$(AB)^2 \equiv AB + AB + AB + ...,$$
AB is a group and is identical with BA.

Ex. 8. If A and B are groups and $AB \equiv BA$, AB is a group.

Ex. 9. If G is an Abelian group of order n and g is any element of order m permutable with every element of G, $\{G, g\}$ is an Abelian group whose order divides nm.

Ex. 10. If p divides the order of an Abelian group G, G contains at least one element whose order is a multiple of p.

§ 3. The elements $g_1, g_2, g_3, ...$ are called *independent* if no one of them can be expressed as a product of any number of the rest; i.e. if g_i is not contained in
$$\{g_1, g_2, ..., g_{i-1}, g_{i+1}, ...\}.$$
for any value of i. In this case $g_1, g_2, g_3, ...$ are called independent *generating elements* or *generators* of $\{g_1, g_2, g_3, ...\}$. A group is said to be given *abstractly* when we know the number of elements it contains and the way in which any two combine. These data are evidently completely given when we know a set of generating elements and the equations connecting them; so that a group is given abstractly by a set of generating elements and certain independent (and mutually consistent) relations which they satisfy. It is in this way that a group is usually defined. Thus, for example, 'the group $a^4 = b^2 = c^2 = (ab)^2 = 1$, $ac = ca$, $bc = cb$' means 'the group $\{a, b, c\}$ generated by the elements a, b, c of orders 4, 2, 2 respectively which are connected by the relations $(ab)^2 = 1$, $ac = ca$, $bc = cb$'.

Two groups G, G' with the same number of elements combining according to the same laws are considered as being one and the same *abstract group* in the pure group-theory, as opposed to its applications. We may denote this by the notation $G = G'$; while $G \equiv G'$ would imply that G and G' contained the same elements and were absolutely identical.

Two groups containing the same number of elements of order 2, the same number of order 3, the same number of order 4, ... are called *conformal*.

Ex. 1. Show that the group of $V1_1$ is generated by a, c where $a^3 = c^2 = (ac)^2 = 1$, or by c, d where $c^2 = d^2 = (cd)^3 = 1$.

Ex. 2. Find generating elements of the groups (i), (iv), (v), (viii), (x) of $V1_{21}$.

Ex. 3. Construct a multiplication table for the group
$a^3 = b^2 = 1$, $ab = ba$, and for $a^4 = 1$, $b^2 = a^2$, $ab = ba^3$.

Ex. 4. The groups $a^n = b^2 = (ab)^2 = 1$ and $a^2 = b^2 = (ab)^n = 1$ are abstractly identical and are of order $2n$.

Ex. 5. The groups $a^3 = b^3 = (ab)^2 = 1$ and $a^2 = b^3 = (ab)^3 = 1$ are abstractly identical.

Ex. 6. Find the group generated by the permutable permutations $(1234)(5678)$ and $(1638)(5274)$.

Ex. 7. Show that (i) reflexions in two planes, (ii) rotations through π about intersecting lines, (iii) inversions in two circles, inclined at an angle $\pi \div n$ generate a group of order $2n$.

Ex. 8. Use Ex. 7 (i) to show that exactly 8 angles are found by taking the supplement and complement of a given angle, the supplement and complement of the angles so obtained, and so on; angles being considered identical when they differ by a multiple of 2π.

Ex. 9. Any element permutable with $a, b, c, \ldots$ is permutable with every element of $\{a, b, c, \ldots\}$.

Ex. 10. If each pair of generators of a group G is permutable, G is Abelian.

Ex. 11. Prove that the following sets of elements form groups of order 4 which are identical when considered as abstract groups:—

(i) The permutations $1, (xy)(zw), (xz)(yw), (xw)(yz)$.

(ii) Rotations through 0 and π about three perpendicular intersecting lines.

(iii) Reflexions in two perpendicular planes and rotations through 0 and π about their intersection.

(iv) Rotations through 0 and π about a line, reflexion in a perpendicular plane, and inversion about their intersection.

(v) The substitutions $x' = \pm x, \pm \dfrac{1}{x}$.

(vi) The substitutions $(\pm x, \pm y)$.

(vii) The substitutions $x' = \dfrac{\beta}{x}, \dfrac{\alpha x - \beta y}{\gamma x - \alpha}, \dfrac{\beta \gamma x - \alpha \beta}{\alpha x - \beta y}$, where α, β, γ are marks of any $GF[p^r]$.

Ex. 12. Prove that the following sets of elements form groups of order 6 which are identical when considered as abstract groups:

(i) The permutations $1, (xyz), (xzy), (yz), (zx), (xy)$.

(ii) Rotations through $0, \dfrac{2\pi}{3}, \dfrac{4\pi}{3}$ about the origin and reflexions in the lines $y = 0, y = +\sqrt{3}x, y = -\sqrt{3}x$.

(iii) The substitutions $x' = x$, $\dfrac{m^2}{m-x}$, $\dfrac{mx-m^2}{x}$, $\dfrac{m^2}{x}$, $\dfrac{mx}{x-m}$, $m-x$.

(iv) The fractional substitutions (x, y), $\left(\dfrac{y}{x}, \dfrac{1}{x}\right)$, $\left(\dfrac{1}{y}, \dfrac{x}{y}\right)$, (y, x), $\left(\dfrac{x}{y}, \dfrac{1}{y}\right)$, $\left(\dfrac{1}{x}, \dfrac{y}{x}\right)$.

(v) The substitutions in the $GF[2]$ (x, y), $(x+y, x)$, $(y, x+y)$, (y, x), $(x+y, y)$, $(x, x+y)$.

(vi) The substitutions in the $GF[3]$ $x' = x$, $x+1$, $x+2$, $2x$, $2x+1$, $2x+2$.

(vii) The substitutions in the $GF[7]$ $x' = x$, $\dfrac{1}{6x+6}$, $\dfrac{6x+6}{x}$, $\dfrac{4x+1}{4x+8}$, $\dfrac{4x+8}{6x+8}$, $\dfrac{6x+8}{4x+1}$.

(viii) The substitutions in the $GF[11]$ $x' = x$, $\dfrac{7x+4}{8x+5}$, $\dfrac{6x+4}{8x+4}$, $\dfrac{4}{8x}$, $\dfrac{x+5}{4x+10}$, $\dfrac{x+9}{x+10}$.

(ix) The substitutions in the $GF[3^2]$ where $P(x) \equiv x^2 + 2x + 2$ $x' = x$, $\dfrac{4}{4x+1}$, $\dfrac{2x+4}{4x}$, $\dfrac{2}{x}$, $\dfrac{8x}{2x+4}$, $\dfrac{8x+2}{4}$.

Ex. 13. Show that the groups (i), (ix), (xi) of $V1_{21}$ are abstractly identical and so are (iv) and (vi).

Ex. 14. The groups $a^{25} = b^5 = 1$, $ab = ba^6$ and $a^{25} = b^5 = 1$, $ab = ba$ are conformal.

Ex. 15. The groups $a^9 = b^3 = c^3 = 1$, $ab = ba^4$, $ac = ca^7$, $bc = cb$ and $a^9 = b^3 = c^3 = 1$, $ab = ba$, $ac = ca$, $bc = cb$ are conformal.

§ 4. It may happen that certain elements of a group G taken by themselves form a group H. In this case H is called a *subgroup* of G, and is said to be 'contained in G'.

The simplest possible group is that which contains only the identical element. It is called the *identical group*, and is denoted by 1 if no confusion is caused thereby. In a sense any group G contains as subgroups both the identical group and G itself; but for the sake of conciseness in enunciating and proving theorems it is sometimes convenient to consider one or both of these as not included among the subgroups of G. It will always be clear from the context whether they are included or not.

The order r of any subgroup H of a group G of finite order n is a factor of n.

Let $1, h_1, h_2, ..., h_{r-1}$ be the elements of H. Let g_1 be any element of G not in H. Then the elements
$$g_1, h_1 g_1, h_2 g_1, ..., h_{r-1} g_1$$
are all distinct from each other and from $1, h_1, h_2, ..., h_{r-1}$. For $h_i g_1 = h_j g_1$ would involve $h_i = h_j$; and $h_i g_1 = h_j$ would involve $g_1 = h_i^{-1} h_j$ which is in H.

Let g_2 be an element of G not included in H or Hg_1. Then the elements $g_2, h_1 g_2, h_2 g_2, ..., h_{r-1} g_2$ may be proved as before to be distinct from each other and the elements of H and Hg_1.

Proceeding in this way we may show that each element of G is included once and only once in a finite number of sets $H, Hg_1, Hg_2, ...$; which proves the theorem. The integer $j = n \div r$ is called the *index* of H in G.

The sets $H, Hg_1, Hg_2, ..., Hg_{j-1}$ may be called *partitions* of G with respect to H. The decomposition of G into these partitions may be expressed by the identity
$$G \equiv H + Hg_1 + Hg_2 + ... + Hg_{j-1},$$
where none of the g's is in H; or, if we prefer it, by
$$G \equiv Hg_1 + Hg_2 + ... + Hg_j,$$
where one and only one of the g's is in H. The decomposition is unaffected by substituting hg_x for g_x, where h is any element of H.

Similarly we may show that we have the identity
$$G \equiv H + \gamma_1 H + \gamma_2 H + ... + \gamma_{j-1} H,$$
or
$$G \equiv \gamma_1 H + \gamma_2 H + ... + \gamma_j H.$$

Ex. 1. In the group $G \equiv \{a, b, c\}$ of V 2_1 where
$$a^4 = b^2 = c^2 = (ab)^2 = 1, \ ac = ca, \ bc = cb,$$
the sets of elements
$$H \equiv 1 + b + c + cb, \ K \equiv 1 + a + a^2 + a^3, \ L \equiv 1 + a^2 + c + ca^2,$$
$$M \equiv 1 + a^2 + b + ba^2, \ N \equiv 1 + a + a^2 + a^3 + b + ba + ba^2 + ba^3,$$
$$O \equiv 1 + a^2 + b + ba^2 + c + ca^2 + cb + cba^2, \ \&c. \text{ form subgroups.}$$
We have
$$G \equiv H + Ha + Ha^2 + Ha^3, \ G \equiv K + Kb + Kc + Kcb,$$
$$G \equiv L + La + Lb + Lba, \ G \equiv M + Ma + Mc + Mca,$$
$$G \equiv N + Nc, \ G \equiv O + Oa, \ \&c.$$

Ex. 2. Any set of elements of a finite group G which satisfy condition (1) of § 1 also satisfy condition (2) and form a subgroup.

Ex. 3. The powers of any element of a finite group form a subgroup.

Ex. 4. The order of every element in a group of order n is a factor of n.

Ex. 5. The only groups not containing a subgroup are those whose order is a prime.

Ex. 6. If
$$G \equiv Hg_1 + Hg_2 + Hg_3 + \ldots,$$
$$G \equiv g_1^{-1}H + g_2^{-1}H + g_3^{-1}H + \ldots.$$

Ex. 7. It is not always possible to divide a given group G into partitions Hg_1, Hg_2, Hg_3, ... with respect to a given subgroup H in such a way that g_1, g_2, g_3, ... form a subgroup of G.

Ex. 8. The p-th power of any element of a group is contained in every subgroup of index p.

Ex. 9. If H and K are groups of orders λ and μ, the order n of $\{H, K\}$ is not necessarily finite. If n is finite, n is a multiple of the L. C. M. of λ and μ.

Ex. 10. If H, K are subgroups of a group G, (i) $\{H, K\}$ is a subgroup of G; (ii) $G \equiv \{H, K\}$ when the order of $G =$ the L. C. M. of the orders of H and K.

Ex. 11. The elements of a group G permutable with every element of G form an Abelian subgroup.

Ex. 12. The elements of G permutable with any given element (or with each of a number of given elements) form a subgroup.

Ex. 13. $\{g_1, g_2, \ldots, g_f\}$ is a subgroup of $\{g_1, g_2, \ldots, g_f, \ldots, g_k\}$.

Ex. 14. Every subgroup of an Abelian group is Abelian.

Ex. 15. Those elements of an Abelian group whose orders divide a given number form a subgroup.

Ex. 16. Those elements of an Abelian group which are q-th powers of some other element of the group form a subgroup.

Ex. 17. The elements of finite order in an infinite Abelian group form a subgroup.

Ex. 18. The elements common to two or more given groups form a subgroup of each.

Ex. 19. (i) A group of permutations containing an odd permutation, (ii) a group of movements containing a rotatory-inversion, (iii) a group of homogeneous orthogonal substitutions containing a substitution with negative determinant, contains a subgroup of index 2.

Ex. 20. The group of rotations bringing a cube to self-coincidence contains as subgroups the group of rotations bringing to self-coincidence (i) a regular tetrahedron, (ii) a right equilateral triangular prism, (iii) an ellipsoid.

Ex. 21. The group of $V 1_{21(i)}$ contains as a subgroup the group of $V 8_{11(i)}$, $V 1_{21(vii)}$ contains $V 1_{21(vi)}$ and $V 8_{11(v)}$, and $V 1_{21(ix)}$ contains $V 8_{11(vi)}$.

Ex. 22. In Ex. 1 divide N and O into partitions with respect to $1 + a^2$ and $1 + b$.

Ex. 23. Divide the group of permutations $\{(12), (1234)\}$ into partitions with respect to $H \equiv \{(12)(34), (13)(24)\}$.

§ 5. The simplest finite group other than the identical group is the group $G \equiv \{a\}$ of order n composed of the powers $a, a^2, ..., a^n$ of a single element of order n. Such a group is called a *cyclic* or *cyclical* group. It is Abelian, since $a^x a^y = a^y a^x$.

Let a^s be the lowest power of a contained in any subgroup H of G, and let a^x be any other element of H, where $(k+1)s > x \geq ks$ (k being a positive integer). Then since a^{x-ks} is in H, $x = ks$. Hence the elements of H are $a^s, a^{2s}, a^{3s}, \dots$. Therefore G contains a single subgroup $\{a^s\}$ of index s, when s is a factor of n.

Ex. 1. Verify the fact that $\{a^s\}$ is the single subgroup of index s in $\{a\}$, taking a as (i) the circular permutation $(1\ 2\ \dots\ n)$, (ii) a rotation through $2\pi \div n$.

Ex. 2. Every subgroup of a cyclic group is cyclic.

Ex. 3. Two cyclic groups of the same order are abstractly identical.

Ex. 4. A cyclic group is abstractly identical with any conformal group.

Ex. 5. Every group of prime order is cyclic.

Ex. 6. Show that (i) $\{a\} \equiv \{a^t\}$ if t is prime to n, (ii) $\{a^r\}$ is a subgroup of index d in $\{a\}$ if d is the H.C.F. of n and r.

Ex. 7. A cyclic group $\{a\}$ of order p^a contains (i) p^r elements whose orders divide p^r ($r \leq a$), (ii) $p^{r-1}(p-1)$ elements of order p^r.

Ex. 8. (i) A cyclic group of order n contains m elements whose orders divide a given factor m of n, and $\phi(m)$ elements of order m. (ii) A group with x cyclic subgroups of order m contains $x\phi(m)$ elements of order m (see footnote on p. 32).

Ex. 9. Every Abelian group whose order is a multiple of p contains an element of order p.

Ex. 10. Every Abelian group whose order is the product of distinct primes is cyclic.

Ex. 11. If the orders of a, b are λ, μ and their orders relative to $\{b\}, \{a\}$ are α, β, while $b^\beta = a^r$; (i) $\lambda \div \alpha = \mu \div \beta$, (ii) α is the H.C.F. of λ and r.

Ex. 12. If in Ex. 11 $ab = ba$, the order of ab is $x\beta$, where x is the smallest integral solution of $x(r + \beta) \equiv 0 \pmod{\lambda}$.

Ex. 13. Find the order of ab when (i) $a^{12} = 1$, $b^7 = a^9$, $ab = ba$, (ii) $a^{20} = 1$, $b^4 = a^6$, $ab = ba$. Find also the order of a relative to $\{b\}$.

Ex. 14. In a $GF[p^r]$ (i) the p integral marks combined by addition, (ii) the powers of any mark combined by multiplication, form a cyclic group.

§ 6. If $g_1, g_2, g_3, \dots$ are the elements of a group G, the transforms of $g_1, g_2, g_3, \dots$ by any element a form a group G'.

This follows at once from the fact that if

$$g_i g_j = g_k, \quad a^{-1} g_i a \cdot a^{-1} g_j a = a^{-1} g_i g_j a = a^{-1} g_k a.$$

We denote G' by $a^{-1}Ga$ and call it the *transform* of G by a ('result of transforming G by a'). If G', G contain the same elements, i.e. are one and the same group, a is said to be *permutable* with G.

If we transform any element h of G by every element of G and obtain thus the distinct elements $h, h_1, h_2, \ldots$ all contained in G; $h, h_1, h_2, \ldots$ are called the *conjugates* of h in G. They are also the conjugates of h_1. For if $g_1, g_2, \ldots$ are elements of G such that

$$g_1^{-1} h g_1 = h_1, \; g_2^{-1} h g_2 = h_2, \ldots,$$

then

$$h = g_1 h_1 g_1^{-1}, \; h_2 = (g_1^{-1} g_2)^{-1} h_1 (g_1^{-1} g_2), \; h_3 = (g_1^{-1} g_3)^{-1} h_1 (g_1^{-1} g_3),$$

and so on: while conversely any conjugate of h_1 such as $g_x^{-1} h_1 g_x = (g_1 g_x)^{-1} h (g_1 g_x)$ is a conjugate of h. Similarly $h, h_1, h_2, \ldots$ are the conjugates of $h_2, h_3, \ldots$. For this reason $h, h_1, h_2, \ldots$ are spoken of as a *conjugate set of elements* in G.

Since $g_t^{-1} h^{-1} g_t = h_t^{-1}$ when $h_t = g_t^{-1} h g_t$, we can easily prove that $h^{-1}, h_1^{-1}, h_2^{-1}, \ldots$ are a conjugate set of elements in G if $h, h_1, h_2, \ldots$ are a conjugate set. The two sets are called *inverse* conjugate sets. If the two sets coincide (i.e. h^{-1} is conjugate to h), $h, h_1, h_2, \ldots$ is called a *self-inverse* conjugate set.

As before, if we transform any subgroup H of G by every element of G and obtain thus the distinct groups $H, H_1, H_2, \ldots$ which are all subgroups of G; $H, H_1, H_2, \ldots$ are the *conjugates* of H in G, while $H, H_1, H_2, \ldots$ form a *conjugate set of subgroups*.

Ex. 1. For example, (i) the elements of $a^4 = b^2 = (ab)^2 = 1$ form the conjugate sets 1, a^2, $a+a^3$, $b+ba^2$, $ba+ba^3$ each set being self-inverse. The subgroups $1+b$ and $1+ba^2$ form a conjugate set. (ii) The elements of $a^7 = b^3 = 1$, $ab = ba^2$ form the conjugate sets 1, $a+a^2+a^4$ and $a^6+a^5+a^3$, $b+ba+ba^2+ba^3+ba^4+ba^5+ba^6$ and $b^2+b^2a^3+b^2a^6+b^2a^2+b^2a^5+b^2a+b^2a^4$. The subgroups $\{b\}$, $\{ba\}$, $\{ba^2\}$, $\{ba^3\}$, $\{ba^4\}$, $\{ba^5\}$, $\{ba^6\}$ form a conjugate set.

Ex. 2. Any transform of a group G is the same as G when considered as an abstract group ($G' \equiv G$).

Ex. 3. Every element or subgroup of a conjugate set has the same order.

Ex. 4. ab is conjugate to ba in $\{a, b\}$.

Ex. 5. If G is a group of order n and a is any element permutable with G, the order of $\{G, a\}$ (i) is np if a is of order p, (ii) divides nq if a is of order q.

Ex. 6. Every element conjugate to h in a group G is of the form hc, where c is the commutator of two elements of G.

Ex. 7. If h^a is conjugate to h in G (i) a is prime to the order m of h; (ii) h^a, h^{a^2}, h^{a^3}, ... are all conjugate to h; (iii) h^{xa_1}, h^{xa_2}, h^{xa_3}, ... are the powers of h conjugate to h^x if h^{a_1}, h^{a_2}, h^{a_3}, ... are the powers of h conjugate to h; x being prime to m.

Ex. 8. If an element of order m is conjugate to t of its powers, t is a factor of $\phi(m)$ (see footnote, p. 82).

Ex. 9. If a subgroup H of G contains no two elements conjugate in G, H is Abelian.

Ex. 10. $g^{-1}\{a, b, c, ...\}g = \{g^{-1}ag, g^{-1}bg, g^{-1}cg, ...\}$ and $g^{-1}\{A, B, C, ...\}g = \{g^{-1}Ag, g^{-1}Bg, g^{-1}Cg, ...\}$; $a, b, c, ...$ being any elements, and $A, B, C, ...$ any sets of elements.

Ex. 11. If H is a subgroup of G, $a^{-1}Ha$ is a subgroup of $a^{-1}Ga$.

Ex. 12. If a^r is the lowest power of a permutable with a group G, r divides the order of a relative to G.

Ex. 13. If an element a of order p is permutable with a group G of order n, but is permutable with no element of G, (i) p is a factor of $n-1$, (ii) $gg_1g_2 ... g_{r-1} = (ga^{-1})^r a^r$, (iii) $gg_1g_2 ... g_{p-1} = 1$, (iv) a is permutable with $\{g_1, g_2, ..., g_{p-1}\}$, where g is any element of G and $ga^i = a^i g_i$.

Ex. 14. If the order of each element of a group is 1 or 3, each element is permutable with every conjugate.

Ex. 15. If each element of a group G is permutable with every conjugate, (i) the commutator of any two of the elements is permutable with both, (ii) those elements of G whose orders divide a given odd number e form a subgroup.

Ex. 16. A group G of even order contains self-inverse conjugate sets.

Ex. 17. The group of $\nabla 8_{11(l)}$ is permutable with every permutation on the symbols x, y, z, w.

Ex. 18. Find the conjugate sets of elements in the groups of $\nabla 1_1$, $\nabla 1_{21(ii)(iv)(ix)}$, $\nabla 2_1$, $\nabla 3_3$, and in the group $a^{11} = b^5 = 1$, $ab = ba^3$.

Ex. 19. Find the subgroups conjugate to $1+c$ in $\nabla 1_1$ and to H in $\nabla 4_1$.

Ex. 20. Find the conjugate sets of elements and the subgroups conjugate to $\{ba\}$ in $a^{24} = b^2 = 1$, $ab = ba^5$.

§ 7. If every element of a group G transforms an element g of G into itself, so that g is permutable with every element of G, g is called a *normal*, *self-conjugate*, or *invariant* element of G (or 'an element normal in G').

NORMAL SUBGROUPS

Similarly, if every element of G transforms a subgroup H into itself, H is called a *normal, self-conjugate,* or *invariant* subgroup of G (or 'a subgroup normal in G').

A group containing no normal subgroup (except itself and identity) is called a *simple* group. A group which contains a normal subgroup (i.e. is not simple) is called *composite*.

If g, h are two elements normal in G, gh is normal in G. For γ being an element of G, $\gamma \cdot gh = g\gamma h = gh \cdot \gamma$. Hence the elements normal in G form a subgroup. This subgroup is called the *central* of G or the 'group of elements self-conjugate in G'. It is evidently Abelian and normal in G.

Ex. 1. For example, $1 + a^2 + b + ba^2$ is a normal subgroup of the group $a^4 = b^2 = (ab)^2 = 1$ of order 8. For the transforms of b and ba^2 by 1, a^2, b, ba^2 are respectively b and ba^2, and their transforms by a, a^3, ba, ba^3 are respectively ba^2 and b; while 1 and a^2 are permutable with every element of the group. Similarly $1 + a + a^2 + a^3$, $1 + a^2 + ba + ba^3$ are normal subgroups. The central of the group is $1 + a^2$.

Ex. 2. Every subgroup of an Abelian group is normal.

Ex. 3. If a cyclic group is simple, its order is prime, and conversely.

Ex. 4. If a group contains only one subgroup of a given order, that subgroup is normal.

Ex. 5. If $h + h_1 + h_2 + \ldots$ is a set of conjugate elements in G, $\{h, h_1, h_2, \ldots\}$ is a normal subgroup of G.

Ex. 6. If $G \equiv g_1 + g_2 + g_3 + \ldots$, $\{g_1^t, g_2^t, g_3^t, \ldots\}$ is a normal subgroup of G.

Ex. 7. If $a, b, c, \ldots$ are the elements of a group G whose orders (i) are equal to, (ii) divide a given number, $\{a, b, c, \ldots\}$ is normal in G.

Ex. 8. If H is a normal subgroup of G, $a^{-1}Ha$ is a normal subgroup of $a^{-1}Ga$.

Ex. 9. A subgroup of $\{a, b, c, \ldots\}$ permutable with $a, b, c, \ldots$ is normal.

Ex. 10. If a normal subgroup H of G contains a subgroup K of G, it contains every subgroup conjugate to K in G.

Ex. 11. The elements common to two or more normal subgroups form a normal subgroup.

Ex. 12. A subgroup of index 2 is always normal.

Ex. 13. If H is a normal subgroup of G, H is normal in any subgroup of G containing H.

Ex. 14. If $c_1, c_2, c_3, \ldots$ are the commutators of all pairs of elements of G, $\{c_1, c_2, c_3, \ldots\}$ is a normal subgroup of G.

Ex. 15. If a cyclic group H is normal in G, so is every subgroup of H.

Ex. 16. If g is any element of $G \equiv Hg_1 + Hg_2 + Hg_3 + \ldots$, where H is a normal subgroup of G, (i) $Hg = gH$, (ii) $H + Hg + Hg^2 + \ldots$ is a subgroup of G, (iii) $G \equiv g_1 H + g_2 H + g_3 H + \ldots$, (iv) every element of $Hg_i \cdot Hg_j$ lies in the same partition of G.

Ex. 17. If H is a normal subgroup of G and the order m of H is prime to its index in G, any element g of G whose order divides m is contained in H.

Ex. 18. If H is a normal subgroup of $\{G, H\}$, the elements of G permutable with every element of H form a normal subgroup of G.

Ex. 19. The central of a group G only coincides with G if G is Abelian.

Ex. 20. A normal subgroup of order 2 is necessarily contained in the central.

Ex. 21. If C is the central of G, (i) $a^{-1}Ca$ is the central of $a^{-1}Ga$; (ii) if G is normal in Γ, so is C.

Ex. 22. The order of the central C of a group G is r. Prove that: (i) If g is any element of G, $\{C, g\}$ is Abelian. (ii) If $g, g', g'', \ldots$ are mutually permutable elements of G, $\{C, g, g', g'', \ldots\}$ is Abelian. (iii) If H is a subgroup of order pr in G containing C, H is Abelian.

Ex. 23. If the central of a group of permutations on m given symbols contains a circular permutation of degree $m-1$ or m, the group is cyclic.

Ex. 24. Every subgroup of the group $a^4 = 1$, $a^2 = (ab)^2 = b^2$ of order 8 is cyclic and normal. Its central is $1 + a^2$.

Ex. 25. The subgroup $1 + b^2 + a^2 b^2 a + ab^2 a^2$ is normal in

$$a^3 = b^4 = (ab)^2 = 1.$$

Ex. 26. $\{a^3, (ba)^2, (ab)^2\}$ and $\{a^2, (ab)^2\}$ are normal subgroups of $a^6 = b^2 = (a^3 b)^2 = (ab)^4 = 1$.

Ex. 27. Those substitutions of a group of homogeneous linear substitutions whose determinant is 1 form a normal subgroup.

Ex. 28. The group of $V\,8_{11(\text{ii})}$ is a normal subgroup of $V\,1_{21(\text{iv})}$ and $V\,3_{11(\text{vi})}$ of $V\,1_{21(\text{ix})}$.

Ex. 29. L is the central of the group G of $V\,4_1$.

Ex. 30. The square of any element not in $\{a\}$ of $a^\lambda = b^2 = 1$, $ab = ba^k$ is in the central of the group.

§ 8. *The elements of a group G permutable with any given element h of G form a subgroup whose index is equal to the number of elements conjugate to h in G.*

If g and g' are any two elements of G permutable with h, $h \cdot gg' = ghg' = gg' \cdot h$, so that gg' is permutable with h. Hence the elements of G permutable with h form a subgroup Γ, which is called the *normaliser* of g in G.

Let $G \equiv \Gamma + \Gamma g_1 + \Gamma g_2 + \ldots$. Then if g is any element of Γ,
$$(gg_i)^{-1} h(gg_i) = g_i^{-1} g^{-1} hgg_i = g_i^{-1} hg_i = h_i \text{ (say)}.$$
Therefore every element of Γg_i transforms h into the same conjugate h_i.

Moreover, $h_i \neq h_j$ unless $i = j$: for if $h_i = h_j$, $g_i^{-1} hg_i = g_j^{-1} hg_j$ and therefore $h \cdot g_i g_j^{-1} = g_i g_j^{-1} \cdot h$; which is only possible if $g_i = g_j$. Hence the index of Γ in G is equal to the number of elements conjugate to h (including h).

Let Γ_i be the subgroup formed by the elements of G permutable with h_i. Then $\Gamma_i = g_i^{-1} \Gamma g_i$. For if a is an element of G such that $a^{-1} h_i a = h_i$, $a^{-1} g_i^{-1} hg_i a = g_i^{-1} hg_i$, and therefore $h \cdot g_i a g_i^{-1} = g_i a g_i^{-1} \cdot h$. Hence $g_i a g_i^{-1}$ is in Γ, and therefore a is in $g_i^{-1} \Gamma g_i$.

Ex. 1. For example, in the group G of V4_1 the subgroup O of index 2 is the normaliser of b, while $b + ba^2$ is a conjugate set of elements in G.

Ex. 2. When h is normal in G, $\Gamma \equiv G$.

Ex. 3. $c^{-1} \Gamma c$ is the normaliser of $c^{-1} hc$ in $c^{-1} Gc$.

Ex. 4. Γ is a subgroup of the normaliser Γ^1 of h^x. If x is prime to the order of h, $\Gamma^1 \equiv \Gamma$.

Ex. 5. Prove a result similar to that of § 8 when h is not in G.

Ex. 6. If an element a of order 2 is permutable with a group G but with no element of G (except 1), (i) every element of $\{G, a\}$ not in G is of order 2, (ii) a transforms every element of G into its inverse, (iii) every element of G is of odd order, (iv) G is Abelian.

Ex. 7. If exactly half the elements of a group G are of order 2 and the remaining elements form a subgroup, this subgroup is Abelian of odd order.

Ex. 8. Find the normaliser of b in the groups of V1_1, V3_3, V6_1, and in $a^9 = b^3 = 1$, $ab = ba^4$.

Ex. 9. Find the normalisers of $(xsuyw)$ in V$1_{21\text{(ii)}}$, of $x' = \dfrac{1}{x}$ and $x' = i\dfrac{x+1}{x-1}$ in V$1_{21\text{(vi)}}$, and of (y, x) in V$1_{21\text{(ix)}}$.

§ 9. *The elements of a group G permutable with a subgroup H form a subgroup of G whose index in G is equal to the number of subgroups conjugate to H in G.*

These statements are proved by putting H for h, H_i for h_i in § 8. As before Γ is called the *normaliser* of H in G.

If $H_i = g_i^{-1} Hg_i$ is one of the subgroups conjugate to H, $g_i^{-1} \Gamma g_i$ is the subgroup formed by the elements of G permutable with H_i.

Ex. 1. For example, the normaliser of $\{a\}$ in the group $a^3 = b^4 = (ab)^2 = 1$ of order 24 is the subgroup $\{a, b^2a^2b\}$ of order 6. The subgroups conjugate to $\{a\}$ are $\{a\}$, $\{b^3ab\}$, $\{b^2ab^2\}$, $\{bab^3\}$.

Ex. 2. When H is normal in G, $\Gamma \equiv G$.

Ex. 3. $c^{-1}\Gamma c$ is the normaliser of $c^{-1}Hc$ in $c^{-1}Gc$.

Ex. 4. Γ contains H normally, and every subgroup of G containing H normally is a subgroup of Γ.

Ex. 5. If r is the order of the normaliser of an element h of order m in G, the order of the normaliser of $\{h\}$ is $r \times$ a factor of $\phi(m)$.

Ex. 6. Prove a result similar to that of § 9 when H is a group not contained in G.

Ex. 7. If n is the order of a group, the number of elements conjugate to any given element or of subgroups conjugate to a given subgroup is a factor of n.

Ex. 8. The central of a group of order $p^a \not\equiv 1$.

Ex. 9. The normalisers of a set of conjugate elements or subgroups form a conjugate set.

Ex. 10. No subgroup of G can contain an element from every conjugate set of elements in G.

Ex. 11. If h is an element of order pr in a group G whose order is prime to $p-1$, the normalisers of h and $\{h\}$ in G are identical.

Ex. 12. If the set of subgroups $H, H_1, H_2, \ldots$ conjugate to H in G is also a conjugate set in $K \equiv \{H, H_1, H_2, \ldots\}$, then every element of G is in $K\Gamma$, where Γ is the normaliser of H in G.

§ 10. *The elements common to two or more groups form a subgroup of each group.*

For if a and b are both contained in each of the groups, so is ab.

This subgroup is called the *greatest common subgroup* (G.C.S.) of the given groups.

Ex. 1. For example, in $V 4_1$ the G.C.S. of N and O is M; and of K, L, M is $1 + a^2$.

Ex. 2. In what case does the G.C.S. of G and H coincide with H?

Ex. 3. The order of the G.C.S. of two or more groups is a factor of the H.C.F. of their orders.

Ex. 4. The G.C.S. of a subgroup of H and a subgroup of K is contained in the G.C.S. of H and K.

Ex. 5. If D is the G.C.S. of $G, H, K, \ldots$, $g^{-1}Dg$ is the G.C.S. of $g^{-1}Gg, g^{-1}Hg, g^{-1}Kg, \ldots$.

Ex. 6. Two groups have only identity in common if their orders are prime to one another.

Ex. 7. Two groups have only identity in common if one is of prime order and is not a subgroup of the other.

Ex. 8. If H, K are subgroups of G, and H is normal, the G. C. S. (D) of H and K is normal in K.

Ex. 9. Find the G. C. S. of (i) $\mathbf{V}\,1_{21(I),\,(II)}$; (ii) $\mathbf{V}\,1_{21(VI)}$ and the group generated by $x' = 1 \div x$, $x' = ix$; (iii) H, M, and N in $\mathbf{V}\,4_1$.

§ 11. *If H, K, L, ... are normal subgroups of a group G, their greatest common subgroup D and $\{H, K, L, ...\}$ are normal subgroups of G.*

If g is any element of G, $g^{-1}Dg$ is evidently the greatest common subgroup of $g^{-1}Hg$, $g^{-1}Kg$, $g^{-1}Lg$, ..., i.e. of H, K, L, ... Hence $g^{-1}Dg \equiv D$, and D is normal in G.

Again, evidently $g^{-1}\{H, K, L, ...\}g \equiv \{g^{-1}Hg, g^{-1}Kg, g^{-1}Lg, ...\} \equiv \{H, K, L, ...\}$; so that $\{H, K, L, ...\}$ is normal in G.

Ex. 1. In $\mathbf{V}\,4_1$ K and M are normal subgroups of G. Hence their G. C. S. $1 + a^2$ and $N \equiv \{K, M\}$ are normal in G.

§ 12. *If H, K, L, ... are a conjugate set of subgroups in a group G, their greatest common subgroup and $\{H, K, L, ...\}$ are normal in G.*

Let g be any element of G. Then no two of the groups $g^{-1}Hg$, $g^{-1}Kg$, $g^{-1}Lg$, ... are identical; for $H \equiv K$ if $g^{-1}Hg \equiv g^{-1}Kg$. Hence these groups are the groups H, K, L, ... in some order or other. The theorem then follows as in § 11.

Ex. 1. In $\mathbf{V}\,4_1$ H and $1 + ba^2 + c + cba^2$ are a conjugate set of subgroups in G. Hence their G. C. S. $1 + c$ and $0 \equiv \{H, 1 + ba^2 + c + cba^2\}$ are normal in G.

Ex. 2. If D is a normal subgroup of G contained in a subgroup H, D is contained in every subgroup conjugate to H.

Ex. 3. If H, H_1, H_2, ... are a conjugate set of subgroups in G; K, K_1, K_2, ... are a conjugate set, and so on, the G. C. S. of H, H_1, H_2, ..., K, K_1, K_2, ..., ... and $\{H, H_1, H_2, ..., K, K_1, K_2, ..., ...\}$ are normal subgroups of G.

Ex. 4. Any simple group G can be generated by a conjugate set of elements of prime order.

§ 13. If G, H are finite groups of orders m, n, and the mn elements GH are the same as the mn elements HG, except possibly as regards arrangement (§ 2), G and H are said to be *permutable*, and $\{G, H\}$ is called a *decomposable* group. It is readily seen that every element of $\{G, H\}$ is included among the elements $GH \equiv HG$.

If G and H are two permutable groups of orders m and n, while the order of their greatest common subgroup D is δ and of $\{G, H\}$ is λ, $mn = \lambda\delta$.

Suppose $H \equiv Dh_1 + Dh_2 + Dh_3 + \ldots$. Then
$$\{G, H\} \equiv Gh_1 + Gh_2 + Gh_3 + \ldots.$$
For every element of $\{G, H\}$ is included among the elements GH, i.e. among $GDh_1 + GDh_2 + GDh_3 + \ldots$, i.e. among $Gh_1 + Gh_2 + Gh_3 + \ldots$. Again, Gh_i and Gh_j have no element in common, since otherwise $h_i h_j^{-1}$ would be contained in both H and G and therefore in D.

Hence $\lambda = m \times (n \div \delta)$ or $mn = \lambda\delta$.

Ex. 1. For example, in $V4_1$ the groups L and M of order 4 are permutable, their G. C. S. $1 + a^2$ is of order 2, and $O \equiv \{L, M\}$ is of order $4 \times 4 \div 2 = 8$.

Ex. 2. A normal subgroup of any group is permutable with every other subgroup.

Ex. 3. If a group is permutable with each of the groups G, H, K, ..., it is permutable with $\{G, H, K, \ldots\}$.

Ex. 4. (i) If G and H are two groups of orders m and n, while their G. C. S. (D) is of order δ and $\{G, H\}$ is of order λ, $mn \leq \lambda\delta$. (ii) If $mn = \lambda\delta$, G and H are permutable.

Ex. 5. Two subgroups H, K of a given group G are permutable if their indices are (i) prime to one another, (ii) both $= p$.

Ex. 6. If G, H are permutable subgroups of orders $q^x r$, $q^y r$ in a group of order $q^z r$, q being prime to r, the order of their G. C. S. is divisible by r.

Ex. 7. If G, H are two permutable groups of orders $q^x r$, $q^y s$, where each of q, r, s is prime to the other two, $\{G, H\}$ is of order $q^z rs$.

Ex. 8. The G. C. S. (D) of two permutable groups A, B is permutable with any group C contained in B and permutable with A.

Ex. 9. If H, K are normal subgroups of G such that H is not contained in a normal subgroup of G and does not contain K, G is decomposable.

Ex. 10. If H, K are subgroups of G such that H is normal, is not contained in any subgroup of G, and does not contain K, G is decomposable.

Ex. 11. The groups H and N of $V4_1$ and the groups of $V6_1$ are decomposable.

§ 14. *If the order a of a subgroup A normal in a group G is prime to the index $n \div a$ of A in G, every subgroup of G whose order divides a is contained in A.*

Let B of order β be a subgroup of G such that β divides α, and let λ, δ be the orders of $\{A, B\}$ and the greatest common subgroup D of A and B. Since A is normal in G, A and B are evidently permutable; and hence $\alpha\beta = \lambda\delta$.

Now $\{A, B\}$ is a subgroup of G, so that λ divides n. Hence $\dfrac{\beta}{\delta} = \dfrac{\lambda}{\alpha}$ divides $\dfrac{n}{\alpha}$. Again, $\dfrac{\beta}{\delta}$ divides α since β divides α.

Therefore $\dfrac{\beta}{\delta} = 1$; for it is a factor of α and $n \div \alpha$ which are prime to one another. Hence D coincides with B; i.e. B is contained in A.

Ex. 1. For example, the group $a^{70} = b^3 = 1$, $ab = ba^{11}$ of order 210 contains a normal subgroup $\{a\}$ of order 70. Therefore the only subgroups of orders 2, 5, 7, 10, 35, 70 are respectively $\{a^{35}\}$, $\{a^{14}\}$, $\{a^{10}\}$, $\{a^7\}$, $\{a^2\}$, $\{a\}$.

Ex. 2. G contains only one subgroup of order α.

Ex. 3. Those elements of G whose orders divide α form a subgroup of order α.

Ex. 4. The $\dfrac{n}{\alpha}$-th power of any element g of G is in A.

Ex. 5. If G is normal in H, so is A.

Ex. 6. If $A, B, C, ..., G, H$ are groups such that each is normal in the succeeding one, while the order of A is prime to its index in G; A is normal in H.

Ex. 7. If G is a group of order $n = \alpha\kappa$, where α is prime to κ, every normal subgroup whose order divides α is contained in all the subgroups of order α in G.

Ex. 8. The order of a subgroup H is prime to its index in G. If Γ is the normaliser of H in G, Γ is its own normaliser in G.

Ex. 9. The group $a^{22} = b^5 = 1$, $ab = ba^3$ contains a single normal subgroup of order 2, 11, 22.

Ex. 10. The group $a^{49} = b^7 = c^3 = 1$, $ab = ba^8$, $bc = cb^2$, $ac = ca$ contains only one subgroup of order 343, and one non-cyclic Abelian subgroup of order 49.

Ex. 11. The group $a^{43} = b^7 = c^3 = 1$, $ab = ba^4$, $bc = cb^2$, $ac = ca^6$ contains only one subgroup of order 301 and one of order 43.

§ 15. If each element of a group G is permutable with every element of a group H, and G, H have only identity in common; $\{G, H\}$ is called the *direct product* of G and H.

More generally, if $G_1, G_2, G_3, ...$ are groups such that for each value of i $P \equiv \{G_1, G_2, G_3, ...\}$ is the direct product of G_i and $\{G_1, G_2, ..., G_{i-1}, G_{i+1}, ...\}$, P is called the *direct product* of the *component* groups $G_1, G_2, G_3, ...$

70 DIRECT PRODUCTS [V 15

Ex. 1. For example, the group G of V 4_1 is the direct product of N and $1+c$.

Ex. 2. The order of a direct product is the product of the orders of the component groups.

Ex. 3. The component groups are normal in their direct product.

Ex. 4. A direct product is 'decomposable'.

Ex. 5. If $\{G_1, G_2, ..., H_1, H_2, ..., K_1, K_2, ..., ...\}$ is the direct product of $G_1, G_2, ..., H_1, H_2, ..., K_1, K_2, ..., ...$, it is the direct product of $\{G_1, G_2, ...\}, \{H_1, H_2, ...\}, \{K_1, K_2, ...\}$.

Ex. 6. The central of a direct product is the direct product of the centrals of the components.

Ex. 7. If two groups contain respectively r and s sets of conjugate elements, their direct product contains rs sets.

Ex. 8. If g is an element of order qr, q being prime to r, $\{g\}$ is the direct product of $\{g^q\}$ and $\{g^r\}$.

Ex. 9. In how many ways can a cyclic group of order 1260 be expressed as a direct product?

Ex. 10. The direct product of Abelian groups is Abelian.

Ex. 11. In an infinite Abelian group G the elements of finite order form a subgroup H and the elements of infinite order form (with 1) a subgroup K, while G is the direct product of H and K.

Ex. 12. An Abelian group G of order p^α each of whose elements is of order p or 1 is the direct product of α cyclic groups of order p.

Ex. 13. If G is the direct product of groups $A, B, C, ...$ whose orders are relatively prime, and the G. C. S. of A and a subgroup G' of G is A', of B and G' is B', of C and G' is C', ..., G' is the direct product of $A', B', C', ...$.

Ex. 14. The semi-group formed by all positive integers, the law of combination being ordinary multiplication, is the direct product of the semi-groups $\{1\}, \{2\}, \{3\}, \{5\}, \{7\}, \{11\}, ...$.

Ex. 15. The group $a^p = b^p = 1$, $ab = ba$ is the direct product of any two of the groups $\{a\}, \{b\}, \{ab\}$, but not of all three.

Ex. 16. In V 4_1 the groups H, L, M, O are direct products.

§ **16.** Suppose that two groups G, Γ are so related that to each element γ of Γ corresponds one or more elements $g, g', g'', ...$ of G, while reciprocally to each element g of G corresponds one or more elements $\gamma, \gamma', \gamma'', ...$ of Γ. Suppose, moreover, that if g_i, g_j are elements of G corresponding to elements γ_i, γ_j of Γ, $g_i g_j$ is an element of G corresponding to $\gamma_i \gamma_j$ in Γ. Then G and Γ are said to be *isomorphic*.

If G and Γ are isomorphic groups, the elements of G corresponding to identity in Γ form a normal subgroup of G.

If g_1, g_2 are any two such elements of G, $g_1 g_2$ corresponds to $1.1 = 1$ in Γ. Moreover, g being any element of G, $g^{-1} g_1 g$ corresponds to $\gamma^{-1} 1 \gamma = 1$ in Γ. Hence the theorem follows.

If G and Γ are isomorphic groups, and L of order l is the subgroup formed by the elements of G corresponding to identity in Γ, l elements of G correspond to each element of Γ.

For if g_i, g_j correspond to the same element γ of Γ, $g_i^{-1} g_j$ corresponds to $\gamma^{-1} \gamma = 1$ in Γ, and hence $g_i^{-1} g_j$ is in L. Therefore the elements corresponding to γ are the l elements $L g_i (\equiv g_i L)$.

If l elements of G correspond to each element of Γ, and λ elements of Γ to each element of G, G and Γ are said to have *an (l, λ) isomorphism* with each other. The most important case is that in which $l = \lambda = 1$. In this case G and Γ are called *simply isomorphic* ('holohedrally isomorphic'). Two simply isomorphic groups are not distinct abstractly speaking.

Another case of importance is that in which $\lambda = 1$, but $l > 1$. Here only one element of Γ corresponds to each element of G, and the order of G is l times the order of Γ. G is said to be *multiply isomorphic* with Γ (or Γ 'merohedrally isomorphic' with G).

Ex. 1. For example, the group (G) $a^{48} = b^3 = 1$, $ab = ba^6$ and the group (Γ) $c^7 = d^3 = 1$, $cd = dc^2$ have a $(48, 7)$ isomorphism; L and Λ being $\{a\}$ and $\{c\}$ respectively. To the elements $b^r a^x (x = 1, 2, \ldots, 48)$ correspond the elements $d^r c^y (y = 1, 2, \ldots, 7)$ and to $d^r c^y$ correspond $b^r a^x$.

Ex. 2. A group is simply isomorphic with any transform.

Ex. 3. Two simple isomorphic groups are simply isomorphic.

Ex. 4. Two groups simply isomorphic with the same group are simply isomorphic with one another.

Ex. 5. If G' is simply isomorphic with G and Γ' with Γ, while G and Γ have an (l, λ) isomorphism, so have G' and Γ'.

Ex. 6. Every Abelian group may be exhibited as simply isomorphic with itself by making each element correspond to its inverse.

Ex. 7. The group G of V 4_1 is multiply isomorphic with that of V 3_{11}.

Ex. 8. The groups $a^{22} = b^5 = 1$, $ab = ba^3$ and $c^{93} = d^5 = 1$, $cd = dc^4$ have a $(22, 93)$ isomorphism.

Ex. 9. The groups of V $14_{10, 11}$ have a $(49, 48)$ isomorphism.

§ 17. *If H is a normal subgroup of G so that*
$$G \equiv Hg_1 + Hg_2 + Hg_3 + \ldots,$$
then the partitions Hg_1, Hg_2, Hg_3, ... may be considered as the elements of a group which is completely defined when G and H are given.

We have first to show that these partitions may be looked upon as elements, i.e. that they have a unique law of combination, &c.

Let $h_1, h_2, h_3, \ldots$ be the elements of H. Then $h_x g_i \cdot h_y g_j$ is an element of the same partition (Hg_k, say) as $g_i g_j$. For since H is normal, $g_i h_y g_i^{-1}$ is in H ($= h_z$, say). Hence $h_x g_i h_y g_j = h_x g_i h_y g_i^{-1} g_i g_j = h_x h_z g_i g_j$, which is in $Hg_i g_j \equiv Hg_k$.

Hence if we denote the partitions by $\gamma_1, \gamma_2, \gamma_3, \ldots$, the γ's obey a unique law of combination defined by $\gamma_i \gamma_j = \gamma_k$ and a similar relation for each pair of γ's.

The γ's also obey the associative law. For if every element of $Hg_i \cdot Hg_j$ is in Hg_k and every element of $Hg_j \cdot Hg_f$ is in Hg_l, the elements $Hg_k \cdot Hg_f$ and the elements $Hg_i \cdot Hg_l$ lie in the same partition, since the elements of G obey the associative law. Hence $\gamma_k \gamma_f = \gamma_i \gamma_l$ or $(\gamma_i \gamma_j) \gamma_f = \gamma_i (\gamma_j \gamma_f)$.

Finally, if g_e is that one of the g's which is in H, and Hg_u is the partition containing g_i^{-1}, $\gamma_i = \gamma_e \gamma_i = \gamma_i \gamma_e$ and $\gamma_e = \gamma_i \gamma_u = \gamma_u \gamma_i$. Therefore $\gamma_1, \gamma_2, \gamma_3, \ldots$ may be treated as elements according to the definition of I 1, γ_e being the identical element and γ_u the inverse of γ_i.

This set of elements evidently forms a group; for the product of any two of the elements is contained in the set and the number of elements is finite.

The group formed by the γ's is called the *quotient* of G by H, and a *factor-group* of G. It is denoted by G/H or $\dfrac{G}{H}$, and is of fundamental importance in the theory of groups. It is evident that G is multiply isomorphic with G/H, the elements of H corresponding in G to identity in G/H, and the elements of Hg_i corresponding to γ_i.

In the above reasoning H is a normal subgroup of G. If H is a subgroup of G but not normal, G/H denotes the same as G/D, where D is the normal greatest common subgroup of all subgroups conjugate to H in G (§ 12). The symbol G/H is, however, very rarely used unless H is normal in G.

Ex. 1. In $\nabla 4_1$ $G \equiv L + La + Lb + Lba \equiv \gamma_1 + \gamma_2 + \gamma_3 + \gamma_4$ (say). Now a^2, b^2, $(ba)^2$ are in γ_1, $b^2 a$ and bab are in γ_2, aba and

ba^2 are in γ_3, ab and ba are in γ_4. Hence the partitions γ_1, γ_2, γ_3, γ_4 may be considered as elements combining according to the multiplication table.

	γ_1	γ_2	γ_3	γ_4
γ_1	γ_1	γ_2	γ_3	γ_4
γ_2	γ_2	γ_1	γ_4	γ_3
γ_3	γ_3	γ_4	γ_1	γ_2
γ_4	γ_4	γ_3	γ_2	γ_1

Therefore G/L is the group of V 3_{11}.

Ex. 2. H and G/H in § 17 do not define G.

Ex. 3. (i) The order of G/H is the index of H in G. (ii) If H is of prime index, G/H is cyclic.

Ex. 4. If $G \equiv H + Hg + Hg^2 + \ldots$, G/H is cyclic.

Ex. 5. $G/H = a^{-1}Ga/a^{-1}Ha$.

Ex. 6. If the order of an element g in G is m, the order of the corresponding element γ of G/H is a factor of m.

Ex. 7. If H and K are conjugate subgroups of a group A, while H is normal in G and G in A, K is normal in G and $G/K = G/H$.

Ex. 8. A factor-group of an Abelian group is Abelian.

Ex. 9. If H is a normal subgroup of G such that G/H is Abelian, H contains the commutator of any pair of elements of G.

Ex. 10. If G is an Abelian group of order n, the elements of G whose orders divide a factor m of n form a subgroup H, and G/H is simply isomorphic with the subgroup of G formed by the m-th powers of all the elements of G.

Ex. 11. (i) If G, G' are isomorphic and L, L' are the subgroups of G, G' corresponding to identity in G', G respectively, G/L and G'/L' are simply isomorphic. (ii) If two groups have an (l, l') isomorphism, their orders are in the ratio $l : l'$.

Ex. 12. If H_1 is a normal subgroup of G_1, H_2 of G_2, ..., while $\{G_1, G_2, \ldots\}$ is the direct product of G_1, G_2, ...,
$$\{G_1, G_2, \ldots\}/\{H_1, H_2, \ldots\}$$
is the direct product of groups simply isomorphic with G_1/H_1, G_2/H_2, ...

Ex. 13. In § 18 $\{G, H\}/G = H/D$.

Ex. 14. If G is the group $a^4 = 1$, $a^2 = (ab)^2 = b^2$ and $H \equiv 1 + a^2$, find G/H.

Ex. 15. Find $\{a, b, c\}/\{a^r, c\}$, where $a^{2r} = b^2 = (ab)^2 = c^2 = 1$, $ac = ca$, $bc = cb$.

Ex. 16. Find $\{a, b\}/\{a^2\}$ and $\{a, b\}/\{a^{11}\}$, where $a^{22} = b^5 = 1$, $ab = ba^3$.

Ex. 17. Find $\{a, b\}/\{a^7\}$, where $a^{49} = b^7 = 1$, $ab = ba^8$.

§ 18. *If H is a normal subgroup of G, to each subgroup Λ of $\Gamma \equiv G/H$ corresponds a subgroup L of G containing H, such that $\Lambda = L/H$. If Λ is normal in Γ, L is normal in G and $G/L = \Gamma/\Lambda$.*

Retaining the notation of § 17, if γ_a, γ_b are any two elements of a subgroup Λ of Γ, each element of $Hg_a \cdot Hg_b$ corresponds to $\gamma_a \gamma_b$. Hence the elements of G corresponding to the elements of Λ form a subgroup L of G, such that L contains H and $\Lambda = L/H$.

Again, if $\gamma^{-1}\gamma_a\gamma$ is in Λ, where γ is any element of Γ, $g^{-1} \cdot Hg_a \cdot g$ is in L, where g is any element of G. Hence if Λ is normal in Γ, L is normal in G. In this case if $\Gamma \equiv \Lambda\gamma_1 + \Lambda\gamma_2 + \Lambda\gamma_3 + \ldots$ and every element of $\Lambda\gamma_i \cdot \Lambda\gamma_j$ is in $\Lambda\gamma_k$, every element of $Lg_i \cdot Lg_j$ is in Lg_k. Hence $G/L = \Gamma/\Lambda$.

Ex. 1. For example, in $V4_1$ to the 8 normal subgroups of $\{a, b, c\}/\{a^2, c\}$ correspond the 8 normal subgroups $\{a, c\}$, $\{a^2, b, c\}$, $\{a^2, ba, c\}$ of $\{a, b, c\}$ containing $\{a^2, c\}$. (See $V17_1$.)

Ex. 2. To a subgroup L of G containing H corresponds a subgroup Λ of Γ. If L is normal in G, Λ is normal in H and $G/L = \Gamma/\Lambda$.

Ex. 3. If Γ is simple, H is contained in no normal subgroup of G; and conversely.

Ex. 4. If $\{H, K\}$ is the direct product of H and K,
$$\{H, K\}/H = K.$$

Ex. 5. If a normal subgroup L of G contains a subgroup H normal in G and G/H is Abelian, so is G/L.

Ex. 6. If H, K are two normal subgroups of G whose G. C. S. is D, G/D contains two normal subgroups H/D, K/D with only identity in common.

Ex. 7. If the G. C. S. of two subgroups H and K of G is D, and H is normal in G, G/H contains a subgroup K' simply isomorphic with K/D. If K is normal in G, K' is normal in G/H and $G/\{H, K\} = (G/H)/K'$.

Ex. 8. Assuming that every group of order $p_1 p_2 \ldots p_{t-1} p_t$ (where $p_1, p_2, \ldots, p_t$ are distinct primes in ascending order of magnitude) has a normal subgroup of order p_t, prove that it contains a normal subgroup of order $p_r p_{r+1} \ldots p_t$ composed of all those elements of the group whose orders divide $p_r p_{r+1} \ldots p_t$.

§ 19. *An Abelian group G whose order is divisible by a prime p contains an element of order p.*

Suppose G is generated by $g_1, g_2, g_3, \ldots$ and let a_1 be the order of g_1, a_2 the order of g_2 relative to $\{g_1\}$, a_3 the order of g_3 relative to $\{g_1, g_2\}$, a_4 the order of g_4 relative to $\{g_1, g_2, g_3\}$, and so on. Then G contains evidently $a_1 a_2 a_3 \ldots$ distinct elements

$$g_1^{\beta_1} g_2^{\beta_2} g_3^{\beta_3} \ldots \; (\beta_i = 1, 2, \ldots, a_i;\; i = 1, 2, 3, \ldots).$$

Hence $a_1 a_2 a_3 \ldots$ is divisible by p, and therefore one of the quantities $a_1, a_2, a_3, \ldots$ is divisible by p. Suppose a_i is divisible by p. Then the order of $g_i = kp$, where k is integral (§ 1); and g_i^k is an element of order p in G.

§ 20. *An Abelian group G of order n contains a subgroup of order r, where r is any factor of n.*

The theorem is readily verified for groups of orders 1, 2, 3, 4, ... Assume it true for all Abelian groups of order $< n$. Let p be any prime factor of r, and let g be an element of order p in G (§ 19).

By the assumption $G/\{g\}$ (which is obviously Abelian of order $n \div p$) contains a subgroup of order $r \div p$; and the corresponding subgroup of G is of order r. The theorem is now at once proved by induction.

Ex. 1. It is not conversely true that a group G of order n is necessarily Abelian if every factor of n is the order of some subgroup of G.

Ex. 2. G is an Abelian group of order $p^\alpha q^\beta r^\gamma \ldots$, $p, q, r, \ldots$ being distinct primes. Prove that (i) G contains one and only one subgroup of order p^α; (ii) G is the direct product of the subgroups $P, Q, R, \ldots$ of orders $p^\alpha, q^\beta, r^\gamma, \ldots$; (iii) G is cyclic if $P, Q, R, \ldots$ are cyclic.

§ 21. *If G is a group of order n, the number N of elements in G whose r-th power is conjugate to a given element a is a multiple of the H.C.F. of n and r.*

We assume the theorem true for all groups of order $< n$, and then deduce the required result by induction.

(1) First suppose that r is a factor of n and that a is not normal in G.

Let H of order m be the normaliser of a in G. If g is an element of G such that $g^r = a$, g is in H. Hence by our assumption the number M of elements such as g is a multiple of the H. C. F. (d) of m and r. Let $b = c^{-1}ac$ be any element conjugate to a in G. Then $(c^{-1}gc)^r = c^{-1}g^r c = c^{-1}ac = b$; and conversely an element g_1 of G whose r-th power $= b$ is the transform by c of the element $cg_1 c^{-1}$ whose r-th power $= a$. Hence G contains M elements whose r-th power $= b$. Now G contains $n \div m$ elements conjugate to a (§ 8). Therefore $N = Mn \div m$. But M is a multiple of d. Hence N is a multiple of r.*

(2) Next suppose that r is a factor of n while a is normal in G. First take the case in which $r = p^a$ (p prime), while the order k of a is divisible by p.

Let g be an element of G such that $g^r = a$. Then

$$g^{kr} = a^k = 1 \text{ and } g^{kp^{a-1}} = a^{k+p} \neq 1,$$

so that g is of order kr. If $(g^s)^r = a$, $a^s = (g^r)^s = (g^s)^r = a$; and therefore $s \equiv 1 \pmod{k}$. Hence $(g^s)^r = a$ if and only if g^s is any one of the distinct elements $g^{1+k}, g^{1+2k}, \ldots, g^{1+rk}$. Moreover in this case $g = (g^s)^e$ where e is chosen so that $se \equiv 1 \pmod{kr}$; which is always possible since s is prime to k, and therefore to p and r. It follows that those elements of G whose r-th power $= a$ can be divided into sets of r elements such that each element of a set is a power of all the rest. Now the number of elements in G whose r-th power $= a$ is N. Hence N is a multiple of r.

(3) Now suppose as in (2) that $r = p^a$ and is a factor of n, while a is normal in G; but that k is not divisible by p.

The normal elements of G whose orders are not divisible by p form an Abelian subgroup K; for if the orders of two permutable elements are prime to p, so is evidently the order of their product.

Let t be the order of K. Find a number u such that $ur \equiv 1 \pmod{t}$; this is always possible since t is prime to p by § 19. Now if $g = a^u h$ is an element of G such that $g^r = a$, $h^r = (ga^{-u})^r = g^r a^{-ur} = g^r a^{-1}$ (since $a^t = 1$) $= 1$; while conversely if $h^r = 1$, $(a^u h)^r = a$. Hence $N =$ the number of elements in G whose r-th power $= 1$. This is true whatever element of K a may be. Hence the number of elements in G whose r-th power is in K is Nt. Now the total number of elements in G is a multiple of r, and by (1) and (2) the number of elements whose r-th power is not in K is a multiple of r. Therefore Nt is a multiple of r. Hence N is a multiple of r, since t is prime to p.

---

* For if $m = m'd$, $r = r'd$, $n = n'r$, $Mn \div m$ is a multiple of $dn \div m = n'r \div m'$: and $n' \div m'$ is integral since $n'r' \div m' = n \div m$ is integral.

(4) Now suppose r is any factor of n, while a is any normal element of G.

Let $r = p^a q$ (q prime to p). If h is an element of G such that $h^q = a$, $(c^{-1}hc)^q = c^{-1}h^q c = c^{-1}ac = a$. Hence the elements of G whose q-th power $= a$ form one or more conjugate sets of elements. Now if g is an element of G such that $g^r = a$, g^{p^a} is an element whose q-th power is a. But by (1), (2), (3) the number of elements whose p^a-th power is an element such as h is a multiple of p^a. Hence N is a multiple of p^a. Similarly N is a multiple of every power of a prime dividing r, so that N is a multiple of r.

(5) Lastly, let r be any positive integer and a any element of G.

Let $n = dn'$ and $r = dr'$, where d is the H.C.F. of n and r. Find integers x, y such that $r'x - n'y = 1$; this is always possible since r' is prime to n'. Then if
$$g^r = a, \; g^d = g^{rx - ny} = g^{rx} = a^x,$$
while conversely if
$$g^d = a^x, \; g^r = a^{r'x} = a^{n'y+1} = a,$$
since
$$a^{n'} = g^{r'n} = 1.$$
But the number of elements of G whose d-th power $= a^x$ is a multiple of d by (1) and (4). Hence the theorem is completely proved in every case.

COROLLARY. If n is the order of a group G, the number of elements in G whose order divides a given factor r of n is a multiple of r.

Ex. 1. For example, in the group $a^3 = b^2 = (ab)^2 = c^3 = 1$, $ac = ca$, $bc = cb$ of order 18 (i) there are 9 elements whose 3rd power is 1 and 9 elements whose 3rd power is conjugate to b; (ii) there are 4 elements whose 10th power is c or c^2, 4 whose 10th power is 1, and 2 whose 10th power is conjugate to a, ca, or $c^2 a$.

Ex. 2. A group of order $2m$ (m odd) contains m elements of odd order.

Ex. 3. (i) If a group G contains q' elements whose orders divide q and r' elements whose orders divide r (q prime to r), G contains at most $q'r'$ elements whose orders divide qr. (ii) If $q' = q$ and $r' = r$, G contains exactly qr elements whose orders divide qr.

Ex. 4. If those elements of a group G of order $\alpha\kappa$ (α prime to κ) whose orders divide α generate an Abelian subgroup H, H is of order α.

Ex. 5. The number of elements in a group G of order n whose r-th power is a is divisible by the H.C.F. of r and the order of the normaliser of a in G.

Ex. 6. If u_x is the number of cyclic subgroups of order p^x in a group G whose order is divisible by p^x,
$$(u_1-1)+(u_2-1)p+(u_3-1)p^2+ \ldots +(u_x-1)p^{x-1} \equiv 0 \pmod{p^x}.$$

Ex. 7. Verify the result of § 21 when $r=3$ in the group of V $6_{1(\text{II})}$.

Ex. 8. V 1_2 is a particular case of the result of § 21.

CHAPTER VI

PERMUTATION-GROUPS

§ 1. A group whose elements are permutations on m given symbols $x_1, x_2, ..., x_m$ is called a *permutation-group of degree m*.

One such group is that containing each of the $m!$ possible permutations on the m symbols. It is called the *symmetric group of degree m*, and is of order $m!$.

Again, there are $\frac{1}{2}m!$ possible even permutations on the m symbols which form a group of order $\frac{1}{2}m!$ called the *alternating group of degree m*. For since the product of two even permutations is even, the even permutations form a group A. Let t be any transposition, and h any odd permutation. Then ht^{-1} being even is in A, so that h is in At. Hence the symmetric group $\equiv A + At$, and A is of order $\frac{1}{2}m!$.

The alternating group is a normal subgroup of the symmetric, since any transform of an even permutation is obviously even (see also V 7_{12}).

If every permutation of a group G is regular, G is called a *regular* permutation-group.

If G contains permutations $\gamma_1, \gamma_2, ..., \gamma_m$ replacing x_1 by each of the symbols $x_1, x_2, ..., x_m$, G contains a permutation (e.g. $\gamma_r^{-1}\gamma_s$) replacing any given symbol x_r by another given symbol x_s. In this case G is called a *transitive* permutation-group; while if G does not contain m such permutations, G is called *intransitive*.

A transitive group containing a permutation replacing any two given symbols by any other two given symbols is called *doubly transitive*. Similarly, a group containing a permutation replacing any 3, 4, ..., k, ... given symbols by any other 3, 4, ..., k, ... given symbols is called *triply, quadruply, ..., k-ply, ... transitive*. A group which is transitive but not doubly, triply, ... transitive is called *simply transitive*.

Ex. 1. Every permutation-group of degree m is a subgroup of the symmetric group of degree m.

Ex. 2. The symmetric group of degree m contains as subgroups every symmetric group of degree $< m$, and the same is true of alternating groups.

Ex. 3. Every symmetric group is decomposable.

Ex. 4. A transitive group of order and degree m can always be found, but there is no transitive group whose order is less than its degree.

Ex. 5. (i) The symmetric group of degree m is m-ply transitive, (ii) the alternating group is $(m-2)$-ply transitive, (iii) there is no $(m-1)$-ply transitive group of degree m.

Ex. 6. If the permutations of an intransitive group G replace x_1 by $x_1, x_2, \ldots, x$, every permutation of G permutes these μ symbols among each other.

Ex. 7. Every subgroup of degree m in an intransitive group of degree m is intransitive.

Ex. 8. If two permutation-groups G, H act on distinct symbols, $\{G, H\}$ is their direct product and is intransitive.

Ex. 9. If a transposition is a normal element of a permutation-group G, G is intransitive and a direct product.

Ex. 10. Prove that $\{(1\,2)(8\,4), (1\,8\,5)(2\,4\,6)\}$ is a transitive group of degree 6 and order 12.

Ex. 11. Find two transitive and one intransitive group of degree and order 4.

Ex. 12. Every two conjugate elements of a permutation-group are similar.

Ex. 13. Any two similar permutations on the same symbols are conjugate in the symmetric group.

Ex. 14. Every conjugate set of elements in the symmetric group is self-inverse.

Ex. 15. (i) A permutation of degree m containing $\alpha, \beta, \gamma, \ldots$ cycles of degree 1, 2, 8, ... has a normaliser Γ of order

$$R \equiv 1^\alpha \alpha!\ 2^\beta \beta!\ 8^\gamma \gamma! \ldots$$

in the symmetric group of degree m. (ii) If $\alpha, \beta, \gamma, \delta, \epsilon, \ldots$ are all 0 or 1, Γ is Abelian. (iii) When is Γ contained in the alternating group?

Ex. 16. Find the number of subgroups conjugate to

$$\{(1\,2)(8\,4)(5\,6\,7)(8\,9\,10\,11)\}$$

in the symmetric group on 1, 2, ..., 14.

Ex. 17. The number of conjugate sets in the symmetric group of degree m is the coefficient of x^m in $1 \div (1-x)(1-x^2)(1-x^3)\ldots$.

Ex. 18. Two similar even permutations a, b are conjugate in the alternating group if a is permutable with an odd permutation c.

Ex. 19. (i) The permutations similar to an even permutation a form two conjugate sets in the alternating group if a is not permutable with any odd permutation. (ii) This is the case if and only if the cycles of a are of odd and distinct degrees.

Ex. 20. (i) An even permutation a of degree m containing α, β, γ, δ, ϵ, ζ, η, θ, ι, κ, λ, ... cycles of degree 1, 2, 3, 4, 5, 6, 7, 8, 9, 10, 11, ... has a normaliser of order $r\,1^\alpha\,\alpha!\,2^\beta\,\beta!\,3^\gamma\,\gamma!\,...\div 2$ in the alternating group of degree m, where

$$r = 1 + \frac{(m-\alpha)(m-1-\alpha)...(2-\alpha)}{(m-1)!\,\{m-\alpha(m-1)\}} \cdot \frac{(m-\beta)...(1-\beta)}{m!}$$
$$\cdot \frac{(m-\gamma)...(2-\gamma)}{(m-1)!\,\{m-\gamma(m-1)\}} \cdot \frac{(m-\delta)...(1-\delta)}{m!}\,...\,.$$

(ii) a is conjugate to a^{-1} in the alternating group when $r = 1$ or when $r = 2$ and $\gamma + \eta + \lambda + ...$ is even.

Ex. 21. (i) The permutation $a \equiv (1\ 2\ 3)(4\ 5\ 6\ 7\ 8\ 9\ 10)$ is conjugate to a, a^4, a^5, a^{16}, a^{17}, a^{20} in the alternating group on 1, 2, ..., 11. (ii) Find the number of subgroups conjugate to $\{a\}$ in the alternating group.

Ex. 22. Those permutations of a group which (i) do not displace (ii) permute among each other any given symbols form a subgroup.

Ex. 23. Those permutations of a group which leave a given function of the symbols unaltered form a subgroup.

Ex. 24. If permutations leaving a function f of the symbols unaltered form a group G and a permutation T changes f into f', every permutation of $T^{-1}GT$ leaves f' unaltered.

Ex. 25. (i) No permutation of

$$G \equiv 1 + (ab)(cd) + (ac)(bd) + (ad)(bc)$$

changes the function (difference of one pair of symbols × difference of the other pair). (ii) Deduce that G is normal in the symmetric group on a, b, c, d.

Ex. 26. (i) Find the group G formed by those permutations on a, b, c, d which leave $ac + bd$ unaltered. (ii) G is the normaliser of $(ac)(bd)$ in the symmetric group on a, b, c, d.

Ex. 27. The function $x_1 + Xx_2 + X^2 x_3 + ... + X^{m-1} x_m$ is in general changed into $m!$ distinct functions by the permutations of the symmetric group on $x_1, x_2, ..., x_m$.

Ex. 28. Construct a function of $x_1, x_2, ..., x_m$ which is unaltered by the permutations of a given group G but by no other permutation on these symbols.

Ex. 29. (i) If a, b, c, $\pi - \alpha$, $\pi - \beta$, $\pi - \gamma$ are the sides and angles of a spherical triangle, and R, $\tfrac{1}{2}\pi - \rho$ are the radii of the circumscribed and inscribed circles; any formula connecting the sides, angles, &c., of a spherical triangle remains true when we apply to it any permutation of the group G generated by $(a\alpha)(b\beta)(c\gamma)(R\rho)$, $(bc)(\beta\gamma)$, $(ca)(\gamma\alpha)$. (ii) G is decomposable, intransitive, and of order 12.

§ 2. *Every abstract group of order n is simply isomorphic with a regular permutation-group of degree and order n.*

Let $g_1, g_2, \ldots, g_n$ be the elements of a group G of order n. Then $g_1 g_i, g_2 g_i, \ldots, g_n g_i$ are the elements $g_1, g_2, \ldots, g_n$ in some order or other. For they are all in G and they are all distinct, since $g_x g_i = g_y g_i$ would involve $g_x = g_y$.

Let S_i denote the permutation $\begin{pmatrix} g_1 & g_2 & \cdots & g_n \\ g_1 g_i & g_2 g_i & \cdots & g_n g_i \end{pmatrix}$ on the symbols $g_1, g_2, \ldots, g_n$. Then since S_i replaces g_x by $g_x g_i$ and S_j replaces $g_x g_i$ by $g_x g_i g_j$, $S_i S_j \equiv \begin{pmatrix} g_1 & g_2 & \cdots & g_n \\ g_1 g_i g_j & g_2 g_i g_j & \cdots & g_n g_i g_j \end{pmatrix}$. Hence if $g_i g_j = g_k$, $S_i S_j = S_k$. Therefore the permutations $S_1, S_2, \ldots, S_n$ form a permutation group P on the symbols $g_1, g_2, \ldots, g_n$ of order and degree n simply isomorphic with G.

The group P is transitive, since it contains a permutation replacing g_1 by any arbitrary symbol g_x; namely, the permutation S_t, where $g_1^{-1} g_x = g_t$.

If g_i is of order e, any cycle of S_i is of the type
$$(g_x g_i \; g_x g_i^2 \cdots g_x g_i^e).$$
Therefore S_i is regular, being the product of $n \div e$ cycles of degree e. Hence P is regular.

Ex. 1. (i) G is simply isomorphic with the group P' formed by the permutations $S_i' \equiv \begin{pmatrix} g_1 & g_2 & \cdots & g_n \\ g_i g_1 & g_i g_2 & \cdots & g_i g_n \end{pmatrix}$. (ii) Each permutation of P' is permutatable with every permutation of P. (iii) The G. C. S. of P and P' is simply isomorphic with the central of G. (iv) The only permutations on $g_1, g_2, \ldots, g_n$ permutable with every element of P are the elements of P'.

Ex. 2. If $a_i = n\left(1 - \dfrac{1}{e_i}\right)$, where e_i is the order of g_i, and $g_x g_y g_z \cdots = g_r$; $a_r - a_x a_y a_z \cdots$ is even.

Ex. 3. The groups P, P' of Ex. 1 are at once derived from the multiplication table of G. Thus S_i is obtained by writing the elements of the column headed g_i under the corresponding elements of the left-hand column, and S_i' is obtained by writing the elements of the row headed g_i under the elements of the top row.

Ex. 4. (i) The multiplication table of a group of order n is a 'latin square of order n', i. e. an array of n rows and n columns formed by n symbols where no row and no column contains the same element twice. (ii) Though we can find in this way a latin square of any given order, we do not obtain all possible latin squares in this way. (iii) Find all possible latin squares of order 2, 3, 4.

§ 3. *If a group G contains a subgroup H of index m, G is isomorphic with a transitive permutation-group of degree m. The isomorphism is simple if H contains no normal subgroup of G.*

Let $G \equiv Hg_1 + Hg_2 + \ldots + Hg_m$. Denote the partitions $Hg_1, Hg_2, \ldots, Hg_m$ by the symbols $\gamma_1, \gamma_2, \ldots, \gamma_m$. Let a, b be any two elements of G. Every element of $Hg_i \cdot a$ lies in the same partition of G (the partition containing $g_i a$); let this partition be γ_i'. Similarly suppose that each element of $\gamma_i' \cdot b$ lies in the partition γ_i''. Let S, T denote the permutations $\begin{pmatrix} \gamma_1 & \gamma_2 & \ldots & \gamma_m \\ \gamma_1' & \gamma_2' & \ldots & \gamma_m' \end{pmatrix}$, $\begin{pmatrix} \gamma_1' & \gamma_2' & \ldots & \gamma_m' \\ \gamma_1'' & \gamma_2'' & \ldots & \gamma_m'' \end{pmatrix}$. Then since every element of $Hg_i \cdot ab$ lies in γ_i'' and $ST \equiv \begin{pmatrix} \gamma_1 & \gamma_2 & \ldots & \gamma_m \\ \gamma_1'' & \gamma_2'' & \ldots & \gamma_m'' \end{pmatrix}$, to the product of a and b corresponds the product of the permutations S and T corresponding to a and b respectively. Hence all the permutations such as $S, T, \ldots$ form a group Q of degree m isomorphic with G. Q is transitive, for we can always find an element g of G (e.g. $g_1^{-1} g_i$) such that $Hg_1 \cdot g$ is γ_i.

Identity is the only element of Q corresponding to identity in G. The elements of G corresponding to identity in Q form a normal subgroup K of G (V 16). Let k be any element of K; then $Hg_i k \equiv Hg_i$ for all the values $1, 2, \ldots, m$ of i. Since one of the g's is in H, $Hk \equiv H$, i.e. k is in H. Therefore H contains the normal subgroup K of G. If H contains no normal subgroup of G, the isomorphism between G and Q is simple.

COROLLARY. *A group G containing a set of m conjugate elements or subgroups $H_1, H_2, \ldots, H_m$ is isomorphic with a transitive permutation-group R of degree m.*

For the normaliser of any one of the conjugate elements or subgroups is of index m.

Ex. 1. Q and R are simply transitive.

Ex. 2. $Q = G/H$. (See end of V 17).

Ex. 3. To the subgroup H of G and to the normaliser of H_1 in G corresponds the subgroup formed by those permutations of Q and R respectively which do not displace one symbol.

Ex. 4. The group R of the corollary may be considered as a transitive permutation-group on the symbols $H_1, H_2, \ldots, H_m$ in which the element $\begin{pmatrix} H_1 & H_2 & \ldots & H_m \\ a^{-1}H_1 a & a^{-1}H_2 a & \ldots & a^{-1}H_m a \end{pmatrix}$ of R corresponds to the element a of G.

84   PERMUTATION-GROUPS   [VI 8

Ex. 5. To identity in R corresponds every element of G permutable with each of $H_1, H_2, \ldots, H_m$.

Ex. 6. The group $a^3 = b^2 = (ab)^3 = 1$ is simply isomorphic with the symmetric group of degree 3.

Ex. 7. Show that $a^3 = b^2 = (ab)^3 = 1$ is simply isomorphic with the alternating group of degree 4.

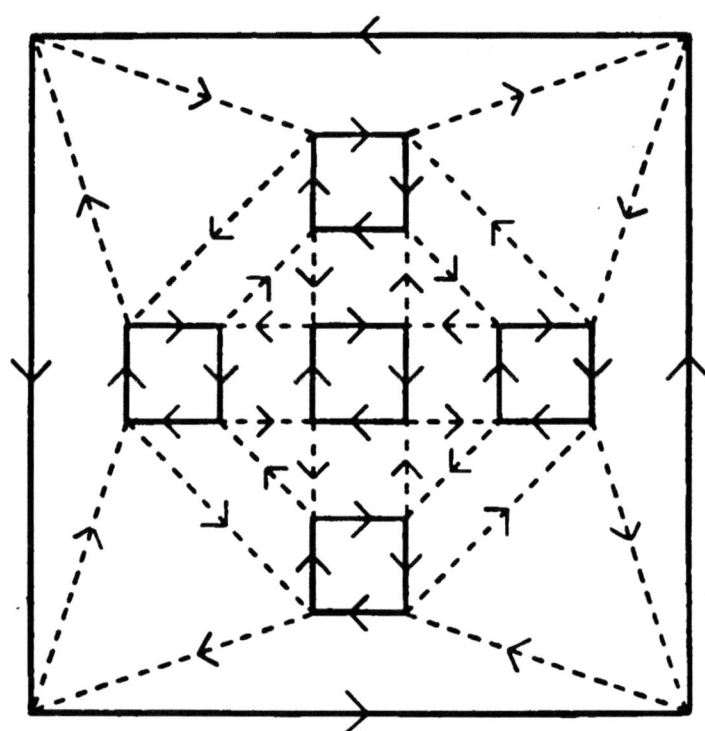

The group $a^3 = b^4 = (ab)^2 = 1$. $a \text{ - - -}, b \text{ ———}$.

Fig. 6.   (See Ex. 8 on this page.)

Ex. 8. If $a^3 = b^4 = (ab)^2 = 1$, (i) $H \equiv \{a, ba^2b^2\}$ is simply isomorphic with the symmetric group of degree 3,

(ii) $\{a, b\} \equiv H + Hb + Hb^2 + Hb^3$

is simply isomorphic with the symmetric group of degree 4.

Ex. 9. If $a^3 = b^5 = (ab)^2 = 1$, (i) $H \equiv \{b, a^3b^2a\}$ is simply isomorphic with the alternating group of degree 4,

(ii) $\{a, b\} \equiv H + Ha + Ha^2 + Ha^3 + Ha^4$

is simply isomorphic with the alternating group of degree 5.

Ex. 10. A group G of order 12 containing a normal subgroup H of order 4 is either Abelian or simply isomorphic with the alternating group of degree 4.

Ex. 11. A group of order 24 (or 60) containing a conjugate set of 4 (5) subgroups of order 6 (12) and containing no normal subgroup of order 2 or 3 is simply isomorphic with the symmetric (alternating) group of degree 4 (5).

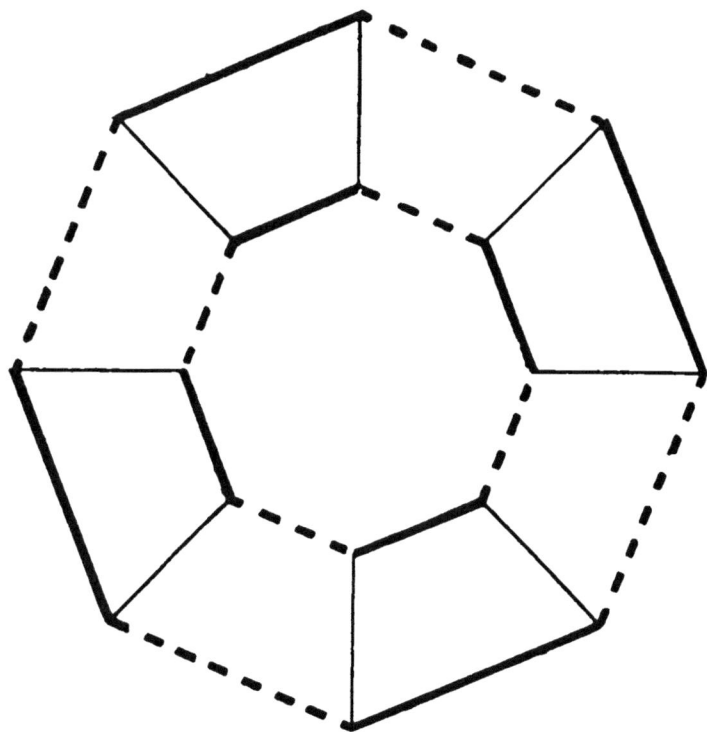

The group $a^2 = b^2 = c^2 = (ab)^4 = 1$, $ac = ca$, $bc = cb$. a---, b━, c—.

Fig. 7.

§ 4. The simple isomorphism between any group G of order n and a regular permutation-group of degree and order n (§ 2) can be shown geometrically as follows.

Represent each element of G by a point. Associate a colour with each element of G (excluding identity); for example, suppose red associated with the element g_i. From each of the points $g_1, g_2, \ldots, g_n$ draw to the points $g_1g_i, g_2g_i, \ldots, g_ng_i$ respectively red lines with arrow-heads to show their direction; and draw similar coloured lines for the other elements. We have then n points joined by $n(n-1)$ lines. One line of each of the $n-1$ colours starts from each of the n points, and one line of each colour ends at each point.

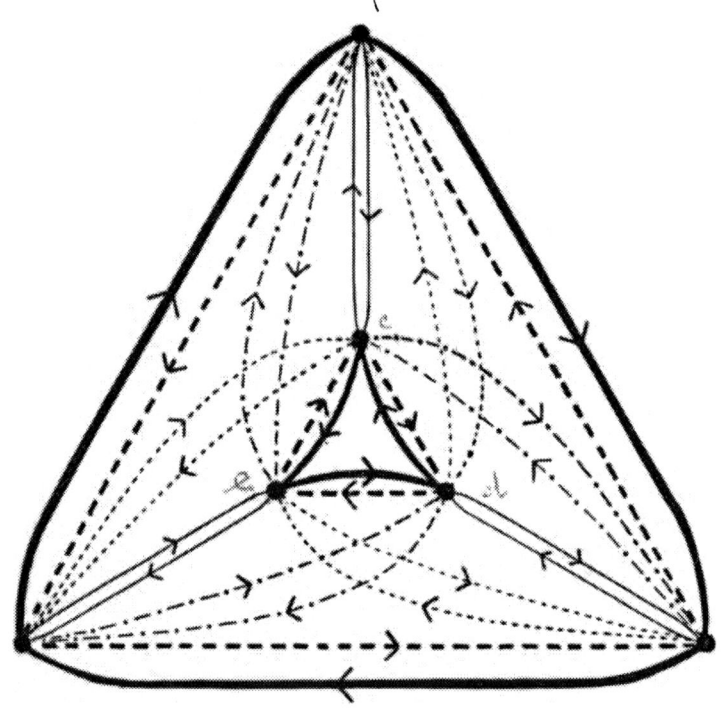

a ---, b ——, c —, d ----, e —·—·—·—·—.

Fig. 8.

A red line runs from a symbol g_x to the symbol g_xg_i replacing it in the permutation S_i (§ 2), and so for the other colours.

The geometrical representations are usually called 'Cayley's colour-groups'. They are somewhat complicated, but may conveniently be simplified by the omission of all the coloured lines except those associated with a set of independent generators of G.

If g_i is one of these generators, red lines run from g_x to $g_x g_i$ and from $g_x g_i^{-1}$ to g_x. If g_i is of order 2, $g_x g_i$ and $g_x g_i^{-1}$ coincide. In this case it is usual to draw only one of the two lines joining g_x and $g_x g_i$ and to suppress the arrow-heads (see Figs. 7, 9, 10).

The simplified diagram enables us to find very readily every relation satisfied by those generators whose colours are retained. For example, if in Fig. 6 we start from any point and

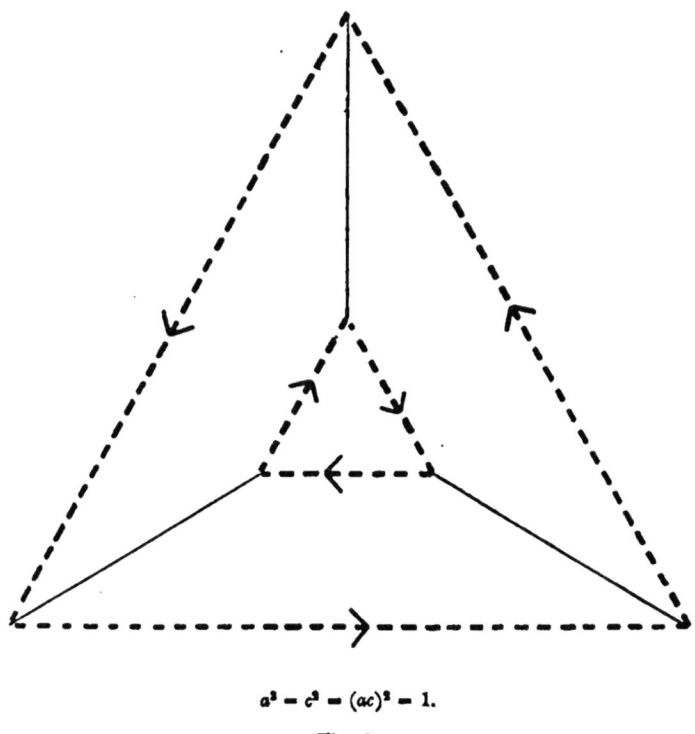

$a^2 = c^2 = (ac)^2 = 1.$

Fig. 9.

pass in the direction of the arrows along the lines in the order ———, - - -, - - -, ———, ———, ———, - - -, - - -, ———, ———, we return to the original point. Hence we have obviously $ba^2b^3a^2b^2 = 1$ or $(ba^2b^2)^2 = 1$. Similarly if in Fig. 7 we pass along the lines in the order - - -, ———, ———, - - -, ———, ———, - - -, ———, ———, - - -, ———, ———, we return to the original point. Hence we have in this case $(abc)^4 = 1$.

Ex. 1. For example, Fig. 8 shows the complete colour-diagram for the group of $\overline{V}1_1$. If we simplify the diagram by retaining only the lines corresponding to the independent generators a and c we get Fig. 9. If we retain only the lines corresponding to c and d we get Fig. 10.

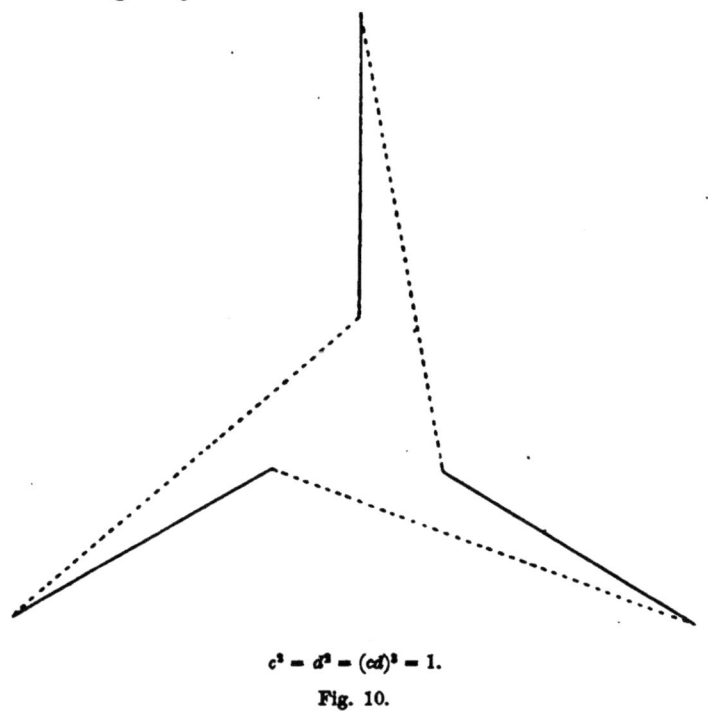

$c^2 = d^2 = (cd)^3 = 1.$

Fig. 10.

Ex. 2. The complete colour-diagram gives immediately the multiplication table of the group.

Ex. 3. In a diagram showing only the colours corresponding to a set of independent generators $\gamma_1, \gamma_2, \gamma_3, \ldots$ of a group G the red lines corresponding to γ_1 are erased. Prove that (i) the diagram breaks up into sets of points $H, g_1H, g_2H, \ldots$, where $G \equiv H + g_1H + g_2H + \ldots$ and $H \equiv \{\gamma_2, \gamma_3, \ldots\}$, so that no two points in different sets are connected by a line; (ii) if H is normal in G, all red lines starting from a given set of points end in the same set.

Ex. 4. In the group of Fig. 6 prove $aba^2b^2a = ba^2b^2$, $ba^2bab^2a = 1$, $a^2bab^2ab = 1$, and find the orders of aba^2b^2, a^2b^2, ab^3a^2.

Ex. 5. In the group of Fig. 7 find the order of bac, $abca$, bab.

Ex. 6. Draw colour-diagrams (simplified) for the groups (i) $a^{10}=1$; (ii) $a^5 = b^2 = 1$, $ab = ba$; (iii) $a^5 = b^2 = (ab)^2 = 1$; (iv) $a^2 = b^2 = (ab)^5 = 1$. Show that (i) and (ii) are the same abstract group, and so are (iii) and (iv).

Ex. 7. Draw a colour-diagram for the group
$$a^4 = b^2 = c^2 = (ab)^2 = 1, \ ac = ca, \ bc = cb$$
of $V4_1$. Show that the group is the same as that of Fig. 7, and that it cannot be represented on a diagram with less than three colours.

Ex. 8. (i) Draw a colour-diagram for the group $a^\lambda = 1$, $b^\beta = a^r$, $ab = ba$. (ii) Prove the results of $V5_{11}$ by means of a colour-diagram.

Ex. 9. Draw colour-diagrams for the groups $a^8 = b^2 = (a^2b)^2 = 1$, $(ab)^2 = (ba)^2$ and $a^8 = b^2 = 1$, $a^2b = ba^2$, $(ab)^2 = (ba)^2$.

Ex. 10. Draw the complete colour-diagrams for the groups (i) $a^6 = 1$, (ii) $a^2 = b^2 = 1$, $ab = ba$.

Ex. 11. ABC is an equilateral triangle and O is its centre; $BC = 5$ in. Points A_2 and A_3, B_2 and B_1, C_1 and C_2 are taken on the sides distant 1 in. from A, B, C. Points D_1 and A_1 are taken on OA distant respectively $\frac{3}{4}$ in. and $1\frac{1}{4}$ in. from O; and points D_2 and B_2, D_3 and C_3 are taken similarly on OB, OC. The black-sided triangles $A_1A_2A_3$, $B_1B_2B_3$, $C_1C_2C_3$, $D_1D_2D_3$ with clockwise arrows and red lines B_1C_1, C_2A_2, A_3B_3, A_1D_1, B_2D_2, C_3D_3 are drawn. What group does the diagram represent?

Ex. 12. A, B, C, D are points of longitude $0°$, $90°$, $180°$, $270°$ on the equator; X, Y, Z, W are points in latitude $45°$ of longitude $45°$, $135°$, $225°$, $315°$. Red triangles XBY, ZDW, and black triangles YCZ, WAX are drawn, and the figure is completed by reflexion in the plane of the equator with interchange of the two colours. If clockwise arrows are inserted round the triangles, what group does the diagram represent?

Ex. 13. Draw two parallel concentric regular m-sided red polygons. Denote the vertices by 1, 2, ..., m and $1'$, $2'$, ..., m'. Turn one polygon through a right angle. Put clockwise arrows round each polygon. Join by black lines the vertices (i) 1 and $1'$, 2 and $2'$, 3 and $3'$, ...; (ii) 1 and $1'$, 3 and $3'$, 5 and $5'$, ..., $2'$ and $\frac{m}{2}+2$, $4'$ and $\frac{m}{2}+4$, $6'$ and $\frac{m}{2}+6$, ... What groups do the diagrams represent?

Ex. 14. Put clockwise arrows round one red polygon of Ex. 13 and counterclockwise round the other. Black lines run (i) as in Ex. 13 (i); (ii) as in Ex. 13 (ii); (iii) with arrows joining 1 and $1'$, 2 and $2'$, 3 and $3'$, ..., $1'$ and $\frac{m}{2}+1$, $2'$ and $\frac{m}{2}+2$, $3'$ and $\frac{m}{2}+3$, ... What groups do the diagrams represent?

Ex. 15. A simplified colour-diagram drawn on a sphere divides up the surface into polygons in such a way that no two of the coloured lines intersect (except at an extremity of both). Prove that (i) the two lines of the same colour meeting at any point are not separated by a line of another colour; (ii) the polygons formed by lines of a given colour contain no vertex in their interior.

Ex. 16. Show that diagrams representing the groups of Ex. 7, 8, 9, 13, 14 can be drawn on an anchor-ring so that no two lines intersect.

§ 5. By definition, a k-ply transitive group on m symbols contains a permutation not displacing any k given symbols. If S and T are any two permutations which do not displace these k symbols, ST does not displace them. Hence:—

Those permutations of a k-ply transitive group G which do not displace k given symbols form a subgroup H.

Ex. 1. The permutations of G not displacing l of the k given symbols form a subgroup of G containing H.

Ex. 2. If the permutations of H do not displace $x_1, x_2, \ldots, x_k$; while g is a permutation of G replacing these symbols by $x_1', x_2', \ldots, x_k'$, the elements of G not displacing $x_1', x_2', \ldots, x_k'$ form the subgroup $g^{-1}Hg$.

Ex. 3. H contains no normal subgroup of G.

Ex. 4. If G is Abelian, $H \equiv 1$.

Ex. 5. Any normal element c of G (i) displaces every symbol, (ii) is regular.

Ex. 6. Every transitive Abelian group is regular.

Ex. 7. Every element of prime degree p normal in a group is circular of order p.

Ex. 8. A permutation S permutable with every element of a group G and acting on the same m symbols displaces all the symbols and is regular.

Ex. 9. The order μ of the central of a transitive group G of degree m is a factor of m.

Ex. 10. (i) The permutations such as S of Ex. 8 form a group whose order is a factor of m. (ii) Find this group when G is the permutation-group P of § 2.

Ex. 11. Find the group H in the case of $\{P, P'\}$ of § 2; and prove that $H = G/C$ where C is the central of G.

§ 6. *The order of a k-ply transitive group G of degree m is $qm(m-1)(m-2)\ldots(m-k+1)$; where q is the order of the subgroup H whose elements do not displace k given symbols.*

Let $g_1, g_2, g_3, \ldots$ be permutations of G each of which replaces the k given symbols by a distinct set of k symbols. The number of such permutations is $m! \div (m-k)!$; for the number of arrangements of m symbols k at a time is $m! \div (m-k)!$. Then $G \equiv Hg_1 + Hg_2 + Hg_3 + \ldots$. For if g, g' are two elements of G replacing the k given symbols by the same k symbols, $g'g^{-1}$ does not displace any one of the k given symbols, and is therefore contained in H. Hence G is of order $q \times m! \div (m-k)!$.

Ex. 1. The elements of G permuting among themselves the k symbols not displaced by the permutations of H form a subgroup of order $q \cdot k!$ containing H normally.

Ex. 2. If $q = 1$, G contains permutations displacing only $m-k+1$ symbols but no permutation displacing less than $m-k+1$ symbols.

Ex. 3. If the degree and order of a transitive group are equal $q = k = 1$. Every group is simply isomorphic with a permutation-group of this type.

Ex. 4. Prove the converse of § 3:—'If a group G is simply isomorphic with a simply transitive permutation-group of degree m, G contains a subgroup of index m containing no normal subgroup of G.'

Ex. 5. The degree of a simply transitive Abelian group = its order.

Ex. 6. In a simply transitive group G of degree m the permutations displacing every symbol (i) are at least $m-1$ in number, (ii) generate a normal subgroup of G.

Ex. 7. If the number of permutations not displacing r given symbols in a transitive group of order n and degree m is ν_r, $n = \sum_0^m \nu_r = \sum_0^m r\nu_r$.

Ex. 8. The elements of a k-ply transitive group displacing every symbol cannot form a group with identity unless $k = 1$ or $k = 2$ and $q = 1$.

Ex. 9. Show that no doubly transitive group of degree 5 is of order less than 20; and prove that $a \equiv (1\ 2\ 3\ 4\ 5)$, $b \equiv (1\ 2\ 4\ 3)$ generate a doubly transitive group of minimum order.

§ 7. Let G be an intransitive group containing permutations which replace the symbol x_1 by $x_1, x_2, \ldots, x_r$ but by no other symbol. Then any permutation g of G replaces x_i by one of the symbols $x_1, x_2, \ldots, x_r$. For let h be an element of G replacing x_1 by x_i, and suppose hg replaces x_1 by x_j. Then g replaces x_i by x_j. Hence the permutations of G permute the symbols of the *transitive set* $x_1, x_2, \ldots, x_r$ among themselves.

Similarly if the permutations of G replace the symbol y_1 by $y_1, y_2, ..., y_s$ only, they permute the symbols of the 'transitive set' $y_1, y_2, ..., y_s$ among themselves; and so on.

Ex. 1. A cycle of any permutation of G only contains symbols from one transitive set.

Ex. 2. G is a subgroup of the direct product of the symmetric groups on the symbols $[x_1, x_2, ..., x_r]$, $[y_1, y_2, ..., y_s]$, ...

Ex. 3. The order of G is a factor of $r! \times s! \times ...$.

Ex. 4. Those permutations of G which do not displace the symbols of certain given transitive sets form a normal subgroup of G.

Ex. 5. Those permutations of G which do not displace x_1 form a subgroup of index r.

Ex. 6. If those cycles of any generator of a permutation-group G which contain one of the symbols $x_1, x_2, ..., x_r$ contain no symbol other than $x_1, x_2, ..., x_r$, G is intransitive; and conversely.

Ex. 7. If in § 2 H is a subgroup of $G \equiv Hg_a + Hg_b + Hg_c + ...$, the corresponding subgroup of P is intransitive, the transitive sets being the symbols $g_a^{-1}H$, $g_b^{-1}H$, $g_c^{-1}H$, ...

Ex. 8. Find the transitive sets of
$\{(1482)(5876)(9\,10), (24)(58)(67)\}$ and of $\{(1284), (24), (56)\}$.

§ 8. Let certain of the transitive sets of symbols affected by an intransitive group G be denoted collectively by σ, and let the remaining sets be denoted collectively by τ. If k, k' are two elements of G permuting only the symbols of σ (displacing no symbol of τ), and if g is any element of G, then evidently kk' and $g^{-1}kg$ do not displace any symbol of τ. Hence those elements of G which permute only the symbols of σ form a normal subgroup K of G. Similarly the elements of G permuting only the symbols of τ form a normal subgroup K' of G.

If we leave out of consideration the effect of G on the symbols of τ, G reduces to a group H on the symbols of σ alone. If g, g' are any two elements of G, while h, h' are elements of H permuting the symbols of σ in the same way as g, g'; then gg' and hh' permute the symbols of σ in the same way. Hence G and H are isomorphic. To the identical element in H correspond the elements of K' in G. Therefore $H = G/K'$. It is evident that H contains K as a normal subgroup.

Now K and K' have only identity in common, and every element of K is permutable with each element of K'. Hence $\{K, K'\}$ is the direct product of K and K'; and it is normal in G, since K and K' are normal in G. It follows that $G/\{K, K'\}$ and H/K have the same order.

Now when we neglect the effect of the elements of G on the symbols of τ, each element of $\{K, K'\}$ reduces to an element of K, and each element of G to an element of H. If k_1, k_2, k_3 are elements of $\{K, K'\}$ and g_1, g_2, g_3 elements of G which reduce respectively to k_1', k_2', k_3' and g_1', g_2', g_3' when we neglect their effect on the symbols of τ, and if $k_1 g_1 \cdot k_2 g_2 = k_3 g_3$; we have evidently $k_1' g_1' \cdot k_2' g_2' = k_3' g_3'$. Hence $G/\{K, K'\}$ and H/K are isomorphic; and the isomorphism is simple since these two groups have the same order (cf. V 18$_7$).

Ex. 1. If H' is the group to which G reduces when we leave out of consideration the effect of its permutations on the symbols of σ, $H/K = H'/K'$.

Ex. 2. The elements of G are found by multiplying each element of H by the corresponding elements of H'.

Ex. 3. Find H, H', K, K' when (i) $G \equiv \{(1\,2\,8\,4), (2\,4), (5\,6)\}$, $\sigma \equiv [1, 2, 3, 4]$; (ii) $G \equiv \{(1\,4\,8\,2)(5\,8\,7\,6)(9\,10), (2\,4)(5\,8)(6\,7)$, $\sigma \equiv [9, 10]$ or $[5, 6, 7, 8, 9, 10]$.

§ 9. Let G be a simply transitive group on m symbols. Suppose that the m symbols may be divided into r sets $\sigma_1, \sigma_2, \ldots, \sigma_r$ each containing s symbols $(m = rs)$, so that every permutation of G either permutes the s symbols of any set σ_i among themselves or replaces them by the s symbols of another set σ_j. Then G is called an *imprimitive* group, and $\sigma_1, \sigma_2, \ldots, \sigma_r$ are called *imprimitive systems*. If no such division of the m symbols into sets is possible, G is said to be *primitive*.

Ex. 1. A k-ply transitive group $(k > 1)$ is primitive.
Ex. 2. A transitive group of prime degree is primitive.
Ex. 3. If a transitive group G of degree m contains a permutation whose order is prime and greater than the largest divisor of m, G is primitive.
Ex. 4. Those permutations of an imprimitive group G which do not displace the imprimitive systems but only permute the symbols of each system form a normal subgroup of G.
Ex. 5. The central of a primitive group $\equiv 1$.
Ex. 6. The central of a k-ply transitive group $\equiv 1$ if $k > 1$.
Ex. 7. No Abelian group is k-ply transitive.
Ex. 8. If H is any subgroup of the group G of § 2 and $G \equiv Hg_1 + Hg_2 + Hg_3 + \ldots$, P is imprimitive in such a way that the symbols of $Hg_1, Hg_2, Hg_3, \ldots$ are imprimitive systems.

Ex. 9. $\{(xyz)(abc), (xa)(yc)(zb)\}$ is an imprimitive group of order 6, the imprimitive systems being either $[x, y, z]$ and $[a, b, c]$ or $[x, a]$, $[y, b]$, and $[z, c]$.

Ex. 10. Find imprimitive systems in the groups (i) $\{(135)(246), (13)(24), (34)(56), (12)(34)\}$ and (ii) $\{(14)(26)(35), (123)(456), (12)(45)\}$.

§ 10. If γ, γ' are two elements of an imprimitive group G which do not displace the imprimitive systems but only permute the symbols of each system, then $\gamma\gamma'$ has evidently the same property. Hence elements such as γ, γ' form a sub-group Γ of G. If $G \equiv \Gamma g_1 + \Gamma g_2 + \Gamma g_3 + ...$, it is obvious that all elements in the partition Γg_i permute the imprimitive systems in the same way.

The group Γ is normal in G. For let g be any element of G, and suppose that g replaces every symbol of any imprimitive system σ_i by a symbol of the system σ_j. Then since γ permutes the symbols of σ_i among themselves, $g^{-1}\gamma g$ permutes the symbols of σ_j among themselves. The group G/Γ may be considered as a permutation-group of degree r on the symbols $\sigma_1, \sigma_2, ..., \sigma_r$.

Ex. 1. Γ is intransitive.
Ex. 2. The index of Γ in G is a divisor of $r!$.
Ex. 3. Find Γ for the groups of VI $9_{9, 10}$.

§ 11. The group Γ of § 10 is an intransitive normal subgroup of the transitive group G. We show in this section that every intransitive normal subgroup of G is contained in a group such as Γ.

Let H be an intransitive normal subgroup of G, and let $x_1, x_2, ...; y_1, y_2, ...; ...$ be the symbols in the transitive sets of H. Then if g is an element of G replacing x_1 by y_1, g^{-1} replaces y_1 by x_1. Hence since $g^{-1}Hg = H$, g replaces every* x by a y; and since $gHg^{-1} = H$, g replaces every y by an x (II 5). Therefore there are as many y's as x's. Similarly we can show that each transitive set of H contains the same number of symbols.

Now since every element of G transforms H into itself, every such element permutes the transitive sets of H among themselves. Therefore G is imprimitive and has the transitive sets of H as imprimitive systems; which proves the above statement.

* For at least one permutation of H contains a cycle of the form $(x_1 x_i ...)$, whatever i may be. If g transforms this cycle into $(y_1 y_i ...)$, g changes x_i into y_i.

Ex. 1. Every normal subgroup of a primitive group is transitive.
Ex. 2. The order of a normal subgroup H of a primitive group G is a multiple of the degree of G.
Ex. 3. Every primitive composite group is decomposable.
Ex. 4. If the group P of § 2 is primitive, it is simple.

§ 12. *The symmetric group is the only primitive group containing a transposition.*

Suppose (1 2) is a transposition contained in a transitive permutation-group G on the m symbols $1, 2, 3, \ldots, m$. Let (1 2), (1 3), …, (1 e) be the only transpositions in G which affect the symbol 1. Then since $(i\,j) = (1\,i)(1\,j)(1\,i)$, G contains $(i\,j)$; where i and j are any two of the set σ of symbols $1, 2, \ldots, e$. Hence, unless G is the symmetric group, the set σ does not include all the m symbols permuted by G.

Let a be a permutation of G replacing 1 by a given symbol f not included in σ and replacing 2 by s (say). Then G contains $a^{-1}(1\,2)\,a = (f\,s)$. Now s is not in σ; for otherwise G would contain $(1\,s)(f\,s)(1\,s) = (1\,f)$. Hence each permutation of G permutes the symbols $1, 2, \ldots, e$ among themselves or replaces them by a completely different set τ.

If σ and τ do not include all the m symbols on which G acts, let b be a permutation of G replacing 1 by a symbol not in σ or τ. Then as before b replaces each symbol of σ by a symbol of a set v having no symbol in common with σ. Now v has no symbol in common with τ either. For if a and b replace two symbols $1'$ and $2'$ of σ by the same symbol, ba^{-1} replaces $2'$ by $1'$. Hence ba^{-1} permutes the symbols of σ among themselves; i.e. $b = ba^{-1} \cdot a$ replaces σ by τ, or τ and v coincide.

Continuing this reasoning we see that the m symbols fall into sets permuted imprimitively by the elements of G; and hence G is imprimitive.

Ex. 1. The symmetric group is the only k-ply transitive group ($k > 1$) or simply transitive group of prime degree containing a transposition.

Ex. 2. G contains as subgroups the symmetric groups on the symbols of $\sigma, \tau, v, \ldots$.

Ex. 3. The symmetric group is the only group of degree m containing the transposition (1 2) and (i) the circular permutation (1 2 3 … m), (ii) a circular permutation b of degree m in which the symbols 1, 2 are separated by $i-1$ symbols, where i is prime to m.

Ex. 4. The symmetric group of degree m is simply isomorphic with a group whose elements are birational substitutions of degree $m-3$.

Ex. 5. The alternating and symmetric groups are the only primitive groups containing a circular permutation of order 8.

Ex. 6. A transitive group G containing a circular permutation of order 8 contains the alternating groups on the symbols of each imprimitive system.

§ 13. *The group G generated by every possible circular permutation of order r on the symbols $1, 2, \ldots, m$ is the alternating or symmetric group on these m symbols according as r is odd or even.*

First take $r = 2$. Since every permutation is the product of transpositions, G contains every possible permutation on the m symbols and is therefore the symmetric group.

Next take $r = 3$; then G contains every possible product of two transpositions on the m symbols. For such a product is either of the form $(1\,2)\,(1\,3) = (1\,2\,3)$ or of the form $(1\,2)\,(3\,4) = (2\,3\,4)\,(1\,2\,3)$; and both these products are in G. Hence G contains every even permutation on the m symbols, and is therefore the alternating group.

Lastly, take $r > 3$; then G contains every circular permutation of order 3 such as $(1\,2\,3)$. For

$$(1\,2\,3) = (1\,3\,2\,4 \ldots r)\,(1\,r \ldots 4\,3\,2)$$

which is in G. If r is even, G contains a circular permutation of even order; i.e. G contains an odd permutation and is the symmetric group. If r is odd, G is the alternating group.

Ex. 1. The group G generated by every permutation of the type $(1\,2)(3\,4)$ on m symbols $(m > 4)$ is the alternating group on the m symbols.

Ex. 2. The theorem in Ex. 1 does not hold if $m = 4$.

Ex. 3. If p is a prime $< m$, the symmetric group of degree m does not contain any subgroup of index $< p$ except the alternating group.

§ 14. *The alternating group G of degree m is simple, unless $m = 4$.*

This is evident when $m = 2$ or 3. When $m = 4$, G has evidently a normal subgroup of order 4 containing the four permutations $1, (1\,2)\,(3\,4), (1\,3)\,(2\,4), (1\,4)\,(2\,3)$; where $1, 2, 3, 4$ are the four symbols on which G acts.

Suppose that when $m > 4$, G contains a normal subgroup H. Let g be that permutation of H which displaces the smallest number of symbols. Let g be decomposed into its cycles. None of these cycles can contain more than three symbols;

THE SYMMETRIC GROUP

for if $g \equiv (1\,2\,3\,...)\,...$, H contains $f = (1\,3\,2)\,g\,(1\,2\,3)$ and also $gf^{-1} \equiv (2)\,(3\,1\,...)$ which displaces fewer symbols than g.

Again, no cycle of g can contain three symbols unless it is the only cycle of g. For if $g \equiv (4\,1\,2)\,(3\,...)\,...$, $gf \equiv (2)\,(1\,3\,...)...$ displaces fewer symbols than g and is in H.

Again, g cannot contain two cycles of two symbols each unless $m = 4$. For if $g \equiv (1\,2)\,(4\,5)\,...$, $gf \equiv (4)\,(5)\,(1\,3\,...)...$ displaces fewer symbols than g and is in H.

We see then that g must be (if $m > 4$) a circular permutation of order 2 or 3. The former is impossible since g is odd. If $g \equiv (1\,2\,3)$, H contains every other circular permutation of order 3 such as $(1'\,2'\,3')$, and is therefore the alternating group (§ 13). For G contains one or other of the two permutations

$$a \equiv \begin{pmatrix} 1 & 2 & 3 & 4 & ... & m \\ 1' & 2' & 3' & 4' & ... & m' \end{pmatrix} \text{ or } b \equiv \begin{pmatrix} 1 & 2 & 3 & 4 & ... & m \\ 2' & 1' & 3' & 4' & ... & m' \end{pmatrix},$$

since $ba^{-1} \equiv (1\,2)$ is odd. Hence $(1'\,2'\,3') = a^{-1}ga = b^{-1}g^2b$ is in H, since H is normal in G.

§ 15. *The symmetric group of degree m can contain no normal subgroup except the alternating group of degree m, unless $m = 4$.*

If $m = 4$, the subgroup of order 4 normal in the alternating group is also normal in the symmetric group. If $m \neq 4$, the proof is exactly the same as that of § 14. We have only to prove in addition that g cannot be a transposition. If $g \equiv (1\,2)$, H contains every other transposition such as $(1'\,2')$ in the m symbols and is therefore the symmetric group; for H contains $a^{-1}ga$.

Ex. 1. A function f_1 of m symbols ($m > 4$) is changed into $f_1, f_2, f_3, ...$ by the elements of the symmetric group on the m symbols. If those permutations which do not alter f_1 do not alter $f_1, f_2, f_3, ...$, they form the alternating or symmetric group.

Ex. 2. The alternating and symmetric groups are the only groups of degree m and order $> (m-1)!$ ($m \neq 4$).

Ex. 3. (i) If G is the symmetric group of degree 4 and H is its normal subgroup of order 4, G/H is simply isomorphic with the group formed by the substitutions $x' = x$, $(1-x)^{-1}$, $(x-1) \div x$, x^{-1}, $x \div (x-1)$, $1-x$. (ii) What is the geometrical interpretation of this result?

CHAPTER VII

SUBSTITUTION-GROUPS

§ 1. A GROUP whose elements are substitutions on m given variables is called a *substitution-group G of degree m*. If the substitutions are homogeneous and linear (III 4), G is called a *homogeneous linear substitution-group*. If the substitutions are fractional and linear (III 9), G is called a *fractional linear substitution-group*. We shall suppose in §§ 1 to 8 that all quantities considered (both coefficients and variables) are ordinary real or complex quantities unless the contrary is stated.

Ex. 1. (i) A permutation-group is a particular case of a homogeneous linear substitution-group. (ii) Each of its substitutions is real and orthogonal.

Ex. 2. The similarities of a homogeneous linear group form a normal Abelian subgroup.

Ex. 3. The determinant of every substitution of a finite homogeneous linear group is a root of unity.

Ex. 4. Those substitutions of a homogeneous linear group whose determinant is a power of a form a normal subgroup.

Ex. 5. (i) The 'group of subtraction and division' generated by $x' = d-x$ and $x' = b \div x$ is of finite order if $\pi \div \phi$ is rational, where $2\sqrt{b} \cos \phi = d$. (ii) If b and d are rational, the group is of order 4, 6, 8, 12, or ∞.

§ 2. If every substitution of a substitution-group G on the m variables $x_1, x_2, ..., x_m$ is expressed in terms of new variables $y_1, y_2, ..., y_m$ (functions of $x_1, x_2, ..., x_m$), we obtain a new substitution-group G' on the m variables $y_1, y_2, ..., y_m$. If now we put x_i for y_i ($i = 1, 2, ..., m$) in the substitutions of G', every substitution of G' will be derived from the corresponding substitution of G by transforming by

$$T \equiv (y_1, y_2, ..., y_m)$$

(III 3). Hence G' becomes $T^{-1}GT$.

Ex. Find $T^{-1}GT$ when G is generated by $x' = 1 \div (1-x)$ and $x' = 1 \div x$, and T is $x' = x-1$.

VII. 1-3] INVARIANTS

§ 3. Suppose that every element of a substitution-group G on the variables $x_1, x_2, ..., x_m$ when operating on any function $f(x_1, x_2, ..., x_m)$ either (i) leaves it unaltered for all values of $x_1, x_2, ..., x_m$ or (ii) merely multiplies it by a constant independent of $x_1, x_2, ..., x_m$. Then $f(x_1, x_2, ..., x_m)$ is called (i) an *absolute invariant* or (ii) a *relative invariant* of G. By an *invariant* we shall mean an 'absolute invariant' unless the contrary is stated.

Every finite group G has invariants. For if the n substitutions $g_1, g_2, ..., g_n$ of G change the function f_1 into $f_1, f_2, ..., f_n$, any symmetric function of $f_1, f_2, ..., f_n$ (e.g. their sum or product) is an invariant of G. In fact g_j changes f_i into f_k, where $g_i g_j = g_k$; so that each substitution of G permutes $f_1, f_2, ..., f_n$.

Ex. 1. For example; x^2y^2 and x^2+y^2 are absolute invariants, xy and x^2-y^2 are relative invariants of the group whose elements are $(x, y), (-y, x), (-x, -y), (y, -x), (x, -y), (y, x), (-x, y), (-y, -x)$.

Ex. 2. If $f(x_1, x_2, ..., x_m)$ is an invariant of G, $f(\Phi_1, \Phi_2, ..., \Phi_m)$ is an invariant of $T^{-1}GT$; where $x_i' = \Phi_i(x_1, x_2, ..., x_m)$ is the substitution T^{-1}.

Ex. 3. An expression is an invariant of G if it is not altered when we perform on it every one of a set of substitutions which generate G.

Ex. 4. Those substitutions of a group which leave unaltered one or more given expressions form a subgroup.

Ex. 5. (i) If a homogeneous linear group has a homogeneous algebraic invariant f of the second degree with non-zero determinant, it can be transformed into a group of orthogonal substitutions. (ii) Illustrate by taking
$$f \equiv x^2 + 2y^2 + 3z^2 + 2sx - 2xy.$$

Ex. 6. $x_1 + x_2 + x_3 + ...$ is a linear invariant of any permutation-group on the symbols $x_1, x_2, x_3, ...$.

Ex. 7. The sum of the symbols in any transitive set of an intransitive permutation-group G is an invariant of G.

Ex. 8. If a homogeneous linear group G has $x_1 x_2 ... x_m$ as a relative invariant, every substitution of G is monomial.

Ex. 9. $x+y-z$ is an invariant of the group generated by $(y, -z, -x)$ and $(x, -z, -y)$.

Ex. 10. $x-y+z$ is a relative invariant of the group generated by $(3x-3y+4z, 2x-3y+4z, -y+z)$ and
$$(-3x+4y-4z, -2x+3y-4z, -z).$$

Ex. 11. $x\bar{x} + y\bar{y}$ is an invariant of the group generated by (i) $(\sin\theta\ x - \cos\theta\ y,\ \cos\theta\ x + \sin\theta\ y)$ and (y, x), (ii) (iy, ix) and $(iy, -ix)$, (iii) $(ix, -iy)$ and (y, x).

Ex. 12. $xy(x^4-y^4)$ and $x^4+y^4\pm 2\sqrt{-8}x^2y^2$ are relative invariants of the group generated by $(ix, -iy)$ and
$$\left(\frac{1-i}{2}x+\frac{1-i}{2}y,\ \frac{-1-i}{2}x+\frac{1+i}{2}y\right).$$

§ 4. If every substitution of a group G on the variables $x_1, x_2, ..., x_e, y_1, y_2, ..., y_f, z_1, z_2, ..., z_g, ...$ changes $x_1, x_2, ..., x_e$ into functions of $x_1, x_2, ..., x_e$ only, G is called 'reducible'. A substitution-group which can be transformed (by a suitable change of variables) into a group such as G is also called *reducible*. A group which cannot be so transformed is called *irreducible*.

Suppose that (i) every substitution of the group G changes $x_1, x_2, ..., x_e$ into functions of $x_1, x_2, ..., x_e$ only; $y_1, y_2, ..., y_f$ into functions of $y_1, y_2, ..., y_f$ only; $z_1, z_2, ..., z_g$ into functions of $z_1, z_2, ..., z_g$ only; and so on: and (ii) that G is irreducible when considered as a group of degree e affecting $x_1, x_2, ..., x_e$ only, and as a group of degree f affecting $y_1, y_2, ..., y_f$ only, and as a group of degree g affecting $z_1, z_2, ..., z_g$ only, &c. Then G is called 'completely reducible'. A substitution-group which can be transformed into a group such as G is also called *completely reducible*.

Ex. 1. If we transform by $(x-y+z, y, z)$ the group G generated by $(3x-3y+4z, 2x-3y+4z, -y+z)$ and $(-3x+4y-4z, -2x+3y-4z, -z)$, we get the group G' generated by $(x, 2x-y+2z, -y+z)$ and $(-x, -2x+y-2z, -z)$. Since every substitution of G' obviously changes x into a function of x, G' and hence G is reducible. If we transform G' by $(x, -x+y-z, x+z)$ we get the group G'' generated by $(x, z, -y)$ and $(-x, y, -z)$. Since every substitution of G'' evidently changes x into a function of x and y, z into functions of y, z while the group generated by $(z, -y)$ and $(y, -z)$ is irreducible (since these two substitutions have no pole in common), G'' is completely reducible. Hence G' and G are completely reducible.

Ex. 2. A homogeneous linear group whose substitutions have a pole in common is reducible.

Ex. 3. Denoting $a_1x_1+a_2x_2+...+a_mx_m$ by f_1 prove that (i) a homogeneous linear group G with f_1 as absolute or relative invariant is reducible; (ii) if the substitutions of an irreducible homogeneous linear group H change f_1 into $f_1, f_2, ..., f_n$, $f_1+f_2+...+f_n \equiv 0$.

Ex. 4. A permutation-group of finite degree is reducible.

Ex. 5. The group generated by (z, x, y) and $(-y, -x, -z)$ is reducible.

§ **5.** If A, B are any two homogeneous linear substitutions and α, β are their determinants, we see at once by III 4 that $\alpha\beta$, β^{-1}, and $\beta^{-1}\alpha\beta = \alpha$ are the determinants of AB, B^{-1}, and $B^{-1}AB$ respectively. Hence if G is any homogeneous linear substitution-group, those elements of G whose determinant $= 1$ form a normal subgroup Γ. If g, h are two elements of G with the same determinant, $g^{-1}h$ is in Γ, since its determinant $= 1$. Hence if $g_1, g_2, g_3, \ldots$ are substitutions of G such that no two have the same determinant,
$$G \equiv \Gamma g_1 + \Gamma g_2 + \Gamma g_3 + \ldots .$$
It is at once proved that the product of two similarities is a similarity, and that a similarity is permutable with any other substitution. Therefore the similarities of G form a subgroup M contained in the central of G.

Let **a**, **b** be the fractional linear substitutions derived from any two substitutions A, B of G (III 9). Then it is at once proved that **ab** is the fractional substitution derived from AB. Hence the fractional substitutions derived from each element of G form a group F isomorphic with G. The identical element of F may obviously be derived from any similarity of G but from no other element of G. Therefore to 1, in F corresponds M in G, so that $F = G/M$.

Ex. 1. For example, in the group G of order 8 generated by $(-y, x)$ and $(x, -y)$ M contains (x, y), $(-x, -y)$, and $F = G/M$ is the group generated by $x' = -1 \div x$ and $x' = -x$.

Ex. 2. If any homogeneous linear substitutions form a group, (i) the transposed substitutions, (ii) the conjugate substitutions, form simply isomorphic groups.

Ex. 3. The monomial substitutions of a group G form a subgroup H, the multiplications of G form a subgroup K of H, and the similarities of G form a subgroup of K.

Ex. 4. (i) The real substitutions of a group G form a subgroup H, the orthogonal substitutions of G form a subgroup K, and the unitary substitutions of G form a subgroup L. (ii) The G.C.S. of K and $L \equiv$ the G.C.S. of L and $H \equiv$ the G.C.S. of H and K.

Ex. 5. The substitutions of G with a given pole or poles form a subgroup.

Ex. 6. A homogeneous linear group of degree m is simply isomorphic with a group of real substitutions of degree $2m$.

Ex. 7. The totality of all substitutions of the type $(ax+cy, \bar{c}x+\bar{a}y)$, where $a\bar{a}-c\bar{c} = 1$, form a group.

Ex. 8. A set of substitutions of the type $x' = (ax+b) \div (cx+d)$ with a pole in common form a finite group. Prove that (i) they have a second pole in common, (ii) the group is cyclic.

Ex. 9. Prove the following properties of the infinite 'modular' group G formed of all substitutions such as $x' = \dfrac{ax+b}{cx+d}$ where a, b, c, d are integers and $ad-bc = 1$. (i) No substitution of G is loxodromic; (ii) every substitution of G is of order 1, 2, 3, or ∞; (iii) the substitutions for which $a \equiv d \equiv 1$, $b \equiv c \equiv 0 \pmod{n}$ form a normal subgroup.

§ 6. *Every finite homogeneous linear group G has a positive Hermitian form as an invariant.*

Let f_1 be any positive Hermitian form
$$(\text{e. g. } x_1\bar{x}_1 + x_2\bar{x}_2 + x_3\bar{x}_3 + ...),$$
and suppose that f_1 is changed into $f_1, f_2, ..., f_n$ by the substitutions of G. By III 5 $f_1, f_2, ..., f_n$ are Hermitian forms, and since f_1 is always positive for all values of the variables (not all zero) so are $f_2, f_3, ..., f_n$. Then
$$f_1 + f_2 + ... + f_n$$
is evidently a positive Hermitian form and is an invariant of G.

Ex. 1. In the group $G \equiv 1 + a + a^2 + a^3 + b + ba + ba^2 + ba^3$ where $a \equiv (-x+2y, -x+y)$, $b \equiv (x-2y, -y)$ take $f_1 \equiv x\bar{x} + y\bar{y}$. Then
$$f_3 \equiv f_1, \quad f_2 \equiv f_4 \equiv 2x\bar{x} + 5y\bar{y} - 3x\bar{y} - 3\bar{x}y,$$
$$f_5 \equiv f_7 \equiv x\bar{x} + 5y\bar{y} - 2x\bar{y} - 2\bar{x}y, \quad f_6 \equiv f_8 \equiv 2x\bar{x} + y\bar{y} - x\bar{y} - \bar{x}y,$$
so that $\quad f_1 + f_2 + ... + f_8 \equiv 12(x\bar{x} + 2y\bar{y} - x\bar{y} - \bar{x}y).$
Hence $x\bar{x} + 2y\bar{y} - x\bar{y} - \bar{x}y$ is a positive Hermitian invariant of G.

Ex. 2. Find a positive Hermitian invariant of the groups of orders 4, 8, 12 generated respectively by (i) $(-x, -y)$ and $(-2x - (\omega-1)y, (\omega^2-1)x + 2y)$, where $\omega^3 = 1$; (ii) $(ix + (1-i)y, -iy)$ and $(x, (1-i)x - y)$ where $i^2 = 1$; (iii) (y, z, x) and $(x, -y, -z)$.

Ex. 3. Every finite homogeneous group can be transformed into a group of unitary substitutions.

Ex. 4. (i) A homogeneous group of degree m with the invariant $x_1\bar{x}_1 + x_2\bar{x}_2 + ... + x_s\bar{x}_s$ is reducible if $s < m$. (ii) A group with a hypohermitian invariant is reducible.

Ex. 5. If an irreducible group G has two positive Hermitian invariants f and f', their ratio is a constant.

§ 7. *Any finite homogeneous linear substitution-group G is either irreducible or completely reducible.*

If G is reducible, it may be transformed by a suitable choice of variables $x_1, x_2, ..., x_k, y_1, y_2, ..., y_l$ so that any substitution g of G is of the form

VII 7]   FINITE HOMOGENEOUS GROUPS

$$x_s' = d_{s1}x_1 + \ldots + d_{sk}x_k,$$
$$y_t' \equiv \beta_{t1}x_1 + \ldots + \beta_{tk}x_k + b_{t1}y_1 + \ldots + b_{tl}y_l$$
$$(s = 1, 2, \ldots, k;\ t = 1, 2, \ldots, l).$$

Let then
$$H \equiv \Sigma p_{ij}\bar{x}_i x_j + \Sigma q_{ef}\bar{y}_e y_f + \Sigma [r_{uv}\bar{x}_u y_v + r_{vu}\bar{y}_v x_u],$$
$$(i, j, u = 1, 2, \ldots, k;\ e, f, v = 1, 2, \ldots, l),$$
be a positive Hermitian invariant of G.

Now express G in terms of $x_1, x_2, \ldots, x_k, z_1, z_2, \ldots, z_l$, where $y_a \equiv z_a + v_{a1}x_1 + v_{a2}x_2 + \ldots + v_{ak}x_k\,(a = 1, 2, \ldots, l)$, and the kl quantities v are chosen so that

$$r_{vu} + q_{v1}v_{1u} + q_{v2}v_{2u} + \ldots + q_{vk}v_{ku} = 0.$$

This is always possible; for by III 5 the determinant

$$\begin{vmatrix} q_{11} & \cdot & \cdot & \cdot & q_{1k} \\ \cdot & \cdot & \cdot & \cdot & \cdot \\ \cdot & \cdot & \cdot & \cdot & \cdot \\ \cdot & \cdot & \cdot & \cdot & \cdot \\ q_{k1} & \cdot & \cdot & \cdot & q_{kk} \end{vmatrix} \neq 0,$$

since H is positive.

Then H takes the form
$$\Sigma p_{ij}'\bar{x}_i x_j + \Sigma q_{ef}\bar{z}_e z_f + \Sigma [(r_{uv} + q_{1v}\bar{v}_{1u} + \ldots + q_{kv}\bar{v}_{ku})\bar{x}_u z_v$$
$$+ (r_{vu} + q_{v1}v_{1u} + \ldots + q_{vk}v_{ku})\bar{z}_v x_u] \equiv \Sigma p_{ij}'\bar{x}_i x_j + \Sigma q_{ef}\bar{z}_e z_f.$$

Now express $\Sigma p_{ij}'\bar{x}_i x_j$ in the canonical form $\sum_{i=1}^{i=k} X_i \bar{X}_i$ (where $X_1, X_2, \ldots, X_k$ are linear functions of $x_1, x_2, \ldots, x_k$) and express $\Sigma q_{ef}\bar{z}_e z_f$ in the canonical form $\Sigma Z_e \bar{Z}_e$.

Suppose that when g is expressed in terms of
$$X_1, \ldots, X_k, Z_1, \ldots, Z_l$$
it takes the form
$$X_s' = a_{s1}X_1 + \ldots + a_{sk}X_k,$$
$$Z_t' = \gamma_{t1}X_1 + \ldots + \gamma_{tk}X_k + c_{t1}Z_1 + \ldots + c_{tl}Z_l.$$
Then if we perform this substitution on $H \equiv \Sigma X_i \bar{X}_i + \Sigma Z_e \bar{Z}_e$, the coefficient of $\bar{X}_u Z_v$ in H becomes
$$\bar{\gamma}_{1u}c_{1v} + \bar{\gamma}_{2u}c_{2v} + \ldots + \bar{\gamma}_{lu}c_{lv}.$$

This must vanish for $v = 1, 2, \ldots, l$, since H is not altered by the substitution g. But the determinant

$$\begin{vmatrix} c_{11} & \cdot & \cdot & \cdot & c_{1l} \\ \cdot & \cdot & \cdot & \cdot & \cdot \\ \cdot & \cdot & \cdot & \cdot & \cdot \\ \cdot & \cdot & \cdot & \cdot & \cdot \\ c_{l1} & \cdot & \cdot & \cdot & c_{ll} \end{vmatrix} \neq 0,$$

since the determinant of $g \neq 0$. Hence
$$\bar{\gamma}_{1u} = \bar{\gamma}_{2u} = \ldots = \bar{\gamma}_{lu} = 0.$$
This holds for each value of u, and therefore every substitution of G is of the type
$$X_s' = a_{s1}X_1 + \ldots + a_{sk}X_k, \quad Z_t' = c_{t1}Z_1 + \ldots + c_{tl}Z_l.$$
If G is irreducible considered as a group affecting $X_1, X_2, \ldots, X_k$ and as a group affecting $Z_1, Z_2, \ldots, Z_l$, the theorem is proved. If not, the process can be repeated until G is transformed into a completely reducible group.

Ex. 1. Any 'Hermitian group' (i. e. a finite or infinite group with a positive Hermitian invariant) is irreducible or completely reducible.

Ex. 2. A finite reducible group of degree 2 is Abelian.

Ex. 3. A permutation-group is completely reducible.

Ex. 4. A finite reducible group of degree 3 has a relative linear invariant.

Ex. 5. The completely reducible group of § 4 can be transformed so that every positive Hermitian invariant is of the form
$$a(x_1\bar{x}_1 + \ldots + x_e\bar{x}_e) + \beta(y_1\bar{y}_1 + \ldots + y_f\bar{y}_f) + \gamma(z_1\bar{z}_1 + \ldots + z_g\bar{z}_g) + \ldots,$$
where $a, \beta, \gamma, \ldots$ are real positive constants.

§ 8. *A finite Abelian homogeneous linear substitution-group G can be transformed into a group each of whose substitutions is a multiplication.*

If all the roots of the characteristic equation of an element A of G are equal, A is a similarity. For find a substitution T such that $T^{-1}AT =$ a multiplication M (III 8). Now M is a similarity, since the roots of its characteristic equation are all equal. Therefore $A = TMT^{-1} = M$. Hence if each element of G is such that all the roots of its characteristic equation are equal, every element of G is a similarity.

Now suppose A is an element of G whose characteristic equation has not all its roots equal. Transform the group G (of degree m, say) into a group G' so that A becomes a multiplication $M \equiv (\omega_1 x_1, \omega_2 x_2, \ldots, \omega_m x_m)$. Suppose $\omega_1 = \omega_2 = \ldots = \omega_r$, but $\omega_1 \neq \omega_{r+1}, \omega_{r+2}, \ldots, \omega_m$ (the reasoning is general). Now if M is permutable with
$$B \equiv (b_{11}x_1 + b_{12}x_2 + \ldots + b_{1m}x_m, \ b_{21}x_1 + b_{22}x_2 + \ldots + b_{2m}x_m, \ldots,$$
$$b_{m1}x_1 + b_{m2}x_2 + \ldots + b_{mm}x_m),$$
$$b_{ij}\omega_j = b_{ij}\omega_i,$$

VII 9]   GENERAL HOMOGENEOUS GROUPS   105

as is evident on comparing MB and BM. Hence $b_{ij} = 0$ if $\omega_i \neq \omega_j$. Therefore every element of G' changes $x_1, x_2, \ldots, x_r$ into functions of $x_1, x_2, \ldots, x_r$ only and changes $x_{r+1}, x_{r+2}, \ldots, x_m$ into functions of $x_{r+1}, x_{r+2}, \ldots, x_m$ only.

Now if we consider the effect of the elements of G' on the variables $x_1, x_2, \ldots, x_r$ only, G' reduces to an Abelian group H_1 of degree r. Similarly if we consider the effect of the elements of G' on the variables $x_{r+1}, x_{r+2}, \ldots, x_m$ only, G' reduces to an Abelian group H_2 of degree $m-r$. Now assume the theorem true for every Abelian group of degree $< m$. Then by the assumption we can find linear functions $y_1, y_2, \ldots, y_r$ of $x_1, x_2, \ldots, x_r$ and functions $y_{r+1}, y_{r+2}, \ldots, y_m$ of $x_{r+1}, x_{r+2}, \ldots, x_m$ such that when H_1 is expressed in terms of $y_1, y_2, \ldots, y_r$ every element of H_1 is a multiplication; and similarly for H_2. Hence G' may be expressed in terms of $y_1, y_2, \ldots, y_m$ so that every element of G' is a multiplication. Then the theorem follows by induction.

Ex. 1. A homogeneous irreducible Abelian group is of degree 1.

Ex. 2. An Abelian group of degree m has m distinct positive Hermitian invariants; and conversely.

Ex. 3. The central of a homogeneous irreducible group consists solely of its similarities.

Ex. 4. Transform the Abelian group of order 8 generated by
$$(19x-12y-24z, \ 10x-7y-12z, \ 10x-6y-13z),$$
$$(25x-18y-30z, \ 8x-5y-10z, \ 16x-12y-19z),$$
and $\quad (5x-6y-6z, \ -2x+y+2z, \ 6x-6y-7z)$
into a group of multiplications.

§ 9. We now consider the case of a group of homogeneous linear substitutions whose coefficients and variables are marks of a $GF[p^r]$. The totality of all possible homogeneous linear substitutions (of non-zero determinant) on m given variables $x_1, x_2, \ldots, x_m$ in a $GF[p^r]$ evidently forms a group G. It is called the *general homogeneous linear substitution-group* in the Field and is of order
$$_m N_r \equiv (p^{mr}-1)(p^{mr}-p^r)(p^{mr}-p^{2r}) \ldots (p^{mr}-p^{(m-1)r}).$$

For the substitutions of G leaving x_1 unchanged form a subgroup H of order $p^{(m-1)r} \times {}_{m-1}N_r$. In fact
$$x_i' = a_{i1}x_1 + a_{i2}x_2 + \ldots + a_{im}x_m \ (i = 1, 2, \ldots, m)$$
is such a substitution when $a_{11} = 1$ and
$$a_{12} = a_{13} = \ldots = a_{1m} = 0,$$

while each of the coefficients $a_{21}, a_{31}, ..., a_{m1}$ is any one of the p^r marks of the Field and $a_{i2}, a_{i3}, ..., a_{im}$ ($i = 2, 3, ..., m$) are marks subject solely to the condition that their determinant $\neq 0$.

Now if g, h are two substitutions changing x_1 into the same linear function $b_{11}x_1 + b_{12}x_2 + ... + b_{1m}x_m$, gh^{-1} is in H. Hence $G \equiv Hg_1 + Hg_2 + ... + Hg_k$, where $g_1, g_2, ..., g_k$ are substitutions each replacing x_1 by a different linear function. Now $k = p^{mr} - 1$, for $b_{11}, b_{12}, ..., b_{1m}$ may be chosen arbitrarily in the Field provided they are not all $= 0$. Therefore

$$_mN_r = (p^{mr} - 1)p^{(m-1)r} \times {_{m-1}N_r},$$

and the required result follows at once by induction.

Ex. 1. The general linear group may be considered as a permutation-group on p^{rm} symbols.

Ex. 2. We denote by P, Q, R the groups formed respectively by all substitutions of the types $x' = x + b$, $x' = ax + b$ ($a \neq 0$), $x' = \dfrac{ax+b}{cx+d}$ ($ad - bc \neq 0$), where x, a, b, c, d are marks of a $GF[p^r]$. Prove that (i) P may be considered as a simply transitive permutation-group of degree p^r and order p^r; (ii) Q may be considered as a doubly transitive group of degree p^r and order $p^r(p^r - 1)$; (iii) R may be considered as a triply transitive group of degree $p^r + 1$ and order $p^r(p^{2r} - 1)$; (iv) every substitution of R is equivalent to a substitution with determinant 1 or ν, where ν is any given not-square of the Field; the substitutions with determinant 1 forming a normal subgroup of index $\frac{1}{2}[8 - (-1)^p]$; (v) Q is the normaliser of P in R; (vi) Q/P is cyclic; (vii) Q contains a cyclic subgroup of order $p^r - 1$ consisting of the substitutions $x' = ax + u(1 - a)$ where u is a given mark of the Field; (viii) by varying u we get a set of p^r conjugate subgroups of Q; (ix) every element of Q is in P or in one of these conjugate subgroups.

Ex. 3. The totality of all substitutions of the type

$$x' = (\mathbf{a}x + \mathbf{b}) \div (\bar{\mathbf{b}}x + \bar{\mathbf{a}}) \text{ where } \mathbf{a}\bar{\mathbf{a}} - \mathbf{b}\bar{\mathbf{b}} = 1$$

(III 11_{10}) form a group.

Ex. 4. In the substitutions $x' = \dfrac{\alpha x + \beta}{\gamma x + \delta}$ each coefficient is of the form $u + vS$, where u, v are marks of a $GF[p]$, and S is a symbol not in the Field defined by $S^2 = 1$ and combining with the marks of the Field under the ordinary laws of addition, &c. Prove that the totality of substitutions for which $\alpha\delta - \beta\gamma = 1$ and (i) $\alpha = a, \beta = b, \gamma = c, \delta = d$ (a, b, c, d being marks of the Field), (ii) $\alpha = 1 + a(1 + S), \beta = b(1 + S), \gamma = c(1 + S), \delta = 1 + d(1 + S)$, (iii) $\alpha = 1 + a(1 - S), \beta = b(1 - S), \gamma = c(1 - S), \delta = 1 + d(1 - S)$ form groups K, H_1, H_2. Every substitution of H_1 is permutable with every substitution of H_2 and $H_1 = H_2 = K$.

§ 10. The remarks of § 5 evidently apply to homogeneous substitution-groups whose coefficients and variables are marks of a $GF[p^r]$.

Let G be the general homogeneous linear group of degree m, and let u be a primitive root of the Field. Then if g is $(ux_1, x_2, x_3, ..., x_m)$, $g^t \equiv (u^t x_1, x_2, x_3, ..., x_m)$ is a substitution of G with determinant u^t. But u^t can be any non-zero mark of the Field; and hence $G \equiv \Gamma g + \Gamma g^2 + ... + \Gamma g^{p^r-1}$. Therefore G/Γ is cyclic of order $p^r - 1$.

Again, if $s \equiv (ux_1, ux_2, ..., ux_m)$, every similarity of G is of the type $s^t \equiv (u^t x_1, u^t x_2, ..., u^t x_m)$. Therefore M is cyclic of order $p^r - 1$.

The greatest common subgroup D of Γ and M is of order d, where d is the H.C.F. of $p^r - 1$ and m. For s^t is in Γ if and only if $u^{tm} = 1$, i.e. $tm \equiv 0 \pmod{p^r - 1}$; and the smallest value of t satisfying this congruence is $(p^r - 1) \div d$.

The fractional linear group Λ of degree $m - 1$ derived from $\Gamma = \Gamma/D$ and is therefore of order ${}_m N_r \div (p^r - 1) d$. It may be shown that Λ is simple unless $m = 2$ and $p^r = 2$ or 3 (i. e. $p = 2$ or 3 and $r = 1$). For the proof of this result, and for a discussion of other simple groups derived from subgroups of the general homogeneous linear group with given invariants, we must refer the reader to Dickson's *Linear Groups* (Teubner, 1901).

Ex. 1. Show that the centrals of G and Γ consist solely of their similarities.

Ex. 2. Show that there are simple groups of orders 60, 168, 504, 660, 1092, 2448, 3420, 4080, 5616.

Ex. 3. Λ is of even order.*

Ex. 4. Those substitutions of G, Γ, Λ whose coefficients are integral marks form a subgroup.

Ex. 5. When $m = 2$ and $r = 1$ every element of Λ is included once and only once among $S^\lambda T S^\mu T S^\nu$ and $T S^\rho T S^\sigma T S^\tau$ (λ, ν, $\tau = 1, 2, ..., p$; $\mu, \sigma = 1, 2, ..., \frac{1}{2}(p-1)$; $\rho\sigma \equiv 1 \pmod{p}$); where S is $x' = x + 1$ and T is $x' = -1 \div x$.

Ex. 6. Show that Λ can be generated by three substitutions of order 2 when $m = 2$, $r = 1$, $p > 3$.

Ex. 7. If $m = 2$ and $p^r = 2$, G contains a normal subgroup of order 3 generated by $(y, x+y)$; and $G \equiv \Gamma = \Lambda$.

Ex. 8. If $m = 2$ and $p^r = 3$, while A, B, C, D, E denote respectively $(2x, x+y)$, $(y, 2x+y)$, $(2y, x)$, $(x+y, x+2y)$, $(2x, 2y)$, show that $\{E\}$, $\{D, E\}$, $\{C, D, E\}$, $\Gamma \equiv \{B, C, D, E\}$, $G \equiv \{A, B, C, D, E\}$ are of orders 2, 4, 8, 24, 48 and that each is normal in its successor.

* No simple non-cyclic group of odd order has yet been discovered.

CHAPTER VIII

GROUPS OF MOVEMENTS

§ 1. WE shall consider in this chapter groups whose elements are geometrical 'movements' of the kind discussed in Ch. IV. Such a group is called a *group of movements*. If each movement of the group leaves a given point O unmoved the group is called a *point-group*.

Ex. 1. A point-group can only contain rotations about lines through O and rotatory-inversions about O and lines through O.

Ex. 2. Every finite group of movements is a point-group.

Ex. 3. If a group contains a rotation through $2\pi \div m$ (m integral) about a line l and a reflexion in a plane through l, it contains reflexions in m planes through l.

Ex. 4. If a point-group contains a rotation through $2\pi \div m$ about l and a rotation through π about a line perpendicular to l, it contains rotations through π about m lines perpendicular to l.

Ex. 5. If a point-group contains rotations through $\tfrac{1}{2}\pi$ about two perpendicular lines, it contains a rotation through $\tfrac{2}{3}\pi$ about a line making an angle $\tan^{-1}\sqrt{2}$ with each.

Ex. 6. If a point-group contains rotations through $\tfrac{2}{3}\pi$ about two lines inclined at an angle $\cos^{-1}\tfrac{1}{3}$, it contains a rotation through π about a line making an angle $\tan^{-1}\sqrt{2}$ with each.

Ex. 7. If a point-group contains rotations through $\tfrac{2}{3}\pi$ about two lines inclined at an angle $\tan^{-1}2$, it contains a rotation through $\tfrac{2}{5}\pi$ about another line.

§ 2. *If G is any group of movements containing rotatory-inversions, the screws of G form a normal subgroup which is of index 2 when G is finite.*

We include rotations and translations as particular cases of 'screws', and reflexions, inversions, gliding-reflexions as particular cases of 'rotatory-inversions' unless the contrary is stated.

By IV 6 the product of two screws is a screw. Hence the screws form a subgroup H. Also the transform of a screw is a screw (IV 9), so that H is normal in G.

Let J be a given rotatory-inversion of G, and let I be any other rotatory-inversion of G. Then IJ^{-1} being a screw, is in H; so that I is in HJ. Hence $G \equiv H + HJ$; and H is of index 2 if G is finite.

§ 3. If any point, line, &c. P is brought to the positions $P, P_1, P_2, \ldots$ by the movements of a group G; $P, P_1, P_2, \ldots$ are said to form an *equivalent system* of points, lines, &c. under G.

If G contains a screw S about a line l, G contains a similar screw (one of equal angle and translation) about every line equivalent to l; since G contains the transform of S by each movement of G (IV 9). These similar screws are the elements conjugate to S in G. A like result holds for the rotatory-inversions of G.

Ex. 1. Points equivalent under a point-group lie on a sphere.

Ex. 2. If G is of finite order n, the number of points, lines, &c. in an equivalent system is in general n.

Ex. 3. (i) If G contains a rotation through $2\pi \div m$ about a line OP, but no rotatory-inversion, there are $n \div m$ points equivalent to P. (ii) If G contains a reflexion in a plane through OP there are $n \div 2m$ points equivalent to P.

Ex. 4. Every movement of G permutes $P, P_1, P_2, \ldots$. These permutations of $P, P_1, P_2, \ldots$ form a permutation-group isomorphic with G.

Ex. 5. Use Ex. 4 to prove the result of VI 2 for a point-group.

Ex. 6. A normal subgroup H of any group of movements G contains a screw about a line l. Show that H contains a similar screw about every line equivalent to l under G; and that a like result holds for rotatory-inversions.

Ex. 7. If a group contains a screw of angle $\frac{1}{2}\pi$ about a line l and a reflexion in a plane through l, it contains reflexions in two other planes through l.

Ex. 8. If a group contains a screw of angle $\frac{2}{3}\pi$ about a line l and a translation perpendicular to l, it contains three independent translations.

§ 4. *The translations of any group G of geometrical movements form a normal subgroup H, and G/H is simply isomorphic with a point-group.*

Since the product of any two translations is a translation, the translations of G form a subgroup H, and since the transform of a translation by any movement is a translation (IV 9), H is normal in G.

If $S_1, S_2, \ldots$ are any screws of G, and $R_1, R_2, \ldots$ are rotations through equal angles about parallel lines through a fixed point O, we can find translations $T_1, T_2, \ldots$ such that $S_1 = R_1 T_1$, $S_2 = R_2 T_2$, ... Moreover we can find a translation T such that $S_i S_j = R_i R_j . T$ (IV $9_{6,7,8,9}$).

Similarly if $J_1, J_2, \ldots$ are any rotatory-inversions of G, and $I_1, I_2, \ldots$ are rotatory-inversions through equal angles about O and parallel lines through O, we can find translations $t_1, t_2, \ldots$ such that $J_1 = I_1 t_1$, $J_2 = I_2 t_2$, ... Moreover we can find a translation t such that $J_i J_j = I_i I_j . t$, or such that $S_i J_j = R_i I_j . t$, or $J_i S_j = I_i R_j . t$.

Hence the group G is multiply isomorphic with the point-group Γ consisting of the movements $R_1, R_2, \ldots, I_1, I_2, \ldots$. To identity in Γ corresponds every translation of G, so that $\Gamma = G/H$.

A group (such as H) each of whose elements is a translation is called a *translation-group*.

Ex. 1. H is infinite unless $H \equiv 1$.

Ex. 2. The group generated by rotations through π about two perpendicular non-intersecting lines is isomorphic with the point-group of $\mathrm{V}\, 3_{11(\text{ii})}$, the subgroup H being generated by a single translation.

§ 5. We proceed now to find all possible types of finite point-group leaving a given point O unmoved. Every element of such a group G is a rotation about a line through O or a rotatory-inversion about O and a line through O. Let R be any rotation about a line l through a positive angle α contained in the group, and suppose that the group contains no rotation about l through a positive angle $< \alpha$. Then $\alpha = \dfrac{2\pi}{n}$ where n is integral. For if $(n+1)\alpha > 2\pi \geq n\alpha$, a rotation through $2\pi - n\alpha$ about l is a movement of the group, so that $2\pi = n\alpha$. Similarly if I is a rotatory-inversion through α about O and l, and the group contains no rotatory-inversion about O and l through an angle $< \alpha$, $\alpha = \dfrac{2\pi}{n}$, where n is integral. We shall speak of R or I as an 'n-al' rotation or rotatory-inversion of G.

Ex. 1. A 1-al rotatory-inversion is equivalent to inversion about O.

VIII 7]   HOLOAXIAL POINT-GROUPS   111

Ex. 2. A 2-al rotatory-inversion about l is equivalent to reflexion in a plane through O perpendicular to l.

Ex. 3. Find the orders of R and I.

Ex. 4. If a group G of order N contains an n-al rotation or rotatory-inversion, $N \div n$ is integral.

Ex. 5. If a group contains an n-al rotatory-inversion, it contains an $\frac{n}{4} \{3-(-1)^n\}$-al rotation about the same line.

§ 6. We first consider a 'holoaxial' point-group G of order n containing only rotations about lines through a point O.

If G contains 2-al rotations about u_2 different lines, 3-al rotations about u_3 different lines, ...,

$$n - 1 = u_2 + 2u_3 + 3u_4 + \ldots.$$

For any point P is brought to coincide with $(m-1)$ other equivalent points by successive rotations through $2\pi \div m$ about any one of the u_m lines round which an m-al rotation of G takes place. We thus get $u_2 + 2u_3 + 3u_4 + \ldots$ points equivalent to P. Also since G contains only rotations, all the points equivalent to P are thus obtained except P itself. But in general there are n points equivalent to and including P.

Ex. If a group G of order n contains 2-al rotations about u_2 lines, 3-al rotations about u_3 lines, ... and rotatory-inversions, $\frac{1}{2}n - 1 = u_2 + 2u_3 + 3u_4 + \ldots$.

§ 7. Let now G contain a-al, b-al, c-al, ... $(a \geq b \geq c \geq \ldots)$ rotations about lines OA, OB, OC, ... no two of which are equivalent under G. We suppose these lines only drawn in one direction from O. The prolongation OA' of OA is included among OB, OC, ... if and only if the two ends of the line $A'OA$ are not equivalent, which is the case if G contains no rotation (through π about a line perpendicular to OA) bringing OA to coincide with OA'. If t is any line through O, there are in general n lines equivalent to t; but if t coincides with OA, these lines coincide in sets of a. Hence there are $n \div a$ lines equivalent to (and including) OA; and G contains a-al rotations about each. A similar result holds for OB, OC, ... Therefore G contains a-al rotations about $n \div a$ equivalent lines, b-al rotations about $n \div b$ equivalent lines, and so on. These lines are the $u_2 + u_3 + u_4 + \ldots$ lines of § 6 reckoned twice over. Thus, for instance, the line $A'OA$ is

112 HOLOAXIAL POINT-GROUPS [VIII 7

reckoned once as OA and once as OA'. Hence

$$2(n-1) = \frac{n}{a}(a-1) + \frac{n}{b}(b-1) + \frac{n}{c}(c-1) + \ldots$$

or
$$2\left(1-\frac{1}{n}\right) = \left(1-\frac{1}{a}\right) + \left(1-\frac{1}{b}\right) + \left(1-\frac{1}{c}\right) + \ldots$$

The term inside each bracket of this equation is <1 but $\geq \frac{1}{2}$. Hence there are on the right-hand side not more than three brackets or less than two.

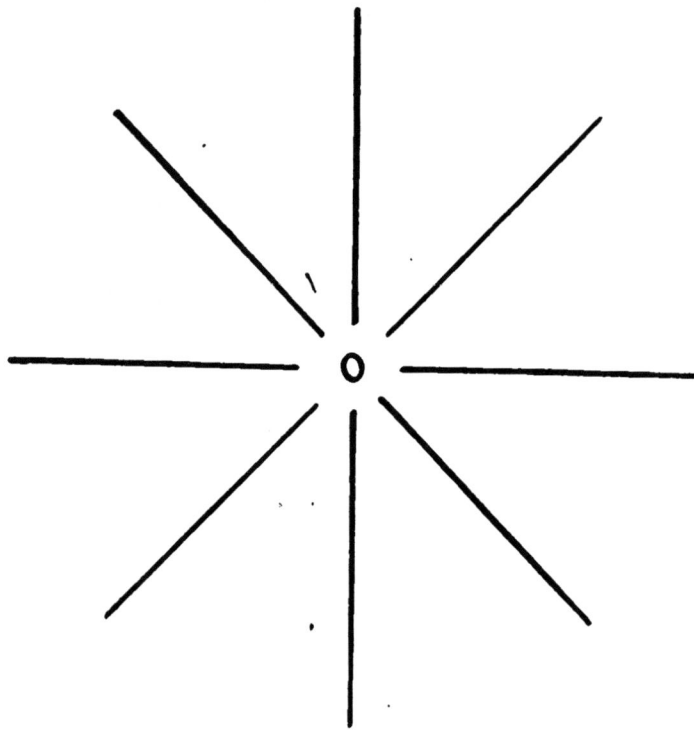

Fig. 11.

The diagram shows the lines about which the 2-al rotations of D_4 take place. The 4-al rotation of D_4 takes place about a line through O perpendicular to the plane of the diagram.

(i) If there are two brackets, we have $\frac{2}{n} = \frac{1}{a} + \frac{1}{b}$. But $\frac{n}{a}$ and $\frac{n}{b}$ are integral; hence $a = b = n$. Then OB is OA',

VIII 7]   HOLOAXIAL POINT-GROUPS   113

and G is a cyclic group (C_a) formed by rotations about a single line.

(ii) If there are three brackets, we have $1 + \frac{2}{n} = \frac{1}{a} + \frac{1}{b} + \frac{1}{c}$. Then $c = 2$; for otherwise n would be negative, since $a \geq b \geq c$. Hence $\frac{1}{2} + \frac{2}{n} = \frac{1}{a} + \frac{1}{b}$. If b also $= 2$, we have $2a = n$, $b = c = 2$. Then OA' is equivalent to OA, and G is the *dihedral* group (D_a) formed by rotations through multiples of $2\pi \div a$ about $A'OA$ and rotations through π about a lines perpendicular to OA each making angles $\pi \div a$ with its neighbours (Fig. 11).

The group D ($\equiv D_2$) formed by rotations through π about three mutually perpendicular intersecting lines is called the 'Quadratic' group (Vierergruppe).

(iii) If $c = 2$ and $b > 2$, $b = 3$; for otherwise $\frac{1}{a} + \frac{1}{b} \leq \frac{1}{2}$. Then $\frac{1}{a} = \frac{1}{6} + \frac{2}{n}$, so that $a \leq 5$.

We can have $n = 12$, $a = b = 3$, $c = 2$. Then G contains rotations through $\tfrac{2}{3}\pi$ about $\frac{1}{2}\left(\frac{n}{a} + \frac{n}{b}\right) = 4$ lines. Each such rotation brings the system of four lines to self-coincidence (§ 3). This is evidently possible only if the four lines lie along the diagonals of a cube. By IV 2 G also contains rotations through π about three lines perpendicular to the faces of the cube. We call G in this case the *tetrahedral* group (**T**).

(iv) Again, we can have $n = 24$, $a = 4$, $b = 3$, $c = 2$. Then as before G contains rotations through $\tfrac{2}{3}\pi$ about four lines lying along the diagonals of a cube. It contains also rotations through $\tfrac{1}{2}\pi$ about the perpendiculars to the cube-faces and rotations through π about the lines joining the middle points of opposite edges. We call G in this case the *octahedral* group (**O**).

(v) Again, we can have $n = 60$, $a = 5$, $b = 3$, $c = 2$. Then G contains rotations through $\tfrac{2}{5}\pi$ about $\frac{1}{2} \cdot \frac{n}{a} = 6$ lines. Each such rotation brings the system of six lines to self-coincidence, and hence the six lines lie along the diagonals of a regular icosahedron. By IV 2 G contains rotations through $\tfrac{2}{3}\pi$ about the ten perpendiculars to the faces of the icosahedron, and rotations through π about the fifteen lines joining the middle points of opposite edges. We call G in this case the *icosahedral* group (**E**).

Ex. 1. Find the groups formed by the rotations bringing to self-coincidence (i) a right regular hexagonal pyramid, (ii) a right regular hexagonal bipyramid, (iii) a rectangular parallelepipedon, (iv) an ellipsoid, (v) a cube, (vi) a regular tetrahedron, (vii) octahedron, (viii) dodecahedron, (ix) icosahedron.

Ex. 2. C_a and D are Abelian.

Ex. 3. (i) C_a is a normal subgroup of D_a, $D_{\frac{a}{2}}$ of D_a (a even), T of O, D of T and O. (ii) E is simple. (iii) $O/D = D_3$.

Ex. 4. D_a contains 1 or 3 conjugate sets of elements of order 2 as a is odd or even.

Ex. 5. If q is a factor of a, D_a contains q subgroups $D_{\frac{a}{q}}$.

Ex. 6. Find the conjugate sets of elements in T.

Ex. 7. O contains 4 subgroups D_3 forming a conjugate set and 3 subgroups D_4 forming a conjugate set.

Ex. 8. E contains 5 subgroups T forming a conjugate set, 10 subgroups D_3 forming a conjugate set, and 6 subgroups D_5 forming a conjugate set.

§ 8. We now consider a point-group G containing rotatory-inversions.* The rotations of G form a normal subgroup H of index 2 (§ 2), and G is completely given when we know H and a single rotatory-inversion of G. We find then all possible point-groups by taking any one of the groups H of § 7 and finding each m-al rotatory-inversion X about O and a line l which (1) brings to self-coincidence the system of lines about which the a-al, b-al, ... rotations of H take place, and (2) is such that H contains a $\frac{m}{4}\{3-(-1)^m\}$-al rotation about l (VIII 5_5).

First we have cyclic groups (c_m) generated by an m-al rotatory-inversion about O and a line l: H is C_m or $C_{\frac{1}{2}m}$ as m is odd or even.

The only other cases in which H is the group C_m are those in which X is an inversion about O, or a reflexion in a plane through the line OA of § 7. We thus get two types of group (Γ_m and δ_m).

Again, we may derive a type (d_m) by combining the group c_m with a rotation through π about a line perpendicular to l: H is D_m or $D_{\frac{1}{2}m}$ as m is odd or even.

The only other case in which H is D_m is that of the type (Δ_m) in which X is an inversion about O.

From T we derive two types (Θ and θ) by taking X as

* Such groups are sometimes called 'extended' groups.

an inversion about O or a reflexion in the plane through two opposite edges of the cube of § 7, (iii).

From each of **O**, **E** we derive a single type (Ω, H) by taking X as an inversion about O.

Ex. 1. Show that d_2 is identical with δ_2, Γ_m with c_m (m odd).

Ex. 2. By taking H as C_m or D_m and X as a reflexion in a plane perpendicular to OA, we get no group not already obtained.

Ex. 3. By taking H as D_m and X as a reflexion in a plane through OA (i) passing through one of the lines about which a 2-al rotation takes place, (ii) bisecting the angle between two such lines, we get no new group.

Ex. 4. Show that we have exhausted all distinct point-groups derivable from **T**, **O**, **E**.

Ex. 5. δ_m contains reflexions in m planes through OA each of which makes angles $\pi \div m$ with its neighbours.

Ex. 6. What are the groups of symmetry-movements of an ellipsoid, a parallelepipedon, a rectangular parallelepipedon, a sphero-conic, an oblique circular cone, a right square prism, a cube, a regular tetrahedron, octahedron, dodecahedron, icosahedron, a tetrahedron with two pairs of opposite edges equal, a tetrahedron with each pair of opposite edges equal, a tetrahedron with two pairs of opposite edges equal and the third pair perpendicular, a square open tank, a bound book, a paraboloid.

Ex. 7. c_m, δ_2, $\Delta (\equiv \Delta_2)$, Γ_m are Abelian.

Ex. 8. $\delta_m = D_m$, $d_m = D_m$ (m even), $O = \theta$, $\Gamma_2 = D = \delta_2$.

Ex. 9. $\theta/D = D_3$, $\theta/D = C_6$, $\Omega/T = D$, $\Omega/D = d_2$.

Ex. 10. Which groups of § 8 are direct products?

§ **9.** We shall now consider briefly the properties of a translation-group H containing no infinitesimal translation. Let O be any point and let OA_1 represent (IV 8) a translation of H such that no other translation of H is represented by a line shorter than OA_1. Let OB_1 represent another translation of H, B_1 being chosen (out of OA_1) so that the area of the parallelogram OA_1DB_1 is as small as possible. Take equidistant points $..., A_{-2}, A_{-1}, O, A_1, A_2, ...$ along OA_1, and through them draw lines parallel to OB_1. Treat OB_1 similarly. The *net* of points so obtained (see Fig. 12) includes all the points in the plane A_1OB_1 which are equivalent to O under H. For if V were such a point situated in a parallelogram r, then evidently the parallelogram OA_1DB_1 (and in fact each parallelogram of Fig. 12) would contain a point F equivalent to V situated with respect to OA_1DB_1 in the same way as V with respect to r. This is impossible; for the parallelogram whose adjacent sides are OF, OA_1 is smaller than OA_1DB_1.

116   TRANSLATION-GROUPS   [VIII 9

Let OC_1 represent another translation of H, C_1 being chosen (out of the plane A_1OB_1) so that the volume of the parallele-

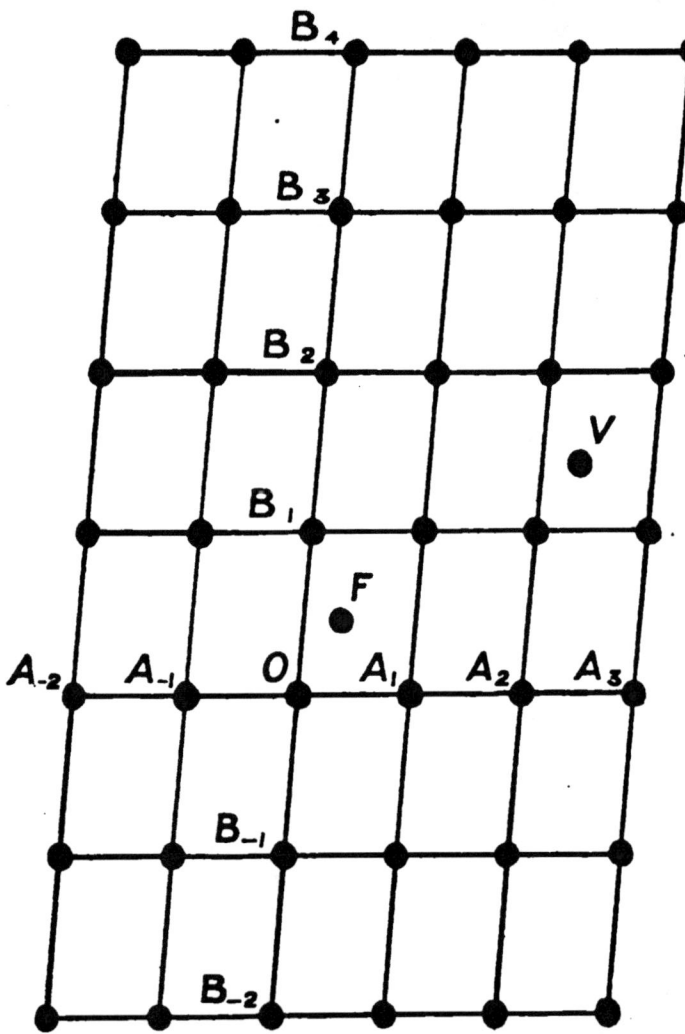

Fig. 12.

pipedon whose adjacent sides are OA_1, OB_1, OC_1 is as small as possible. Take equidistant points $..., C_{-2}, C_{-1}, O, C_1, C_2, ...$ along OC_1 and through them draw planes parallel to OA_1B_1.

Treat the lines OA_1, OB_1 similarly. Then just as before we see that the *lattice* of points formed by the intersections of these three sets of parallel planes (Fig. 13) includes all the points equivalent to O under H. Hence H is generated by the translations represented by OA_1, OB_1, OC_1; and therefore:—

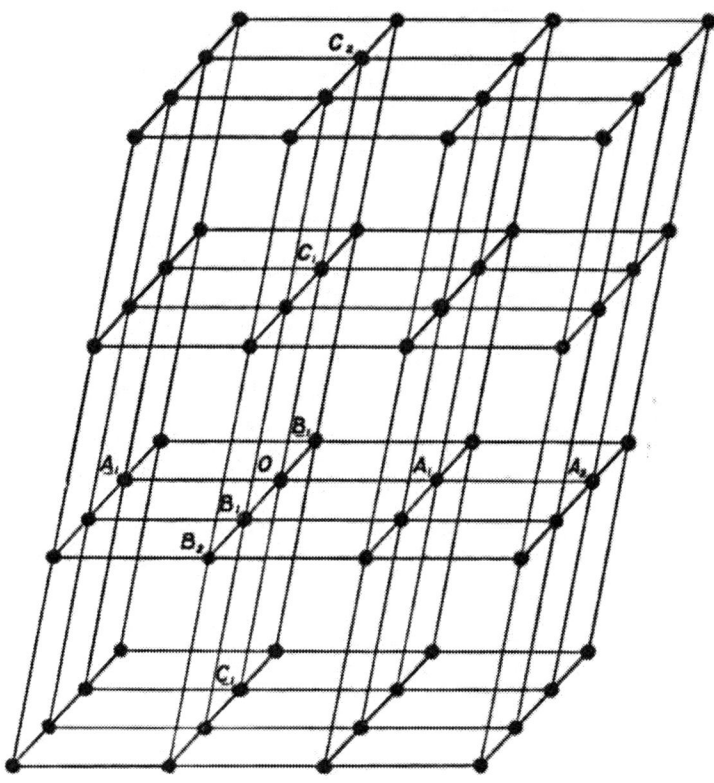

Fig. 13.

Every translation-group containing no infinitesimal translation is generated by not more than three independent translations.

Ex. 1. Every translation of H is represented by a line drawn from any given point of the lattice to some other point of the lattice.

Ex. 2. The straight line joining two points of a net (or lattice) passes through an infinite number of points of the net (or lattice).

Ex. 3. The plane through three non-collinear points of a lattice contains a net of points in the lattice.

Ex. 4. If t_1, t_2, t_3 are the translations represented by OA_1, OB_1, OC_1 in § 9, (i) prove that $t_1^{\alpha_1} t_2^{\beta_1}$ and $t_1^{\alpha_2} t_2^{\beta_2}$ are independent if $\alpha_1 \beta_2 - \alpha_2 \beta_1 \neq 0$ and generate a subgroup of $\{t_1, t_2\}$ which only coincides with $\{t_1, t_2\}$ if $\alpha_1 \beta_2 - \alpha_2 \beta_1 = \pm 1$; (ii) find the condition that $\tau_1 \equiv t_1^{\alpha_1} t_2^{\beta_1} t_3^{\gamma_1}$, $\tau_2 \equiv t_1^{\alpha_2} t_2^{\beta_2} t_3^{\gamma_2}$, $\tau_3 \equiv t_1^{\alpha_3} t_2^{\beta_3} t_3^{\gamma_3}$ should be independent; (iii) show that $K \equiv \{\tau_1, \tau_2, \tau_3\}$ is a subgroup of H and find the condition that $H \equiv K$; (iv) show that $\{t_1, t_2, t_3\}/\{t_1^x, t_2^y, t_3^z\}$ is an Abelian group of order xyz generated by three permutable elements of orders x, y, z.

Ex. 5. Find every group of movements such that H is generated by a single translation.

Ex. 6. No function of the complex quantity $x + \sqrt{-1}y$ can have more than two independent periods.

§ 10. Let H be the normal subgroup formed by the translations of any group of movements G (§ 4). Let G contain a screw S through an angle $2\pi \div n$ (but through no smaller angle) round any line. Let R be the rotation through $2\pi \div n$ about a parallel line l through O. Now S transforms every translation of G into another translation of G, and hence S at most moves the lattice of § 9 parallel to itself. Hence R brings the lattice to self-coincidence.

Let E_1 be a point of the lattice such that no point of the lattice is nearer l than E_1 (excluding points on l). Let the rotations R, R^2, ..., R^{n-1} bring E_1 to $E_2, E_3, ..., E_n$. Complete the parallelogram $E_1 E_2 E_3 D$. Then $E_1, E_2, ..., E_n$ are points of the lattice, and therefore $E_2 E_1$, $E_2 E_3$ represent translations of H. Hence $E_2 D$ represents a translation of H; so that D is a point of the lattice. Therefore D lies on l, or else is outside the polygon $E_1 E_2 ... E_n$. We see at once that this is only possible if $n = 2, 3, 4,$ or 6.

A similar result holds for the rotatory-inversions of G. Hence:—

If the subgroup H formed by the translations of a group G contains no infinitesimal translation, the point-group simply isomorphic with G/H contains only 2-al, 3-al, 4-al, and 6-al rotations and rotatory-inversions.

G is not necessarily given when H and G/H are given. If H is generated by three finite independent translations, G is one of 230 different types (of which 165 contain rotatory-inversions). For the discussion of these we must refer to Schoenflies' *Krystallsysteme und Krystallstructur*, or Hilton's *Mathematical Crystallography*.

Ex. 1. G/H is one of 32 different types.

Ex. 2. The movements bringing a net to self-coincidence and not displacing O form one of the groups Γ_2, Δ, Δ_4, Δ_6.

Ex. 3. The movements bringing a lattice to self-coincidence and not displacing O form one of the groups c, Γ_2, Δ, Δ_3, Δ_4, Δ_6, Ω.

Ex. 4. The only type of lattice brought to self-coincidence by Δ_6 is that in which
$$OA_1 = OB_1, \ A_1OB_1 = 120°, \ C_1OA_1 = C_1OB_1 = 90°$$
(§ 9).

Ex. 5. There are two types of lattice brought to self-coincidence by Δ_4; that in which
 (i) $OA_1 = OB_1, \ A_1OB_1 = C_1OA_1 = C_1OB_1 = 90°$;
 (ii) $OA_1 = OB_1, \ A_1OB_1 = 90°$,
and the line joining C_1 to the middle point of A_1B_1 is perpendicular to the plane OA_1B_1.

Ex. 6. If $C_1OA_1 = C_1OB_1 = 90°$ and $G/H = \mathbf{C}_2$, G is one of two possible types. If $G/H = \mathbf{c}_2$, G is one of two types.

Ex. 7. If $A_1OB_1 = 120°$, $C_1OA_1 = C_1OB_1 = 90°$, and $G/H = \mathbf{C}_3$, G is one of three types.

Ex. 8. There is only one type of group for which $G/H = \mathbf{c}_6$.

Ex. 9. Find the groups in which H is generated by only two independent translations and G/H is $\mathbf{C}_2$, $\mathbf{C}_3$, $\mathbf{C}_4$, or $\mathbf{C}_6$.

§ 11. If a given movement brings any point P to the position P', P and P' have a one-to-one correspondence. Therefore a movement may be considered as a particular case of collineation. If (x', y', z') and (x, y, z) are the coordinates of P' and P referred to the same Cartesian axes of reference, we have evidently relations of the form

$$x' = a_1x + b_1y + c_1z + d_1, \ y' = a_2x + b_2y + c_2z + d_2,$$
$$z' = a_3x + b_3y + c_3z + d_3$$

(for if P is at infinity so is P'). These relations may be considered as defining a substitution. Hence any group of movements G may be looked upon as a group of collineations, while the corresponding substitutions evidently form a substitution-group of degree 3 simply isomorphic with G.

If G is a holoaxial point-group whose elements leave a point O unmoved, G is simply isomorphic with a fractional linear substitution-group of degree 1.

For let Σ be any sphere with centre O, and et a point P on Σ be brought to Q by a rotation of G equivalent to successive reflexions in two planes through O meeting Σ in the great circles j, k. Let P', Q', j', k' be the stereographic projections of P, Q, j, k. Then P' is brought to Q' by successive inversions in the circles j', k' (IV 11). Let the coordinates of P', Q' referred to rectangular axes be (x, y), (x', y'); and let $z = x + iy$, $z' = x' + iy'$ ($i = \sqrt{-1}$). Let j', k' be the circles

$$x^2 + y^2 + 2gx + 2fy + e = 0, \quad x^2 + y^2 + 2g_1 x + 2f_1 y + e_1 = 0;$$

and let (X, Y) be the inverse of (x, y) in j' or of (x', y') in k'. We verify at once that

$$X = \frac{(g^2 + f^2 - e)(x + g)}{(x+g)^2 + (y+f)^2} - g, \quad Y = \frac{(g^2 + f^2 - e)(y + f)}{(x+g)^2 + (y+f)^2} - f.$$

Hence

$$X - iY = \frac{z(-g + if) - e}{z + (g + if)} = \text{(similarly)} \frac{z'(-g_1 + if_1) - e_1}{z' + (g_1 + if_1)} \quad \ldots\ldots(\text{i})$$

Solving (i) we have a substitution S of the form $z' = \dfrac{az + b}{cz + d}$ (where a, b, c, d are complex quantities) which is not altered by multiplying a, b, c, d by a common factor (not 0 or ∞). It is usual to take $ad - bc = 1$. The substitutions similar to S form a substitution-group G' simply isomorphic with G. If we change the vertex of stereographic projection or the axes of reference, we obtain a transform of G' by some substitution.

Ex. 1. A point-group is simply isomorphic with a group of homogeneous orthogonal substitutions.

Ex. 2. (i) The substitutions of a homogeneous orthogonal group of degree 3 whose determinant is 1 form a normal subgroup H of index 1 or 2. (ii) If H is finite, it can be transformed into one of 5 given types of group.

Ex. 3. Find the simplest substitution-groups of degree 8 simply isomorphic with Δ, $\mathbf{d}_3$, $\mathbf{D}_4$, $\mathbf{T}$, the group generated by an inversion and three independent translations, and the group generated by two screws through π and of equal translations about two parallel lines.

Ex. 4. Find the simplest substitution-groups of degree 2 simply isomorphic with δ_4, the group generated by two rotations through π about parallel lines, and the group generated by a reflexion in a plane and a rotation through π about a parallel line.

Ex. 5. Find the simplest fractional substitution-groups of degree 1 simply isomorphic with $\mathbf{C}_m$, $\mathbf{D}_m$, $\mathbf{T}$.

Ex. 6. Show that there are only 5 possible types of finite fractional linear substitution-groups of degree 1.

Ex. 7. By what substitution is the group G' of § 11 transformed if (i) the plane of stereographic projection is turned through an angle α about the axis of y, the origin being at O; (ii) the axes of reference are turned through an angle β about the origin, the plane of projection remaining unaltered?

Ex. 8. Show that a point-group containing rotatory-inversions is simply isomorphic with a group composed of substitutions such as $x' = (ax+b) \div (cx+d)$ and 'pseudo-substitutions' such as $x' = (a\bar{x}+b) \div (c\bar{x}+d)$.

§ 12. We shall conclude this chapter by working out in detail one example showing the connexion between certain groups of movements, collineations, permutations, and substitutions.

Consider the octahedral group **O** formed by the rotations bringing a cube to self-coincidence (§ 7 (iv)). Take as Cartesian reference-axes the lines through the centre O of the cube perpendicular to the faces. The group **O** may obviously be generated by a rotation a through $\frac{1}{2}\pi$ about $x = y = 0$ and a rotation b through π about $y = 0$, $x = z$.

Now let (x, y, z) be the coordinates of any point P. Then if the rotation a brings P to coincide with the point P_1 and b brings P to coincide with P_2, the coordinates of P_1 and P_2 are $(-y, x, z)$ and $(z, -y, x)$. Hence **O** is simply isomorphic with the homogeneous linear substitution-group of degree 3 generated by $x' = -y$, $y' = x$, $z' = z$ and $x' = z$, $y' = -y$, $z' = x$.

Take OP as unit of length and project points on the sphere $x^2 + y^2 + z^2 = 1$ stereographically from the point $(0, 0, -1)$ on to the plane $z = 0$. Let $(\mathbf{x}, \mathbf{y})$, $(\mathbf{x}_1, \mathbf{y}_1)$, $(\mathbf{x}_2, \mathbf{y}_2)$ be the coordinates of the stereographic projections of P, P_1, P_2 and let $\mathbf{z} = \mathbf{x} + \sqrt{-1}\,\mathbf{y}$, $\mathbf{z}_1 = \mathbf{x}_1 + \sqrt{-1}\,\mathbf{y}_1$, $\mathbf{z}_2 = \mathbf{x}_2 + \sqrt{-1}\,\mathbf{y}_2$. The rotation a is equivalent to successive reflexions in the planes $y = 0$, $x = y$ and b is equivalent to successive reflexions in the planes $y = 0$, $x = z$. These planes meet the sphere in great circles whose projections are $y = 0$, $x = y$ and $y = 0$, $x^2 + y^2 + 2x = 1$.* Hence it follows by equations (i) of § 11 that $\mathbf{z}_1 = \sqrt{-1}\,\mathbf{z}$, $\mathbf{z}_2 = (1-\mathbf{z}) \div (1+\mathbf{z})$. Hence **O** is simply isomorphic with the fractional substitution-group generated by $x' = \sqrt{-1}\,x$ and $x' = \dfrac{1-x}{1+x}$.

Again, every rotation of **O** interchanges the four lines

* The circle through $(0, \pm 1)$ cutting $x = 0$ at an angle of $\dfrac{\pi}{4}$.

$x = \pm y = \pm z$ (the diagonals of the cube) while evidently no rotation of **O** except identity brings each such diagonal to self-coincidence. Hence **O** being of order 4! must be simply isomorphic with the symmetric group of degree 4.

Again, suppose a rotation r of **O** brings any line l to coincide with l'. Let l, l' meet a given plane in Q, Q'; and let the lines $x = \pm y = \pm z$ meet the plane in the corners of a quadrangle $ABCD$. Then the rotation r establishes a collinear transformation of the plane $ABCD$ such that Q' corresponds to Q. This collineation interchanges the points A, B, C, D and therefore transforms the quadrangle $ABCD$

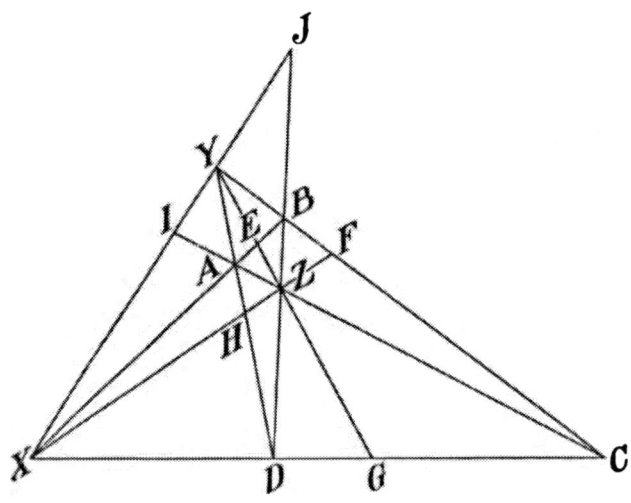

Fig. 14.

into itself. Moreover since a collineation of a plane is completely determined when four pairs of corresponding points are given and A, B, C, D can be interchanged in 4! ways, **O** is simply isomorphic with the group formed by all those collineations of a plane which transform a given quadrangle into itself. The collineations of order 2 in this group are at once seen from Fig. 14 to be the perspective collineations whose fixed point and line are X and YZ, Y and ZX, Z and XY, E and CD, F and DA, G and AB, H and BC, I and BD, J and AC. These correspond to the rotations through π contained in **O** as explained in IV 13.

Ex. 1. Show that **θ** is also simply isomorphic with the symmetric group of degree 4.

Ex. 2. Show that **E** is simply isomorphic with the alternating group of degree 5 and with the group generated by those collineations of a plane of order 2 which transform into itself the figure formed by a regular pentagon and the line at infinity.

Ex. 3. Show that an Abelian group composed of collineations of order 2 transforming (i) a straight line, (ii) a plane into itself is of order ≤ 4.

Ex. 4. Show that an Abelian group generated by perspective collineations of order 2 is of order ≤ 8.

Ex. 5. Show that in an Abelian group of collineations of order 2 the non-perspective collineations form with identity a normal subgroup of index 1 or 2.

Ex. 6. Discuss the groups generated by (i) two perspective collineations with a common fixed point; (ii) four perspective collineations with a common fixed plane; (iii) three non-perspective collineations of order 2 with one fixed line in common and the other fixed lines concurrent.

CHAPTER IX

GENERATORS OF GROUPS

§ 1. We defined 'an independent set of generators' in V 3. A group may have several such sets, but the group is completely determined when we know any one such set of generators and all independent relations between them. So far our knowledge of the properties of generators is confined to isolated theorems (see the examples below) except in the case of Abelian groups which are discussed in §§ 3 to 6. We shall suppose the number of generators to be always finite; this is the case for all finite groups.

Ex. 1. The group $a^m = b^n = 1$ is infinite.

Ex. 2. If a, b denote (i) permutations on any finite number of symbols, (ii) linear substitutions in a $GF[p^r]$, a and b are connected by relations other than the equations $a^m = b^n = 1$ giving their orders.

Ex. 3. (i) The relations $a^\lambda = 1$, $b^\beta = a^r$, $ab = ba^k$ * are inconsistent unless $k^\beta - 1 \equiv r(k-1) \equiv 0 \pmod{\lambda}$. (ii) If they are consistent, $\{a, b\}$ is of order $\lambda\beta$. (iii) $a^p = b^p = 1$, $ab = ba^k$ are inconsistent unless $k = 1$.

Ex. 4. If $\{a, b\}$ is finite and $b^2 = (ab)^2$, $\{a, b\}$ is of the type $a^\lambda = b^{2\mu} = 1$, $aba = b$ or $a^{2\lambda} = 1$, $b^{2\mu} = a^\lambda$, $aba = b$.

Ex. 5. The relations $ab = ba^k$, $ba = ab^l$ define (if consistent) a finite group.

Ex. 6. If a and b are of finite order and are both permutable with their commutator c, $\{a, b\}$ is finite and each of its elements is of the form $a^x b^y c^z$.

Ex. 7. If $a^p = b^p = c^2 = 1$, $ab = ba$, $ca = bc$; $\{a, b, c\}$ is of order $2p^2$.

Ex. 8. $a^{2m} = b^3 = (ab)^2 = c^2 = 1$, $ac = ca$, $bc = cb$ cannot be generated by < 3 generators.

Ex. 9. Find in their simplest form the elements of
(i) $a^3 = b^3 = 1$, $ba = a^2b^2$; (ii) $a^3 = b^4 = 1$, $ba = a^2b^2$.

Ex. 10. (i) Prove that if $a^4 = b^4 = 1$ and $ba = a^2b^2$, $ab = (ba)^2$

* This implies that λ is the order of a, β the order of b relative to $\{a\}$, $\lambda > k > 0$.

and $(ba)^5 = 1$. (ii) Deduce that $a^4 = b^4 = 1$, $ba = a^2 b^2$ is the same abstract group as $g^4 = h^5 = 1$, $hg = gh^2$ and find its order.

Ex. 11. Prove that $a^5 = b^5 = 1$, $ba = a^2 b^2$ is the same abstract group of order 55 as $g^5 = h^{11} = 1$, $hg = gh^3$.

Ex. 12. $a^{2m} = b^2 = (a^2 b)^2 = 1$, $(ab)^r = (ba)^r$ and $a^{2m} = b^2 = 1$, $a^2 b = ba^2$, $(ab)^r = (ba)^r$ are of order $4mr$.

Ex. 13. Find the orders of (i) $a^4 = b^4 = (ab)^2 = a^2 b^2 ab^3 = 1$, (ii) $a^2 = b^2 = c^2 = (abc)^2 = (ac)^5 (cb)^2 = (ac)^3 (cb)^3 = 1$.

Ex. 14. Find the orders of
(i) $a^3 = b^2 = (ab)^3 = 1$, (ii) $a^4 = b^3 = (ab)^2 = 1$,
(iii) $a^5 = b^2 = (ab)^3 = 1$, (iv) $a^7 = b^2 = (ab)^3 = (a^4 b)^4 = 1$.

§ 2. Suppose we are given a finite or infinite group G generated by any given elements $g_1, g_2, g_3, \ldots$ connected by given mutually consistent relations $g_l^\lambda g_m^\mu \ldots = 1$, $g_r^\rho g_s^\sigma \ldots = 1$, &c. Consider the group Γ generated by elements $\gamma_1, \gamma_2, \gamma_3, \ldots$ connected by the relations $\gamma_l^\lambda \gamma_m^\mu \ldots = 1$, $\gamma_r^\rho \gamma_s^\sigma \ldots = 1$, &c., and also by any number of further relations $\gamma_a^\alpha \gamma_b^\beta \ldots = 1$, $\gamma_d^\delta \gamma_e^\epsilon \ldots = 1$, &c., not in general all independent but consistent with each other and with $\gamma_l^\lambda \gamma_m^\mu \ldots = 1$, $\gamma_r^\rho \gamma_s^\sigma \ldots = 1$, &c. Now G and Γ are evidently isomorphic; for to the product of any two generators g_i, g_j of G corresponds the product of γ_i, γ_j in Γ, and conversely. To each element of G corresponds only one element of Γ, while to identity in Γ corresponds every element of G contained in the normal subgroup H whose elements are 1, $g_a^\alpha g_b^\beta \ldots$, $g_d^\delta g_e^\epsilon \ldots$, &c. Hence $\Gamma = G/H$.

Ex. 1. (i) The addition of $g_a{}^\alpha g_b{}^\beta \ldots = 1$ to the relations connecting the generators $g_1, g_2, g_3, \ldots$ of any group G involves $h = 1$, where h is any element conjugate to $g_a{}^\alpha g_b{}^\beta \ldots$ in G. (ii) If $g_a{}^\alpha g_b{}^\beta \ldots$ is normal in G and of order ν, the addition of the relation $g_a{}^\alpha g_b{}^\beta \ldots = 1$ reduces the order of G to $1 \div \nu$ its original value.

Ex. 2. $a^{2n} = a^n b^2 = 1$, $aba = b$ is a subgroup of index 2 in $a^{2n} = b^4 = 1$, $aba = b$.

Ex. 3. Prove that in § 1, Ex. 14 the group (i) is simply isomorphic with the alternating group of degree 4, the group $\Lambda(m = 2)$ in the $GF[3]$ (see VII 10), and the tetrahedral group $\mathbf{T}$; that (ii) is simply isomorphic with the symmetric group of degree 4 and the groups $\mathbf{O}$, $\mathbf{\theta}$; that (iii) is simply isomorphic with the alternating group of degree 5, the group $\Lambda(m = 2)$ in the $GF[5]$ and the group $\Lambda(m = 2)$ in the $GF[2^2]$, and the group $\mathbf{E}$; that (iv) is simply isomorphic with the group generated by $(1\,2\,3\,4\,5\,6\,7)$ and $(12)(47)$, the group $\Lambda(m = 2)$ in the $GF[7]$ and the group $\Lambda(m = 8)$ in the $GF[2]$.

Ex. 4. Prove that in § 1, Ex. 14 the group (i) is simply isomorphic with that generated by $x' = \dfrac{4}{x+1}$ and $x' = \dfrac{8x}{x+2}$ in the $GF[5]$, and the group (iii) with that generated by $x' = \dfrac{8x}{4}$ and $x' = \dfrac{x+9}{x+10}$ in the $GF[11]$.

Ex. 5. Prove that the group $a^3 = b^2 = (ab)^2 = 1$ is simply isomorphic with the symmetric group of degree 3, the group $\Lambda(m=2)$ in the $GF[2]$, and the groups $\mathbf{D}_3$, $\boldsymbol{\delta}_3$.

Ex. 6. Show that $a^6 = b^2 = (ab)^3 = (a^3b)^2 = 1$ is simply isomorphic with the permutation-group generated by
$$\mathbf{a} \equiv (1\ 2\ 3\ 4\ 5\ 6) \text{ and } \mathbf{b} \equiv (3\ 6).$$

Ex. 7. Show that $a^8 = b^3 = (ab)^2 = (a^5b)^2 = 1$ is simply isomorphic with the general homogeneous linear group of degree 2 in the $GF[3]$.

Ex. 8. Prove that $a^5 = b^2 = (ab)^4 = (a^4bab)^3 = 1$ is simply isomorphic with the symmetric group of degree 5.

Ex. 9. Find abstract groups generated by two elements simply isomorphic with Θ, Ω, H.

§ 3. *As independent generating elements of an Abelian group G of order n, we can always find elements $g_1, g_2, g_3, \ldots$ satisfying the following conditions:*—$g_i g_j = g_j g_i$ *for all values of i and j and $g_i{}^{n_i} = 1$, where* (i) *the order n_i of g_i is a factor of n_{i-1} and is the order of g_i relative to $\{g_1, g_2, \ldots, g_{i-1}\}$;* (ii) g^{n_i} *is in* $\{g_1, g_2, \ldots, g_{i-1}\}$, g *being any element of G;* (iii) $n = n_1 n_2 n_3 \ldots$.

(1) If n_1 is the L.C.M. of the orders of all the elements of G, G contains an element whose order is n_1. For let $n_1 = p^\alpha q^\beta r^\gamma \ldots$, where $p, q, r, \ldots$ are prime numbers. Then G contains an element g whose order is $p^\alpha m$ (m integral); and therefore G contains an element g^m of order p^α. Similarly G contains elements of orders $q^\beta, r^\gamma, \ldots$; and the product g_1 of these permutable elements of orders $p^\alpha, q^\beta, r^\gamma, \ldots$ is of order n_1. If g is any element of G, we have $g^{n_1} = 1$.

(2) Let the L.C.M. of the orders of all the elements of $G_1 \equiv G/\{g_1\}$ be n_2. Any factor-group of an Abelian group is evidently Abelian; in particular G_1 is Abelian. Then G_1 contains an element h' of order n_2. Let h be an element of G corresponding to h' in G_1. Then n_2 is the order of h relative to $\{g_1\}$. The order of any element of G relative to $\{g_1\}$ is a factor of n_2; for it is equal to the order of the corresponding element of G_1. Hence g^{n_2} is $\{g_1\}$, where g is any element of G.

IX 4] BASES AND INVARIANTS 127

Let $h^{n_2} = g_1{}^t$. Then $t \div n_2 (= e, $ say$)$ is integral. For $g_1{}^{n_1 e} = h^{n_1} = 1$ by (1); which is only possible if e is integral. Put $g_2 = h g_1{}^{-e}$. Then $g_2{}^{n_2} = (h g_1{}^{-e})^{n_2} = h^{n_2} g_1{}^{-e n_2} = h^{n_2} g_1{}^{-t} = 1$. Moreover h^s is not in $\{g_1\}$ $(s < n_2)$, and therefore $g_2{}^s = (h g_1{}^{-e})^s = h^s g_1{}^{-es}$ is not in $\{g_1\}$, if s is a positive integer $< n_2$. Hence n_2 is the order of g_2 and is its order relative to $\{g_1\}$.

Since n_2 divides the order of h which divides n_1, n_2 divides n_1 (the case $n_2 = n_1$ is not excluded). It is evident that the order of $\{g_1, g_2\}$ is $n_1 n_2$, and that each of its elements is of the form $g_1{}^{\beta_1} g_2{}^{\beta_2}$.

(3) Let the L.C.M. of the orders of all the elements of $G_2 \equiv G/\{g_1, g_2\}$ be n_3. Then G_2 contains an element of order n_3. Let k be a corresponding element of G. Then as in (2) n_3 is the order of k relative to $\{g_1, g_2\}$, and g^{n_3} is in $\{g_1, g_2\}$, g being any element of G.

Let $k^{n_3} = g_1{}^v g_2{}^w$. Then $v \div n_3$ and $w \div n_3$ $(= q$ and r, say$)$ are integral. For $g_1{}^{n_2 q} g_2{}^{n_2 r} = k^{n_3}$ is in $\{g_1\}$ by (2); which is only possible if r is integral; and $g_1{}^{n_1 q} g_2{}^{n_1 r} = k^{n_1} = 1$ by (1); which is only possible if q is integral. Put $g_3 = k g_1{}^{-q} g_2{}^{-r}$. Then as in (2) $g_3{}^{n_3} = k^{n_3} g_1{}^{-v} g_2{}^{-w} = 1$, and $g_3{}^s = h^s g_1{}^{-qs} g_2{}^{-rs}$ is not in $\{g_1, g_2\}$ $(s < n_3)$. Hence n_3 is the order of g_3 and is its order relative to $\{g_1, g_2\}$.

Since k^{n_3} is in $\{g_1, g_2\}$ and n_3 is the order of k relative to $\{g_1, g_2\}$, n_3 divides n_2 (V 1).

(4) We now apply to $\{g_1, g_2, g_3\}$ the process applied in (3) to $\{g_1, g_2\}$ and so on.

All the elements of G will then be included among the $n_1 n_2 \ldots n_x$ elements

$$g_1{}^{\beta_1} g_2{}^{\beta_2} \ldots g_x{}^{\beta_x} \; (\beta_i = 1, 2, \ldots, n_i; \; i = 1, 2, \ldots, x).$$

These elements are all distinct. For if $g_1{}^{\alpha_1} g_2{}^{\alpha_2} \ldots g_x{}^{\alpha_x} = g_1{}^{\beta_1} g_2{}^{\beta_2} \ldots g_x{}^{\beta_x}$, $g_x{}^{\alpha_x - \beta_x}$ is in $\{g_1, g_2, \ldots, g_{x-1}\}$ and hence $\alpha_x = \beta_x$; and then similarly $\alpha_{x-1} = \beta_{x-1}$, &c. Therefore $n = n_1 n_2 \ldots n_x$.

§ 4. The elements $g_1, g_2, g_3, \ldots$ are said to form a *base* $[g_1, g_2, g_3, \ldots]$ of the Abelian group G. The base may be chosen in many different ways; but, however the base is chosen, the quantities $n_1, n_2, n_3, \ldots$ are always the same. For this reason $n_1, n_2, n_3, \ldots$ are called *invariants* of G, and G is said to be of *the type* $(n_1, n_2, n_3, \ldots)$.* Two Abelian

---

* An Abelian group of the type $(p^\alpha, p^\beta, p^\gamma, \ldots)$ is said by some authors to be of the type $(\alpha, \beta, \gamma, \ldots)$; see § 7.

groups of the same type are simply isomorphic and two simply isomorphic Abelian groups are of the same type; so that an Abelian group is completely defined as an abstract group when its invariants are given. Abelian groups of every possible type exist. These statements we shall now prove (§§ 5 and 6).

§ 5. *The orders of the elements of two different bases of an Abelian group G are respectively equal.*

If $[g_1, g_2, g_3, ...]$ and $[\gamma_1, \gamma_2, \gamma_3, ...]$ are the bases, g_i being of order n_i and γ_i of order ν_i, we wish to prove
$$n_i = \nu_i, \; (i = 1, 2, 3, ...).$$
Now $n_1 = \nu_1$ by § 3 (1). If therefore we can prove $n_i = \nu_i$ when we assume $n_1 = \nu_1, n_2 = \nu_2, ..., n_{i-1} = \nu_{i-1}$, the theorem can be proved by induction.

Consider the elements obtained by raising every element of G to the n_ith power. They form a subgroup H of G, since $g^{n_i} h^{n_i} = (gh)^{n_i}$, g and h being any elements of G. Every element of H is included in
$$g_1^{\beta_1 n_i} g_2^{\beta_2 n_i} ... g_{i-1}^{\beta_{i-1} n_i} g_i^{\beta_i n_i} g_{i+1}^{\beta_{i+1} n_i} ...$$
$$(\beta_t = 1, 2, ..., n_t; \; t = 1, 2, 3, ...);$$
i.e. in
$$g_1^{\beta_1 n_i} g_2^{\beta_2 n_i} ... g_{i-1}^{\beta_{i-1} n_i} \; (\beta_t = 1, 2, ..., n_t; \; t = 1, 2, ..., i-1),$$
since
$$g_i^{n_i} = g_{i+1}^{n_i} = g_{i+2}^{n_i} = ... = 1.$$

Now $g_t^{\beta_t n_i} (\beta_t = 1, 2, ..., n_t)$ takes $n_t \div n_i$ distinct values, and therefore H is of order $\dfrac{n_1}{n_i} \cdot \dfrac{n_2}{n_i} \cdot ... \cdot \dfrac{n_{i-1}}{n_i}$.

Again, the elements
$$\gamma_1^{\beta_1 n_i} \gamma_2^{\beta_2 n_i} ... \gamma_{i-1}^{\beta_{i-1} n_i} \; (\beta_t = 1, 2, ..., \nu_t; \; t = 1, 2, ..., i-1)$$
are all in H and are $\dfrac{n_1}{n_i} \cdot \dfrac{n_2}{n_i} \cdot ... \cdot \dfrac{n_{i-1}}{n_i}$ in number on the assumption $n_1 = \nu_1, n_2 = \nu_2, ..., n_{i-1} = \nu_{i-1}$. Hence every element of H is included among these elements and is therefore in $\{\gamma_1, \gamma_2, ..., \gamma_{i-1}\}$. But $\gamma_i^{n_i}$ is in H and is only in $\{\gamma_1, \gamma_2, ..., \gamma_{i-1}\}$ if ν_i divides n_i. Hence ν_i divides n_i, and similarly n_i divides ν_i. Therefore $n_i = \nu_i$, and the proof by induction can be completed.

It should be noted in particular that every base contains the same number of elements.

§ 6. *Two Abelian groups with the same invariants are simply isomorphic.*

Let $[g_1, g_2, g_3, \ldots]$, $[\gamma_1, \gamma_2, \gamma_3, \ldots]$ be bases of the two Abelian groups. The g's are connected by precisely the same relations as the γ's and therefore $\{g_1, g_2, g_3, \ldots\} = \{\gamma_1, \gamma_2, \gamma_3, \ldots\}$.

Two simply isomorphic Abelian groups G and Γ have the same invariants.

Let $[g_1, g_2, g_3, \ldots]$ be a base of G and let γ_i in Γ correspond to g_i in G. Since the γ's are connected by the same relations as the g's, the γ's satisfy the conditions of § 3 and therefore form a base of Γ precisely similar to $[g_1, g_2, g_3, \ldots]$.

An Abelian group of any given type can always be found.

Let the type be $(n_1, n_2, n_3, \ldots)$. Taking for g_1 the cyclical permutation $(a_1 a_2 \ldots a_{n_1})$, for g_2 $(b_1 b_2 \ldots b_{n_2})$, for g_3 $(c_1 c_2 \ldots c_{n_3})$, &c., the required group is the permutation-group $\{g_1, g_2, g_3, \ldots\}$.

Ex. 1. An infinite Abelian group is not of necessity generated by a finite number of elements.

Ex. 2. The group G of § 4 is the direct product of $H \equiv \{g_1, g_2, g_4, g_8, \ldots\}$ and $K \equiv \{g_3, g_5, g_6, g_7, g_9, \ldots\}$ or of any two similar subgroups.

Ex. 3. Every Abelian group is the direct product of cyclic subgroups.

Ex. 4. Two conformal Abelian groups are simply isomorphic.

Ex. 5. The subgroup formed by those elements of G whose orders divide n_i is of the type $(n_i, n_i, \ldots, n_i, n_{i+1}, n_{i+2}, \ldots, n_x)$.

Ex. 6. The subgroup formed by the n_i-th powers of the elements of G is of the type $\left(\dfrac{n_1}{n_i}, \dfrac{n_2}{n_i}, \dfrac{n_3}{n_i}, \ldots\right)$.

Ex. 7. If $n_1 = p^{a_1} m_1$, $n_2 = p^{a_2} m_2$, ..., $n_x = p^{a_x} m_x$, where $m_1, m_2, \ldots, m_x$ are prime to p, $[g_1^{m_1}, g_2^{m_2}, \ldots, g_x^{m_x}]$ is a base of the subgroup of order $p^{a_1 + a_2 + \cdots + a_x}$ in G.

Ex. 8. Find a base and the invariants of (i) $a^4 = b^3 = 1$, $ab = ba$; (ii) $a^{30} = b^{24} = 1$, $ab = ba$; (iii) $a^{12} = 1$, $b^6 = a^{10}$, $ab = ba$; (iv) $a^{45} = 1$, $b^{20} = a^{30}$, $ab = ba$; (v) $a^{15} = b^{10} = c^6 = 1$, $bc = cb$, $ca = ac$, $ab = ba$; (vi) $a^{18} = 1$, $b^{12} = a^{15}$, $c^7 = a^9 b^9$, $bc = cb$, $ca = ac$, $ab = ba$.

Ex. 9. Find the types of the Abelian groups $\mathbf{C}_m$, δ_2, Δ, Γ_m.

§ 7. If $[g_1, g_2, ..., g_x]$ is a base of an Abelian group G of order p^a (p prime), the orders of $g_1, g_2, ..., g_x$ are evidently all powers of p. If these orders are $p^{a_1}, p^{a_2}, ..., p^{a_x}$, $a_1, a_2, ..., a_x$ are often called the *invariants* of G instead of $p^{a_1}, p^{a_2}, ..., p^{a_x}$ as in § 4; and G is said to be of *the type* $(a_1, a_2, ..., a_x)$ instead of the type $(p^{a_1}, p^{a_2}, ..., p^{a_x})$ as in § 4. No ambiguity will arise if we are careful to state in this case that the order of G is a power of p. Thus 'an Abelian group of the type $(n_1, n_2, ..., n_x)$' has generators of orders $n_1, n_2, ..., n_x$; while 'an Abelian group *of order p^a* and of the type $(n_1, n_2, ..., n_x)$' has generators of orders $p^{n_1}, p^{n_2}, ..., p^{n_x}$.

Any element g of the group G of order p^a with base $[g_1, g_2, ..., g_x]$ and invariants $a_1, a_2, ..., a_x$ is of the form $g_1^{\beta_1} g_2^{\beta_2} ... g_x^{\beta_x}$ ($\beta_t = 1, 2, ..., p^{a_t}$). Suppose $a_i \geq \lambda \geq a_{i+1}$. Then $g^{p^\lambda} = 1$ if and only if β_1 is a multiple of $p^{a_1-\lambda}$, β_2 of $p^{a_2-\lambda}$, ..., β_i of $p^{a_i-\lambda}$. Hence G contains $p^{i\lambda+a_{i+1}+a_{i+2}+...+a_x}$ elements whose orders divide p^λ. If $a_j \geq \lambda - 1 \geq a_{j+1}$ ($i \geq j$), G contains $p^{j(\lambda-1)+a_{j+1}+a_{j+2}+...+a_x}$ elements whose orders divide $p^{\lambda-1}$ and therefore G contains

$$p^{i\lambda+a_{i+1}+a_{i+2}+...+a_x} - p^{j(\lambda-1)+a_{j+1}+a_{j+2}+...+a_x}$$

($\equiv L$ say) elements of order p^λ.

Ex. 1. G contains $p^x - 1$ elements of order p.

Ex. 2. If $a_i \geq \lambda > \lambda - 1 \geq a_{i+1}$, G contains
$$p^{i(\lambda-1)+a_{i+1}+a_{i+2}+...+a_x}(p^i - 1)$$
elements of order p^λ.

Ex. 3. G contains $L \div p^{\lambda-1}(p-1)$ cyclic subgroups of order p^λ.

Ex. 4. An Abelian group G contains $L, M, N, ...$ elements and $L', M', N', ...$ subgroups of orders $p^\lambda, q^\mu, r^\nu, ...$ respectively; $p, q, r, ...$ being distinct primes. How many elements, subgroups, and cyclic subgroups of order $p^\lambda q^\mu r^\nu ...$ does G contain?

Ex. 5. (i) Every element of an Abelian group of order p^a and type $(1, 1, ..., 1)$ is of order 1 or p; (ii) conversely, if every element of an Abelian group G except identity has the same order, G is of this type; (iii) every subgroup and factor-group of G is of this type.

Ex. 6. If every element of an Abelian group G is contained in one of a set of subgroups of G no two of which have an element in common, G is of the type $(1, 1, ..., 1)$.

Ex. 7. If an element a of prime order q is permutable with an Abelian group G of order p^a but with no subgroup of G, q is $> a$.

Ex. 8. (i) A group G whose elements are all of order < 3 is Abelian of order 2^a and type $(1, 1, ..., 1)$. (ii) If a is an element of order r permutable with G, $\{G, a\}$ is of order $2^{a-1}r$ or $2^a r$.

Ex. 9. (i) In the group $a^r = b^2 = 1$, $bb_1 = b_m$ ($b_t \equiv a^{-t}ba^t$) prove that $b_s b_{s+1} = b_{s+m}$ and $bb_s = a^{-m}(bb_1 b_2 \ldots b_{s-1})a^m$. (ii) Show that the group contains a normal Abelian subgroup of order 2^k and type $(1, 1, \ldots, 1)$ where $k \leq m$.

Ex. 10. If $[g_1, g_2, \ldots, g_m]$ is a base of an Abelian group G, find the condition that

$$h_1 \equiv g_1^{a_{11}} g_2^{a_{12}} \ldots g_m^{a_{1m}}, \quad h_2 \equiv g_1^{a_{21}} g_2^{a_{22}} \ldots g_m^{a_{2m}}, \ldots,$$
$$h_m \equiv g_1^{a_{m1}} g_2^{a_{m2}} \ldots g_m^{a_{mm}}$$

may (1) be independent, (2) form a base of G in the two cases where the invariants are (i) infinite, (ii) all $= p$.

Ex. 11. The marks of a $GF[p^r]$ form an Abelian group of order p^r and type $(1, 1, \ldots, 1)$ when combined by addition.

§ **8.** Let G be an Abelian group of order p^a and type $(1, 1, \ldots, 1)$. Then evidently a base of G contains a generators, every element of G except identity is of order p, and every subgroup of G is of order p^r ($r \leq a$) and type $(1, 1, \ldots, 1)$.

A base $[h_1, h_2, \ldots, h_r]$ of some subgroup of order p^r in G may be chosen in

$$X \equiv (p^a - 1) \times p(p^{a-1} - 1) \times p^2(p^{a-2} - 1) \times \ldots \times p^{r-1}(p^{a-r+1} - 1)$$

ways. For h_1 may be any one of the $p^a - 1$ elements of order p in G; h_2 may be any one of the $(p^a - 1) - (p - 1) = p(p^{a-1} - 1)$ elements of G not contained in $\{h_1\}$; h_3 may be any one of the $(p^a - 1) - (p^2 - 1) = p^2(p^{a-2} - 1)$ elements of G not contained in $\{h_1, h_2\}$; h_4 may be any one of the $(p^a - 1) - (p^3 - 1) = p^3(p^{a-3} - 1)$ elements of G not contained in $\{h_1, h_2, h_3\}$; and so on.

Putting $a = r$ in X we see that, when a subgroup of order p^r is given, its base may be chosen in

$$Y \equiv (p^r - 1) \times p(p^{r-1} - 1) \times p^2(p^{r-2} - 1) \times \ldots \times p^{r-1}(p - 1)$$

ways. Hence the total number ${}_a N_r$ of subgroups of order p^r in G is

$$\frac{X}{Y} = \frac{(p^a - 1)(p^{a-1} - 1) \ldots (p^{a-r+1} - 1)}{(p^r - 1)(p^{r-1} - 1) \ldots (p - 1)}.$$

Ex. 1. ${}_a N_r = {}_a N_{a-r}$.

Ex. 2. ${}_a N_r \times p^{\frac{1}{2}r(r+1)} =$ the coefficient of x^r in
$$(1 + px)(1 + p^2 x) \ldots (1 + p^a x).$$

Ex. 3. An Abelian group G of order p^a and type $(a_1, a_2, \ldots, a_x)$ contains $(p^x - 1)(p^{x-1} - 1) \ldots (p^{x-r+1} - 1) \div (p^r - 1)(p^{r-1} - 1) \ldots (p - 1)$ subgroups of order p^r and type $(1, 1, \ldots, 1)$.

Ex. 4. The G. C. S. of all the subgroups of index p in G (§ 8) $\equiv 1$.

Ex. 5. If an element s of prime order q is permutable with an Abelian group G of order p^a and type $(1, 1, ..., 1)$, but with no subgroup of $(G, s)N_r \equiv 0 \pmod{q}$, and $q > a$.

Ex. 6. Find the number of subgroups of order p^y in an Abelian group of order p^{2y+z} and type $(2, 2, ..., 2, 1, 1, ..., 1)$:—$y$ 2's and z 1's.

Ex. 7. Find the number of subgroups of the type $(2, 1)$ in an Abelian group of order p^6 and type $(2, 2, 1, 1)$.

Ex. 8. Find the number of subgroups of the type $(3, 3, 2)$ in an Abelian group of order p^{15} and type $(3, 3, 3, 2, 2, 1, 1)$.

Ex. 9. Find the number of distinct bases of an Abelian group of order $p^{\frac{1}{2}m(m+1)}$ and type $(m, m-1, ..., 2, 1)$.

CHAPTER X

THE COMMUTANT AND GROUP OF AUTOMORPHISMS

THE COMMUTANT

§ 1. THE commutator of any two elements of a group G will be called for brevity a *commutator of G*. (See I 4.)

Let $h, k, l, \ldots$ be these commutators; then the subgroup $\Delta \equiv \{h, k, l, \ldots\}$ of G is called the *commutant, commutator subgroup*, or *first derived group* of G. Though Δ contains every commutator of G, it is not in general true that every element of Δ is a commutator of G; for the product of two commutators of G is not necessarily a commutator of G.

If Δ coincides with G, G is called a *perfect* group.

Ex. 1. $\Delta \equiv 1$, if and only if G is Abelian.
Ex. 2. The commutant of a subgroup of G is a subgroup of Δ.
Ex. 3. The commutant of the direct product of any number of groups is the direct product of their commutant.
Ex. 4. The direct product of perfect groups is perfect.
Ex. 5. If Δ is of order δ, no conjugate set of G contains more than δ elements.
Ex. 6. If Δ is a subgroup of the central of G, any two elements conjugate in G are permutable.
Ex. 7. If G contains a normal cyclic subgroup K, each element of Δ is permutable with each element of K.
Ex. 8. If $ba = ab^\beta$ and $ab = ba^\alpha$, the commutant of $\{a, b\}$ is cyclic.
Ex. 9. Find the commutants of the groups of V 4_1 and IX 1_3.

§ 2. *The commutant Δ of a group G is normal in G.*

Let a, b be two elements of G; then $a^{-1}b^{-1}ab$ is in Δ. Let g be any other element of G; then

$$g^{-1}(a^{-1}b^{-1}ab)g = (g^{-1}ag)^{-1}(g^{-1}bg)^{-1}(g^{-1}ag)(g^{-1}bg)$$

is in Δ, for it is the commutator of $g^{-1}ag$ and $g^{-1}bg$ which are elements of G. Again, if $h, k, l, \ldots$ are commutators of G,

$g^{-1}hkl\ldots g = g^{-1}hg \cdot g^{-1}kg \cdot g^{-1}lg \ldots$ is the product of commutators of G, and is therefore in Δ. Hence the transform of any element of Δ by any element of G is in Δ, i.e. Δ is normal in G.

Ex. 1. Every simple group is perfect.
Ex. 2. The direct product of any number of simple groups is perfect.
Ex. 3. The commutant of $a^{-1}Ga$ is $a^{-1}\Delta a$.
Ex. 4. The commutant of the symmetric group of degree m is the alternating group of degree m, and this alternating group is perfect unless $m = 4$.
Ex. 5. In VII 10 Γ is the commutant of G except when $m = 2$, $p^r = 2$ or 3.

§ 3. *If H is any normal subgroup of a group G and Δ is the commutant of G, $\{H, \Delta\}/H$ is the commutant of G/H.*

Let Δ' be the commutant of $\Gamma \equiv G/H$. Let a, b be any two elements of G, and α, β the corresponding elements of Γ. Then to the commutator $\alpha^{-1}\beta^{-1}\alpha\beta$ of α and β correspond the elements of $Ha^{-1}b^{-1}ab$, while to each commutator of G corresponds a commutator of Γ. It follows that to the product of any number of commutators of Γ correspond the products of elements of H and commutators of G, and conversely. Hence the subgroup Δ' of Γ corresponds to the subgroup $\{H, \Delta\}$ of G, and therefore $\Delta' = \{H, \Delta\}/H$ (V 18).

COROLLARY I. *If any normal subgroup H of a group G coincides with or contains the commutant Δ of G, $\Gamma \equiv G/H$ is Abelian.*

For in this case the commutant Δ' of $\Gamma = \{H, \Delta\}/H \equiv 1$, and therefore Γ is evidently Abelian.

COROLLARY II. *Conversely, if Γ is Abelian, H coincides with or contains Δ.*

For if Γ is Abelian, $\Delta' = 1$.

Ex. 1. Every factor-group of a perfect group is perfect.
Ex. 2. Every perfect group is isomorphic with a simple non-cyclic group.
Ex. 3. We can always find a group G such that G/Δ is simply isomorphic with any given Abelian group K.
Ex. 4. The G. C. S. of all normal subgroups of index p in any group G contains Δ.

Ex. 5. (i) A normal subgroup H containing the commutators of each pair of generators of G contains Δ. (ii) If these commutators generate a subgroup K and K, K_1, K_2, ... are the conjugates of K in G, $\Delta \equiv \{K, K_1, K_2, ...\}$.

Ex. 6. If the commutant of a group G is Abelian, the commutant of any factor-group Γ is Abelian.

Ex. 7. Find the commutants of the groups of V $14_{10, 11}$ and IX 1_{12}.

Ex. 8. Find the commutants of $\mathbf{D}_m$, $\mathbf{T}$, $\mathbf{O}$, $\mathbf{H}$.

The Group of Inner Automorphisms

§ 4. If C is the central of a group G, $A \equiv G/C$ is called the *group of inner automorphisms*, the *group of cogredient isomorphisms*, the *first cogredient*, or the *first adjoined group* of G. (See V 7.)

The group of inner automorphisms A of a group G is not cyclic, unless G is Abelian when $A \equiv 1$.

If A is generated by a single element a of order e, and g is an element in G corresponding to a in A; the elements $C + Cg + Cg^2 + \ldots + Cg^{e-1}$ are all distinct and include every element of G. Hence if A is cyclic, G is Abelian: for any two elements such as $c_i g^x$, $c_j g^y$ are permutable (c_i and c_j being in C), since $c_i g^x . c_j g^y = c_i c_j g^x g^y = c_j c_i g^y g^x = c_j g^y . c_i g^x$. But if G is Abelian $G \equiv C$, and hence $A \equiv 1$.

Ex. 1. No element of A is a power of each of the others.

Ex. 2. h is an element of G corresponding to an element of order t normal in A, and g is any other element of G. Prove that (i) h is permutable with every commutator of G; (ii) $c = g^{-1} h^{-1} g h$ is in C; (iii) $g h^s = c^s h^s g$; (iv) $g h^t = h^t g$; (v) $c^t = 1$; (vi) if C is of order p^a, it is possible to choose h so that c is of order t.

Ex. 3. The group of inner automorphisms of a direct product is the direct product of groups simply isomorphic with the groups of inner automorphisms of the component groups.

Ex. 4. The orders of a group G, its commutant, and its central C are n, δ, γ. If the group G/C contains an element a of order ϵ, G contains a subgroup of index $\leq \delta$ with a central of order $\geq \epsilon \gamma$.

Ex. 5. Find the groups of inner automorphisms of the groups of V 3_3, V 4_1, and V 14_{10}.

§ 5. If the group of inner automorphisms of a group G is Abelian, G is called *Metabelian*. It follows at once from § 3 that the commutant of a metabelian group is contained in its central; and conversely, that if the commutant of a group is contained in its central, the group is metabelian.

Ex. 1. If the group of inner automorphisms A of a group G is metabelian, its commutant is Abelian.

Ex. 2. If $\{a\}$, $\{b\}$, $\{c\}$, ... are normal in $G \equiv \{a, b, c, ...\}$, G is metabelian.

Ex. 3. a, b are two elements of a metabelian group G and c is their commutator. Prove that the order of c is a factor of the order of ab and of the orders of a, b relative to $\{b\}$, $\{a\}$.

Ex. 4. (i) Every metabelian group of odd order is conformal with an Abelian group. (ii) This is not true of every metabelian group of even order.

Ex. 5. $a^{2m} = b^2 = 1$, $a^2 b = ba^2$, $(ab)^2 = (ba)^2$ is metabelian.

The Group of Automorphisms

§ 6. If the elements $g_1, g_2, g_3, \ldots$ of a group G are transformed by an element γ permutable with G into $g_1', g_2', g_3', \ldots$; then $g_i g_j$ is transformed into $g_i' g_j'$ since

$$\gamma^{-1} g_i \gamma \cdot \gamma^{-1} g_j \gamma = \gamma^{-1} g_i g_j \gamma.$$

The transformation by γ exhibits G as simply isomorphic with itself, g_i' corresponding to g_i in the isomorphism. If γ_1 transforms g_i' into g_i'', $\gamma \gamma_1$ evidently transforms g_i into g_i''. Therefore to the isomorphisms of G with itself given by γ and γ_1 corresponds a definite isomorphism of G with itself given by $\gamma \gamma_1$. A simple isomorphism of G with itself is often called an *automorphism* of G. It is defined as an *inner* or *cogredient* automorphism, if the isomorphism can be obtained by transforming G by an element contained in G; if not, as an *outer* or *contragredient* automorphism.

If every possible outer automorphism of G is obtained by transforming G by $\gamma, \gamma_1, \gamma_2, \ldots$, $\Gamma \equiv \{G, \gamma, \gamma_1, \gamma_2, \ldots\}$ is a group (not necessarily finite) containing G as a normal subgroup. Those elements of Γ which transform each element of G into itself evidently form a subgroup H of Γ. If h is permutable with each element of G and a is any element of Γ, $a^{-1}ha$ is permutable with each element of G; and therefore H is normal in Γ. The greatest common subgroup of G and H is obviously the central C of G.

If the same automorphism of G is exhibited on transforming by two elements a, b of Γ, ab^{-1} transforms each element of G into itself, and is therefore in H. Let

$$\Gamma \equiv H a_1 + H a_2 + H a_3 + \ldots.$$

Then each element of $H a_i$ transforms the elements of G in the same way, while the elements of $H a_i$, $H a_j$ transform the elements of G in different ways ($i \neq j$). Let a_i' be the element of Γ/H corresponding to the elements Ha_i of Γ. Then if the elements $Ha_i.Ha_j$ transform the elements of G in the same way as the elements Ha_k, $a_i a_j = a_k$. Hence Γ/H is a perfectly definite group such that to each element of Γ/H corresponds one and only one automorphism of G. It is called the *group of automorphisms* or *group of isomorphisms* of G.

If any two elements g, g' of G transform the elements of G in the same way, $g'g^{-1}$ is in H and G, and is therefore in C. Hence (changing the notation) if
$$G \equiv Cg_1 + Cg_2 + \ldots + Cg_r,$$
$$\Gamma \equiv Hg_1 + Hg_2 + \ldots + Hg_r + H\gamma + H\gamma_1 + H\gamma_2 + \ldots$$
(where γ, γ_1, γ_2, ... are not in G). Now
$$E \equiv Hg_1 + Hg_2 + \ldots + Hg_r$$
is a normal subgroup of Γ, for $E \equiv \{H, G\}$ and H, G are normal subgroups of Γ. The automorphism of G exhibited by transforming the elements of G by an element g of Γ is inner or outer according as E does or does not contain g. Therefore the group of automorphisms Γ/H contains a normal subgroup $E/H = G/C$ corresponding to the inner automorphisms of G. This is the reason why G/C is called the 'group of inner automorphisms' of G. If
$$\Gamma \equiv Eb_1 + Eb_2 + Eb_3 \ldots,$$
the r outer automorphisms exhibited by transforming the elements of G by each element of Eb_i are said to form a *class* of outer automorphisms.

If G admits of no outer automorphisms and the central $C \equiv 1$, G is called a *complete* group.

Ex. 1. The identical element corresponds to itself in every automorphism of a group G.

Ex. 2. Those elements of G which correspond to themselves in a given automorphism of G form a subgroup.

Ex. 3. In any automorphism of G a conjugate set of elements corresponds to a conjugate set.

Ex. 4. An Abelian group may be exhibited as automorphic by making each element correspond to its inverse.

Ex. 5. A complete group is simply isomorphic with its group of automorphisms.

Ex. 6. If L is the group of automorphisms of the direct product G of two complete groups A and B, $G = L$, unless $A = B$ when G is normal and of index 2 in L.

Ex. 7. If L_1, L_2, L_3, ... are the groups of automorphisms of groups G_1, G_2, G_3, ... such that the orders of any two are prime to one another, while $\{G_1, G_2, G_3, ...\}$ is their direct product; the group of automorphisms of $\{G_1, G_2, G_3, ...\}$ is the direct product of groups simply isomorphic with $L_1, L_2, L_3, ...$.

Ex. 8. In § 6 those elements of Γ which are permutable with a given subgroup X of G form a subgroup Ξ of Γ. Those elements of Γ which transform each partition of G with respect to X into itself form a normal subgroup of Ξ.

Ex. 9. If the complete group K is a normal subgroup of a group G, the elements of G not lying in K form (with 1) a subgroup M of G; and G is the direct product of K and M.

Ex. 10. If $a, b, c, ...$ are generators of a group G satisfying certain relations, and $a', b', c', ...$ are elements of G satisfying precisely similar relations but no relations independent of these, then an automorphism of G exists in which a' corresponds to a, b' to b, c' to c, ...

Ex. 11. The group of automorphisms of a cyclic group of order p^a is a cyclic group of order $p^{a-1}(p-1)$ excluding the case $p = 2$, $a > 2$.

Ex. 12. The group of automorphisms of a cyclic group of order $2^a (a > 2)$ is Abelian of order 2^{a-1} and type $(a-2, 1)$.

Ex. 13. Find the group of automorphisms of any cyclic group.

Ex. 14. (i) If $h_i g_i$ corresponds to g_i in an automorphism of an Abelian group $G \equiv g_1 + g_2 + g_3 + ...$ (h_i in G), g_i corresponds to h_i in an isomorphism of G with a subgroup. (ii) Every Abelian group (of order > 4) is isomorphic with a subgroup in such a way that no element corresponds to its inverse.

Ex. 15. G is an Abelian group with base $[g_1, g_2, ..., g_x]$. Prove that (i) if h_i corresponds to $g_i (i = 1, 2, ..., x)$ in any automorphism of G, $[h_1, h_2, ..., h_x]$ is a base of G; (ii) if $[h_1, h_2, ..., h_x]$ is a base of G, an automorphism of G exists such that h_i corresponds to g_i; (iii) the order of the group of automorphisms of an Abelian group is equal to the number of distinct bases: apply this to the group of IX 8.

Ex. 16. (i) If an Abelian group G of order p^m and type $(1, 1, ..., 1)$ with base $[g_1, g_2, ..., g_m]$ admits of an automorphism in which $g_1^{a_1 r} g_2^{a_2 r} ... g_m^{a_{mr}}$ corresponds to g_r, $g_1^{x_1'} g_2^{x_2'} ... g_m^{x_m'}$ corresponds to $g_1^{x_1} g_2^{x_2} ... g_m^{x_m}$ in this automorphism; where $x_i' = a_{i1} x_1 + a_{i2} x_2 + ... + a_{im} x_m$ in the $GF[p]$. (ii) The group of automorphisms of G is simply isomorphic with the general homogeneous linear group of degree m in the $GF[p]$.

Ex. 17. If an element of prime order q is permutable with an Abelian group G of order p^a and type $(1, 1, ..., 1)$, a is $\geq s$, where s is the smallest integer such that $p^s \equiv 1 \pmod{q}$.

Ex. 18. If $a^p = b^p = 1$, and the commutator c of a and b is permutable with a and b, every element of $\{a, b\}$ is of the form $a^x b^y c^z$ and is of order $p (p > 2)$. Prove that $a' = a^x b^y c^z$ can correspond to a and $b' = a^r b^s c^t$ to b in some automorphism of

$\{a, b\}$ if and only if $xs - yr \not\equiv 0 \pmod{p}$. Find the order of the group and of its group of automorphisms.

Ex. 19. Find the order of the group of automorphisms of
(i) $a^3 = b^2 = (ab)^3 = 1$, (ii) $a^4 = b^3 = (ab)^2 = 1$,
(iii) $a^5 = b^3 = (ab)^2 = 1$.

§ 7. If the group H of § 6 is itself simply isomorphic with G, Γ is called the *holomorph* of G. For the proof that this holomorph always exists we refer to § 8, where we shall show how to construct a permutation-group simply isomorphic with the holomorph of any given group.

If every element permutable with G is permutable with a subgroup K of G, K is called a *characteristic* subgroup of G. In every automorphism of G each element of K corresponds to itself or some other element of K. A characteristic subgroup of G is evidently a normal subgroup of the group Γ of § 6; and conversely, each normal subgroup of Γ contained in G is a characteristic subgroup of G.

Ex. 1. Every characteristic subgroup of a group G is normal in G, but not every normal subgroup is necessarily characteristic.

Ex. 2. A simple group has no characteristic subgroup.

Ex. 3. The central and commutant of any group are characteristic.

Ex. 4. If B is the only subgroup in G of a given order, B is characteristic.

Ex. 5. Every subgroup of a cyclic group is characteristic.

Ex. 6. The subgroup generated by those elements of a group whose orders divide a given number is characteristic.

Ex. 7. An Abelian group of order $p^\alpha q^\beta r^\gamma \ldots$ (p, q, r, ... being distinct primes) has characteristic subgroups of order p^α, q^β, r^γ, ...

Ex. 8. The subgroup formed by the k-th powers of the elements of an Abelian group is characteristic.

Ex. 9. A characteristic subgroup K of an Abelian group G cannot contain an element g of maximum order in G.

Ex. 10. (i) Every characteristic subgroup of an Abelian group is contained in the subgroup formed by all the elements not of maximum order. (ii) What is the condition that an Abelian group of order p^α may contain a characteristic subgroup of index p?

Ex. 11. If a group is the direct product of characteristic subgroups, its group of automorphisms is the direct product of groups simply isomorphic with the groups of automorphisms of these subgroups.

Ex. 12. The order of the holomorph of a group G is the product of the order of G and the order of the group of automorphisms of G.

Ex. 13. The holomorph of a complete group of order n is of order n^2.

Ex. 14. The holomorph of the direct product of two simply isomorphic complete groups of order n is of order $2n^2$.

Ex. 15. The holomorph of the holomorph of a complete group of order n is of order $2n^4$.

Ex. 16. Find the order of the holomorph of a cyclic group.

Ex. 17. The general linear group Γ of degree m in the $GF[p]$ formed by substitutions of the type
$$x_i' = a_{i1}x_1 + a_{i2}x_2 + \ldots + a_{im}x_m + b_i$$
is simply isomorphic with the holomorph of an Abelian group of order p^m and type $(1, 1, \ldots, 1)$.

§ 8. If $g_1, g_2, \ldots, g_n$ are the elements of a group G of order n, we can readily construct permutation-groups on the symbols $g_1, g_2, \ldots, g_n$ simply isomorphic with the group of automorphisms and the holomorph of G.

If **a**, **b** are elements of Γ (§ 6) such that
$$\mathbf{a}^{-1}g_i\mathbf{a} = g_i', \quad \mathbf{b}^{-1}g_i'\mathbf{b} = g_i''; \quad (\mathbf{ab})^{-1}g_i(\mathbf{ab}) = g_i''.$$
Again, if σ, τ denote the permutations
$$\begin{pmatrix} g_1 & g_2 & \ldots & g_n \\ g_1' & g_2' & \ldots & g_n' \end{pmatrix}, \quad \begin{pmatrix} g_1' & g_2' & \ldots & g_n' \\ g_1'' & g_2'' & \ldots & g_n'' \end{pmatrix},$$
$\sigma\tau$ replaces g_i by g_i''. Hence the permutations $\sigma, \tau, \ldots$ corresponding to each distinct transformation of G by an element of Γ form a group L such that Γ is multiply isomorphic with L, while to each element of L corresponds one automorphism of G, and conversely. Therefore $L = \Gamma/H$ and is simply isomorphic with the group of automorphisms of G.

Consider now the group P (VI 2) simply isomorphic with G formed by the permutations $S_i \equiv \begin{pmatrix} g_1 & g_2 & \ldots & g_n \\ g_1g_i & g_2g_i & \ldots & g_ng_i \end{pmatrix}$.

Let $T \equiv \begin{pmatrix} g_1 & g_2 & \ldots & g_n \\ e_1g_1 & e_2g_2 & \ldots & e_ng_n \end{pmatrix}$ (where $e_1, e_2, \ldots, e_n$ are elements of G) be a permutation on the symbols $g_1, g_2, \ldots, g_n$ permutable with every element of P. Then TS_i replaces g_x by $e_xg_xg_i$; and S_iT replaces g_x by $e_ug_xg_i$ if $g_xg_i = g_u$. Now because $TS_i = S_iT$, $e_x = e_u$. But since g_i may be any element whatever of G, g_u may also be any element of G. Therefore $e_x = e_u$ ($u = 1, 2, \ldots, n$); and T is permutable with every element of P if and only if $e_1 = e_2 = \ldots = e_n$. Hence the only permutations on $g_1, g_2, \ldots, g_n$ permutable with every element of P are the n permutations of the type
$$S_i' \equiv \begin{pmatrix} g_1 & g_2 & \ldots & g_n \\ g_ig_1 & g_ig_2 & \ldots & g_ig_n \end{pmatrix},$$
which are readily shown (as in VI 2) to form a group P' simply isomorphic with G or P.

The permutation $v_i \equiv \begin{pmatrix} g_1 & g_2 & \cdots & g_n \\ g_ig_1g_i^{-1} & g_ig_2g_i^{-1} & \cdots & g_ig_ng_i^{-1} \end{pmatrix}$ is in L, and $v_iS_i = S_i'$. Therefore the group $K \equiv \{L, P\}$ contains P' as a subgroup. Now P and P' are normal subgroups of K,

since $$S_i\sigma = \sigma \times \begin{pmatrix} g_1 & g_2 & \cdots & g_n \\ g_1g_i' & g_2g_i' & \cdots & g_ng_i' \end{pmatrix}$$

and $$S_i'\sigma = \sigma \times \begin{pmatrix} g_1 & g_2 & \cdots & g_n \\ g_i'g_1 & g_i'g_2 & \cdots & g_i'g_n \end{pmatrix},$$

as is easily verified. Again, L and P have only identity in common; for no permutation of L displaces that one of the symbols $g_1, g_2, \ldots, g_n$ which represents the identical element of G, while each permutation of P (except identity) displaces every symbol. Similarly L and P' have only identity in common. Hence if $\sigma_1, \sigma_2, \sigma_3, \ldots$ are the permutations of L, $K \equiv \{L, P'\} \equiv \{L, P\} \equiv P\sigma_1 + P\sigma_2 + P\sigma_3 + \ldots$ and $K/P' = L$. But the elements of K permutable with every element of P are the elements of P', and $P' = P$. Hence K is the holomorph of P, and is therefore simply isomorphic with the holomorph of G.

Ex. 1. L is intransitive, K transitive.

Ex. 2. (i) K is not contained in any permutation-group on the symbols $g_1, g_2, \ldots, g_n$ which contains P normally. (ii) Every permutation on these symbols permutable with P is in K.

Ex. 3. The group of automorphisms and the holomorph of a non-cyclic Abelian group of order 4 are simply isomorphic with the symmetric group of degree 3 and the symmetric group of degree 4.

Ex. 4. (i) The group of automorphisms of $a^m = b^2 = (ab)^2 = 1$ is $c^m = d^{\phi(m)} = 1$, $cd = dc^k$; k being prime to m and such that $k^t \not\equiv 1 \pmod{m}$, $t < \phi(m)$. (ii) When $m = 3$, 4, or 6 the group and its group of automorphisms are simply isomorphic.

CHAPTER XI

PRIME-POWER GROUPS

§ 1. We shall devote this chapter to the properties of a group whose order is the power of a prime. Such a group will be called a *prime-power* group.

Every prime-power group contains normal elements other than identity.

Let G be a group of order p^a, p being prime. Then the order of every element and subgroup of G is a power of p. Let C of order ν be the central of G. Let the conjugate sets of elements in G (other than the ν sets containing only one element apiece) contain respectively $\epsilon_1, \epsilon_2, \epsilon_3, \ldots$ elements. Then $p^a = \nu + \epsilon_1 + \epsilon_2 + \epsilon_3 + \ldots$. Now by V 8 G contains a subgroup of order $p^a \div \epsilon_i$, and therefore each ϵ is a power of p. Hence ν is a power of p and is $\neq 1$; which proves the theorem.

COROLLARY. *Every group of order p^2 is Abelian.*

A group G of order p^2 can only contain elements of orders 1, p, p^2. If G contains an element of order p^2, G is cyclic and is therefore Abelian. If G contains no element of order p^2, let g be an element of order p normal in G. Let h be another element of G of order p, not contained in $\{g\}$. Then the p^2 elements $g^x h^y$ ($x, y = 1, 2, \ldots, p$) are all in G, are all permutable, and are all distinct.

For $g^r h^s \cdot g^x h^y = g^x h^y \cdot g^r h^s$ since $gh = hg$; and $g^r h^s = g^x h^y$ only when $h^{y-s} = g^{r-x}$, i.e. when $x \equiv r$ and $y \equiv s$ (mod p). Hence all the elements of G are included among the p^2 permutable elements $g^x h^y$, and therefore G is Abelian.

Ex. 1. The direct product of prime-power groups has a central $\not\equiv 1$.
Ex. 2. No prime-power group is simple unless its order is prime.
Ex. 3. No prime-power group is complete.
Ex. 4. In § 1 the order of the commutant of G is $\geq$ the greatest of the quantities $\epsilon_1, \epsilon_2, \epsilon_3, \ldots$.

Ex. 5. If a group G of order p^3 contains more than one normal subgroup of order p, G is Abelian and non-cyclic.

Ex. 6. If a group G has a commutant of index p^2, it contains no other normal subgroup of this index.

Ex. 7. The G. C. S. of all normal subgroups of index p or p^2 in any group G contains the commutant of G.

Ex. 8. A normal subgroup of a prime-power group G has elements in common with the central C of G.

Ex. 9. The commutant of the group of inner automorphisms of a prime-power group G is of lower order than the commutant of G.

Ex. 10. The central C of a group G of order p^a contains at least p commutators of G.

Ex. 11. If the commutant of a prime-power group G is of prime order, each commutator of G is normal in G.

Ex. 12. Every group G of order p^a contains (i) a normal subgroup of index p, (ii) subgroups of orders $p, p^2, ..., p^{a-1}$.

Ex. 13. No prime-power group is perfect.

Ex. 14. An element of order p in a group G of order p^a is conjugate to none of its powers except the first.

Ex. 15. If a, b are two elements of a group G of order p^a having each p conjugates in G, their commutator c is of order p and is permutable with a and b.

Ex. 16. The elements of those conjugate sets of a group G of order $p^a (p > 2)$ which contain 1 or p elements of order $\leq p^\beta$ form with identity a characteristic subgroup of G.

Ex. 17. If the central C of a group G of order p^a is of order p^x, and g corresponds in G to an element of order p in G/C, $\{C, g\}$ is Abelian of order p^{x+1} and is the central of a subgroup of index $\leq p^x$ in G.

Ex. 18. A group of order p^a whose central is of order p^x contains a subgroup of index $p^{\frac{1}{2}\beta(2x+\beta-1)}$ whose central is of order $\geq p^{x+\beta}$, if $a \geq \frac{1}{2}(2x+\beta)(\beta+1)$.

Ex. 19. A group G of order p^a whose central is of order p^x contains an Abelian subgroup of order $p^{x+\epsilon}$ if $a > \frac{1}{2}\epsilon(2x+\epsilon-1)$.

Ex. 20. A group of order p^{15} whose central is of order p^2 contains an Abelian subgroup of order p^6, and a group of order p^{16} whose central is of order p^4 contains an Abelian subgroup of order p^7.

§ 2. *In any group G of order p^a we can always find a series of subgroups of orders $p, p^2, p^3, ...$ such that each is normal in G and in all the subgroups of the series which follow it.*

Let c be any element of order p^e normal in G; then $g_1 = c^{p^{e-1}}$ is an element of order p normal in G, and $\{g_1\}$ is a normal subgroup of G of order p. Now $G/\{g_1\}$ is of order

p^{a-1} and similarly contains a normal element γ_2 of order p. Let g_2 in G correspond to γ_2 in $G/\{g_1\}$. Then $g_2{}^p$ is in $\{g_1\}$; and, if g is any element of G and γ the corresponding element of $G/\{g_1\}$, $\gamma^{-1}\gamma_2^{-1}\gamma\gamma_2 = 1$ and therefore $g^{-1}g_2^{-1}gg_2$ is in $\{g_1\}$. It follows at once that $\{g_1, g_2\}$ is a normal subgroup of G. It is of order p^2 containing the p^2 elements

$$g_1{}^{\beta_1}g_2{}^{\beta_2} \ (\beta_1, \beta_2 = 1, 2, \ldots, p)$$

which may be shown to be distinct as in the Corollary of § 1.

Let γ_3 be an element of order p normal in $G/\{g_1, g_2\}$, and let g_3 be a corresponding element of G. Then as before $g_3{}^p$ and $g^{-1}g_3^{-1}gg_3$ are in $\{g_1, g_2\}$, while $\{g_1, g_2, g_3\}$ is a normal subgroup of G containing the p^3 elements

$$g_1{}^{\beta_1}g_2{}^{\beta_2}g_3{}^{\beta_3} \ (\beta_1, \beta_2, \beta_3 = 1, 2, \ldots, p).$$

These elements are all distinct, since $g_1{}^x g_2{}^y g_3{}^z = g_1{}^r g_2{}^s g_3{}^t$ would involve $g_3{}^{z-t}$ lying in $\{g_1, g_2\}$.

We now take an element γ_4 of order p normal in $G/\{g_1, g_2, g_3\}$ and proceed as before. Finally we show that every element of G is included once and only once among the p^a elements $g_1{}^{\beta_1}g_2{}^{\beta_2}\ldots g_a{}^{\beta_a} (\beta_i = 1, 2, \ldots, p; i = 1, 2, \ldots, a)$, where for all values of i $g_i{}^p$ and $g^{-1}g_i{}^{-1}gg_i$ (i.e. the commutator of g and g_i, g being any element whatever of G) are contained in $\{g_1, g_2, \ldots, g_{i-1}\}$. Any one of the subgroups $\{g_1\}, \{g_1, g_2\}, \{g_1, g_2, g_3\}, \ldots$ of orders $p, p^2, p^3, \ldots$ is normal in all the subgroups succeeding it.

Ex. 1. If G is the direct product of prime-power groups and m is any factor of the order of G, G contains a normal subgroup whose order is m.

Ex. 2. Any normal subgroup Γ of order p^s in a group G of order p^a is contained in normal subgroups of orders p^{s+1}, p^{s+2}, $\ldots$, p^{a-1}.

Ex. 8. A group G of order n contains a normal subgroup H of index p^β. Prove that (i) G contains a normal subgroup of index p^γ, $\gamma < \beta$; (ii) any normal subgroup K of index p^γ contains a normal subgroup of index p^β.

§ 3. *Every subgroup H of order p^s in a group G of order p^a is contained normally in a subgroup of order p^{s+1}.*

Using the notation of § 2, if H does not contain g_1, $\{H, g_1\} \equiv H + Hg_1 + Hg_1{}^2 + \ldots + Hg_1{}^{p-1}$ is evidently the subgroup of order p^{s+1} required. If H contains $\{g_1, g_2, \ldots, g_i\}$ but not g_{i+1}, $\{H, g_{i+1}\} \equiv H + Hg_{i+1} + Hg_{i+1}^2 + \ldots + Hg_{i+1}^{p-1}$ is

the subgroup required. For g_{i+1}^2 is in H; and so is $g_{i+1}^{-1} h g_{i+1}$ (h being any element of H), since $h^{-1} g_{i+1}^{-1} h g_{i+1}$ is in
$$\{g_1, g_2, \ldots, g_i\}.$$

COROLLARY. *Every subgroup of index p in a group of order p^a is a normal subgroup.*

Ex. 1. Every subgroup of order p^s in G is contained in some subgroup of given order p^β where $\alpha > \beta > s$.

Ex. 2. If $K_1, K_2, K_3, \ldots$ are conjugate subgroups of G, $\{K_1, K_2, K_3, \ldots\} \not\equiv G$.

Ex. 3. If every subgroup of order p^r in G is Abelian, every subgroup of lower order is Abelian.

Ex. 4. If two subgroups H, K of index p in G are Abelian and G is non-Abelian, (i) the G.C.S. of H and K is the central C of G, (ii) the commutant and group of inner automorphisms of G are Abelian of the type $(1, 1, \ldots, 1)$.

Ex. 5. *Any* group containing two Abelian subgroups of index p is Abelian or metabelian.

Ex. 6. If the commutant of G (§ 3) is of order p, the G.C.S. D of all subgroups of index p is in the central of G.

Ex. 7. If G contains only one subgroup Γ of index p, G is cyclic.

Ex. 8. If G contains only one subgroup K of order p^s, K is cyclic.

§ 4. *If p^δ is the order of the greatest common subgroup D of the subgroups of index p in a group G of order p^a, G contains $(p^{a-\delta}-1) \div (p-1)$ such subgroups of index p.*

Let $H_1, H_2, H_3, \ldots$ be the subgroups of index p. Since they are all normal in G (§ 3), D is normal in G (V 11). Now $G/H_1, G/H_2, G/H_3, \ldots$ are of order p and are therefore Abelian. Hence $H_1, H_2, H_3, \ldots$ all contain the commutant Δ of G (X 3). Therefore D contains Δ, and G/D is Abelian.

Let g be any element whatever of G, γ_1 the corresponding element of G/H_1, and γ the corresponding element of G/D. Since $\gamma_1^p = 1$, g^p is in H_1. Similarly g^p is in $H_2, H_3, \ldots$, so that g^p is in D. Therefore $\gamma^p = 1$. Hence every element of G/D is of order 1 or p, and G/D is of the type $(1, 1, \ldots, 1)$.

It follows from IX 8 that G/D contains $(p^{a-\delta}-1) \div (p-1)$ subgroups of index p, each corresponding to one of the subgroups $H_1, H_2, H_3, \ldots$ in G. Hence G contains
$$(p^{a-\delta}-1) \div (p-1)$$
subgroups of index p.

Ex. 1. The number of subgroups of index p in a prime-power group $\equiv 1 \pmod{p}$.

Ex. 2. If Δ is the commutant of a non-cyclic group G of order p^a, G/Δ is non-cyclic.

Ex. 3. G (§ 4) contains no element of order $> p^{\beta+1}$.

Ex. 4. If E is a normal subgroup of G such that G/E is Abelian of type $(1, 1, ..., 1)$, E contains D.

Ex. 5. If P is the normal subgroup generated by the p-th powers of the elements of G, prove that (i) $G/\{\Delta, P\}$ is Abelian of type $(1, 1, ..., 1)$, (ii) $\{\Delta, P\} \equiv D$.

Ex. 6. G contains 0, 1, or $p+1$ Abelian subgroups of index p, unless G is Abelian.

Ex. 7. It is possible to choose the elements $g_1, g_2, ..., g_a$ of § 2 so that g_a may be any given element in G but not in D.

Ex. 8. *Any* group G contains (i) $(p^t-1) \div (p-1)$ normal subgroups of index p, (ii) $(p^t-1)(p^{t-1}-1) \div (p^2-1)(p-1)$ normal subgroups $K_1, K_2, K_3, ...$ of index p^2 such that G/K_1, G/K_2, G/K_3, ... are non-cyclic, (iii) pt non-normal subgroups of index p or p^2; t being zero or a positive integer.

§ 5. *The number of subgroups of order p^β in a group G of order $p^a \equiv 1 \pmod{p}$.*

The number of subgroups conjugate to any subgroup H not normal in G (including H) $\equiv 0 \pmod{p}$; for the index of the normaliser of H in G is a multiple of p. Hence the number of subgroups of order p^β not normal in $G \equiv 0 \pmod{p}$, and we must prove that the number of those normal in $G \equiv 1 \pmod{p}$.

By § 2 G contains at least one normal subgroup of order p^β. Suppose that the normal subgroups of order p^β are $B_1, B_2, ..., B_s$; and that the subgroups of order p^{a-1} are $A_1, A_2, ..., A_r$. By § 4 $r \equiv 1 \pmod{p}$, and we wish to prove $s \equiv 1 \pmod{p}$.

Let a_i be the number of subgroups B contained in A_i, and let b_j be the number of subgroups A which contain B_j. Then $b_1 + b_2 + ... + b_s = a_1 + a_2 + ... + a_r$; for each side of this equation represents the number of subgroups A when each is counted once for every subgroup B which it contains.

Now $b_j \equiv 1 \pmod{p}$. For the groups A containing B_j are the subgroups of G corresponding to the subgroups of index p in G/B_j. Hence $a_1 + a_2 + ... + a_r \equiv s \pmod{p}$.

We know that the number of normal subgroups of order p^β in a group of order $p^{\beta+1} \equiv 1 \pmod{p}$. We shall assume the same true for groups of orders $p^{\beta+2}, p^{\beta+3}, ..., p^{a-1}$, and then by induction prove it true for the group G of order p^a. By the assumption the number of normal subgroups of order p^β contained in $A_i \equiv 1 \pmod{p}$. These subgroups include a_i of the groups B together with other subgroups $C_1, C_2, \ldots, C_t$ not normal in G. Since A_i is normal in G, A_i contains every subgroup conjugate to $C_1, C_2, \ldots$ in G. Hence $t \equiv 0 \pmod{p}$ as before; and therefore $a_i \equiv 1 \pmod{p}$. It follows that $s \equiv a_1 + a_2 + \ldots + a_r \equiv r \pmod{p}$. But $r \equiv 1 \pmod{p}$, and hence $s \equiv 1 \pmod{p}$. Therefore the proof by induction holds good.

Ex. 1. The total number of subgroups of G (including 1 and G) $\equiv 1 + a \pmod{p}$.

Ex. 2. A subgroup H of order $p^{\beta+1}$ normal in G contains a subgroup of order p^β normal in G.

Ex. 3. The number of Abelian subgroups of order $p^{\beta+1}$ in G which contain a given Abelian subgroup K of order p^β is zero or $\equiv 1 \pmod{p}$.

Ex. 4. The number of subgroups of index p^λ in *any* group $G \equiv 1$ or $\equiv 0 \pmod{p}$ according as G does or does not contain a normal subgroup of this index.

§ 6. *If a group G of order p^a contains only one subgroup H of order p^s, G is cyclic unless $p = 2$, $s = 1$, $a > 2$.*

(1) First suppose $s = a - 1$. If g is any element of G not in H, g is of order p^a. For otherwise $\{g\}$ being contained in some subgroup of order p^{a-1} would be contained in H. Hence if $s = a - 1$, $G \equiv \{g\}$ and is cyclic.

(2) If all the subgroups $A, B, C, \ldots$ of index p in a group L of order p^λ are cyclic, L contains a single subgroup of index p^2.

For let X be the greatest common subgroup of $A, B, C, \ldots$, and let a be an element of order $p^{\lambda-1}$ in L. Then a^p is in X (§ 4), and hence $X \equiv \{a^p\}$ is a cyclic subgroup of index p^2 in L. If Y is any subgroup of index p^2, Y is contained in one of the subgroups $A, B, C, \ldots$ (§ 3) and therefore coincides with X; since a cyclic group of order $p^{\lambda-1}$ contains only one subgroup of order $p^{\lambda-2}$ (see also XI 3_4).

(3) Suppose that G contains a single subgroup of order p^s but more than one subgroup of order p^{s+1}.

G contains a non-cyclic subgroup K of order p^{s+2} by (2). Let a be any element of K not in H. Then as in (1) a must be of order p^{s+1}, for otherwise $\{a\}$ would be in H. Moreover, the group $\{a^p\} \equiv H$ since it is of order p^s. Similarly, if b is any element of K not in $\{a\}$, b is of order p^{s+1} and $\{b^p\} \equiv H$. Suppose $a^p = b^{up}$, where u is prime to p, since a and b are of the same order. Now $c = a^{-1}b^{-1}ab$ is in $\{a\}$ and $\{b\}$ by § 4 and is therefore in H. Hence c is permutable with a and b. Therefore by I 4 $c^p = a^{-p}b^{-1}a^p b = 1$ (since $a^p = b^{up}$) and $(b^{-u}a)^p = b^{-up}a^p c^{\frac{1}{2}up(1-p)} = c^{\frac{1}{2}up(1-p)}$.

If $c = 1$ (K is Abelian), or if $c \neq 1$ but p is odd, $(b^{-u}a)^p = 1$. Now $b^{-u}a$ is not in H, since a is not in $\{b\}$. Hence K contains a subgroup $\{b^{-u}a\}$ of order p not contained in H. This is impossible, since every subgroup of order $\leq p^s$ is contained in H.

Similarly if $c \neq 1$, $p = 2$, $(b^{-u}a)^4 = b^{-4u}a^4 c^{-6u} = 1$. Hence K contains a subgroup of order 4 not contained in H, which is impossible if $s > 1$.

§ 7. *There is one and only one abstract non-Abelian group of order p^a containing an element of order p^{a-1}, if $p > 2$ and $a > 2$.*

Let a be an element of order p^{a-1} in a group G of order p^a. Now by § 6 G contains an element g of order p not contained in $\{a\}$. Since $\{a\}$ is normal in the non-Abelian group $G \equiv \{a, g\}$ by § 3, $g^{-1}ag = a^k$, where k is an integer such that $p^{a-1} > k > 1$; and then $g^{-p}ag^p = a^{k^p}$ (I 3). But $g^{-p}ag^p = a$, and hence $k^p \equiv 1$ (mod p^{a-1}).

Now from $k^p \equiv 1$ (mod p) and $k^p \equiv k$ (mod p) [Fermat's theorem] we deduce $k \equiv 1$ (mod p). Let $k = 1 + vp^t$, where t is an integer such that $a - 1 > t > 0$ and v is a positive integer prime to p. Then
$$k^p - 1 \equiv [1 + vp^t]^p - 1 \equiv p^{t+1}[v + p^t \cdot \tfrac{1}{2}v^2(p-1)$$
$$+ \text{a multiple of } p] \equiv 0 \pmod{p^{a-1}}.$$
This is only possible if $t = a - 2$; since $\tfrac{1}{2}v^2(p-1)$ is integral.

Now $g^{-x}ag^x = a^{k^x}$; and $k^x = (1 + vp^{a-2})^x = 1 + vxp^{a-2} + $ a multiple of p^{a-1}, since $a > 2$. Hence, choosing x so that $vx \equiv 1$ (mod p), we have $g^{-x}ag^x = a^{1+p^{a-2}}$. Putting $g^x = b$ we obtain the unique group $G \equiv \{a, b\}$, where
$$a^{p^{a-1}} = b^p = 1, \quad ab = ba^{1+p^{a-2}}.$$

Since $b^{-1}a^p b = a^{p+p^{a-1}} = a^p$, b is permutable with a^p. Therefore a and b are permutable with $c = a^{-1}b^{-1}ab = a^{p^{a-2}}$ and $c^p = a^{-p}b^{-1}a^p b = 1$. Hence by I4 $(b^y a)^t = b^{yt}a^t c^{\frac{1}{2}t(t-1)} = a^t$, if t is a multiple of p. Therefore $b^y a$ is of order p^{a-1}. Hence G contains p cyclic subgroups $\{b^y a\}$ ($y = 0, 1, 2, ..., p-1$) and one Abelian non-cyclic subgroup $\{a^p, b\}$ of index p. Since the greatest common subgroup of the subgroups of index p in G is $\{a^p\}$ by § 6 (2), G contains no subgroup of index p other than these (§ 4). Now every subgroup of G of order p^{a-2} is contained in some subgroup of order p^{a-1}, while every subgroup of $\{b^y a\}$ is contained in $\{a^p\}$ and therefore in $\{a^p, b\}$. But $\{a^p, b\}$ is of order p^{a-1} and contains an element a^p of order p^{a-2}. Hence G contains p cyclic subgroups $\{b^y a^p\}$ and one non-cyclic Abelian subgroup $\{a^{p^2}, b\}$ of index p^2. Repetition of this process shows at once that G contains exactly p cyclic subgroups $\{b^y a^{p^{\lambda-1}}\}$ and one Abelian subgroup $\{a^{p^\lambda}, b\}$ (non-cyclic if $\lambda \neq a-1$) of index p^λ.

Ex. 1. The central of G is $\{a^p\}$, and the commutant is $\{a^{p^{a-2}}\}$.
Ex. 2. Find the conjugate sets of elements in G.
Ex. 3. Every subgroup of G is Abelian.
Ex. 4. G is metabelian and conformal with an Abelian group of order p^a and type $(a-1, 1)$.
Ex. 5. Every non-cyclic subgroup of G is characteristic.
Ex. 6. G contains only p non-normal subgroups.
Ex. 7. Every factor-group of G is Abelian.
Ex. 8. Any two subgroups of G are permutable.
Ex. 9. Find the order of the group of automorphisms of G.
Ex. 10. Every non-cyclic group of order p^a contains at least one normal non-cyclic subgroup of order $p^s (s > 1)$.
Ex. 11. Find every type of group of order $p^3 (p > 2)$.

§ 8. *There are four and only four abstract non-Abelian groups of order 2^a containing an element of order 2^{a-1}, if $a > 3$.*

(1) Let a be an element of order 2^{a-1} in a non-Abelian group G of order 2^a. First suppose that G contains an element b of order 2 not contained in $\{a\}$.

Since $\{a\}$ is normal in G, $b^{-1}ab = a^k (2^{a-1} > k > 1)$; and then $b^{-2}ab^2 = a^{k^2}$, so that $k^2 \equiv 1 \pmod{2^{a-1}}$. Now k is odd; suppose $k = 1 + v2^t$, where t is an integer such that $a-1 > t > 0$ and v is an odd positive integer. Then

$k^2 - 1 \equiv (1 + v2^t)^2 - 1 \equiv 2^{t+1}(v + v^2 2^{t-1}) \equiv 0 \pmod{2^{a-1}}$.

This is only possible if

(i) $t = a-2$, (ii) $t = 1$ and $v(1+v) \equiv 0 \pmod{2^{a-3}}$.

In case (i) we have $k = 1 + v2^{a-2}$; hence $v = 1$ and $k = 1 + 2^{a-2}$, since $2^{a-1} > k$. In case (ii) we may put $v = -1 + l2^{a-3}$ and get $k = -1 + l2^{a-2}$. Since $2^{a-1} > k$, we have $l = 1$ or 2 and $k = 2^{a-2} - 1$ or $2^{a-1} - 1$. We obtain thus three types of non-Abelian group:—

(I) $a^{2^{a-1}} = b^2 = 1$, $bab = a^{1+2^{a-2}}$;

(II) $a^{2^{a-1}} = b^2 = 1$, $a^{2^{a-2}} = (ab)^2$;

(III) $a^{2^{a-1}} = b^2 = (ab)^2 = 1$.

Type (III) is a 'dihedral' group.

(2) Now suppose G does not contain an element of order 2 not contained in $\{a\}$. Let b be any other element of G; so that $G \equiv \{a\} + \{a\}b$ and $b^{-1}ab = a^k$, $b^2 = a^r$. Then $r \not\equiv 0 \pmod{2^{a-1}}$, since $b^2 \neq 1$: we may suppose $2^{a-1} > r > 0$. Since $a^r = b^2 = b^{-1}b^2b = b^{-1}a^rb = a^{rk}$, $r(k-1) \equiv 0 \pmod{2^{a-1}}$. Now as in (1) there are three cases to consider, since
$$a = b^{-2}ab^2 = a^{k^2}.$$

(i) $k = 1 + 2^{a-2}$. Then $r \equiv 0 \pmod{2}$; let $r = 2h$. Choose x so that $h + x(1 + 2^{a-3}) \equiv 0 \pmod{2^{a-2}}$. Then
$$(ba^x)^2 = b^2 . b^{-1}a^xb . a^x = a^{r+x(k+1)} = 1;$$
which is impossible since ba^x is not in $\{a\}$.

(ii) $k = -1 + 2^{a-2}$. Then $r \equiv 0 \pmod{2^{a-2}}$, and therefore $r = 2^{a-2}$ since $2^{a-1} > r$. Hence $(ba)^2 = a^{r+k+1} = 1$; which is impossible.

(iii) $k = -1 + 2^{a-1}$. Then as in (ii) $r = 2^{a-2}$. We have then the type—

(IV) $a^{2^{a-1}} = 1$, $a^{2^{a-2}} = (ab)^2 = b^2$.

Ex. If $a = 3$, there are only two distinct non-Abelian groups of order 2^a, i.e. $a^4 = b^2 = (ab)^2 = 1$ and $a^4 = 1$, $a^2 = (ab)^2 = b^2$.

§ **9.** *A group G of order 2^a containing only one subgroup of order 2 is cyclic or dicyclic.*

A dicyclic group is defined by the relations $a^{2m} = 1$, $a^m = (ab)^2 = b^2$. Every element of this group not in $\{a\}$ is evidently of the form ba^x, while $\{a\}$ is a normal subgroup. Since $(ba^x)^2 = b^2 . b^{-1}a^xb . a^x = b^2$, a^m is the square of every element not in $\{a\}$.

(1) The theorem is obvious if $a = 2$; suppose $a = 3$. If G is non-cyclic, G contains two elements a and b of order 4 such that $\{a^2\} = \{b^2\}$ and therefore $a^2 = b^2$. Since $\{a\}$ is normal in G, $b^{-1}ab = a$ or a^3. Now $b^{-1}ab \neq a$, i.e. G is not Abelian and non-cyclic; for then ab^{-1} would be an element of order 2 not contained in $\{a\}$. Hence $(ab)^2 = b^2$, and G is dicyclic.

(2) Now assume in the general case that every group of order 2^β ($\beta < a$) containing only one subgroup of order 2 is

cyclic or dicyclic. We shall show that on this assumption G is cyclic or dicyclic. By § 8 (2) it is sufficient to prove that G contains an element of order 2^{a-1}. Then induction may be applied to prove the theorem true universally.

Now if G is non-cyclic, some subgroup of order 2^β in G is non-cyclic ($\beta > 2$), for otherwise by § 6 (2) G would contain only one subgroup of order $2^{\beta-1}$. Hence G contains a dicyclic subgroup of order 2^β and is non-Abelian.

(i) First take $a = 4$. The subgroups of order 4 in G are all cyclic; for otherwise G would contain more than one subgroup of order 2. Let a be an element generating a normal subgroup $\{a\}$ of order 4, and let b be any element of order 4 in G but not in $\{a\}$. Then $H \equiv \{a, b\}$ is the dicyclic group $a^4 = 1$, $a^2 = (ab)^2 = b^2$ of index 2 in G.

(ii) Now take $a > 4$. Let a subgroup H of index 2 in G be dicyclic, so that $H \equiv \{a, b\}$ where $a^{2^{a-2}} = 1$, $a^{2^{a-3}} = (ab)^2 = b^2$. Since $\{a\}$ is the only cyclic subgroup of order 2^{a-2} in H and H is normal in G, $\{a\}$ is normal in G.

In cases (i) and (ii) let g be an element of G not in H, so that $G \equiv H + Hg$ and g^2 is in H. Let $g^{-1}ag = a^k$. Now g^2 is not of the form ba^x. For otherwise

$$a^{k^2} = g^{-2}ag^2 = a^{-x}b^{-1}aba^x = a^{-1},$$

and therefore $k^2 + 1 \equiv 0 \pmod{2^{a-2}}$. But this is impossible when $a > 3$; for as in § 8 (1) $k^2 - 1 \equiv 0 \pmod{2^{a-2}}$. Hence g^2 is in $\{a\}$, and as in § 8 (2) $k \equiv \pm 1$ or $\pm 1 + 2^{a-3} \pmod{2^{a-2}}$.

If $k = +1 + 2^{a-3}$ we show as in § 8 (2) that $\{a, g\}$ contains an element of order 2 not in $\{a\}$, which is impossible.

Similarly if
$$k = -1 + 2^{a-3}, (bg)^{-1}a(bg) = g^{-1}a^{-1}g = a^{1-2^{a-3}} = a^{1+2^{a-3}};$$
and $\{a, bg\}$ contains an element of order 2 not in $\{a\}$.

If $k = 1$, $\{a, g\}$ is of order 2^{a-1} and is Abelian. This is impossible unless $\{a, g\}$ is cyclic, when G contains an element of order 2^{a-1}.

If $k = -1$, $(bg)^{-1}a(bg) = a$; and therefore $\{a, bg\}$ is cyclic of order 2^{a-1}.

CHAPTER XII

SYLOW'S THEOREM

§ 1. SYLOW's theorem is of fundamental importance in the theory of finite groups. It may be enunciated as follows:—

If p^a is the highest power of a prime p which divides the order n of a group G, G contains $kp+1$ subgroups of order p^a (k being integral), and these form a conjugate set of subgroups. If $p^a m$ is the order of the normaliser in G of any one of the subgroups of order p^a, $n = p^a m (kp+1)$.

(1) G contains at least one subgroup of order p^a.

When $n' = 2, 3, 4, \ldots$ it may be easily verified that a group of order n' contains a subgroup of order $p^{a'}$ if this is the highest power of p which divides n'. We assume the statement true for all values of $n' < n$, and use induction to prove it true for the group G.

Let ν be the order of the central C of G, and let the elements of G not contained in C be divided up into conjugate sets containing respectively $\epsilon_1, \epsilon_2, \epsilon_3, \ldots$ elements.

(i) Suppose one of the quantities $\epsilon_1, \epsilon_2, \epsilon_3, \ldots$ (ϵ_i say) not divisible by p. By V 8 G contains a subgroup Γ of order $n \div \epsilon_i$. Now $n \div \epsilon_i$ is $< n$, and is divisible by p^a but not by p^{a+1}. Hence by our assumption Γ contains a subgroup of order p^a, and therefore so does G.

(ii) Suppose each of the quantities $\epsilon_1, \epsilon_2, \epsilon_3, \ldots$ is divisible by p; then ν is divisible by p since $n = \nu + \epsilon_1 + \epsilon_2 + \epsilon_3 + \ldots$. Hence C contains an element c of order p (V 19), and $G/\{c\}$ being of order $n \div p$ contains by our assumption a subgroup of order p^{a-1}. Corresponding to this subgroup of $G/\{c\}$ we have a subgroup of order p^a in G.

(2) The subgroups of order p^a are $(kp+1)$ in number, and are all conjugate.

This is obvious if G contains a single subgroup H of order p^a; then $k = 0$, and H is a normal subgroup of G. Now suppose that G contains at least two subgroups H, H_1 of order p^a. Let D of order p^β be the greatest common subgroup of H and H_1, and let $H \equiv Dh_1 + Dh_2 + Dh_3 + \ldots (h_1 = 1)$. Form the

XII 1] SYLOW SUBGROUPS 153

$p^{\alpha-\beta}$ groups $H_1 \equiv h_1^{-1} H_1 h_1$, $H_2 \equiv h_2^{-1} H_1 h_2$, $H_3 \equiv h_3^{-1} H_1 h_3$, ... all conjugate to H_1. Then:—

(i) H_1, H_2, H_3, ... are all distinct.

Let Γ_1 be the normaliser of H_1 in G. The order of $h_i h_j^{-1}$ is a power of p, since H is of order p^α. If $h_i h_j^{-1}$ were permutable with H_1, it would be contained in Γ_1, and the corresponding element of Γ_1/H_1 would be a power of p. This is impossible; for the order of Γ_1/H_1 is not divisible by p. Hence $h_i h_j^{-1} H_1 \not\equiv H_1 h_i h_j^{-1}$, i.e. $h_i^{-1} H_1 h_i \not\equiv h_j^{-1} H_1 h_j$ or $H_i \not\equiv H_j$.

(ii) Every element of the partition Dh_i transforms H_1 into H_i. For if d is any element of D,

$$(dh_i)^{-1} H_1 (dh_i) \equiv h_i^{-1} (d^{-1} H_1 d) h_i \equiv h_i^{-1} H_1 h_i \equiv H_i.$$

Hence on transforming H_1 by all the elements of H we get $p^{\alpha-\beta}$ and only $p^{\alpha-\beta}$ distinct subgroups conjugate to H_1 (including H_1).

Let K_1 be a subgroup of G conjugate to H_1 not included among these $p^{\alpha-\beta}$ subgroups (if such exists); and let E, the greatest common subgroup of H and K_1 be of order p^γ. Then by splitting H up into the partitions $Ek_1 + Ek_2 + Ek_3 + ...$ and proceeding as before we get $p^{\alpha-\gamma}$ more subgroups of G conjugate to H_1. These are distinct from H_1, H_2, H_3, ... ; for since $K_1 \not\equiv (h_i k_j^{-1})^{-1} H_1 (h_i k_j^{-1})$, $k_j^{-1} K_1 k_j \not\equiv h_i^{-1} H_1 h_i$.

This process may be continued till all the subgroups conjugate to H_1 are exhausted.

We have shown that H_1 is not normal in G. If we had taken H as one of the subgroups conjugate to H_1, we should have deduced the fact that G contains $p^{\alpha-\beta} + p^{\alpha-\gamma} + ...$ subgroups conjugate to H_1 including H_1 but not H; i.e. that the total number of subgroups conjugate to H_1 and including H and H_1 is $1 + p^{\alpha-\beta} + p^{\alpha-\gamma} + ...$ If, however, it had been possible to take H as a subgroup of order p^α not conjugate to H_1, we should have deduced that the total number of subgroups conjugate to and including H_1 is $p^{\alpha-\beta} + p^{\alpha-\gamma} + ...$ These two statements are inconsistent, and we conclude that H cannot be a subgroup not conjugate to H_1. Hence all the subgroups of order p^α are conjugate, and they are

$$1 + p^{\alpha-\beta} + p^{\alpha-\gamma} + ... = kp + 1$$

in number.

(3) $n = p^\alpha m (kp + 1)$.

For the index of Γ_1 in G = the number of subgroups conjugate to $H_1 = kp + 1$.

The $kp+1$ subgroups of order p^α are known as *Sylow subgroups* of G.

COROLLARY I. *If p^r is a power of a prime p which divides the order of a group G, G contains a subgroup of order p^r.*

For each Sylow subgroup of order p^a in G contains a subgroup of order p^r.

COROLLARY II. *Every subgroup of order p^r in G is contained in a subgroup of order p^a.*

Take H, H_1 as subgroups of orders p^r, p^a respectively; and as in the proof of § 1 obtain all subgroups conjugate to H_1, $p^{r-\beta} + p^{r-\gamma} + \ldots$ in number. Since the number of subgroups conjugate to H_1 is $kp + 1$, one of the quantities $\beta, \gamma, \ldots = r$. Hence the greatest common subgroup of H and some subgroup of order p^a is of order p^r; i.e. H is contained in some subgroup of order p^a.

COROLLARY III. *A group G containing $kp+1$ Sylow subgroups of order p^a is isomorphic with a transitive permutation-group of degree $kp+1$.*

This is a particular case of the corollary of VI 3, since the Sylow subgroups form a conjugate set.

COROLLARY IV. *If every Sylow subgroup of a group G is normal in G, G is the direct product of these Sylow subgroups.*

Let G_1, G_2, G_3, ... be the Sylow subgroups of orders $p_1^{a_1}$, $p_2^{a_2}$, $p_3^{a_3}$, ... respectively. Let g_i, g_j be elements of G_i, G_j. Then $c = g_i^{-1} g_j^{-1} g_i g_j$ is in G_i since $g_j^{-1} g_i g_j$ is in G_i, and is in G_j since $g_i^{-1} g_j^{-1} g_i$ is in G_j. Hence the order of c divides the orders of G_i and G_j, and therefore $c = 1$; i.e. $g_i g_j = g_j g_i$. Moreover, G_i and G_j have only identity in common since their orders are relatively prime. Hence $\{G_i, G_j\}$ is the direct product of G_i and G_j and is of order $p_i^{a_i} p_j^{a_j}$. Similarly we show that every element of $\{G_i, G_j\}$ is permutable with every element of G_k, and that G_k and $\{G_i, G_j\}$ have only identity in common. Hence $\{G_i, G_j, G_k\}$ is the direct product of G_k and $\{G_i, G_j\}$ and is of order $p_i^{a_i} p_j^{a_j} p_k^{a_k}$. Continuing this process we show that G is the direct product of G_x and $\{G_1, G_2, \ldots, G_{x-1}, G_{x+1}, \ldots\}$ for all values of x, and hence G is the direct product of $G_1, G_2, G_3, \ldots$.

In particular we notice that every Abelian group is the direct product of its Sylow subgroups.

Ex. 1. Two Sylow subgroups are conjugate in any subgroup K of G containing both.

Ex. 2. A normal subgroup of order p^β in G is contained in every Sylow subgroup of order p^α.

Ex. 3. The subgroup of G generated by the elements of the Sylow subgroups of order p^α is characteristic.

Ex. 4. (i) The normalisers $\Gamma_1, \Gamma_2, \Gamma_3, \ldots$ of $H_1, H_2, H_3, \ldots$ in § 1 are all distinct; (ii) they form a conjugate set; (iii) each is its own normaliser in G; (iv) every subgroup of Γ_i whose order is a power of p is in H_i.

Ex. 5. Each subgroup of order p^r in G is contained in $lp+1$ Sylow subgroups of order p^α.

Ex. 6. If $k_\beta p^{\alpha-\beta}$ is the number of subgroups conjugate to H and having with H a G.C.S. of order p^β, the total number of subgroups of order p^α is $k_1 p^{\alpha-1} + k_2 p^{\alpha-2} + \ldots + 1$.

Ex. 7. If a group is the direct product of its Sylow subgroups, so is every subgroup.

Ex. 8. The number of subgroups of order $p^x q^y r^z \ldots$ ($p, q, r, \ldots$ being distinct primes) in a group which is the direct product of its Sylow subgroups $=$ the product of the number of subgroups of orders $p^x, q^y, r^z, \ldots$.

Ex. 9. Find the number of subgroups (i) of order 84 in an Abelian group of the type (42, 6, 2), (ii) of order p^2qr in an Abelian group of the type ($p^2q^2r^2, p^2qr, p^2q, pq, p, p$).

Ex. 10. If the commutator of any two elements of a group G is permutable with both elements, G is the direct product of its Sylow subgroups.

Ex. 11. G is a group of order $p_1^\alpha p_2^\beta p_3^\gamma \ldots$ and $G_1, G_2, G_3, \ldots$ are Sylow subgroups of orders $p_1^\alpha, p_2^\beta, p_3^\gamma, \ldots$ respectively. If the commutant Δ of G is of order p_1^λ, show that (i) $G_2, G_3, \ldots$ are Abelian; (ii) $\{\Delta, G_i\}$ is the direct product of Δ and G_i provided $i > 1$ and $p_1^\epsilon \not\equiv 1 \pmod{p_i}$, $\epsilon \leq \lambda$.

Ex. 12. (i) If a group G contains cyclic Sylow subgroups of even order, G contains a normal subgroup of index 2. (ii) If the order of a group is divisible by 2 but not by 4, the elements of odd order form a subgroup of index 2.

Ex. 13. A group of order $p^\alpha q^\beta$ (p and q prime) is decomposable.

Ex. 14. Use the method of § 1 to prove that every subgroup of index p in a group G of order p^α is normal.

Ex. 15. (i) If $p^\alpha s$ is the degree of a transitive permutation-group G of order $p^\alpha st$ (s and t being prime to p), a Sylow subgroup H of order p^α has s transitive sets each containing p^α symbols. (ii) If $s = 1$, G is decomposable and H transitive.

Ex. 16. Those elements of a group G of order n whose orders divide a factor e of n generate a group L whose order λ is a multiple of e.

Ex. 17. If two conjugate subgroups E and F of G are both normal in a Sylow subgroup H, they are conjugate in the normaliser Γ of H.

Ex. 18. If $p^a e$ is the order of a group G, where $e \not\equiv 0$ and $\not\equiv 1$ (mod p), G contains a normal subgroup of order p^a.

Ex. 19. Show that the only possible types of abstract group of order pq, p and q being primes such that $p > q$, are (1) a cyclic group; (2) the group $a^p = b^q = 1$, $ab = ba^\kappa$; where κ is a positive integer $< p$ such that $\kappa^q \equiv 1 \pmod{p}$, but $\kappa^e \not\equiv 1 \pmod{p}$ if $e < q$.*

Ex. 20. Find all possible groups of orders $2p$, 35, 39, 55, 57, 133, 185, 889.

Ex. 21. Show that a group of order 825 contains normal subgroups of orders 25 and 11, but not necessarily one of order 3.

Ex. 22. Show that there is no simple group of order 200, 204, 260, 330, 364, 2228, 2540, 3042, 9075.

Ex. 23. Show that a group of order 1001, 3325, 6125 is the direct product of its Sylow subgroups; and find every group of this order.

Ex. 24. Show that there is no simple group of order 520, 80, 330, 495, 546.

Ex. 25. Show that there is no simple group of order 616, 56, 351.

Ex. 26. There is no simple group of order 450, 12, 80, 150, 300, 12375.

Ex. 27. There is no simple group of order 90 or 306.

Ex. 28. Find every abstract group of order < 16.

Ex. 29. Find the Sylow subgroups of (i) $a^3 = b^2 = (ab)^3 = 1$, (ii) $a^{49} = b^7 = c^3 = 1$, $ab = ba^3$, $bc = cb^2$, $ac = ca$.

Ex. 30. Find the Sylow subgroups of the alternating group of degree 4.

Ex. 31. There is a homogeneous linear group of order $p^{\frac{1}{2}m(m-1)r}$ and degree m with coefficients in the $GF[p^r]$. No one of its substitutions except identity can be transformed into a multiplication.

Ex. 32. The normaliser of a Sylow subgroup of order 3 in the point-group Ω is d_3.

§ 2. *If the order n of a group G is divisible by p^r, G contains $lp + 1$ subgroups of order p^r (l integral).*

Let p^a be the highest power of p which divides n; then G contains a subgroup H of order p^a by § 1. The theorem is true if $r = a$, suppose then $r < a$. Now H contains $xp + 1$ subgroups of order p^r, x being integral (XI 5); it is then only

---

* κ is called a 'primitive root of the congruence $x^q \equiv 1 \pmod{p}$'. It is readily shown that such a root exists only if q is a factor of $p-1$, and that the roots of the congruence are $\kappa, \kappa^2, \kappa^3, \ldots, \kappa^q$. If we replace κ by another primitive root κ^i in the relations $a^p = b^q = 1$, $ab = ba^\kappa$, we only obtain group (2) in another form; for since $ab^i = b^i a^{\kappa i}$ the new relations are obtained from the old by writing b for b^i.

necessary to prove that G contains yp subgroups of order p^r besides these.

Let H_1 be a subgroup of order p^r not contained in H (if such exists). If a, b are two elements of H permutable with H_1, ab is also permutable with H_1. Hence those elements of H which are permutable with H_1 form a subgroup F of H.

Let p^β be the order of F, and let p^κ be the order of the greatest common subgroup of F and H_1. Since every element of F is permutable with H_1, F and H_1 are evidently permutable groups. Hence $\{F, H_1\}$ is of order $p^{r+\beta-\kappa}$ (V 13). But $\{F, H_1\}$ is a subgroup of G, and therefore $r+\beta-\kappa \leq \alpha$. Since $\kappa < r$, $\beta < \alpha$.

Now let $H \equiv Fh_1 + Fh_2 + Fh_3 + \ldots$, and let $h_i^{-1} H_1 h_i = H_i$. Then just as in § 1 we see that on transforming H_1 by the elements of H we get $p^{\alpha-\beta}$ and only $p^{\alpha-\beta}$ distinct subgroups of order p^r not contained in H. Taking now any other subgroup K_1 of order p^r not contained in H, we derive $p^{\alpha-\gamma}$ ($\gamma < \alpha$) more subgroups of order p^r not contained in H. Repeating the process we obtain $p^{\alpha-\beta} + p^{\alpha-\gamma} + \ldots = yp$ subgroups of G not contained in H.

Ex. The subgroups of order p^r do not necessarily form a conjugate set.

CHAPTER XIII

SERIES OF GROUPS

§ 1. WE shall discuss in this chapter the properties of various series of groups which may be derived from a given group G; namely, the composition-series, chief-series, series of derived groups, and series of adjoined groups.

THE COMPOSITION-SERIES

§ 2. If G_1 is a normal subgroup of G not contained in any other normal subgroup (other than G itself), G_1 is called a *maximum* normal subgroup of G. This does not imply that there is no subgroup normal in G of greater order than G_1; only that if such a subgroup exists, it does not contain G_1. Let G_2 be a maximum normal subgroup of G_1, G_3 of G_2, G_4 of G_3, &c. Then the series $G, G_1, G_2, G_3, \ldots$ is called a *composition-series* of G. It should be noticed (i) that G may have more than one distinct composition-series, (ii) that every composition-series terminates with the identical group, (iii) that G_i, though normal in G_{i-1}, is not necessarily normal in G_{i-2}.

It will be proved in § 3 that, whatever composition-series of G is taken, the groups $G/G_1, G_1/G_2, G_2/G_3, \ldots$ are always the same (considered as abstract groups) except as regards the sequence in which they occur. They are known as *composition-factor-groups* of G, and their orders are called *composition-factors* of G. These groups are all simple; for to a normal subgroup of G_i/G_{i+1} would correspond a normal subgroup of G_i containing G_{i+1}; and this does not exist. Conversely, if G_1 is a normal subgroup of G, G_2 of G_1, G_3 of $G_2, \ldots$, and $G/G_1, G_1/G_2, G_2/G_3, \ldots$ are all simple; $G, G_1, G_2, G_3, \ldots$ is a composition-series of G.

Ex. 1. For example, $G, O, H, \{b\}, 1$ is a composition-series for the group G of $V 4_1$. O is normal in G, H in O (but not in G), $\{b\}$ in H. The groups $G/O, O/H, H/\{b\}, \{b\}$ are simple, being all of order 2.

Ex. 2. $G_i, G_{i+1}, G_{i+2}, \ldots$ is a composition-series of G_i.

§ **3.** *The composition-factor-groups of any two composition-series of a group G are identical except as regards the sequence in which they occur.*

(1) Let $G, G_1, \ldots, G_i, G_{i+1}, \ldots$ and $G, G_1, \ldots, G_i, F_{i+1}, \ldots$ be two composition-series of G. Let D be the greatest common subgroup of G_{i+1} and F_{i+1}; then D and $\{G_{i+1}, F_{i+1}\}$ are normal in G_i (V 11). Since $\{G_{i+1}, F_{i+1}\}$ is normal in G_i and contains G_{i+1}, $G_i \equiv \{G_{i+1}, F_{i+1}\}$.

Let $G_{i+1} \equiv Dg_1 + Dg_2 + Dg_3 + \ldots$ Since F_{i+1} is normal in $\{G_{i+1}, F_{i+1}\}$, all the elements of $G_i \equiv \{G_{i+1}, F_{i+1}\}$ are included among the elements $F_{i+1} G_{i+1}$, i.e. among $F_{i+1} Dg_1 + F_{i+1} Dg_2 + F_{i+1} Dg_3 + \ldots$, i.e. among $F_{i+1} g_1 + F_{i+1} g_2 + F_{i+1} g_3 + \ldots$. Moreover, $F_{i+1} g_t$ and $F_{i+1} g_s$ have no element in common ($t \neq s$); for otherwise $g_t g_s^{-1}$ would be contained in both G_{i+1} and F_{i+1}, and therefore in D. Hence $G_i \equiv F_{i+1} g_1 + F_{i+1} g_2 + F_{i+1} g_3 + \ldots$ (see V 13).

It follows at once that $G_i/F_{i+1} = G_{i+1}/D$. Similarly $G_i/G_{i+1} = F_{i+1}/D$.

(2) D is a maximum normal subgroup of G_{i+1} and F_{i+1}.

For since F_{i+1} is a maximum normal subgroup of G_i, G_i/F_{i+1} is simple. Hence G_{i+1}/D is simple; and therefore D is a maximum normal subgroup of G_{i+1}, and similarly of F_{i+1}.

(3) By (1) and (2) the two composition-series $G, G_1, \ldots, G_r, G_{r+1}, G_{r+2}, \ldots$ and $G, G_1, \ldots, G_r, F_{r+1}, F_{r+2}, \ldots$ have the same composition-factor-groups if G_{r+1} and F_{r+1} have only identity in common so that $G_{r+2} \equiv F_{r+2} \equiv 1$. We shall show that they have the same factor-groups when $r = i$, on the assumption that they have the same factor-groups when $r < i$. Then the required theorem follows at once by induction.

Let two composition-series of G be

(i) $G, G_1, \ldots, G_i, G_{i+1}, G_{i+2}, G_{i+3}, \ldots$

and (ii) $G, G_1, \ldots, G_i, F_{i+1}, F_{i+2}, F_{i+3}, \ldots$.

Let D be the greatest common subgroup of G_{i+1} and F_{i+1}; then

(iii) $G, G_1, \ldots, G_i, G_{i+1}, D, D_1, D_2, \ldots$

and (iv) $G, G_1, \ldots, G_i, F_{i+1}, D, D_1, D_2, \ldots$

are also composition-series of G by (2), if $D, D_1, D_2, \ldots$ is part of a composition-series of G.

Now by our assumption the two composition-series (i) and (iii) have the same factor-groups, and the two series (ii) and (iv) have the same factor-groups. But since $G_i/F_{i+1} = G_{i+1}/D$ and $G_i/G_{i+1} = F_{i+1}/D$ the two series (iii) and (iv) have the same factor-groups (two factor-groups being interchanged). Hence the two series (i) and (ii) have the same factor-groups; and the proof by induction can be completed.

COROLLARY I. *The composition-factors of any two composition-series are identical except as regards their sequence.*

COROLLARY II. *The order of a group is equal to the product of its composition-factors.*

Ex. 1. A composition series of G can always be found containing a given subgroup H, if H is normal; but not in general if H is not normal.

Ex. 2. (i) A prime-power cyclic group has only one distinct composition-series. (ii) Conversely a prime-power group G with only one distinct composition-series is cyclic.

Ex. 3. The only composition-series of a simple group G is $G, 1$.

Ex. 4. A non-cyclic group G of order pq (where p, q are primes such that $p > q$) has only one composition-series.

Ex. 5. The symmetric group has only one composition-series unless it is of degree four.

Ex. 6. Use § 8 to prove that the symmetric group G of degree m ($m \neq 4$) contains only one normal subgroup, assuming that the alternating group H of degree m is simple.

Ex. 7. Every composition-factor of an Abelian group G is prime, and a composition-series of G can always be formed in which the composition-factors occur in any given sequence.

Ex. 8. A cyclic group has only one composition-series in which the composition-factors occur in an assigned sequence.

Ex. 9. (i) A cyclic group G of order $p^\alpha q^\beta r^\gamma \ldots$ ($p, q, r, \ldots$ being distinct primes) has $e \equiv (\alpha + \beta + \gamma + \ldots)! \div \alpha! \times \beta! \times \gamma! \times \ldots$ distinct composition-series. (ii) An Abelian group K of order $p^\alpha q^\beta r^\gamma \ldots$ with only e distinct composition-series is necessarily cyclic.

Ex. 10. Show that a non-cyclic group G of order $p^\alpha (p > 2)$ containing an element of order $p^{\alpha-1}$ has $(\alpha-1)p+1$ distinct composition-series.

Ex. 11. Show that an Abelian group G of order p^α and type $(1, 1, \ldots, 1)$ has $(p^\alpha - 1)(p^{\alpha-1} - 1)(p^{\alpha-2} - 1) \ldots (p-1) \div (p-1)^\alpha$ composition-series.

Ex. 12. Any group in a composition-series of a group G whose order is prime to its index in G is normal in G.

Ex. 13. If a group G has a composition-series in which each of the last α composition-factors is p, while every other composition-factor is prime to p, G contains a normal subgroup of order p^α.

Ex. 14. (i) If every subgroup of G is contained in some composition-series of G, G is the direct product of prime-power groups. (ii) Conversely, if G is the direct product of its Sylow subgroups, every subgroup of G is contained in some composition-series of G.

Ex. 15. Find the number of composition-series of each group of order 8.

Ex. 16. Find all composition-series of the groups d_3, Ω, H.

§ 4. *Given any normal subgroup H of a group G, a composition-series of G which includes H can always be found. The composition-factor-groups of G are the composition-factor-groups of G/H together with those of H.*

Let $G/H \equiv \Gamma$, and let $\Gamma, \Gamma_1, \Gamma_2, \Gamma_3, \ldots$ be a composition-series of Γ. Let $G_1, G_2, G_3, \ldots$ be the subgroups of G corresponding to the subgroups $\Gamma_1, \Gamma_2, \Gamma_3, \ldots$ of Γ. Then
$$G/G_1 = \Gamma/\Gamma_1, \ G_1/G_2 = \Gamma_1/\Gamma_2, \ G_2/G_3 = \Gamma_2/\Gamma_3, \ldots \text{(V 18)}.$$
But $\Gamma/\Gamma_1, \Gamma_1/\Gamma_2, \Gamma_2/\Gamma_3, \ldots$ are simple, and hence G/G_1, G_1/G_2, G_2/G_3, ... are simple. Therefore $G, G_1, G_2, G_3, \ldots$ is a composition-series of G including H, and its composition-factor-groups are those of Γ together with those of H.

Ex. 1. If $G, H, K, L, \ldots$ is a series of groups each normal in its predecessor, a composition-series of G can be found containing $H, K, L, \ldots$. The composition-factor-groups of G are those of $G/H, H/K, K/L, \ldots$.

Ex. 2. $G, G_1, G_2, G_3, \ldots$ is a composition-series of G, and H is a subgroup contained in G_{r-1} but not in G_r. If H_1 is the G. C. S. of G_r and H, prove that $\{G_r, H\}/G_r = H/H_1$.

Ex. 3. If H is any subgroup of a group G, every composition-factor-group of H is simply isomorphic with a subgroup of some composition-factor-group of G.

Ex. 4. Find the composition-factor-groups of the group G of VII 10.

§ 5. A group all of whose composition-factors are primes is called a *soluble* group. Evidently all its composition-factor-groups are cyclic. Since every group of order p^a contains a normal subgroup of index p, every prime-power group is soluble. Every Abelian group is also soluble; for if p is any prime dividing the order of an Abelian group G, G contains a normal subgroup of index p (V 20).

Ex. 1. No soluble non-cyclic group is simple.
Ex. 2. No perfect group is soluble.

Ex. 3. Every subgroup of a soluble group is soluble.
Ex. 4. Every group of order pq is soluble (p and q being prime).
Ex. 5. The direct product of soluble groups is soluble.
Ex. 6. The direct product of any number of groups, one of which is insoluble, is insoluble.
Ex. 7. No perfect group is the direct product of groups one of which is soluble.
Ex. 8. Every factor-group of a soluble group is soluble.
Ex. 9. The group $a^\lambda = 1$, $b^\beta = a^r$, $ab = ba^k$ is soluble.
Ex. 10. The groups of V $14_{10, 11}$ are soluble.
Ex. 11. Every finite point-group except E and H is soluble.

§ 6. *If G is a minimum normal subgroup of a group Γ, the composition-factor-groups of G are all simply isomorphic.*

By a 'minimum' normal subgroup of Γ we mean one containing no normal subgroup of Γ except itself and identity.

Let H_1 be a maximum normal subgroup of G; and let $H_1, H_2, H_3, \ldots$ be the subgroups conjugate to H_1 in Γ. If γ is any element of Γ, evidently $\gamma^{-1}H_1\gamma$ is normal in $\gamma^{-1}G\gamma \equiv G$; while $G/\gamma^{-1}H_1\gamma \equiv \gamma^{-1}G\gamma/\gamma^{-1}H_1\gamma = G/H_1$, and is simple. Hence $H_1, H_2, H_3, \ldots$ are all maximum normal subgroups of G, and $G/H_1 = G/H_2 = G/H_3 = \ldots$.

Denote by $H_{rst\ldots}$ the greatest common subgroup of $H_r, H_s, H_t, \ldots$. Then as in § 3 we have $H_1/H_{12} = G/H_2$, and therefore $H_1/H_{12} = G/H_1$. Similarly $H_1/H_{1r} = G/H_1$.

Now the greatest common subgroup of $H_1, H_2, H_3, \ldots \equiv 1$, for it is normal in G (V 11). Hence H_{12} cannot contain all of $H_{13}, H_{14}, H_{15}, \ldots$ unless $H_{12} \equiv 1$. Suppose H_{12} does not contain H_{1r}. Then as in § 3 $G, H_1, H_{12}, H_{12r}, \ldots$ and $G, H_1, H_{1r}, H_{12r}, \ldots$ are composition-series of G, and $H_{12}/H_{12r} = H_1/H_{1r} = G/H_1$.

As before H_{12r} does not contain all of $H_{123}, H_{124}, H_{125}, \ldots$ unless $H_{12r} \equiv 1$. If H_{12r} does not contain H_{12s}, we may repeat the above reasoning and prove that $G, H, H_{12}, H_{12r}, H_{12rs}, \ldots$ is a composition-series of G and that $H_{12r}/H_{12rs} = G/H_1$. By repetition of this process we may establish the theorem.

Each group of the composition-series is normal in G, for it is the greatest common subgroup of normal subgroups.

COROLLARY I. *G is the direct product of groups simply isomorphic with its composition-factor-groups.*

Let $B \equiv G_t$ be the group of a composition-series $G, G_1, G_2, \ldots$ of G preceding 1. Then B is simple, is normal in G, and is simply isomorphic with any one of the composition-factor-groups of G. Let $B, B_1, B_2, \ldots$ be conjugate groups in Γ. Then $\{B, B_1, B_2, \ldots\}$ being a group normal in Γ and contained in G must coincide with G.

Since B and B_1 are normal in G, their greatest common subgroup is normal in G and therefore in B. But B is simple, and hence B and B_1 have only identity in common. Moreover, every element of B is permutable with every element of B_1. For let b be any element of B, and b_1 any element of B_1. Then $b^{-1}b_1^{-1}bb_1$ is in B since $b_1^{-1}bb_1$ is in B, and is in B_1 since $b^{-1}b_1^{-1}b$ is in B_1. Hence $b^{-1}b_1^{-1}bb_1 = 1$. Therefore $\{B, B_1\}$ is the direct product of B and B_1.

Now let B_2 be one of the groups conjugate to B which is not contained in $\{B, B_1\}$. Then just as before, since B_2 and $\{B, B_1\}$ are both normal in G, we may show that B_2 and $\{B, B_1\}$ have only identity in common and that every element of B_2 is permutable with every element of $\{B, B_1\}$. Similarly B and $\{B_1, B_2\}$ have only identity in common, and every element of B is permutable with every element of $\{B_1, B_2\}$; and so for B_1 and $\{B, B_2\}$. Hence $\{B, B_1, B_2\}$ is the direct product of $B, B_1,$ and B_2. Now let B_3 be a group conjugate to B not contained in $\{B, B_1, B_2\}$. Then as before $\{B, B_1, B_2, B_3\}$ is the direct product of the simply isomorphic groups B, B_1, B_2, B_3; and, proceeding in this way, we show that G is the direct product of $t+1$ simply isomorphic groups

$$B, B_1, B_2, \ldots, B_t.$$

COROLLARY II. *Let G, H be normal subgroups of a group Γ, such that G contains H, but contains no normal subgroup of Γ containing H. Then the composition-factor-groups of G/H are all simply isomorphic, and G/H is the direct product of groups simply isomorphic with these composition-factor-groups.*

For G/H is evidently a minimum normal subgroup of Γ/H.

Ex. 1. If G (§ 6) is a prime-power group, it is Abelian.

Ex. 2. If G is of order pr (p prime to r), G is simple.

Ex. 3. Assuming that the symmetric group of degree m ($m \neq 4$) contains no normal subgroup except the alternating group of degree m, deduce from § 6 that this alternating group is simple.

Ex. 4. If P is a primitive permutation-group of degree pk and order pr (p prime to r), the group H generated by the elements of order p in P is a minimum normal subgroup of P and is simple.

The Chief-Series

§ 7. Let H_1 be a maximum normal subgroup of a group G, and let $H_1, H_2, H_3, \ldots$ be a series of normal subgroups of G such that H_i contains H_{i+1} but contains no normal subgroup of G containing H_{i+1}. Then $G, H_1, H_2, H_3, \ldots$ is called a *chief-series* or *chief-composition-series* of G. The group G may have several distinct chief-series; each such series ends with the identical group.

As in § 4 we may prove that a chief-series of G can always be found containing any given normal subgroup of G.

The groups $G/H_1, H_1/H_2, H_2/H_3, \ldots$ are called *chief-factor-groups* of G. The first G/H_1 is simple, each of the others is simple or is the direct product of simply isomorphic simple groups. This follows at once from § 6, Corollary II. If $I_1, I_2, I_3, \ldots, I_t$ are the subgroups of H_i corresponding to the members of a composition-series of H_i/H_{i+1}; $G, H_1, \ldots, H_i, I_1, I_2, I_3, \ldots, I_t, H_{i+1}, \ldots$ is a composition-series of G. The chief-factor-group H_i/H_{i+1} is the direct product of $t+1$ groups simply isomorphic with any one of the composition-factor-groups $H_i/I_1, I_1/I_2, I_2/I_3, \ldots, I_t/H_{i+1}$.

The orders of the chief-factor-groups are called *chief-factors* of G.

Ex. 1. For example; $G, N, K, \{a^2\}, 1$ and $G, O, L, \{c\}, 1$ are chief-series of the group G of $V\,4_1$, each group of either series being normal in G.

Ex. 2. $H_i, H_{i+1}, H_{i+2}, \ldots$ is not necessarily a chief-series of H_i.

§ 8. *The chief-factor-groups of any two chief-series of a group G are identical except as regards the sequence in which they occur.*

(1) Let $G, H_1, \ldots, H_i, H_{i+1}, \ldots$ and $G, H_1, \ldots, H_i, K_{i+1}, \ldots$ be two chief-series of G. Let D be the greatest common subgroup of H_{i+1} and K_{i+1}; then D and $\{H_{i+1}, K_{i+1}\}$ are normal in G (V 11). Since $\{H_{i+1}, K_{i+1}\}$ is a normal subgroup of G containing H_{i+1}, $H_i \equiv \{H_{i+1}, K_{i+1}\}$. Then as in § 3 (1) we prove $H_i/K_{i+1} = H_{i+1}/D$ and $H_i/H_{i+1} = K_{i+1}/D$.

(2) H_{i+1} contains no normal subgroup of G containing D.

For if J were such a subgroup, $\{J, K_{i+1}\}$ would be a normal subgroup of G contained in and not identical with $\{H_{i+1}, K_{i+1}\} \equiv H_i$. Similarly K_{i+1} contains no normal subgroup of G containing D.

(3) The proof of the theorem is now completed exactly as in § 3 (3).

Ex. 1. A composition-series can always be found containing the terms of any chief-series.

Ex. 2. It is not always possible to obtain a chief-series by suppressing terms of a given composition-series.

Ex. 3. Any element permutable with a given group transforms every chief-series into a chief-series and every composition-series into a composition-series.

Ex. 4. Every composition-series of an Abelian-group is also a chief-series.

Ex. 5. If a group has only one composition-series it has only one chief-series.

Ex. 6. Every chief-series of a prime-power group is a composition-series, but not conversely. The same holds for the direct product of prime-power groups.

Ex. 7. Every chief-series of a group G of order p^a ends with the groups K, 1, where K is some subgroup of order p in the central of G.

Ex. 8. If H is a normal subgroup of G, the chief-factor-groups of G are the chief-factor-groups of G/H together with direct products of groups simply isomorphic with the chief-factor-groups of H.

Ex. 9. (i) If every chief-factor-group of a group G is cyclic, the same is true of G/H, H being any normal subgroup of G. (ii) Every element of the group preceding 1 in any chief-series of G is permutable with each commutator of G.

Ex. 10. A non-Abelian group of order $p^a (p > 2, a > 2)$ containing an element of order p^{a-1} has $(a-2)p+1$ chief-series.

Ex. 11. Find the number of chief-series of each group in XIII $8_{15, 16}$.

The Characteristic-Series

§ 9. Let G be any group, and let $J_1, J_2, J_3, \ldots$ be characteristic subgroups of G, such that J_i contains J_{i+1}, but contains no characteristic subgroup of G containing J_{i+1}. Then $G, J_1, J_2, J_3, \ldots$ is called a *characteristic-series* of G.

Let Γ be the holomorph of G or any finite group containing G of the type described in X 6. Then $G, J_1, J_2, J_3, \ldots$ is part of a chief-series of Γ, so that properties of a characteristic-series can be deduced from those of a chief-series.

Ex. 1. A group with no characteristic subgroup is the direct product of simply isomorphic simple groups.

Ex. 2. Show that J_i/J_{i+1} is the direct product of simply isomorphic simple groups.

Ex. 3. A characteristic-series can always be formed containing any given characteristic subgroup.

Ex. 4. A chief-series can always be formed containing every member of a given characteristic-series.

Ex. 5. Every characteristic-series of a complete group is also a chief-series.

Ex. 6. Every composition-series of a cyclic group is also a chief-series and a characteristic-series.

Ex. 7. If a group has only one chief-series, it is also a characteristic series.

The Series of Derived Groups

§ 10. If Δ_1 is the first derived group (commutant) of any group G, Δ_2 the first derived group of Δ_1, Δ_3 the first derived group of Δ_2, &c., $\Delta_2, \Delta_3, \ldots$ are called respectively the 'second, third, ... derived groups' of G.

All the derived groups are characteristic subgroups of G.

The proof of X 2 shows at once that $h^{-1}\Delta_1 h$ is the commutant of $h^{-1}Gh$, whatever element h may be. Hence any element permutable with G is permutable with Δ_1. Similarly any element permutable with Δ_1 is permutable with Δ_2, and so on. Hence any element permutable with G is permutable with $\Delta_1, \Delta_2, \Delta_3, \ldots$; i.e. $\Delta_1, \Delta_2, \Delta_3, \ldots$ are characteristic subgroups of G.

§ 11. Each of the groups $G, \Delta_1, \Delta_2, \Delta_3, \ldots$ is contained in the one preceding it. Hence there are two possibilities only; (i) for some value of i Δ_i is perfect, and (ii) for some value of i $\Delta_i \equiv 1$. We shall prove that in case (ii) G is soluble.

If the series of derived groups of a group G ends with the identical group, G is soluble.

For since all the derived groups are normal in G, a composition-series of G may be formed containing all the groups $\Delta_1, \Delta_2, \Delta_3, \ldots$; while the composition-factors of G are the composition-factors of $G/\Delta_1, \Delta_1/\Delta_2, \Delta_2/\Delta_3, \ldots$ (an obvious extension of § 4). But these latter groups are Abelian (IX 3), and are therefore soluble (§ 5). Hence G is soluble.

Ex. 1. If a group G is soluble, its series of derived groups ends with identity.

Ex. 2. Every soluble group contains a characteristic Abelian subgroup.

Ex. 3. If Δ_i is perfect, G/Δ_i is soluble.

The Series of Adjoined Groups

§ 12. If A_1 is the first adjoined group (group of inner automorphisms) of a group G, A_2 the first adjoined group of A_1, A_3 the first adjoined group of A_2, &c.; A_2, A_3, ... are called respectively the 'second, third, ... adjoined groups' (or 'cogredients') of G. If any one of these A_{i-1} is Abelian (of order > 1), $A_i \equiv 1$ and G is said to be of *class* or *speciality* i. In this case none of the groups G, A_1, A_2, ..., A_{i-2} can be Abelian.

Since A_{i-1} is the first adjoined group of the non-Abelian group A_{i-2}, A_{i-1} is non-cyclic (X 4); hence:—

No adjoined group of a non-Abelian group is cyclic.

If the centrals of G, A_1, A_2, ..., A_{i-1} are of the types
$(\lambda, \mu, \nu, ...), (\lambda_1, \mu_1, \nu_1, ...), (\lambda_2, \mu_2, \nu_2, ...), ..., (\lambda_{i-1}, \mu_{i-1}, \nu_{i-1}, ...),$
G is said to be of the type
$(\lambda, \mu, \nu, ...)(\lambda_1, \mu_1, \nu_1, ...)(\lambda_2, \mu_2, \nu_2, ...) ... (\lambda_{i-1}, \mu_{i-1}, \nu_{i-1}, ...).$
There are in general several distinct groups of a given type.

Let C_1 be the central of G; and let C_2 be the normal subgroup of G corresponding to the central B of A_1, so that $B = C_2/C_1$. Then $G/C_2 = G/C_1/C_2/C_1 = A_1/B = A_2$ (V 18). Let C_3 be the normal subgroup of G corresponding to the central of A_2. Then as before $G/C_3 = A_3$. Let C_4 be the normal subgroup of G corresponding to the central of A_3, then $G/C_4 = A_4$, and so on. The central C_1 is sometimes called the 'first central' of G, while $C_2, C_3, ...$ are called the 'second, third, ... centrals' of G.

Ex. 1. The direct product of prime-power groups is of finite class.

Ex. 2. A metabelian group is of class 2, and conversely.

Ex. 3. The commutant of a group of class 2 or 3 is Abelian.

Ex. 4. Every non-Abelian group of order p^3 is of the type $(1)(1, 1)$.

Ex. 5. If G is of class i, (i) $\mu_{i-1} \neq 0$ unless $i = 1$, (ii) $C_i \equiv G$, (iii) the class of A_x is $i-x$.

Ex. 6. If G is of class i, (i) C_{i-1} contains Δ_1, (ii) C_{i-2} contains Δ_2.

Ex. 7. If G is of order p^α and Δ_1 of order p^β, the class of $G \leq \beta + 1$.

Ex. 8. Every element of C_x is of the form $c_1 c_2 ... c_x$ where c_t is in C_t but not in C_{t-1}. The commutator of c_t and any element of G is in C_{t-1}.

§ 13. *If the first adjoined group A of a group G is the direct product of its Sylow subgroups, G is also the direct product of its Sylow subgroups.*

Let G be of order $p^\alpha q^\beta r^\gamma ...$; $p, q, r, ...$ being distinct primes. Let $P, Q, R, ...$ be Sylow subgroups of orders $p^\alpha, q^\beta, r^\gamma, ...$

The order of A is a factor of the order of G. Let A be of order $p^{\alpha_1} q^{\beta_1} r^{\gamma_1} ....$ Then A must be the direct product of prime-power groups $P_1, Q_1, R_1, ...$ of orders $p^{\alpha_1}, q^{\beta_1}, r^{\gamma_1}, ...$

Let a, b be elements of P and Q respectively; and let a_1, b_1 in A correspond to a, b in G. Then the order of a_1 is a power of p and the order of b_1 is a power of q. But A is the direct product of $P_1, Q_1, R_1, ...$, and therefore $b_1^{-1} a_1 b_1 = a_1$. From this we deduce $b^{-1} ab = ca$, where c is some element in the central of G. Hence if m is the order of a,

$$1 = b^{-1} a^m b = (ca)^m = c^m a^m = c^m \text{ (since } ca = ac).$$

It follows that the order of c is a factor of m and is therefore a power of p. Similarly from $a^{-1} b^{-1} a = cb^{-1}$ we see that the order of c is a power of q; and hence $c = 1$.

Therefore every element of P is permutable with every element of Q, and similarly with every element of R, &c. Hence every element of P is permutable with every element of $\{Q, R, ...\}$, and these two groups have only identity in common. The same is true of Q and $\{P, R, ...\}$, &c. Hence G is the direct product of $P, Q, R, ...$

COROLLARY. *If one of the adjoined groups of a group G is identity, G is the direct product of its Sylow subgroups.*

If $A_i \equiv 1$, A_{i-1} is Abelian, and is therefore the direct product of its Sylow subgroups (XII 1, Corollary IV). Now A_{i-1} is the first adjoined group of A_{i-2}, and therefore A_{i-2} is also the direct product of its Sylow subgroups. The same reasoning may be extended to show that $A_{i-3}, A_{i-4}, ..., A_1, G$ are all direct products of their Sylow subgroups.

Ex. 1. A group of finite class is soluble.

Ex. 2. If each chief-factor-group of a group G is cyclic, the commutant Δ of G is the direct product of its Sylow subgroups.

CHAPTER XIV

SOME WELL-KNOWN GROUPS

§ 1. Suppose that $\{a\}$ is a normal cyclic subgroup of the group $G \equiv \{a, b\}$ generated by the elements a and b. Let λ, μ be the orders of a, b; and let α, β be their orders relative to $\{b\}$, $\{a\}$ respectively. Suppose

$$a^\alpha = b^s, \quad b^\beta = a^r, \quad b^{-1}ab = a^k.$$

It follows at once from the relation $b^{-1}ab = a^k$ that every element of G is included once and only once among

$$b^y a^x \, (x = 1, 2, \ldots, \lambda; \; y = 1, 2, \ldots, \beta),$$

and hence that G is of order $\lambda\beta$.

Since a^r is in $\{b\}$, $r \div \alpha$ and similarly $s \div \beta$ are integral (V 1). Hence $b^{\beta\lambda+\alpha} = a^{r\lambda+\alpha} = 1$, and therefore $\lambda \div \alpha$ is a multiple of $\mu \div \beta$. Similarly $\mu \div \beta$ is a multiple of $\lambda \div \alpha$, so that $\lambda \div \alpha = \mu \div \beta$.

Now the order of $b^\beta = \mu \div \beta = \lambda \div \alpha$, while the order of a^r is evidently $\lambda \div$ (the H.C.F. of λ and r). Hence α is the H.C.F. of λ and r, and similarly β is the H.C.F. of μ and s.

Since $a^{-1}b^{-1}ab = a^{k-1}$, we have by I 4

$$1 = a^{-\alpha}b^{-1}a^\alpha b = a^{\alpha(k-1)}.$$

Hence $\alpha(k-1) \equiv 0 \pmod{\lambda}$ or $r(k-1) \equiv 0 \pmod{\lambda}$, since α is the H.C.F. of λ and r.

Since $b^{-1}ab = a^k$, $b^{-y}ab^y = a^{k^y}$ (I 3); hence b^y is permutable with a if and only if $k^y \equiv 1 \pmod{\lambda}$. If b^ϵ is the lowest power of b permutable with a, ϵ is the smallest positive integer such that $k^\epsilon \equiv 1 \pmod{\lambda}$, i.e. k is a 'primitive root of the congruence $x^\epsilon \equiv 1 \pmod{\lambda}$'. Since b^β is permutable with a, it follows as in V 1 that ϵ is a factor of β and $k^\beta \equiv 1 \pmod{\lambda}$.

We shall show in § 5 that every group whose Sylow subgroups are cyclic is of the same type as G: the converse is not true.

Ex. 1. Every element of G is included among $a^x b^y$ ($x = 1, 2, \ldots, \lambda; \; y = 1, 2, \ldots, \beta$), or among $a^x b^y$ ($x = 1, 2, \ldots, \alpha; \; y = 1, 2, \ldots, \mu$).

Ex. 2. If d is the H.C.F. of λ and $k-1$, (i) the central of G is $\{a^{\lambda+d}\}$; (ii) the commutant of G is $\{a^d\}$; (iii) G is metabelian if λ is a factor of d^2.

Ex. 3. Find a group of the type of § 1 with non-cyclic Sylow subgroups.

Ex. 4. $\{a^l\}$ and $\{a, b^l\}$ are normal subgroups of G; $\{a^l, b\}$ is normal only if it contains the commutant of G.

Ex. 5. Every subgroup of G is of the type $\{a^l, b^y a^x\}$ where y is a factor of β, l is a factor of λ and $r + x(k^\beta - 1) \div (k^y - 1)$, and $l > x \geq 0$. No two such subgroups are identical.

Ex. 6. Every subgroup and factor-group of G is of the same type.

Ex. 7. (i) G is soluble. (ii) The chief-factors of G are prime.

Ex. 8. If every Sylow subgroup of G is cyclic, k is a primitive root of $x^\beta \equiv 1 \pmod{\lambda}$, provided a and b are chosen so that G is not generated by two elements $\mathbf{a}, \mathbf{b}$ where $\{\mathbf{a}\}$ is normal in G and of order greater than λ.

§ 2. The following four important groups are included among the groups of § 1:—

(I) $a^{4m} = b^2 = 1$, $bab = a^{1+2m}$;
(II) $a^{4m} = b^2 = 1$, $a^{2m} = (ab)^2$;
(III) $a^m = b^2 = (ab)^2 = 1$;
(IV) $a^{2m} = 1$, $a^m = (ab)^2 = b^2$.

Group III is the *dihedral* group of order $2m$, and group IV is the *dicyclic* group of order $4m$. The case in which m is a power of 2 has been discussed in XI 8.

Ex. 1. Find the centrals and commutants of the four types.

Ex. 2. (i) Every element of any one of the four groups is of the form a^x or ba^x. (ii) Find the order of each element. (iii) Find the conjugate sets of elements.

Ex. 3. (i) $\{a^x\}$ is a normal subgroup of each type. (ii) Every non-cyclic subgroup is of the form $\{a^l, ba^x\}$.

Ex. 4. Every subgroup of group I is Abelian or of the type I.

Ex. 5. In group II the subgroups $\{a^l, ba^x\}$ are of the type II, III, IV according as l is odd, l and x even, l even and x odd.

Ex. 6. In groups III and IV the subgroups $\{a^l, ba^x\}$ are respectively dihedral and dicyclic, and they form one or two conjugate sets for a given value of l as l is an odd or even factor of m.

Ex. 7. Find the orders of the groups of automorphisms of the four types.

Ex. 8. (i) If $m = 2^\gamma 3^\delta 5^\epsilon 7^\zeta \ldots$, the number of composition-series of III is $2^\gamma u_\gamma t! \div \delta! \, \epsilon! \, \zeta! \ldots$, where u_γ is the coefficient of x^γ in the expansion of $(1-x)^{-1}(1-\tfrac{1}{2}x)^{-t-1}$ and $t = \delta + \epsilon + \zeta + \ldots$

(ii) The number of chief-series is
$$(3\gamma+t)\times(\gamma+t-1)! \div \gamma!\,\delta!\,\epsilon!\,\zeta!\,....$$
(iii) Find similar theorems for group IV.

Ex. 9. (i) The dihedral and dicyclic groups are the only groups generated by a and b, where $a^r = (ab)^2 = b^2$. (ii) A group of order $2p^a$ with cyclic Sylow subgroups is either cyclic or dihedral ($p > 2$).

§ 3. Another important special case of the group in § 1 is the *metacyclic* group $G \equiv \{a, b\}$ where $a^p = b^{p-1} = 1$, $ab = ba^k$; k being a primitive root of the congruence $x^{p-1} \equiv 1 \pmod{p}$. As in § 1 G is of order $p(p-1)$.

Every automorphism of $\{a\}$ is completely given when we know the power of a corresponding to a in the automorphism. Now $k, k^2, \ldots, k^{p-1}$ leave different remainders when divided by p; for $k^e \equiv k^f \pmod{p}$ ($p > e > f > 0$) would involve $k^{e-f} \equiv 1 \pmod{p}$, contrary to the hypothesis that k is a primitive root of $x^{p-1} \equiv 1 \pmod{p}$. Hence these remainders are the numbers $1, 2, \ldots, p-1$ in some order or other. But $b^{-y}ab^y = a^{k^y}$ (I 3), so that every automorphism of $\{a\}$ is established by transforming $\{a\}$ by a power of b, and no two powers of b establish the same automorphism. Hence $\{b\}$ = the group of automorphisms of $\{a\}$. Also since the only elements of G permutable with a are the elements of $\{a\}$, G is the holomorph of $\{a\}$.

Ex. 1. The commutant of G is $\{a\}$ and the central is 1.

Ex. 2. There is only one abstract metacyclic group of order $p(p-1)$.

Ex. 3. The order of $b^y a^x$ is $(p-1) \div$ (the H.C.F. of y and $p-1$), unless $y \equiv 0 \pmod{p}$.

Ex. 4. The subgroups of G are cyclic subgroups $\{b^y a^x\}$ not normal in G, a normal cyclic subgroup $\{a\}$, and normal subgroups $\{a, b^y\}$, where y is any factor of $p-1$ and $x = 1, 2, \ldots,$ or p.

Ex. 5. A metacyclic group contains a dihedral subgroup.

Ex. 6. Every Sylow subgroup of a metacyclic group is cyclic.

Ex. 7. Every composition-series of G is a chief-series.

Ex. 8. If $p-1 = 2^\gamma 3^\delta 5^\epsilon 7^\zeta \ldots$, G has
$$(\gamma+\delta+\epsilon+\ldots)! \div \gamma!\,\delta!\,\epsilon!\,\ldots$$
composition-series.

Ex. 9. Every metacyclic group is complete.

Ex. 10. G is simply isomorphic with the group of automorphisms of a dihedral group of order $2p$.

Ex. 11. G is simply isomorphic with the doubly-transitive permutation-group of degree p generated by $S \equiv (1\,2\,\ldots\,p)$ and $T \equiv (k_1 k_2 \ldots k_{p-1})$, where k_s is that one of the symbols $1, 2, \ldots, p-1$ which satisfies $k_s \equiv k^s \pmod{p}$.

Ex. 12. G is simply isomorphic with the substitution-group in the $GF[p]$ generated by $x' = x+1$, $x' = kx$; i.e. with the group in the $GF[p]$ composed of every substitution of the form
$$x' = ax + b.$$

§ 4. *If the Sylow subgroups of a group G are cyclic groups of orders $p_1^{a_1}, p_2^{a_2}, \ldots, p_m^{a_m}$ ($p_1 < p_2 < \ldots < p_m$), G contains a normal subgroup of order $p_r^s p_{r+1}^{a_{r+1}} p_{r+2}^{a_{r+2}} \ldots p_m^{a_m}$ containing every element of G whose order divides*

$$p_r^s p_{r+1}^{a_{r+1}} p_{r+2}^{a_{r+2}} \ldots p_m^{a_m} \quad (s \leq a_r).$$

(1) Let $n \equiv p_1^{a_1} p_2^{a_2} \ldots p_m^{a_m}$ be the order of G. The number of elements in G whose orders divide n is n, and by the corollary of V 21 the number of elements in G whose orders divide $n \div p_1$ is $\lambda n \div p_1$ (λ integral). Let g of order $p_1^{a_1} k$ be one of the $(p_1 - \lambda) p_1^{a_1-1} p_2^{a_2} \ldots p_m^{a_m}$ elements of G whose orders divide n but not $n \div p_1$. Such an element exists; for G contains by hypothesis an element of order $p_1^{a_1}$. Then the order of g^e ($p_1^{a_1} k > e > 0$) divides n but not $n \div p_1$ if and only if e is one of the $p_1^{a_1-1}(p_1-1)k$ integers less than $p_1^{a_1}k$ and prime to p_1.

Let h of order $p_1^{a_1} l$ be one of the $(p_1 - \lambda) p_1^{a_1-1} p_2^{a_2} \ldots p_m^{a_m}$ elements of G whose orders divide n but not $n \div p_1$ which is not a power of g (if such an element exists). Then as before $p_1^{a_1-1}(p_1-1)l$ of the powers of h divide n but not $n \div p_1$. Now take one of the $(p_1 - \lambda) p_1^{a_1-1} p_2^{a_2} \ldots p_m^{a_m}$ elements whose orders divide n but not $n \div p_1$ which is not a power of g or h and reason as before. Continuing the process till all the $(p_1 - \lambda) p_1^{a_1-1} p_2^{a_2} \ldots p_m^{a_m}$ elements are exhausted, we see that $(p_1 - \lambda) p_1^{a_1-1} p_2^{a_2} \ldots p_m^{a_m}$ is a multiple of $p_1^{a_1-1}(p_1-1)$ and is not zero. Since $p_1 - 1$ is prime to $p_2^{a_2} \ldots p_m^{a_m}$, we must have $\lambda = 1$.

(2) By (1) and the Corollary of V 21 the number of elements in G whose orders divide $n \div p_1$ but not $n \div p_1^2$ is $(p_1 - \mu) p_1^{a_1-2} p_2^{a_2} \ldots p_m^{a_m}$ (μ integral). Then exactly as in (1) we may show that $(p_1 - \mu) p_1^{a_1-2} p_2^{a_2} \ldots p_m^{a_m}$ is a multiple of $p_1^{a_1-2}(p_1-1)$ and is not zero; from which it follows that $\mu = 1$.

(3) This reasoning may be repeated to show that G contains exactly $p_r^s p_{r+1}^{a_{r+1}} \ldots p_m^{a_m}$ elements whose orders divide $p_r^s p_{r+1}^{a_{r+1}} \ldots p_m^{a_m}$; and finally that G contains exactly $p_m^{a_m}$

XIV 4] CYCLIC SYLOW SUBGROUPS 173

elements whose orders divide $p_m^{a_m}$. Hence G contains only one Sylow subgroup P_m of order $p_m^{a_m}$; for if G contained two, G would contain more than $p_m^{a_m}$ elements whose orders are powers of p_m. Since P_m is the only subgroup of order $p_m^{a_m}$ in G, P_m is normal in G.

(4) If Γ is any factor-group of G, the Sylow subgroups of Γ are cyclic. For that Sylow subgroup of Γ whose order is a power of p_x is generated by an element of Γ corresponding to an element of order $p_x^{a_x}$ in G.

Hence G/P_m contains a normal subgroup of order $p_{m-1}^{a_{m-1}}$. The corresponding subgroup P_{m-1} of G is of order $p_{m-1}^{a_{m-1}} p_m^{a_m}$ and is normal in G. Again, G contains a normal subgroup P_{m-2} of order $p_{m-2}^{a_{m-2}} p_{m-1}^{a_{m-1}} p_m^{a_m}$ corresponding to the normal subgroup of order $p_{m-2}^{a_{m-2}}$ in G/P_{m-1}. Continuing this process we see that G contains a normal subgroup P_{r+1} of order $p_{r+1}^{a_{r+1}} p_{r+2}^{a_{r+2}} \ldots p_m^{a_m}$. The group G/P_{r+1} contains a normal cyclic subgroup of order $p_r^{a_r}$, and hence G/P_{r+1} contains a normal cyclic subgroup of order p_r^s. The corresponding subgroup P of G is of order $p_r^s p_{r+1}^{a_{r+1}} \ldots p_m^{a_m}$ and consists of those $p_r^s p_{r+1}^{a_{r+1}} \ldots p_m^{a_m}$ elements of G whose orders divide $p_r^s p_{r+1}^{a_{r+1}} \ldots p_m^{a_m}$.

Ex. 1. If G is Abelian, it is cyclic.

Ex. 2. The subgroup P is characteristic.

Ex. 3. If $g_1, g_2, \ldots, g_m$ are elements of orders $p_1^{a_1}, p_2^{a_2}, \ldots, p_m^{a_m}$ in G, $P \equiv \{g_r^u, g_{r+1}, \ldots, g_m\}$, where $u = p_r^{a_r-s}$.

Ex. 4. Any subgroup H of G has all its Sylow subgroups cyclic.

Ex. 5. The result of § 4 holds good even if the Sylow subgroup of order $p_m^{a_m}$ is non-cyclic, provided $r \neq m$.

Ex. 6. Prove that G is soluble. This is true even if the Sylow subgroup of order $p_m^{a_m}$ is non-cyclic.

Ex. 7. The chief-factors of G are prime.

Ex. 8. Assuming only that G contains a normal subgroup of order $p_m^{a_m}$, deduce from V 14 that G contains exactly $p_r^{a_r} p_{r+1}^{a_{r+1}} \ldots p_m^{a_m}$ elements whose orders divide $p_r^{a_r} p_{r+1}^{a_{r+1}} \ldots p_m^{a_m}$.

Ex. 9. If a group G (with non-cyclic Sylow subgroups) contains exactly $p_r^s p_{r+1}^{a_{r+1}} \ldots p_m^{a_m}$ elements whose orders divide $p_r^s p_{r+1}^{a_{r+1}} \ldots p_m^{a_m}$, G contains exactly $p_{r+1}^{a_{r+1}} \ldots p_m^{a_m}$ elements whose orders divide $p_{r+1}^{a_{r+1}} \ldots p_m^{a_m}$; where $p_1^{a_1} p_2^{a_2} \ldots p_m^{a_m}$ is the order of G and $s < a_r$.

§ 5. *A group G with cyclic Sylow subgroups is generated by two elements a, b such that $\{a\}$ is normal in G and contains every normal cyclic subgroup of G, while the lowest power of b permutable with a is in $\{a\}$.*

(1) We assume that the result is true for any group whose order is the product of powers of $m-1$ distinct primes. We shall then prove that the result is true for a group G whose order is the product of powers of m distinct primes. Then the theorem can be proved by induction; for it is evidently true when $m=1$ (b being identity). Let G be the group of § 4. It contains a subgroup H of index $p_1^{a_1}$ with cyclic Sylow subgroups formed of those elements of G whose orders divide $n \div p_1^{a_1}$. Since H is the only subgroup of its kind in G, every element permutable with G is evidently permutable with H; i.e. H is a characteristic subgroup of G. By our assumption $H \equiv \{a, b\}$, where $a^\lambda = 1$, $b^\beta = a^r$, $ab = ba^k$; while $\{a\}$ is normal in H and contains every normal cyclic subgroup of H, and b^β is the lowest power of b permutable with a. Since every element permutable with $\{a\}$ is permutable with each subgroup of $\{a\}$, $\{a\}$ contains no cyclic subgroup not normal in H; and since $\{a\}$ is the only subgroup of its kind in H, every element permutable with H is permutable with $\{a\}$; i.e. $\{a\}$ is a characteristic subgroup of H.

(2) Let a cyclic Sylow subgroup of order $p_1^{a_1}$ in G be generated by an element g; and let g^ρ be the lowest power of g such that $\{g^\rho\}$ is normal in G. As in V 1 ρ is a factor of $p_1^{a_1}$. Since H and $\{g^\rho\}$ are normal in G, $g^{-\rho}b^{-1}g^\rho b$ is both in H and in $\{g^\rho\}$. Hence $g^{-\rho}b^{-1}g^\rho b = 1$; for H and $\{g^\rho\}$ have only identity in common, since their orders are prime to one another. Therefore g^ρ is permutable with b, and similarly with a.

Since the orders of a and g^ρ are prime to one another, the order of ag^ρ = the order of the Abelian group $\{a, g^\rho\}$; and hence $\{a, g^\rho\} \equiv \{ag^\rho\}$ is cyclic.

(3) Since $\{a\}$ and $\{g^\rho\}$ are normal in G, $\{ag^\rho\}$ and every subgroup of $\{ag^\rho\}$ is normal in G. Conversely, every normal cyclic subgroup of G is contained in $\{ag^\rho\}$. For suppose h generates such a subgroup of order $p_1^\epsilon m$, where m is prime to p_1. Then $\{h^{p_1^\epsilon}\}$, being a normal cyclic subgroup of order m, is in $\{a\}$; while $\{h^m\}$, being a normal cyclic subgroup of order p_1^ϵ, is in $\{g^\rho\}$. Hence $\{h\} \equiv \{h^{p_1^\epsilon}, h^m\}$ is in $\{ag^\rho\}$.

(4) Now g^ρ is the lowest power of g permutable with a. For if g^σ is permutable with a, $b^{-1}g^\sigma b$ is permutable with $b^{-1}ab = a^k$ and therefore with a^{ke}. Hence $b^{-1}g^\sigma b$ is permutable with a; for we can choose e such that $ke \equiv 1 \pmod{\lambda}$, since k is prime to λ. Now since g^σ is permutable with H, every element of $\{g^\sigma, H\}$ is of the form $g^{z\sigma}b^y a^x$, which is not permutable with a unless $y = 0$. Hence $b^{-1}g^\sigma b$ is of the form $g^{z\sigma}a^x$. But since the order of g^σ is prime to the order of a, we must have $x = 0$, so that b is permutable with $\{g^\sigma\}$ and $\{g^\sigma\}$ is normal in G.

(5) Again, g is permutable with $\{a\}$; suppose $g^{-1}ag = a^l$. Then since g^ρ is the lowest power of g permutable with a, l is a primitive root of $x^\rho \equiv 1 \pmod{\lambda}$. Now

$$(bg)^{-1}a(bg) = g^{-1}a^k g = a^{kl};$$

hence by I 3

$$(bg)^{-t}a(bg)^t = a^{(kl)^t} = a^{k^t l^t}.$$

If $(bg)^t$ is permutable with a, $k^t l^t \equiv 1 \pmod{\lambda}$; and then $1 \equiv (k^t l^t)^\rho \equiv k^{t\rho}$ and $1 \equiv (k^t l^t)^\beta \equiv l^{t\beta} \pmod{\lambda}$. Since β and ρ are prime to one another, we deduce that t is a multiple both of β and ρ if $(bg)^t$ is permutable with a. Hence the lowest power of bg permutable with ag^ρ is a multiple of $\beta\rho$; for b and g are permutable with g^ρ.

(6) Write now **a** for ag^ρ, **b** for bg. Then $\{\mathbf{a}\}$ is normal in $\{\mathbf{a}, \mathbf{b}\}$, and the order of $\{\mathbf{a}, \mathbf{b}\} \equiv \{\mathbf{a}\} + \{\mathbf{a}\}\mathbf{b} + \{\mathbf{a}\}\mathbf{b}^2 + \ldots$ is $\geq n$. For the order of **a** is $n \div \beta\rho$; while the order of **b** relative to $\{\mathbf{a}\}$ is $\geq \rho\beta$, since the lowest power of **b** permutable with **a** is a multiple of $\rho\beta$. But $\{\mathbf{a}, \mathbf{b}\}$ is a subgroup of G. Hence $\mathbf{b}^{\rho\beta}$ is in $\{\mathbf{a}\}$, and $G \equiv \{\mathbf{a}, \mathbf{b}\}$ where $\{\mathbf{a}\}$ is normal in G and contains every normal cyclic subgroup of G, while the lowest power of **b** permutable with **a** is in $\{\mathbf{a}\}$.

Ex. 1. A group Γ whose order contains no square factor is of the type $a^\lambda = b^\mu = 1$, $ab = ba^k$, where k is a primitive root of $x^\mu \equiv 1 \pmod{\lambda}$ and λ is prime to μ.

Ex. 2. (i) Find the conditions that $b^\sigma a^\rho$ should correspond to a, $b^y a^x$ to b in an automorphism of H. (ii) Find the order of the group of automorphisms of Γ in Ex. 1.

Hamiltonian Groups

§ 6. A non-Abelian group all of whose subgroups are normal is called a *Hamiltonian group*. The simplest type of Hamiltonian group is the *quaternion group* $a^4 = 1$,

$a^2 = (ab)^2 = b^2$ which is identical with the dicyclic group of order 8. It contains one subgroup $\{a^2\}$ of order 2, and three subgroups $\{a\}, \{b\}, \{ab\}$ of order 4.

Ex. 1. Verify directly that every subgroup of the quaternion group is permutable with a and b.

Ex. 2. Every subgroup of a Hamiltonian group is Hamiltonian or Abelian.

Ex. 3. Every element of order 2 in a Hamiltonian group is normal.

Ex. 4. A Hamiltonian group is the direct product of its Sylow subgroups.

Ex. 5. Every factor-group of a Hamiltonian group is Hamiltonian or Abelian.

Ex. 6. If $a^2 = (ab)^2 = b^2$, $\{a, b\}$ is Abelian of order 4 or quaternion.

Ex. 7. If $bab = a$ and $ab = ba^3$, $\{a, b\}$ is Abelian of order 4 or quaternion.

Ex. 8. The quaternion group is the holomorph of a cyclic group of order 4.

Ex. 9. (i) The group of inner automorphisms of a quaternion group is non-cyclic of order 4. (ii) The group of automorphisms is simply isomorphic with the symmetric group of degree 4.

Ex. 10. The quaternion group is not the group of inner automorphisms of any other group.

§ 7. *The direct product G of an Abelian group A of odd order x, an Abelian group B of order 2^m and type $(1, 1, ..., 1)$, and the quaternion group C is Hamiltonian.*

Let H be any subgroup of G, let $h = abc$ be any element of H, and let $g = \alpha\beta\gamma$ be any element of G; where a and α are in A, b and β in B, and c and γ in C. Then
$$g^{-1}hg = \gamma^{-1}\beta^{-1}\alpha^{-1}abc\alpha\beta\gamma = \gamma^{-1}abc\gamma = \gamma^{-1}c\gamma ab.$$
Now since $c^4 = 1$ and $\{c\}$ is normal in C, $\gamma^{-1}c\gamma = c$ or c^3. Hence $g^{-1}hg = h$ or c^2h. But H contains
$$h^{2x} = (abc)^{2x} = a^{2x}b^{2x}c^{2x} = c^{2x} = c^2 \text{ (since } c^4 = 1 \text{ and } x \text{ is odd)}.$$
Hence H contains $g^{-1}hg$ and is normal in G.

The converse of this theorem is proved in § 9.

Ex. 1. Every element of $\{B, C\}$ is of order 1, 2, or 4.

Ex. 2. The central of G is the direct product of A and H, where $H \equiv \{B, e\}$ is Abelian of order 2^{m+1} and type $(1, 1, ..., 1)$, e being the element of order 2 in C.

HAMILTONIAN GROUPS

§ 8. *There is no Hamiltonian group of order p^a if $p > 2$. If $p = 2$, there is one and only one abstract Hamiltonian group of order p^a ($a > 2$); it is the direct product of the quaternion group and an Abelian group of the type $(1, 1, \ldots, 1)$.*

(1) Let G be a Hamiltonian group of order p^a. Let g of order p^λ be an element of G which is not normal in G but is such that every element of lower order in G is normal. Let h of order p^μ ($\mu \geq \lambda$) be any element of G not permutable with g.

Let $c = g^{-1}h^{-1}gh$. Since G is Hamiltonian $h^{-1}gh$ is in $\{g\}$, and therefore c is a power of g. Similarly, c is a power of h. Hence c lies in the greatest common subgroup D of $\{g\}$ and $\{h\}$. Since $c \neq 1$, D contains the subgroups $\{g^{p^{\lambda-1}}\}$ and $\{h^{p^{\mu-1}}\}$ of order p in $\{g\}$ and $\{h\}$. Therefore $g^{p^{\lambda-1}} = h^{up^{\mu-1}}$ where u is prime to p. Since h is not permutable with g, $D \not\equiv \{g\}$ and hence $\lambda > 1$.

Now by 14 $g^{-p}h^{-1}g^p h = c^p$. But g^p is normal in G by hypothesis, and hence $c^p = 1$. Again, $(h^y g)^t = h^{yt} g^t c^{\frac{1}{2}yt(t-1)}$. Putting $y = -up^{\mu-\lambda}$, $t = p^{\lambda-1}$, we have $(h^y g)^t = c^{\frac{1}{2}yt(t-1)}$. Hence if p is odd, or if $p = 2$ and y is even or $\lambda > 2$, $(h^y g)^t = 1$. Now since $h^y g$ is not permutable with h, we cannot have $(h^y g)^t = 1$; otherwise $h^y g$ would be of lower order than g contrary to hypothesis. Hence $p = 2$, y is odd and therefore $\lambda = \mu$, and $\lambda = 2$. Therefore $\lambda = \mu = 2$ and $g^4 = h^4 = 1, g^2 = h^2$. The group $\{g, h\}$ is evidently a quaternion group.

(2) We have shown that any two non-permutable elements of a Hamiltonian group G of order 2^a generate a quaternion subgroup. Now every element of order 2 in G is normal; for if g is such an element, $\{g\}$ is normal. These elements of order 2 form an Abelian subgroup H of the type $(1, 1, \ldots, 1)$. Let $a^4 = 1$, $a^2 = (ab)^2 = b^2$ be any quaternion subgroup C. If d is any element not permutable with a, $\{a, d\}$ is a quaternion group and $d^2 = a^2$.

Let γ be any element of G permutable with a and b. Then γb is not permutable with a, and hence $a^2 = (\gamma b)^2 = \gamma^2 b^2 = \gamma^2 a^2$. Therefore $\gamma^2 = 1$ and γ is in H.

If γ is an element of G not permutable with a and b, three cases can arise since γ is permutable with $\{a\}$ and $\{b\}$, namely (i) $\gamma^{-1} a \gamma = a, \gamma^{-1} b \gamma = b^3$, (ii) $\gamma^{-1} a \gamma = a^3, \gamma^{-1} b \gamma = b$, (iii) $\gamma^{-1} a \gamma = a^3, \gamma^{-1} b \gamma = b^3$. It is at once proved that a and b are both permutable with (i) $a\gamma$, (ii) $b\gamma$, (iii) $ab\gamma$. Hence as before H contains (i) $a\gamma$, (ii) $b\gamma$, (iii) $ab\gamma$. In each case γ is in

CH. Hence $G \equiv \{C, H\}$, and H is the central of G. The greatest common subgroup of C and H is $\{a^2\}$. Let B be a subgroup of index 2 in H not containing $\{a^2\}$. Then $G \equiv \{B, C\}$ and is the direct product of B and C, i.e. of an Abelian group of order 2^{a-3} and type $(1, 1, ..., 1)$ and the quaternion group.

Ex. 1. The commutant of G is $\{a^2\}$.

Ex. 2. G contains $2^{a-2}-1$ subgroups of order 2, $3 \cdot 2^{a-3}$ of order 4, $2^{a-1}-1$ of index 2, $\frac{1}{3}(2^{a-1}-1)(2^{a-2}-1)$ of index 4, and 2^{2a-6} quaternion subgroups.

Ex. 3. If every subgroup of order $> p$ in a non-Abelian and non-Hamiltonian group K of order p^a is normal ($p > 2$), K contains only one normal subgroup of order p.

§ 9. *Every Hamiltonian group is the direct product of an Abelian group of odd order, an Abelian group of order 2^m and type $(1, 1, ..., 1)$, and the quaternion group.*

By Corollary IV of XII 1 a Hamiltonian group G is the direct product of its Sylow subgroups. Now each of these subgroups is evidently Hamiltonian or Abelian. Hence by § 8 the Sylow subgroups of odd order are Abelian, and therefore their direct product is an Abelian group A of odd order. Again by § 8 the Sylow subgroup of even order is the direct product of an Abelian group B of order 2^m and type $(1, 1, ..., 1)$ and the quaternion group C. Hence G is the direct product of A, B, and C; which proves the theorem.

Ex. 1. The commutant of G is of order 2.
Ex. 2. The central of G is of index 4.
Ex. 3. G is metabelian.

CHAPTER XV

CHARACTERISTICS

§ 1. If a group G is simply or multiply isomorphic with irreducible homogeneous linear substitution-groups $S, S', S'', \ldots$ (VII 4), then $S, S', S'', \ldots$ are called *representations* of G.

Let g be any element of G, and let s, s' be the corresponding substitutions of S, S' respectively. Then if a fixed substitution t can be found such that $t^{-1}st = s'$ whatever element of G g may be, S and S' are called *equivalent* representations of G; if not, S and S' are called *distinct* representations.

Every substitution conjugate to s in S has the same characteristic equation (III 6). Hence the substitutions of S corresponding to each element conjugate to g in G have the same characteristic equation; for to an element of G conjugate to g evidently corresponds an element of S conjugate to s. The sum of the roots of the characteristic equation of s is called the *characteristic* in the representation S of the set of elements conjugate to g.

Suppose S is of degree m. Let s be transformed into the multiplication $(\omega_1 x_1, \omega_2 x_2, \ldots, \omega_m x_m)$ (III 8); then s^{-1} is transformed into $(\omega_1^{-1} x_1, \omega_2^{-1} x_2, \ldots, \omega_m^{-1} x_m)$. If s is of order q; $\omega_1, \omega_2, \ldots, \omega_m$ are q-th roots of unity and are the roots of the characteristic equation of s. Hence the characteristics $\omega_1 + \omega_2 + \ldots + \omega_m$ and $\omega_1^{-1} + \omega_2^{-1} + \ldots + \omega_m^{-1}$ of the sets of elements conjugate to g and g^{-1} are conjugate imaginaries; for ω_i is conjugate to ω_i^{-1}. If the conjugate set containing g is self-inverse (V 6), its characteristic is real.

If $g = 1$, s is $(x_1, x_2, \ldots, x_m)$. Hence the characteristic of 1 is the degree m of S.

If we replace each coefficient of every substitution of S by the conjugate imaginary, the substitutions so obtained obviously form a group $\bar{S}$ simply isomorphic with S which is also a representation of G: S and $\bar{S}$ are called *inverse* representations. If S and $\bar{S}$ are equivalent representations, S is called a *self-inverse* representation.

Ex. 1. The following table shows the 3 distinct representations and the corresponding characteristics for the group
$$a^3 = b^2 = (ab)^2 = 1.$$

Elements of group	Substitutions of the representation			Characteristic in		
	S	S'	S''	S	S'	S''
1	x	x	(x, y)	1	1	2
a	x	x	$\left(-\frac{1}{2}x - \frac{\sqrt{3}}{2}y,\ \frac{\sqrt{3}}{2}x - \frac{1}{2}y\right)$	1	1	-1
a^2	x	x	$\left(-\frac{1}{2}x + \frac{\sqrt{3}}{2}y,\ -\frac{\sqrt{3}}{2}x - \frac{1}{2}y\right)$			
b	x	$-x$	$(x, -y)$	1	-1	0
ba	x	$-x$	$\left(-\frac{1}{2}x + \frac{\sqrt{3}}{2}y,\ \frac{\sqrt{3}}{2}x + \frac{1}{2}y\right)$			
ba^2	x	$-x$	$\left(-\frac{1}{2}x - \frac{\sqrt{3}}{2}y,\ -\frac{\sqrt{3}}{2}x + \frac{1}{2}y\right)$			

Ex. 2. One and the same group of linear substitutions may give rise to two or more representations of G.

Ex. 3. The characteristic of a set of elements of order 2 is integral.

Ex. 4. Every representation of G is simply isomorphic with a factor-group of G.

Ex. 5. Every representation of a factor-group of G is a representation of G.

Ex. 6. The substitution-group of degree and order 1 is a representation of every group.

Ex. 7. Every representation of an Abelian group is of degree 1.

Ex. 8. A group is not necessarily simply isomorphic with any one of its representations.

§ 2. Suppose G is a group whose elements form r conjugate sets of which the first is the set containing only identity. Denote the elements of the k-th conjugate set by C_k ($C_1 \equiv 1$).

Let $S_1, S_2, S_3, \ldots$ be the distinct representations of G; where S_1 is the homogeneous linear group of degree and order 1, which is evidently a representation of every group.

We denote by $\chi_k{}^i$ the characteristic of C_k in the representation S_i. Then $\chi_1{}^i$ is the degree of S_i, and $\chi_k{}^1 = 1$.

We denote by $\chi_k{}^j$ the characteristic in S_i of the set inverse to C_k. Then $\chi_k{}^i, \chi_k{}^j$ are conjugate imaginaries, and are real and equal if C_k is a self-inverse set.

We denote by $\chi_k{}^{i'}$ the characteristic of C_k in the representation inverse to S_i. Then $\chi_k{}^i$ and $\chi_k{}^{i'}$ are conjugate imaginaries, and are real and equal if S_i is a self-inverse representation.

The r characteristics $\chi_1{}^i, \chi_2{}^i, \ldots, \chi_r{}^i$ are called the *set of characteristics* of G in the representation S_i.

Ex. 1. $\chi_k{}^{i'} = \chi_k{}^i$ and $\chi_{k'}{}^{i'} = \chi_k{}^i$.
Ex. 2. The modulus of $\chi_k{}^i \leq \chi_1{}^i$.
Ex. 3. If $\chi_1{}^i = \chi_a{}^i = \chi_b{}^i = \ldots$, S_i is simply isomorphic with G/H, where $H \equiv C_1 + C_a + C_b + \ldots$.
Ex. 4. Let $\chi_1, \chi_2, \chi_3, \ldots$ be a set of characteristics for the conjugate sets $E_1, E_2, E_3, \ldots$ of a factor-group Γ of G; and let $C_k, C_k', C_k'', \ldots$ be the conjugate sets of G corresponding to the elements E_k of Γ. Then there is a set of characteristics of G in which χ_k is the characteristic of each of
$$C_k, C_k', C_k'', \ldots \quad (k = 1, 2, 3, \ldots).$$
Ex. 5. Every characteristic of a symmetric group is real.

§ 3. Suppose G is an Abelian group of order n. Then $r = n$, and each conjugate set contains one element only. Any representation S_i of G (being irreducible) is of degree 1 by VII 8; hence $\chi_1{}^i = 1$.

Let $[g_1, g_2, \ldots, g_t]$ be a base of G, and let a_e be the order of g_e. Let $x' = \omega_e x$ be the substitution of S_i corresponding to g_e; so that $\omega_e{}^{a_e} = 1$ and ω_e is the characteristic of g_e in the representation S_i. Then the substitution of S_i corresponding to $g_1^{\beta_1} g_2^{\beta_2} \ldots g_t^{\beta_t}$ is $x' = \omega_1^{\beta_1} \omega_2^{\beta_2} \ldots \omega_t^{\beta_t} x$, and $\omega_1^{\beta_1} \omega_2^{\beta_2} \ldots \omega_t^{\beta_t}$ is the characteristic of $g_1^{\beta_1} g_2^{\beta_2} \ldots g_t^{\beta_t}$ in the representation S_i.

Now ω_e may be any one of the a_e a_e-th roots of unity; hence there are $a_1 a_2 \ldots a_t = n$ distinct representations of G. If θ_e is any primitive a_e-th root of unity (so that $\theta_e{}^{a_e} = 1$, $\theta_e{}^y \neq 1$ if $y < a_e$), the characteristics of $g_1^{\beta_1} g_2^{\beta_2} \ldots g_t^{\beta_t}$ in the n representations are

$$\theta_1^{\beta_1 k_1} \theta_2^{\beta_2 k_2} \ldots \theta_t^{\beta_t k_t} \quad (k_e = 1, 2, \ldots, a_e;\ e = 1, 2, \ldots, t).$$

The representations of G may be considered as elements if we define the product $S_i S_j$ as follows. Let the characteristics of $g_1 g_2 \ldots g_t$ in the representations S_i, S_j be respectively $\theta_1{}^{i_1}\theta_2{}^{i_2} \ldots \theta_t{}^{i_t}, \theta_1{}^{j_1}\theta_2{}^{j_2} \ldots \theta_t{}^{j_t}$; then the product $S_i S_j$ is defined as the representation in which the characteristic of $g_1 g_2 \ldots g_t$ is $\theta_1{}^{i_1+j_1}\theta_2{}^{i_2+j_2} \ldots \theta_t{}^{i_t+j_t}$. It is at once seen that the representations considered as elements form a group Σ simply isomorphic with G, the element $g_1^{i_1} g_2^{i_2} \ldots g_t^{i_t}$ in G corresponding to the element S_i in Σ.

Ex. 1. If every characteristic of an element g in an Abelian group is real, $g^2 = 1$.

Ex. 2. The number of representations of any group G of the first degree = the index of its commutant Δ.

Ex. 3. The substitution-group $x' = x, -x$ stands for $2^\alpha - 1$ distinct representations of an Abelian group of order 2^α and type $(1, 1, \ldots, 1)$.

Ex. 4. The multiplication table of an Abelian group of order n considered as a determinant of n^2 elements is the product of n linear factors.

Ex. 5. (i) The multiplication table of any group considered as a determinant has q linear factors, where q is the index of the commutant. (ii) Find these linear factors in $V 1_1$.

Ex. 6. The sum of the characteristics in any given representation of all the elements of an Abelian group is 0, unless each characteristic is 1.

Ex. 7. The sum of the characteristics of a given element of an Abelian group in every representation is 0, unless the element is identity.

§ 4. Let H be any subgroup of the Abelian group
$$G \equiv H\gamma_1 + H\gamma_2 + \ldots + H\gamma_u,$$
and let S be one of the u distinct representations of G/H. Since G is multiply isomorphic with G/H and G/H with S, S is a representation of G. The characteristic of every element of H in the representation S of G is 1. Conversely, if the characteristic of every element of H in the representation S of G is 1, S is a representation of G/H. For evidently in this case the characteristic of every element in $H\gamma_i . H\gamma_j$ is the same.

Now let $\theta_1{}^{k_1}\theta_2{}^{k_2} \ldots \theta_t{}^{k_t}$ be the characteristic of $g_1 g_2 \ldots g_t$ in the representation S. Then the u elements of the type $g_1{}^{k_1} g_2{}^{k_2} \ldots g_t{}^{k_t}$ form a subgroup K simply isomorphic with G/H. For they evidently form a subgroup simply isomorphic with the group L whose elements are the u representations of G/H, $g_1{}^{k_1} g_2{}^{k_2} \ldots g_t{}^{k_t}$ corresponding to S: and $L = G/H$ (§ 3).

The subgroup H bears the same relation to K that K does to H. For $g_1^{l_1} g_2^{l_2} \ldots g_t^{l_t}$ is in H if and only if $\theta_1^{k_1 l_1} \theta_2^{k_2 l_2} \ldots \theta_t^{k_t l_t} = 1$ for each of the u sets of values of $k_1, k_2, \ldots, k_t$. Again, $\theta_1^{l_1} \theta_2^{l_2} \ldots \theta_t^{l_t}$ is the characteristic of $g_1 g_2 \ldots g_t$ in a representation of G/K if and only if $\theta_1^{l_1 k_1} \theta_2^{l_2 k_2} \ldots \theta_t^{l_t k_t} = 1$ for each of the u sets of values of $k_1, k_2, \ldots, k_t$; which is the same condition as before. For this reason H and K are called *reciprocal* subgroups of G.

Ex. 1. The subgroup of G reciprocal to H depends on the base $[g_1, g_2, \ldots, g_t]$ and on the quantities $\theta_1, \theta_2, \ldots, \theta_t$.

Ex. 2. K is a subgroup of the group reciprocal to any subgroup of H.

Ex. 3. An Abelian group contains as many subgroups of index q as it does subgroups of order q.

Ex. 4. An Abelian group contains as many subgroups with given invariants as it has factor-groups with those invariants.

Ex. 5. An Abelian group of order p^a with t invariants has
$$(p^t-1)(p^{t-1}-1)\ldots(p^{t-q+1}-1) \div (p^q-1)(p^{q-1}-1)\ldots(p-1)$$
factor-groups of the type $(1, 1, 1, \ldots$ to q terms$)$.

Ex. 6. An Abelian group of order p^a of the type $(2, 2, 2, \ldots, 1, 1, 1, \ldots)$—$y$ 2's and s 1's—contains
$$\frac{(p^{y+s}-1)(p^{y+s-1}-1)}{(p^2-1)(p-1)} + \frac{p^y-1}{p-1} p^{y+s-1}$$
subgroups of index p^2.

Ex. 7. (i) Any group contains
$$\frac{(p^{y+s}-1)(p^{y+s-1}-1)}{(p^2-1)(p-1)} + \frac{p^y-1}{p-1} p^{y+s-1}$$
normal subgroups of index p^2 where y and s are zero or positive integers. (ii) Find y and s in the group of XI 7.

§ 5. The discussion of the properties of characteristics of non-Abelian groups is too difficult to be included in an elementary treatise. We shall confine ourselves to a statement of the fundamental relations between the characteristics and to one application.

Using the notation of § 2 it may be proved that there are r distinct representations of G.[*] Let h_k be the number of elements C_k; so that $n = h_1 + h_2 + \ldots + h_r$. Now if any element g is contained among the $h_k h_l$ elements $C_k C_l$, we prove immediately that $C_k C_l \equiv C_l C_k$ includes every element

---

[*] For a proof of these important theorems see two papers by Prof. W. Burnside; *Acta Mathematica*, xxviii (1904), p. 369 and *Proc. London Math. Soc.*, 2 i (1903), p. 117.

conjugate to g. Suppose that the $h_k h_l$ elements $C_k C_l$ include the elements C_1 c_{kl1} times, the elements C_2 c_{kl2} times, ..., the elements C_r c_{klr} times; i.e. $C_k C_l \equiv c_{kl1} C_1 + c_{kl2} C_2 + ... + c_{klr} C_r$, where $c_{kl1}, c_{kl2}, ..., c_{klr}$ are zero or positive integers. Then

$$h_k h_l \chi_k^i \chi_l^i = \chi_1^i (c_{kl1} h_1 \chi_1^i + c_{kl2} h_2 \chi_2^i + ... + c_{klr} h_r \chi_r^i) \quad \ldots\ldots\ldots (i)*$$

$$h_1 \chi_1^i \chi_1^j + h_2 \chi_2^i \chi_2^j + ... + h_r \chi_r^i \chi_r^j = n \text{ or } 0$$
$$\text{as } j = i'$$
$$\text{or } j \neq i' \quad \ldots\ldots\ldots (ii)*$$

In (ii) keep i fixed and let j take the r values $1, 2, ..., r$. Solving the r equations so obtained we get $h_k \chi_k^i X = n X_k^{i'}$, where $X_k^{i'}$ is the co-factor of $\chi_k^{i'}$ in

$$X \equiv \begin{vmatrix} \chi_1^1 & \chi_2^1 & \cdots & \chi_r^1 \\ \chi_1^2 & \chi_2^2 & \cdots & \chi_r^2 \\ \vdots & \vdots & & \vdots \\ \chi_1^r & \chi_2^r & \cdots & \chi_r^r \end{vmatrix}.$$

Now $X_k^{1'} \chi_l^1 + X_k^{2'} \chi_l^2 + ... + X_k^{r'} \chi_l^r$
$$= X_k^{1'} \chi_{l'}^{1'} + X_k^{2'} \chi_{l'}^{2'} + ... + X_k^{r'} \chi_{l'}^{r'} = X \text{ or } 0$$

according as $l' = k$ or $l' \neq k$, i.e. as $l = k'$ or $l \neq k'$. Hence

$$\chi_k^1 \chi_l^1 + \chi_k^2 \chi_l^2 + ... + \chi_k^r \chi_l^r = \frac{n}{h_k} \text{ or } 0 \text{ as } l = k' \text{ or } l \neq k' \quad \ldots\ldots (iii)$$

In (i) keep k fixed and let l take the r values $1, 2, ..., r$. Eliminating $h_1 \chi_1^i, h_2 \chi_2^i, ..., h_r \chi_r^i$ between the r equations so obtained we get

$$\begin{vmatrix} c_{k11} - \kappa & c_{k12} & \cdots & c_{k1r} \\ c_{k21} & c_{k22} - \kappa & \cdots & c_{k2r} \\ \vdots & \vdots & & \vdots \\ c_{kr1} & c_{kr2} & \cdots & c_{krr} - \kappa \end{vmatrix} = 0,$$

$$\text{where } \kappa = \frac{h_k \chi_k^i}{\chi_1^i} \quad \ldots\ldots\ldots (iv)$$

Ex. 1. The alternating group on the symbols 1, 2, 3, 4 contains 4 conjugate sets
$$C_1 \equiv 1, \ C_2 \equiv (1\ 2)(3\ 4) + (1\ 3)(2\ 4) + (1\ 4)(2\ 3),$$
$$C_3 \equiv (1\ 2\ 3) + (1\ 4\ 2) + (1\ 3\ 4) + (2\ 4\ 3),$$
$$C_4 \equiv (1\ 3\ 2) + (1\ 2\ 4) + (1\ 4\ 3) + (2\ 3\ 4).$$

* See footnote on p. 183.

XV 5]   PROPERTIES OF CHARACTERISTICS   185

The table gives the value of c_{kle}. Putting $k=8$ in (iv) we have $\kappa^4 = 64\kappa$. Hence $\kappa = 4, 4\omega, 4\omega^2$, or 0, where $2\omega = -1 + \sqrt{-3}$. Putting these values of κ in the 8 equations (i) where $k=8$ and $l=2, 3, 4$ we get for the ratios $h_1\chi_1{}^i : h_2\chi_2{}^i : h_3\chi_3{}^i : h_4\chi_4{}^i$ the four values $1:8:4:4, 1:8:4\omega:4\omega^2, 1:8:4\omega^2:4\omega$, and $1:-1:0:0$. Substituting in the result of Ex. 4 (noting that C_1 and C_2 are self-

Value of e.

Values of k, l.	1	2	3	4
1,1.	1	0	0	0
1,2.	0	1	0	0
1,3.	0	0	1	0
1,4.	0	0	0	1
2,2.	3	2	0	0
2,3.	0	0	3	0
2,4.	0	0	0	3
3,3.	0	0	0	4
3,4.	4	4	0	0
4,4.	0	0	4	0

Value of $C_{kle} = C_{lke}$

Value of k

Value of i	1	2	3	4
1	1	1	1	1
2	1	1	ω	ω^2
3	1	1	ω^2	ω
4	3	-1	0	0

Value of χ_k^i

inverse, while C_3 is inverse to C_4) we obtain the values 1, 1, 1, 3 for $\chi_1{}^i$ respectively. Hence we get the above table for $\chi_k{}^i$.

The corresponding representations are those generated by $x' = x$, $x' = \omega x$, $x' = \omega^2 x$, (y, z, x) and $(x, -y, -z)$. Of these S_1 and S_4 are self-inverse representations, while S_2 is inverse to S_3. There are 8 representations of degree 1, since the commutant $C_1 + C_2$ is of index 8 (cf. XV 8_2).

Ex. 2. (i) $h_i = h_i'$; (ii) $k_k h_l = c_{kl1} h_1 + c_{kl2} h_2 + \ldots + c_{klr} h_r$; (iii) $c_{kls} = c_{lks}$; (iv) $c_{kls} = c_{k'l'q'}$; (v) $c_{1l_e} = 1$ or 0, as $e = l$ or $e \neq l$; (vi) $c_{kl1} = h_k$ or 0, as $l = k'$ or $l \neq k'$; (vii) $c_{kk'_e} = 0$ if C_e is not in the commutant; (viii) $c_{kls} h_s = c_{ks'l'} h_l$.

Ex. 3. Prove $h_1 \chi_1^{\ i} + h_2 \chi_2^{\ i} + \ldots + h_r \chi_r^{\ i} = 0 \ (i \neq 1)$.

Ex. 4. Prove $h_1 \chi_1^{\ i} \chi_1^{\ i'} + h_2 \chi_2^{\ i} \chi_2^{\ i'} + \ldots + h_r \chi_r^{\ i} \chi_r^{\ i'} = n$.

Ex. 5. Verify (i) when the elements C_k and C_l are in the normal subgroup of G corresponding to identity in S_i.

Ex. 6. Verify (i) and (ii) for an Abelian group.

Ex. 7. Find the characteristics and corresponding representations for the group (i) $a^p = b^2 = (ab)^2 = 1$; (ii) $a^4 = b^2 = (ab)^2 = 1$; (iii) $a^6 = b^2 = (ab)^2 = 1$.

Ex. 8. Find the characteristics for the groups
(i) $a^6 = 1$, $a^3 = (ab)^2 = b^2$; (ii) $a^4 = 1$, $a^2 = (ab)^2 = b^2$.

Ex. 9. Find the characteristics for the group $a^7 = b^3 = 1$, $ab = ba^2$.

Ex. 10. Find the characteristics for the symmetric group of degree 4.

Ex. 11. Find the characteristics for (i) the alternating group, (ii) the symmetric group of degree 5.

§ 6. *No simple group contains a conjugate set of p^s elements.*

Suppose that in the group G of § 5 the conjugate set C_k contains p^s elements, i.e. $h_k = p^s$. Put $l = 1$ in § 5 (iii) then
$$\chi_1^{\ 1} \chi_k^{\ 1} + \chi_1^{\ 2} \chi_k^{\ 2} + \ldots + \chi_1^{\ r} \chi_k^{\ r} = 0 \ldots\ldots\ldots\ldots(i)$$

If $\chi_1^{\ i} = 1 \ (i \neq 1)$, the representation S_i is of degree 1 and is therefore Abelian. Hence G, being isomorphic with S_i, is not simple.

Next suppose $\chi_1^{\ i} \neq 1$ unless $i = 1$. Since $\chi_1^{\ 1} \chi_k^{\ 1} = 1$, it follows from (i) that not all of $\chi_1^{\ 2} \chi_k^{\ 2}, \chi_1^{\ 3} \chi_k^{\ 3}, \ldots, \chi_1^{\ r} \chi_k^{\ r}$ can be divisible by p. Suppose $\chi_1^{\ i} \chi_k^{\ i}$ not divisible by p.

Let σ of order q be an element of S_i corresponding to an element of C_k. Then σ can be transformed into a multiplication of the form $(\omega^{a_1} x_1, \omega^{a_2} x_2, \omega^{a_3} x_3, \ldots)$ where ω is a primitive q-th root of unity, and $\chi_k^{\ i} = \omega^{a_1} + \omega^{a_2} + \omega^{a_3} + \ldots$. Denote by $\omega_1 (= \chi_k^{\ i}), \omega_2, \ldots, \omega_{q-1}, \omega_q (= \chi_1^{\ i})$ the quantities obtained by putting $\omega^1, \omega^2, \ldots, \omega^{q-1}, \omega^q$ for ω in $\chi_k^{\ i}$. Let
$$(x - \omega_1)(x - \omega_2) \ldots (x - \omega_q) \equiv x^q + t_1 x^{q-1} + \ldots + t_q.$$
Then $t_1, t_2, \ldots, t_q$ are integers; for they are integral symmetric functions of the roots of $x^q = 1$.

Now by § 5 (iv) $h_k \chi_k^{\ i} \div \chi_1^{\ i}$ is a root of an equation of the form $x^r + p_1 x^{r-1} + \ldots + p_r = 0$, where $p_1, p_2, \ldots, p_r$ are integers.

Then the H. C. F. of $x^r + p_1 x^{r-1} + \ldots + p_r$ and

$$x^q + t_1 \left(\frac{h_k}{\chi_1^i}\right) x^{q-1} + \ldots + t_q \left(\frac{h_k}{\chi_1^i}\right)^q$$

is of the form $x^f + q_1 x^{f-1} + \ldots + q_f$, where $q_1, q_2, \ldots, q_f$ are rational; f is $\neq 0$ since the H. C. F. is divisible by $x - \frac{h_k \chi_k^i}{\chi_1^i}$.

Let $x^r + p_1 x^{r-1} + \ldots + p_r$
$$\equiv (x^f + q_1 x^{f-1} + \ldots + q_f)(x^e + r_1 x^{e-1} + \ldots + r_e),$$

where $r = e + f$. Then q_f is integral. For let λ and μ be the L. C. M.'s of the denominators of the rational fractions $q_1, q_2, \ldots, q_f$ and of $r_1, r_2, \ldots, r_e$ respectively. Then
$$\lambda \mu (x^r + p_1 x^{r-1} + \ldots + p_r)$$
$$\equiv (\lambda x^f + \lambda q_1 x^{f-1} + \ldots + \lambda q_f)(\mu x^e + \mu r_1 x^{e-1} + \ldots + \mu r_e),$$
and therefore by Gauss' theorem * $\lambda = \mu = 1$.

Now the integer q_f is the product of f quantities
$$\frac{h_k \omega_1}{\chi_1^i}, \frac{h_k \omega_a}{\chi_1^i}, \frac{h_k \omega_b}{\chi_1^i}, \ldots$$

Since $h_k = p^s$ and χ_1^i is prime to p, the product $\frac{\omega_1}{\chi_1^i} \cdot \frac{\omega_a}{\chi_1^i} \cdot \frac{\omega_b}{\chi_1^i} \ldots$ must be integral. But since $\omega_1, \omega_a, \omega_b, \ldots$ are each the sum of χ_1^i quantities with unit modulus, the moduli of $\omega_1, \omega_a, \omega_b, \ldots$ are each $\leq \chi_1^i$.† Hence the modulus of $\frac{\chi_k^i}{\chi_1^i} = \frac{\omega_1}{\chi_1^i}$ is integral, since the modulus of $\frac{\omega_1}{\chi_1^i} \cdot \frac{\omega_a}{\chi_1^i} \cdot \frac{\omega_b}{\chi_1^i} \cdot \ldots$ is integral. This is only possible if $a_1 = a_2 = a_3 = \ldots$, and then the substitution σ is a similarity. Hence S_i contains a normal element σ and is not simple. Therefore G being isomorphic with S_i is not simple.

Ex. Prove that a group G of order $p^\alpha q^\beta$ (p and q prime) is (i) composite, (ii) soluble.

---

* 'If the coefficients of $a_0 x^m + a_1 x^{m-1} + \ldots + a_m$ are integers with no common factor, and the same is true of $b_0 x^n + b_1 x^{n-1} + \ldots + b_n$, the coefficients of their product $c_0 x^{m+n} + c_1 x^{m+n-1} + \ldots + c_{m+n}$ have no common factor.' In fact, since $c_i = a_0 b_i + a_1 b_{i-1} + \ldots + a_{i-1} b_1 + a_i b_0$, a given prime dividing $a_0, a_1, \ldots, a_{g-1}$ and $b_0, b_1, \ldots, b_{h-1}$ but not a_g or b_h divides $c_0, c_1, \ldots, c_{g+h-1}$ but not c_{g+h}.

† For the sum of the moduli of two or more quantities $\geq$ the modulus of their sum. This is at once evident from the graphical representation of complex quantities.

HINTS FOR THE SOLUTION OF THE EXAMPLES

CHAPTER I

§ 1. Ex. 2. (i) $a \cdot a\alpha = e\alpha = ae$, $\therefore a\alpha = e$. (ii) $ga\alpha = ha\alpha$, $\therefore g = h$.

Ex. 3. $ab \ldots kl \cdot l^{-1}k^{-1} \ldots b^{-1}a^{-1} = ab \ldots k \cdot k^{-1} \ldots b^{-1}a^{-1} = \ldots = ab \cdot b^{-1}a^{-1} = a \cdot a^{-1} = 1$.

Ex. 4, 5. Prove as in ordinary algebra.

Ex. 6. $a^2b = aba = baa = ba^2$; and this can be at once extended.

Ex. 7. Prove as in Ex. 6.

Ex. 8, 9. Prove when $n = 1$, and then use induction.

Ex. 10, 11. The identical element is zero when the law of combination is that of addition, unity when the law is that of multiplication.

§ 2. Ex. 4. (ii) If $x = kn + l$ $(n > l \geq 0)$, $1 = a^{x-kn} = a^l$. $\therefore l = 0$.

Ex. 7. Use I $1_{7(1)}$.

Ex. 8. (i) If $x = kn + l$ $(n > l \geq 0)$, a^{x-kn} is permutable with b. $\therefore l = 0$. (ii) Prove as in (i). (iii) Find integers x and y such that $xr \equiv 1 \pmod{n}$ and $ys \equiv 1 \pmod{m}$. Then since a^r and b^s are permutable, so are $a^{xr} = a$ and $b^{ys} = b$.

Ex. 9. $ab \cdot ba = ab^2a = a^2 = 1$.

Ex. 10. $ba = ba \cdot abab = ba^2bab = b^2ab = ab$.

Ex. 11. (i) Find integers x and y such that $xr + yq = 1$ and put $a = xr$, $\beta = yq$. (ii) $a^q = (bc)^q = b^q c^q = c^q$.
$$\therefore a^\beta = a^{yq} = c^{yq} = c^{1-xr} = c.$$

Ex. 12. Use I $1_{8(1) \text{ and } (1v)}$.

Ex. 13. Use I 1_9, putting $t = 1$.

§ 3. Ex. 1. If $a^n = 1$, $(b^{-1}ab)^n = b^{-1}a^n b = b^{-1}b = 1$, and conversely.

Ex. 3. $ab = b^{-1}(ba)b$. Now use Ex. 1.

Ex. 4. $c^{-1}(ab)c = c^{-1}ac \cdot c^{-1}bc$.

Ex. 5. If $a^{-1}ca = b^{-1}cb$, $ba^{-1} \cdot c = c \cdot ba^{-1}$ and $ab^{-1} \cdot c = c \cdot ab^{-1}$.

Ex. 6. (i) Use induction;
(ii) $(b^s a^r)^{-1}(b^y a^x)(b^s a^r) = b^y \cdot b^{-y}a^{-r}b^y \cdot b^{-s}a^x b^s \cdot a^r$. Now use § 3.

Ex. 7. Put $y = m$ in $b^{-y}ab^y = a^{k^y}$.

Ex. 8. 1 or 31.

Ex. 9. $k^{p-1} \equiv 1 \pmod{p}$ for all values of k prime to p.
Ex. 10. $b^{-1}ab = a^{-1}$ and $a^{-1}ba = b^{-1}$,
$$\therefore b^2 = b \cdot aba = bab \cdot a = a^2.$$
Hence $b^2 = a^2 = a^{-1}a^2a = a^{-1}b^2a = b^{-2}$ and $\therefore b^4 = 1$.
Ex. 11. If $a^{-1}ca = c^\alpha$ and $b^{-1}cb = c^\beta$, $(ab)^{-1}c(ab) = b^{-1}c^\alpha b$
$$= c^{\alpha\beta} = (ba)^{-1}c(ba).$$

§ 4. **Ex. 2.** $a^{-1}b^{-1}ab \cdot b^{-1}a^{-1}ba = 1$.
Ex. 3. $g^{-1}(a^{-1}b^{-1}ab)g$ is the commutator of $g^{-1}ag$ and $g^{-1}bg$.
Ex. 4. If $b = a^{-1}b^{-1}ab$, $b = 1$.
Ex. 5. Use I 3_4.
Ex. 6. $a^{-1}b^{-1}ab = (ba)^{-1} \cdot (ab)$. Now use I 3_3.
Ex. 7. $a^{-1}b^{-1}ab = (ba)^{-1}(aba^{-1}b^{-1})ba$.
Ex. 8. $a^{-1}b^{-1}ab = abab$.
Ex. 9. If $aga^{-1} = g^r$ and $bgb^{-1} = g^s$, $g = a^{-1}g^ra = b^{-1}g^sb$.
Hence $c^{-1}gc = b^{-1}a^{-1}ba \cdot g \cdot a^{-1}b^{-1}ab = b^{-1}a^{-1}b \cdot g^r \cdot b^{-1}ab$
$$= b^{-1}a^{-1} \cdot g^{rs} \cdot ab = b^{-1}g^sb = g.$$
Ex. 10. Put α = the order of a in $a^{-\alpha}b^{-1}a^\alpha b = c^\alpha$.
Ex. 11. (i) and (ii). Use induction or **Ex. 2.** (iii) **Making** repeated use of $a^\alpha b^\beta = b^\beta a^\alpha c^{\alpha\beta}$ we have
$$b^{-y}a^{-x} \cdot b^{-s}a^{-r} \cdot a^x b^y \cdot a^r b^s = b^{-y}a^{-x}b^{-s}a^x b^y c^{-yr} b^s = c^{xs-yr}.$$
Ex. 12. Use induction and $g_i^* g_j = g_j g_i^* c_{ij}^*$.
Ex. 13. (i) $a^{z(k^p-1)-r(k^q-1)}$. (ii) $a^{z(k^{q+s}-k^q)-r(k^{q+s}-k^q)}$.

CHAPTER II

§ 1. **Ex. 2.** 6.
Ex. 4. Call the rows of the board $1, 2, \ldots, m$ and call the files $\alpha, \beta, \ldots, \mu$. Place a queen on the square common to each row and file with the same name.

§ 2. **Ex. 7.** Of $(a\ b)$ and $(b\ c)$.

§ 3. **Ex. 1.** $(1\ 8\ 6\ 4\ 9)(2\ 8\ 5)(7\ 10)$, $(1\ 11\ 10\ 9\ 6\ 2\ 7\ 3\ 5)(4\ 12\ 8)(13\ 14)$, and $(a\ e)(b\ g\ c\ f)$.
Ex. 5. (i) $(a\ b\ \ldots\ l)(m\ n\ \ldots\ x)$, (ii) $(a\ b\ c\ \ldots\ x\ y\ z\ \ldots)$.
Ex. 6. Use Ex. 5.
Ex. 8. (i) $(h\ j\ x\ y\ z \ldots i\ \xi\ \eta\ \zeta \ldots)$, (ii) $(h\ j\ \xi\ \eta\ \zeta \ldots)(i\ k\ x\ y\ z \ldots)$.
Ex. 9. S^t replaces a_x by a_{x+t}.
Ex. 10. $(a\ b\ c\ \ldots\ l)(\alpha\ \beta\ \gamma\ \ldots\ \lambda)(A\ B\ C\ \ldots\ L) \ldots$ containing k cycles $= (a\ \alpha\ A\ \ldots\ b\ \beta\ B\ \ldots\ c\ \gamma\ C\ \ldots\ \ldots\ l\ \lambda\ L\ \ldots)^k$.
Ex. 11. $(1\ 2\ 4\ 3\ 7\ 8\ 5\ 6\ 10\ 12\ 11\ 9)^2$.

§ 4. **Ex. 2.** 6, 20, 2. Resolve into cycles.
Ex. 3. By II 3_7 the statement is true for circular permutations. Suppose $S = ABC\ldots$, where $A, B, C, \ldots$ are circular permutations, no two of which have a symbol in common; and let

SOLUTIONS. CH. II 191

$A = A_1 A_2$, $B = B_1 B_2$, $C = C_1 C_2$, ..., where $A_1, A_2, B_1, B_2, C_1, C_2,$ ... are of order 2. Then $S = A_1 A_2 B_1 B_2 C_1 C_2 ... = (A_1 B_1 C_1 ...)(A_2 B_2 C_2 ...)$, which is of order 2.

Ex. 4. $m! \div rst ...$ is integral if $r+s+t+ ... = m$.

§ 5. Ex. 1. (5 6 8 4) (9 8 1) (2 7), (4 1 8) (7 8) (6 2).
Ex. 3. If $A \equiv (a\ b\ c\ ...)\ (k\ l\ m\ ...)\ ...$ and
$$B = (\alpha\ \beta\ \gamma\ ...)\ (\kappa\ \lambda\ \mu\ ...)\ ...$$
are the two similar permutations, $B = T^{-1}AT$ where
$$T = \begin{pmatrix} a\ b\ c\ ... k\ l\ m\ ...\ ... \\ \alpha\ \beta\ \gamma\ ... \kappa\ \lambda\ \mu\ ...\ ... \end{pmatrix}.$$

Ex. 4. C is the commutator of A and T.
Ex. 5. Let $A \equiv (a\ b\ c\ ...\ l)\ (m\ n\ o\ ...)\ ...$ and $B \equiv (\alpha\ \beta\ \gamma\ ...)\ ...$ be the permutations. Then $A^{-1}B^{-1}AB = A^{-1} \cdot B^{-1}AB = (c\ b\ a\ l\ ...)\ (o\ n\ m\ ...)\ ... \cdot (\beta b\ c\ ...\ l)\ (m\ n\ o\ ...)\ ... = (a\beta b)$.

Ex. 6. If the 2 symbols are not consecutive in a cycle of either permutation, the commutator is of order 3 as in Ex. 5. Similarly, if they are consecutive in (i) both, (ii) one and not the other, the commutator is of order (i) 2, (ii) 5.

Ex. 7. By § 5 if $T^{-1}ST = S$, T is a power of S.
Ex. 8. If $A \equiv (a\ b\ c\ d\ e)$, $B \equiv (1\ 2\ 3\ 4\ 5)$, the permutations required are the 25 permutations of the form $A^r B^s$ together with the 25 transforming A into B and B into A, i.e. 20 of the form $(a\ 2\ d\ 5\ b\ 3\ e\ 1\ c\ 4)$ and 5 of the form $(a\ 3)\ (b\ 4)\ (c\ 5)\ (d\ 1)\ (e\ 2)$.

§ 6. Ex. 2. (1 3) (1 6) (1 4) (1 9) (2 8) (2 5) (7 10) and
$(a\ c)\ (a\ e)\ (a\ f)\ (b\ h)\ (b\ i)\ (b\ d)$.
Ex. 3. $(rs) = (1\ r)\ (1\ s)\ (1\ r)$.
Ex. 4. Assume the result true for the product of any number of transpositions $< k$. Let $T_1, T_2, ..., T_k$ be transpositions whose product is a permutation C of degree m with s cycles. Then $T_1 T_2 ... T_{k-1} = CT_k$ has by II $8_{4, 5}$ $s \pm 1$ cycles; so that $k - 1 \geq m - s \mp 1$ and ∴ $k \geq m - s$. Now use induction.
Ex. 5. Use § 6 and Ex. 4.
Ex. 6. Use Ex. 4, 5.

§ 7. Ex. 2. Use § 6.
Ex. 3. Use Ex. 2.
Ex. 5. By II 6_3, any permutation can be expressed as the product of transpositions all having a symbol in common, and the product of any two of these is circular of order 3.
Ex. 6. By Ex. 5 every even permutation is the product of permutations of the type $(1\ r\ s)$, and $(1\ r\ s) = (1\ 2\ s)\ (1\ 2\ r)\ (1\ 2\ s)^2$.
Ex. 8. If it contains a cycle of even degree, it is permutable with that cycle considered as a circular permutation. If it contains two cycles of equal odd degree, use II 5_9.

CHAPTER III

§ 2. Ex. 4. $x' = (-dx+b) \div (cx-a)$, $(5x+8y, 8x+13y)$, and $(-4x+3y+5z, x-y-z, 5x-3y-6z)$.

Ex. 6. 2, 2, 3, 3, 12, 6, 4, 2, 4.

Ex. 7. Its n-th power is $x' = a^n x + b(a^n - 1) \div (a-1)$. Hence the required condition is that a should be a root of unity and $\neq 1$.

Ex. 8. $(a^n x, na^{n-1}bx + a^n y, na^{n-1}cx + a^n z)$.

Ex. 9. $(a^n x, \dfrac{a^n - d^n}{a-d} cx + d^n y)$. a and d are roots of unity, and if $a = d$, $c = 0$.

Ex. 10. $(-x+2y+2z, y, z)$; $(-3x+7y+8z, -x+y+3z, -2x+7y+5z)$.

Ex. 12. (i) Prove by induction. (ii) $\phi \div \pi$ is rational but not integral.

Ex. 13. $x' = \dfrac{1}{c}\left\{ a - \dfrac{\Delta}{a+d-} \dfrac{\Delta}{a+d-} \cdots \dfrac{\Delta}{-cx+d} \right\}$ to $n+1$ convergents, where $\Delta = ad - bc$.

Ex. 14. Put in the form $\dfrac{x'-a}{x'-b} = k\dfrac{x-a}{x-b}$.

Ex. 15. T^n is derived from S^n by putting $d_4 = 1$, $a_4 = b_4 = c_4 = d_1 = d_2 = d_3 = 0$. $\therefore T^n = 1$ if $S^n = 1$.

Ex. 16. (i) $y_1' = -y_1 \div (y_1+1)$, $y_2' = y_2 \div (y_1+1)$, $y_3' = y_3$, ..., $y_{m-2}' = y_{m-2}$ and $y_1'' = y_2$, $y_2'' = y_3$, ..., $y_{m-4}'' = y_{m-3}$, y_{m-3}''

$$= -1 + \dfrac{y_{m-3}}{-1} + \dfrac{y_{m-4}}{-1} + \cdots + \dfrac{y_1}{-1}.$$

(ii) Obvious from (i); or notice that the $m! \div 4!$ anharmonic ratios of m points in a line are equivalent to $m-3$ independent anharmonic ratios, i.e. each such ratio can be expressed rationally in terms of any $m-3$ independent ratios.

§ 3. Ex. 2. (i) $x' = [(a\alpha + b\gamma)x + (a^2\beta - ab\alpha + ab\delta - b^2\gamma)] \div [\gamma x + (a\delta - b\gamma)]$;

(ii) and (iii) $(\omega_1 x_1, \omega_2 x_2, ..., \omega_m x_m)$, (iv) $(x, 2y, 3z)$;

(v) $(-32x - 25y, 41x + 32y)$.

§ 4. Ex. 1. $b_{i1}a_{1j} + b_{i2}a_{2j} + \ldots + b_{im}a_{mj} = a_{i1}b_{1j} + a_{i2}b_{2j} + \ldots + a_{im}b_{mj}$.

Ex. 2. The determinant of AA^{-1} is 1.

Ex. 3. The determinant of $B^{-1}AB$ is $|b|^{-1} \cdot |a| \cdot |b| = |a|$.

Ex. 4. The determinant of A^n is $\{|a|\}^n$.

Ex. 5. Prove by induction.

Ex. 9. Use Ex. 5 or Ex. 3.

Ex. 10. (ii) If $AA' = BB' = 1$, $CC' = ABB'A' = 1$ by Ex. 3; or note that since A and B leave $x_1^2 + x_2^2 + \ldots + x_m^2$ unaltered so does AB. (iii) Prove as in (ii).

SOLUTIONS. CH. III

Ex. 11. (i) If $A \equiv \bar{A}$ and $AA' = 1$, $A\bar{A}' = AA' = 1$; (ii) and (iii) prove as in (i).

Ex. 15. (ii) If $C = A\bar{A}'$ we have readily $\bar{c}_{ij} = c_{ji}$ and $c(x, \bar{x}) = x_1'\bar{x}_1' + x_2'\bar{x}_2' + \ldots + x_m'\bar{x}_m'$.

Ex. 16. (i) By Ex. 7 the determinant of AA' is $\{|a|\}^2$; (ii) the product of $|a|$ and its conjugate is 1; (iii) $|a|$ is not altered by changing a_{ij} into a_{ij}; see also § 5.

Ex. 17. If A is orthogonal, so is A'.

Ex. 21. (i) Use Ex. 10 (i); (ii) $B'AB$ is symmetric if A is symmetric by Ex. 5; and if B is orthogonal, $B' = B^{-1}$; (iii) prove as in (ii).

Ex. 22. $x_1' = a_1 x_1 + a_2 x_2 + \ldots + a_m x_m$, $x_i' = a_i x_1 + \dfrac{a_i a_2}{a_1 \pm 1} x_2 + \dfrac{a_i a_3}{a_1 \pm 1} x_3 + \ldots + \left(\dfrac{a_i^2}{a_1 \pm 1} \mp 1\right) x_i + \ldots + \dfrac{a_i a_m}{a_1 \pm 1} x_m$.

Ex. 23. (i) Let $x_i = \beta_{i1} \xi_1 + \beta_{i2} \xi_2 + \ldots + \beta_{im} \xi_m$. Then $a(x, y) \equiv \sum_{i,j} a_{ij} y_i x_j \equiv \sum_{k,l} \left[\sum_{i,j} \beta_{ik} a_{ij} \beta_{jl}\right] \eta_k \xi_l \equiv \sum_{k,l} \left[\sum_{i,j} b_{ki} a_{ij} \beta_{jl}\right] \eta_k \xi_l \equiv d(\xi, \eta)$ by Ex. 5. (ii) As in (i).

§ 5. Ex. 3. If $a(x, \bar{x}) \equiv a_1 X_1 \bar{X}_1 + \ldots + a_r X_r \bar{X}_r - a_{r+1} X_{r+1} \bar{X}_{r+1} - \ldots - a_m X_m \bar{X}_m \equiv \beta_1 Y_1 \bar{Y}_1 + \ldots + \beta_s Y_s \bar{Y}_s - \beta_{s+1} Y_{s+1} \bar{Y}_{s+1} - \ldots - \beta_m Y_m \bar{Y}_m$

where all the a's and β's are positive, then
$a_1 X_1 \bar{X}_1 + \ldots + a_r X_r \bar{X}_r + \beta_{s+1} Y_{s+1} \bar{Y}_{s+1} + \ldots + \beta_m Y_m \bar{Y}_m$
$\equiv a_{r+1} X_{r+1} \bar{X}_{r+1} + \ldots + a_m X_m \bar{X}_m + \beta_1 Y_1 \bar{Y}_1 + \ldots + \beta_s Y_s \bar{Y}_s$.
Now if $m - s + r > m - r + s$ we can choose $x_1, x_2, \ldots, x_m$ so that
$$X_{r+1} = \ldots = X_m = Y_1 = \ldots = Y_s = 0,$$
while not all of $X_1, \ldots, X_r, Y_{s+1}, \ldots, Y_m$ are zero. This is impossible, and therefore $r \leq s$. Similarly $r \geq s$; and $\therefore r = s$.

Ex. 4. Every positive form is > 0, and $\therefore$ the sum of any number of positive forms is > 0.

§ 6. Ex. 2. $|a| \neq 0$.

Ex. 8. Use equations (iii) of § 6.

Ex. 9. Transform A and B so that $(1, 0, 0, \ldots, 0)$ is the common pole. Then using Ex. 6 the result is obvious.

Ex. 10. Use Ex. 9.

Ex. 11. $\theta(\lambda)$ is not altered by writing a_{ij} for a_{ij}.

Ex. 12. Put λX_i for x_i', X_i for x_i in III 4_{14}.

Ex. 14. $\Sigma XZ = \dfrac{1}{\lambda} \Sigma (a_{i1} X_1 + a_{i2} X_2 + \ldots + a_{im} X_m) Z_i$
$= \dfrac{1}{\lambda} \Sigma (a_{1j} Z_1 + a_{2j} Z_2 + \ldots + a_{mj} Z_m) X_j = \dfrac{\mu}{\lambda} \Sigma XZ$.

Ex. 15. If $x_i' = a_{i1} x_1 + a_{i2} x_2 + \ldots + a_{im} x_m$, $b_{i1} x_1' + b_{i2} x_2' + \ldots + b_{im} x_m' = c_{i1} x_1 + c_{i2} x_2 + \ldots + c_{im} x_m$. Now put λX_i for x_i', X_i for x_i in these equations and eliminate $X_1, X_2, \ldots, X_m$.

Ex. 16. (i) Use Ex. 10, 18 and $A' = A^{-1}$. (ii) Use Ex. 10, 14.
Ex. 17. $\Sigma \lambda \bar{\lambda} X_i \bar{X}_i = \Sigma (a_{i1} X_1 + \ldots + a_{im} X_m)(\bar{a}_{i1} \bar{X}_1 + \ldots + \bar{a}_{im} \bar{X}_m) = \Sigma X_i \bar{X}_i$. $\therefore \lambda\bar{\lambda} = 1$.
Ex. 18, 19. Put $y_i = \bar{X}_i$ in Ex. 12; noticing that, if $B = D^{-1}$, B is real and symmetric or Hermitian when D is.
Ex. 20. Prove as in Ex. 19.
Ex. 21. Use equations (iii) of § 6.
Ex. 22. Let $TAT^{-1} = L$. TA changes x_i into $(a_{i1}X_1 + a_{i2}X_2 + \ldots + a_{im}X_m)x_1 + \ldots = \lambda X_i x_1 + \ldots$; and LT changes x_i into $(X_i l_{11} + l_{21} t_{i2} + \ldots + l_{m1} t_{im}) x_1 + \ldots$. Hence $\lambda X_i = X_i l_{11} + l_{21} t_{i2} + \ldots + l_{m1} t_{im}$, $(i = 1, 2, \ldots, m)$. Solving these m equations for $l_{11}, l_{21}, \ldots, l_{m1}$ we get $l_{11} = \lambda$, $l_{21} = l_{31} = \ldots = l_{m1} = 0$. Hence by Ex. 6 $(1, 0, 0, \ldots, 0)$ is a pole of TAT^{-1}.
Ex. 23. Use equations (iii) of § 6.
Ex. 24. Use Ex. 23 and III $4_{21, 22}$.
Ex. 25. (i) $e^{\pm \theta i}$; $(\pm i, 1)$. (ii) $\pm i$; $(1, 0), (1+i, 2)$. (iii) ± 1; $(1, 1), (i, 1)$. (iv) $1, 2, 8$; $(1, 1, 0), (1, -1, 1), (1, 0, 1)$. (v) $1, -1, -1$; $(3, -2, 4), (1, -1, Z)$ for all values of Z. (vi) $-1, -1, -1$; $(3, 1, 2)$.

§ 7. Ex. 6. The n-th power of $(a_1 x, a_2 x, \ldots, a_m x_m)$ is $(a_1^n x_1, a_2^n x_2, \ldots, a_m^n x_m)$.
Ex. 7. Use Ex. 6.
Ex. 12. If $S^{-1}AS = A$, $a_{21} = a_{31} = \ldots = a_{m1} = 0$. Hence $(1, 0, 0, \ldots, 0)$ is a pole of A.

§ 8. Ex. 2. The substitution is obtained by transforming a similarity and is therefore a similarity.
Ex. 3. The a's and e's are the roots of the characteristic equation of either substitution.
Ex. 4. The practical method of § 8 can always be carried out in this case.
Ex. 5. Transform one of the substitutions with two distinct poles into a multiplication.
Ex. 6. Transform by (i) $(5x-(8-i)y, 5x-(8+i)y)$;
  (ii) $(2x-(1+i)y, y)$; (iii) $(x-iy, x-y)$;
(iv) $(x-z, x-y-z, -x+y+2z)$; (v) $(x+y, 2x+y-z, 4x+4y-z)$;
  (vi) $(x_1, \epsilon_2 x_1 + (\omega_2 - \omega_1) x_2, \ldots, \epsilon_m x_m + (\omega_m - \omega_1) x_m)$.
Ex. 7. (i) If $L \equiv (\lambda_1 x_1, \lambda_2 x_2, \ldots, \lambda_m x_m)$, where $\lambda_1, \lambda_2, \ldots, \lambda_m$ are the roots of $\theta(\lambda) = 0$ corresponding to the m poles, we prove at once $TA = LT$. (ii) In equations (iii) of § 6 the determinant formed by the Y's $= |b| \times$ the determinant formed by the X's.
Ex. 8. (ii) Use III $4_{20, 21}$; (iii) use III 6_{14}.
Ex. 9, 10. Prove by induction exactly as in § 8.
Ex. 11. (i) Prove by induction as in § 8, using III 6_{24} and noting that the product of two orthogonal substitutions is orthogonal. (ii) Use III 4_{22}.

Ex. 12. Prove by induction as in § 8.
Ex. 14. Transform by (i) $(3x+2y, 4x+3y)$,
  (ii) $(-4x+8y+5z, x-y-z, 5x-8y-6z)$.

§ 9. Ex. 5. Use III 8_9.
Ex. 7. Use § 6.
Ex. 8. (i) α, β are roots of $cx^2+(d-a)x-b = 0$.
  (ii) $x'-\alpha = \dfrac{ax+b}{cx+d} - \dfrac{a\alpha+b}{c\alpha+d} = \dfrac{x-\alpha}{(cx+d)(c\alpha+d)}$.
(iv) Use (ii). (v) Transform S by $x' = \dfrac{1}{x-\alpha}$. (vi) Use (ii).
(vii) Transform S by $x' = \dfrac{x-\alpha}{x-\beta}$. (viii) and (ix) Use (vii). (x) If $e^{2\theta i}=re^{\theta i}$, where r and θ are real, S is the product of $\dfrac{x'-\alpha}{x'-\beta} = r\dfrac{x-\alpha}{x-\beta}$ and $\dfrac{x'-\alpha}{x'-\beta} = e^{\lambda i}\dfrac{x-\alpha}{x-\beta}$, which are respectively hyperbolic and elliptic. (xi) Use (vii) or prove directly. (xii) Use (xi) and Ex. 7. (xiii) Transform S into a multiplication. (xiv) Use (vii).

§ 10. Ex. 1. $u_0, u_{p^\rho(p-\lambda)}, u_{p^r-t-1}$.
Ex. 2, 3. Every other function of the type $x^2+p_1x+p_2$ is reducible mod p.

Ex. 4 (i)

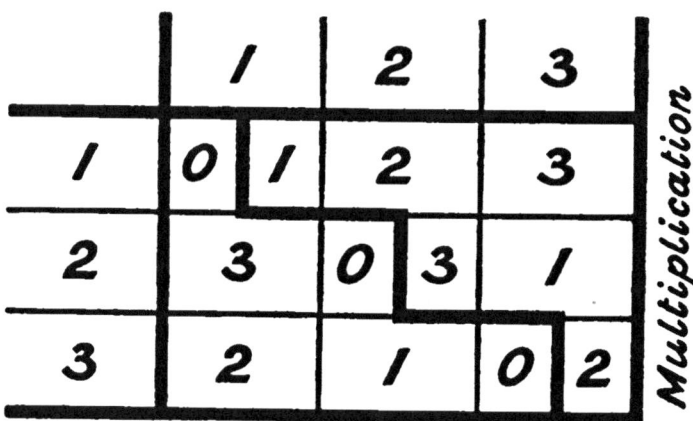

Addition
$p=2$, $P(x) \equiv x^2+x+1$

(ii)

	1	2	3	4	5	6	7	8
1	2|1	2	3	4	5	6	7	8
2	0	1|1	6	8	7	3	5	4
3	4	5	6|4	7	1	8	2	5
4	5	3	7	8|2	3	5	6	1
5	3	4	8	6	7|8	2	4	6
6	7	8	0	1	2	3|4	1	7
7	8	6	1	2	0	4	5|8	3
8	6	7	2	0	1	5	3	4|2

Addition / Multiplication

$p' = 3$; $P(x) \equiv x^2 + 2x + 2$

Ex. 5. u_2 and u_5, u_6 and u_7, u_5 and u_6. Use the table.

Ex. 7 (ii). Express $\dfrac{\sin n\phi}{\sin \phi}$ (n odd) or $\dfrac{\sin n\phi}{\sin 2\phi}$ (n even) in descending powers of $4\cos^2\phi$; then put $4\cos^2\phi = \dfrac{(a+d)^2}{ad-bc}$ and we get the required condition; cf. III 2_{12}.

Ex. 8. The number of substitutions on given variables with coefficients in a given Field is limited.

Ex. 9. 8, 4.
Ex. 10. 2, 2, 5.
Ex. 11. 2, 2, 2, 4, 8, 7.
Ex. 12. 2, 2, 2, 5, 6, 11.
Ex. 13. 2, 5.
Ex. 14. 8, 4.
Ex. 15. If we equate two of these marks we get an equation for u of degree lower than k.
Ex. 16. Use Ex. 15.
Ex. 18. (i) Assume the result true; replace $F(u)$ by $(u - u_{k+1}) \cdot F(u)$; and use induction. (ii) and (iii) Prove as in the case of ordinary equations, using (i).

§ 11. Ex. 1. Use III $2_{7, 8, 9}$.
Ex. 2. 82, 108.
Ex. 3. Use III $10_{16, 17}$.

SOLUTIONS. CH. IV

Ex. 5. Every power of an integral mark is integral.
Ex. 6. (i) 2, 6, 7, 8; 5. (ii) 8, 5, 6, 7; 4.
Ex. 7. (i) It is a power of $(ux_1, ux_2, ..., ux_m)$ where u is any primitive root.
Ex. 8. If a given mark u^s is the square of u^x, $2x \equiv s \pmod{p^r - 1}$. We can always find an integer x satisfying this congruence if $p = 2$; but only when s is even if $p > 2$.
Ex. 9. Prove as in Ex. 8.
Ex. 10. (i) $a\bar{a} = a_1^2 - a_2^2 u$ which is the difference of a square and a not-square unless $a_1 = a_2 = 0$.
(ii) If $a \neq 0$, $a\bar{a} b = a\bar{a} b_1 + a\bar{a} b_2 i \neq 0$ unless $b_1 = b_2 = 0$.
(iii) $(a_1 + a_2 i)^{p^r} \equiv a_1^{p^r} + a_2^{p^r} i^{p^r} \pmod{p} = a_1 + a_2 i u^{(p^r-1)+2}$
$$= a_1 - a_2 i = \bar{a}.$$
(iv) Prove as in (iii) that $\bar{a}^{p^r} = a$.

CHAPTER IV

§ 2. Ex. 4. OC lies in the plane AOB and $\sin BOC = m \sin AOC$.
Ex. 5. Let O be at infinity.
Ex. 7, 8. Put $\beta = -a$ in Ex. 5.
Ex. 10. OA, OB, OC are brought into the positions Oa, Ob', Oc' by a rotation through π about OA followed by a rotation about OD. $\therefore D_1 OA$, DOA are perpendicular and DOD_1 bisects the angle between DOA and DOa. Now consider the intersection of all lines and planes of the figure with a plane perpendicular to OD.

§ 4. Ex. 1. (i) The point about which the inversion of the equivalent rotatory-inversion takes place. (ii) When the rotatory-inversion reduces to a reflexion or gliding-reflexion.
Ex. 2. $S \equiv (a).(b).(c)$, where a and b are parallel planes and c is a plane perpendicular to them. Let d be a plane perpendicular to a, b, c. Then $S \equiv (a).(d).(d).(b).(c)$, and $(a).(d) \equiv$ a rotation through π, $(d).(b).(c) \equiv$ an inversion.

§ 6. Ex. 3. Rotations about lines through O; rotatory-inversions whose inversions take place about O (including inversion about O and reflexion in planes through O as special cases).

§ 7. Ex. 1. The product is equivalent to successive reflexions in $4r + 8s$ planes.
Ex. 4. $\dfrac{n}{2}[3 - (-1)^n]$.

§ 8. Ex. 1. A screw is equivalent to successive rotations through π about two straight lines. Take a pair of such lines to represent the screw (§ 5).

§ 9. Ex. 3. $t = S^{-1}TS$.

Ex. 4. If the lines Ox, Oy represent T and t geometrically, R is a rotation through the angle xOy about a line perpendicular to Ox and Oy.

Ex. 5. T is a translation bringing l to coincide with l'. $s = T^{-1}ST$; now use Ex. 3.

Ex. 6. $R = s\tau$, where s is a screw about l' similar to S and τ is a translation parallel to l. Now use Ex. 5.

Ex. 8. Find by Ex. 6 translations t, τ such that $S = Rt$, $s = r\tau$; then find τ' such that $tr = r\tau'$. Then
$$Ss = Rtr\tau = Rr \cdot \tau'\tau = Rr \cdot T.$$

Ex. 10. Use Ex. 8.

Ex. 12. Use Ex. 10, taking a vertex of the parallelepipedon as O'.

Ex. 13. Use Ex. 10, taking O' as the point on a at a distance $2x$ from the point of a nearest to b.

Ex. 14. Use Ex. 10 and 11 taking A as the point O'. A rotation through π about a line through D perpendicular to AD and making an angle of 80° with CD.

§ 10. Ex. 1. The lines through the centre perpendicular to the faces are 4-al rotation-axes; the lines joining the middle points of opposite edges are 2-al rotation-axes.

Ex. 2. (ii) The axis of a spheroid.

§ 11. Ex. 1. The circles in which the inversions take place are (i) two intersecting straight lines, (ii) two parallel straight lines, (iii) two concentric circles.

Ex. 2. Invert the circles into a pair of straight lines or a pair of concentric circles according as they meet in real or imaginary points, and use the theorem 'a circle and a pair of inverse points inverts into a circle and a pair of inverse points'.

Ex. 3. Use stereographic projection and § 2.

Ex. 4. Prove as in § 9.

Ex. 5. (i) Inversion about $(\tfrac{1}{2}d, 0)$, (ii) Inversion in $x^2 + y^2 = b$ followed by reflexion in $y = 0$. Replace inversion about $(\tfrac{1}{2}d, 0)$ by successive reflexions in $x = \tfrac{1}{2}d$, $y = 0$, and use Ex. 2.

Ex. 6. See VIII 11.

Ex. 7. If j is $x^2 + y^2 + 2gx + 2fy + m = 0$ and l is
$$x\cos\theta + y\sin\theta = t,$$
we have
$$\frac{a}{c} = 2te^{i\theta} + e^{2i\theta}(g - if),\ \frac{b}{c} = 2te^{i\theta}(g + if) + me^{2i\theta},\ \frac{d}{c} = g + if;$$
whence the result follows.

SOLUTIONS. CH. V   199

Ex. 8. (i) Use Ex. 7. (ii) Prove for the case in which $ad-bc = 1$ noting that $(a+d)^2$ is real. Now multiplying a, b, c, d by the same quantity is equivalent to magnifying the figure $ABCD$ with respect to the origin and turning the axes of reference through some angle.

§ 12. Ex. 1. We have $x' = (l_1x+m_1y+n_1) \div (Lx+My+N)$, $y' = (l_2x+m_2y+n_2) \div (Lx+My+N)$, &c.

Ex. 2. If x', x are the distances of corresponding points from fixed points of the lines, we have a relation of the form
$$x' = (ax+b) \div (cx+d).$$

Ex. 5. The points whose coordinates are the poles of the substitution defining the relations between the coordinates of corresponding points when referred to the same (i) points, (ii) triangle, (iii) tetrahedron of reference. Exceptions:—a rotation, reflexion, translation, screw.

Ex. 6. (i) O and the circular points, (ii) the point at ∞ on l and the circular points in a plane perpendicular to l, (iii) O, the point at ∞ on l, and the circular points in a plane perpendicular to l.

Ex. 7. Use § 6.

Ex. 8. Referring to rectangular Cartesian axes with corresponding points as origins the collineation is represented by a homogeneous substitution multiplying $x^2+y^2+z^2$ by a constant, since the plane at infinity and the cone $x^2+y^2+z^2 = 0$ are fixed.

§ 13. Ex. 1. Put $a+d = 0$ in the solution of IV 12_2.

Ex. 4. The two fixed lines are l and the line at ∞ in a plane perpendicular to l.

Ex. 5. The fixed point or fixed plane are at ∞.

Ex. 6, 7, 8. Prove as in § 9.

Ex. 9. Use Ex. 8; or transform one collineation so that it is defined by $x' = -x$.

Ex. 10. Use Ex. 6; or transform σ_1 into the plane at ∞.

Ex. 12. The collineations can be transformed into (i) inversions, (ii) reflexions in parallel planes, (iii) rotations through π about parallel lines.

Ex. 18. Transform the intersection of the given plane and conicoid into the circle at infinity.

CHAPTER V

§ 1. Ex. 4. $g = a^{-1}b$, $h = ba^{-1}$.

Ex. 8. See § 6.

Ex. 9, 10. The elements of order > 2 can be divided into pairs each consisting of 2 elements inverse to one another.

Ex. 11. Let $a^2 = b^2 = (ab)^2 = 1$. Then $a^{-1}b^{-1}ab = abab = 1$.
Ex. 12. See VI 2.
Ex. 22. (viii), (x), (xii).
Ex. 23. 2, 4, 6, 8.

§ 2. Ex. 4. $b^y a^x$ ($x = 1, 2, 3, 4, 5$; $y = 1, 2, 3$).
Ex. 5. Use I 3.
Ex. 6. Since $a_i A \equiv A$ and contains r distinct elements, A contains a_i^{-1}, &c.
Ex. 7. $(AB)^2$ contains $1 b_j . a_i 1$; $\therefore BA \equiv AB$, &c.
Ex. 9. $\{G, g\} \equiv Gg + Gg^2 + \ldots + Gg^r$, where r is the order of g relative to G.
Ex. 10. See § 19.

§ 3. Ex. 4. Put $AB = a$, $B = b^{-1}$ in $a^n = b^2 = (ab)^2 = 1$. Every element of the group is of the form $ABABAB \ldots$.
Ex. 5. Put $AB = a$, $B = b^{-1}$ in $a^3 = b^3 = (ab)^2 = 1$.
Ex. 8. Let POX be the angle, P_1OX and P_2OX its supplement and complement. Then OP_1 and OP_2 are the reflexions of OP in lines through O making angles of $\frac{1}{2}\pi$ and $\frac{1}{4}\pi$ with OX.
Ex. 14. Any element of either group is of the form $b^y a^x$. Its order is found by I 3.
Ex. 15. Prove as in Ex. 14 using I 4_{12}.

§ 4. Ex. 4. Use Ex. 3.
Ex. 6. If $g_i^{-1}H$ and $g_j^{-1}H$ have an element in common $g_j g_i^{-1}$ is contained in H, and $\therefore i = j$.
Ex. 7. Take L in Ex. 1 as an instance.
Ex. 8. If H is such a subgroup and g is in G but not in H, $G \equiv H + Hg + Hg^2 + \ldots + Hg^{p-1}$.
Ex. 15, 16, 17. Use I 2_7.
Ex. 19. The subgroup composed of (i) the even permutations, (ii) the screws, (iii) the substitutions with determinant 1.
Ex. 22. $N \equiv (1 + a^2)(1 + a + b + ba) \equiv (1 + b)(1 + a + a^2 + a^3)$.
$O \equiv (1 + a^2)(1 + b + c + cb) \equiv (1 + b)(1 + a^2 + c + ca^2)$.
Ex. 23. $H + H(234) + H(243) + H(1234) + H(1324) + H(14)$.

§ 5. Ex. 6 (ii). Let $n = n'd$, $r = r'd$. Choose integers x, y such that $r'x - n'y = 1$. Then $\{a^r\}$ contains $a^{rx} = a^{d + ny} = a^d$.
Ex. 7. (i) They are $a^{xp^{a-r}}$ ($x = 1, 2, \ldots, p^r$). (ii) $\{a\}$ contains p^r elements whose orders divide p^r and p^{r-1} whose orders divide p^{r-1}, and $\therefore p^r - p^{r-1}$ of order p^r.
Ex. 8. (i) Prove as in Ex. 7. (ii) No two subgroups have an element of order m in common.
Ex. 9. See § 19.

SOLUTIONS. CH. V 201

Ex. 10. If $a, b, c, \ldots$ are elements of prime orders $p, q, r, \ldots$ in an Abelian group of order $pqr \ldots$ (Ex. 9), $abc \ldots$ is an element of order $pqr \ldots$.
Ex. 11. See XIV 1.
Ex. 12. $(ab)^{x\beta} = a^{x\beta}b^{x\beta} = a^{x(r+\beta)}$.
Ex. 13. 21, 8. 3, 2.

§ 6. Ex. 3. See I 8_1.
Ex. 4. $ba = a^{-1}(ab)a$.
Ex. 5. $\{G, a\} \equiv Ga + Ga^2 + Ga^3 + \ldots + Ga^r$ where r is the order of a relative to G.
Ex. 6. $g^{-1}hg = h \cdot h^{-1}g^{-1}hg$.
Ex. 7. (i) Use Ex. 8. (ii) If $g^{-1}hg = h^a$, $g^{-t}hg^t = h^{a^t}$.
Ex. 8. Use Ex. 7, noticing that $a^{\phi(m)} \equiv 1 \pmod{m}$.
Ex. 9. If h, h_1 are elements of H, $h_1^{-1}hh_1 = h$ (being in H and conjugate to h).
Ex. 12. Prove as in § 1.
Ex. 13. (i) The elements of G excluding 1 can be divided into sets of p elements such as $g, g_1, \ldots, g_{p-1}$. (iii) $(ga^{-1})^p = gg_1 \ldots g_{p-1}$ is permutable with ga^{-1} and $\therefore$ with a.
Ex. 14. Let $a^3 = b^3 = (ab^2)^3 = (ba)^3 = 1$. $\therefore ab^2ab^2ab^2 = 1$, $ab^2ab = ba^2b^2 = b^2aba$, since $bababa = 1$ or $baba = a^2b^2$. Hence $a \cdot b^{-1}ab = b^{-1}ab \cdot a$.
Ex. 15. (i) If a is permutable with $b^{-1}ab$, a is permutable with the product $c = a^{-1}b^{-1}ab$ of a^{-1} and $b^{-1}ab$. (ii) By I 4 if $a^e = b^e = 1$, $c^e = a^{-e}b^{-1}a^eb = 1$ and $(ba)^e = b^ea^ec^{\frac{1}{2}e(e-1)} = 1$.
Ex. 16. G contains an element of order 2 by V 1_9.
Ex. 19. $1+c, 1+d, 1+e$ and $\{b, c\}$, $\{ba^2, c\}$.
Ex. 20. 1, a^6 and a^{18}, a^{12}, $a+a^5$ and $a^{23}+a^{19}$, a^2+a^{10} and $a^{22}+a^{14}$, a^3+a^{15}, $a^{21}+a^9$ and a^4+a^{20}, a^7+a^{11} and $a^{17}+a^{13}$, a^8+a^{16}, ba^{4x}, ba^{2+4x}, ba^{1+4x} and ba^{3+4x}. $\{ba\}$, $\{ba^3\}$, and $\{ba^5\}$.

§ 7. Ex. 5. See § 12.
Ex. 10. $H \equiv g^{-1}Hg$ contains $g^{-1}Kg$, g being any element of G.
Ex. 11. See § 11.
Ex. 12. If H is of index 2 in G, $G \equiv H + Hg \equiv H + gH$ where g is any element of G not in H. $\therefore Hg \equiv gH$ or $g^{-1}Hg \equiv H$.
Ex. 14. See X 2.
Ex. 16. See § 17.
Ex. 17. $H + Hg + Hg^2 + \ldots$ is a subgroup of G, and $\therefore$ its order k divides the order of G. Now $k = m \times$ a factor of the order of g (§ 1), &c.
Ex. 18. Let g, g_1 be any elements of G, h and $ghg^{-1} = h_1$ elements of H. If
$$g_1h_1 = h_1g_1, \ g^{-1}g_1g \cdot h = g^{-1}g_1h_1g = h \cdot g^{-1}g_1g, \ \&c.$$
Ex. 23. The only permutations permutable with the circular permutation are its powers.

Ex. 25. The subgroup is obviously permutable with a and b, and therefore with $\{a, b\}$.

Ex. 26. Since
$b^{-1}a^2b = (ab)^2 \cdot a^4$, $b^{-1}a^3b = a^3$, $a^{-1}(ab)^2a = b^{-1}(ab)^2b = a^2(ab)^2a^4$,
the subgroups are permutable with a and b and hence with $\{a, b\}$.

Ex. 30. $(ba^x)^2 = a^{(k+1)x}$ which is permutable with a and b by I 8.

§ 8. Ex. 5. Let G be of order n. Then $\{G, a\} \equiv G + Ga$, and the elements Ga are the n elements conjugate to a in $\{G, a\}$. (i) The order of each element of $Ga =$ the order of $a = 2$. (ii) If g is an element of G, $a^{-1}ga = (a^{-1}g)^{-1}a = g^{-1}$. (iii) g is not of order $2m$, for otherwise $a^{-1}g^m a = g^{-m} = g^m$. (iv) If g and h are elements of G, a transforms gh into $g^{-1}h^{-1}$ and also into $(gh)^{-1}$. Hence $gh = hg$.

Ex. 7. Let $g_1, g_2, g_3, \ldots$ be the remaining elements and a an element of order 2 in G. Then $g_i a$ is of order 2; $\therefore g_i a^{-1} g_i a = 1$ and $a^{-1} g_i a = g_i^{-1}$. Hence $(g_i g_j)^{-1} = g_i^{-1} g_j^{-1}$ and $g_i g_j = g_j g_i$ as in Ex. 6.

Ex. 8. $1 + a + b$, $\{a, b\}$ and $\{b\}$, $\{a^2, b\}$ and $\{b\}$, $\{a^3, b\}$.

§ 9. Ex. 5. Use V 6_8.
Ex. 8. See XI 1.
Ex. 9. Use Ex. 8.

Ex. 10. Let $H_1, H_2, \ldots, H_k$ be a set of conjugate subgroups of order m in a group G of order n. Then $H_1, H_2, \ldots, H_k$ contain at most $k(m-1) + 1$ distinct elements between them, since each contains identity. Now $k(m-1) + 1 < n$; for $m - 1 <$ the order $n \div k$ of the normaliser of H_1 in G. Hence H_1 does not contain an element from every conjugate set in G.

Ex. 11. If g is an element of order q in G such that $g^{-1}hg = h^k$, $h = g^{-q}hg^q = h^{k^q}$; and $\therefore k^q \equiv 1 \pmod{p}$. But $k^{p-1} \equiv 1 \pmod{p}$ and $\therefore k = 1$.

Ex. 12. Let g be any element of G. Then we can find an element k of K such that $g^{-1}Hg = k^{-1}Hk$; i.e. H is permutable with gk^{-1}. Hence g is in $k\Gamma$.

§ 10. Ex. 2. When H is a subgroup of G.
Ex. 8. If k is an element of K, $k^{-1}Dk$ is the G. C. S. of $k^{-1}Hk \equiv H$ and $k^{-1}Kk \equiv K$. $\therefore k^{-1}Dk \equiv D$.

Ex. 9. (i) $1 + (xw)(yz)$. (ii) $x' = \pm x, \pm \dfrac{1}{x}$. (iii) $1 + b$.

§ 12. Ex. 4. If g is any element of prime order in G and $g, g_1, g_2, \ldots$ are the conjugates of g, $G \equiv \{g, g_1, g_2, \ldots\}$.

§ 13. Ex. 4. If
$G \equiv Dg_1 + Dg_2 + Dg_3 + ...$, $H \equiv Dh_1 + Dh_2 + Dh_3 + ...$,
$\{G, H\}$ contains the $mn \div \delta$ distinct elements $Gh_1 + Gh_2 + Gh_3 + ...$.
If $\lambda\delta = mn$, $\{G, H\} \equiv Gh_1 + Gh_2 + Gh_3 + ... \equiv Hg_1 + Hg_2 + Hg_3 + ...$,
and $\therefore GH \equiv HG$.

Ex. 5. (i) If the indices are q, r and the order of G is n; the order of the G. C. S. of the subgroups $\leq n \div qr$. But the order of $\{H, K\} \leq n$; now use Ex. 4. (ii) As in (i).

Ex. 6. By § 13 the order of the G. C. S. is $q^{x+y-1}r$, where $q^l r$ is the order of $\{G, H\}$.

Ex. 7. Prove as in Ex. 6.

Ex. 8. If d is an element of D and c of C, $dc = c_1 a$, where c_1 is in C and a in A. But $a = c_1^{-1}dc$ is in B and $\therefore$ in D. Hence $DC = CD$.

Ex. 9, 10. $G \equiv \{H, K\}$ and H, K are permutable.

§ 14. Ex. 4. $(g^{n+a})^a = 1$ and $\therefore g^{n+a}$ is in A.

Ex. 5. If h is any element of H, $h^{-1}Ah$ is of order a in $h^{-1}Gh \equiv G$. Hence $h^{-1}Ah \equiv A$.

Ex. 6. Use Ex. 5 repeatedly to prove that A is normal first in C, then in D, ...

Ex. 7. Let A be a subgroup of order a, and B a normal subgroup whose order β divides a. Now proceed as in § 14.

Ex. 8. Let g be an element of G not in Γ. Then $g^{-1}\Gamma g \not\equiv \Gamma$, for otherwise Γ would contain two subgroups H and $g^{-1}Hg$ of order prime to index, H being normal.

Ex. 9. $\{a^{11}\}$, $\{a^2\}$, $\{a\}$.
Ex. 10. $\{a, b\}$, $\{a^7, b\}$.
Ex. 11. $\{a, b\}$, $\{a\}$.

§ 15. Ex. 9. 7; use Ex. 8.

Ex. 12. Take any element g_1 of G, take any element g_2 of G not in $\{g_1\}$, take any element g_3 of G not in $\{g_1, g_2\}$, &c. Then G is the direct product of $\{g_1\}$, $\{g_2\}$, $\{g_3\}$, ...

Ex. 13. Let a, b, c, ... be elements of A, B, C, ... such that $abc...$ is in G'. Then G' contains $(abc...)^t = a^t$, where t is the order of $bc...$. Hence G' contains a, since t is prime to the order of a (V 5_6); and similarly G' contains b, c, ... Hence G' is contained in $A'B'C'...$, and $\therefore$ since G' contains $A'B'C'...$, $G' \equiv A'B'C'...$.

§ 16. Ex. 6. If $ab = c = ba$, $a^{-1}b^{-1} = c^{-1}$.

§ 17. Ex. 6. The order of γ is the order of g relative to H.

Ex. 7. If a is an element of A such that $a^{-1}Ha = K$, K is normal in $a^{-1}Ga \equiv G$ and $G/H = a^{-1}Ga/a^{-1}Ha$.

Ex. 8. If $g_i^{-1}g_j^{-1}g_ig_j = 1$, $\gamma_i^{-1}\gamma_j^{-1}\gamma_i\gamma_j = 1$.

Ex. 9. If $\gamma_i^{-1}\gamma_j^{-1}\gamma_i\gamma_j = 1$, $g_i^{-1}g_j^{-1}g_ig_j$ is in H.

Ex. 10. If $G \equiv Hg_1 + Hg_2 + Hg_3 + \ldots$ and $\gamma_i = g_i^m$, $\gamma_i \neq \gamma_j$; for then $(g_i g_j^{-1})^m = 1$ and $g_i g_j^{-1}$ is in H. Again, if $g_i g_j = h g_k$ where h is in H, $\gamma_i \gamma_j = h^m \gamma_k = \gamma_k$. Hence $\gamma_1, \gamma_2, \gamma_3, \ldots$ are the elements of G/H.

Ex. 11. Let
$$G \equiv Lg_1 + Lg_2 + Lg_3 + \ldots \text{ and } G' \equiv L'g_1' + L'g_2' + L'g_3' + \ldots.$$
Then if g_i corresponds to g_i' so does every element of Lg_i, while since g_i' corresponds to g_i so does every element of $L'g_i'$. Hence the above partitions have a (1, 1) correspondence.

Ex. 14. $a^2 = b^2 = (ab)^2 = 1$.
Ex. 15. $a^r = b^2 = (ab)^2 = 1$.
Ex. 16. $a^2 = b^5 = 1$, $ab = ba$ and $a^{11} = b^5 = 1$, $ab = ba^3$.
Ex. 17. $a^7 = b^7 = 1$, $ab = ba$.

§ 18. Ex. 5. $G/L = G/H/L/H$ and a factor-group of an Abelian group is Abelian.

Ex. 7. If $\quad K \equiv Dk_1 + Dk_2 + \ldots + Dk_r,$
$$G \equiv Hk_1 + Hk_2 + \ldots + Hk_r + Hg_1 + Hg_2 + \ldots.$$
The partitions Hk_i combine according to the same laws as Dk_i.

Ex. 8. Assume that such a group G contains a normal subgroup H of order $p_{r+1} \ldots p_t$. Then since G/H is of order $p_1 p_2 \ldots p_r$ it contains a normal subgroup of order p_r, and to this corresponds a normal subgroup of order $p_r p_{r+1} \ldots p_t$ in G. Now use induction; and then V 14$_3$.

§ 20. Ex. 2. (i) If G contained two subgroups P, P' of order p^a, $\{P, P'\}$ would be a subgroup of order p^k, $k > a$. (ii) P and Q have only identity in common. (iii) If $a, b, c, \ldots$ are elements of order $p^a, q^\beta, r^\gamma \ldots$ in G, $G \equiv \{abc \ldots\}$.

§ 21. Ex. 3. (i) Each element of order qr can be put into the form $ab = ba$ where a, b are of orders q, r (I 2$_{11}$). (ii) G contains at least qr elements whose orders divide qr; now use (i).

Ex. 4. H is of order $\geq a$ by § 21. Again, H is of order $\leq a$, for otherwise H would contain an element whose order divides κ by V 19.

Ex. 6. Since no two cyclic groups of order p^s have an element of order p^s in common, the number of elements of order p^s in G is $(p^s - p^{s-1}) u_s$. Now put $r = p^x$ in the corollary of § 21, and use induction.

Ex. 7. There are in the group 15 elements whose 3rd power is 1, and 8 whose 3rd power is conjugate to a or a^5.

CHAPTER VI

§ 1. Ex. 3. The symmetric group of degree $m \equiv \{A, (1\,2\ldots m)\}$, where A is the symmetric group on 1, 2, ..., $m-1$. A and $\{(1\,2\ldots m)\}$ are permutable by V 18$_{4(ii)}$.

SOLUTIONS. CH. VI

Ex. 4. $\{(1\ 2\ \ldots\ m)\}$ is a transitive group of order m.

Ex. 5. (ii) Since either $\begin{pmatrix} 1 & 2 & \ldots & (m-2) & (m-1) & m \\ 1' & 2' & \ldots & (m-2)' & (m-1)' & m' \end{pmatrix}$ or $\begin{pmatrix} 1 & 2 & \ldots & (m-2) & (m-1) & m \\ 1' & 2' & \ldots & (m-2)' & m' & (m-1)' \end{pmatrix}$ is even we can find a permutation of the alternating group replacing $1, 2, \ldots, m-2$ by any given symbols $1', 2', \ldots, (m-2)'$.

Ex. 6. If g_i is a permutation of G replacing x_1 by x_i, h replaces x_i by x_j; where $g_i h = g_j$.

Ex. 9. Any permutation permutable with the transposition $(1\ 2)$ has the cycle $(1\ 2)$ or $(1)(2)$. Hence G is the direct product of $\{(1\ 2)\}$ and a group acting on symbols $3, 4, 5, \ldots$.

Ex. 11. $\{(1\ 2\ 3\ 4)\}$, $\{(1\ 2)(3\ 4),\ (1\ 3)(2\ 4)\}$, $\{(1\ 2),\ (3\ 4)\}$.

Ex. 12, 13. Use II $5_2, _3$.

Ex. 15. (i) The number of distinct permutations on the m symbols with the given cycles is evidently $m! \div R$. (ii) If $C_1, C_2, C_3, \ldots$ are the cycles, every permutation of Γ is of the form $C_1^{a_1} C_2^{a_2} C_3^{a_3} \ldots$ ($a_i = 1, 2, \ldots, i$). (iii) When $a, \gamma, \epsilon, \ldots = 0$ or 1, $\beta = \delta = \zeta = \ldots = 0$.

Ex. 16. 87,887,800.

Ex. 17. The number of ways in which $a, \beta, \gamma, \ldots$ can be chosen so that $a + 2\beta + 3\gamma + \ldots = m$.

Ex. 18. If $g^{-1}bg = a$, $(gc)^{-1}b(gc) = a$; and either g or gc is even.

Ex. 19. (i) The two conjugate sets are the transforms of a by the odd and even permutations respectively. (ii) Use II 7_3.

Ex. 20. Use Ex. 15, 19.

Ex. 21. (ii) 158,400.

Ex. 24. T^{-1} changes f' into f, a permutation of G leaves f unchanged, T changes f into f'.

Ex. 25. (ii) Use Ex. 24.

Ex. 26. (i) $1 + (ac)(bd) + (ab)(cd) + (ad)(bc) + (abcd) + (ac) + (adcb) + (bd)$.

Ex. 27. Let the function be changed into $f_1, f_2, f_3, \ldots$ by the permutations of the symmetric group. Choose X so that the discriminant of $(x-f_1)(x-f_2)(x-f_3)\ldots = 0$ is not zero.

Ex. 28. Let the function of Ex. 27 be changed into $f_1, f_2, \ldots, f_r$ by the permutations of G; $f_1 f_2 \ldots f_r$ is a solution of the problem if X is suitably chosen.

Ex. 29. Use the properties of the polar triangle.

§ 2. Ex. 1. See X 8.

Ex. 2. a_i is odd or even as S_i is odd or even, since S_i contains $n \div e_i$ cycles of degree e_i.

Ex. 4. (iii)

$a\ b$	$a\ b\ c$	$a\ b\ c\ d$	$a\ b\ c\ d$	$a\ b\ c\ d$	$a\ b\ c\ d$
$b\ a'$	$b\ a\ c,$	$b\ a\ d\ c$	$b\ a\ d\ c$	$b\ d\ a\ c$	$b\ c\ d\ a$,
	$c\ b\ a$	$c\ d\ b\ a'$	$c\ d\ a\ b'$	$c\ a\ d\ b'$	$c\ d\ a\ b'$
		$d\ c\ a\ b$	$d\ c\ b\ a$	$d\ c\ b\ a$	$d\ a\ b\ c$

and those obtained by permuting rows in these squares.

§ 3. Ex. 6. The subgroup $\{b\}$ is of index 8 and order 2, and it contains no normal subgroup.

Ex. 7. $\{a, b\} \equiv H + Hb + Hba + Hba^2$, where $H \equiv \{a\}$. Denoting the partitions by 1, 2, 3, 4 we have a corresponding to $(2\ 3\ 4)$ and b to $(1\ 2)(3\ 4)$; since $bab = a^2 \cdot ba^2$, $ba^2 b = a \cdot ba$.

Ex. 8. (i) $a^3 = (ba^2 b^2)^2 = (ba^2 b^2 \cdot a)^2 = 1$; now use Ex. 6. (ii) Denoting the partitions by 1, 2, 3, 4, a corresponds to $(4\ 3\ 2)$, b to $(1\ 2\ 3\ 4)$; since $ba = a^2 \cdot b^3$, $b^2 a = ba^2 b^2 \cdot b$, $b^3 a = a \cdot ba^2 b^2 \cdot b^2$.

Ex. 9. (i) $b^3 = (a^3 b^2 a)^2 = (b \cdot a^3 b^2 a)^3 = 1$; now use Ex. 7. (ii) Denoting the partitions by 1, 2, 3, 4, 5, a corresponds to $(1\ 2\ 3\ 4\ 5)$ and b to $(2\ 5\ 4)$; since $ab = b^2 \cdot a^4$, $a^2 b = b^2 \cdot a^3 b^2 a \cdot a^2$, $a^3 b = a^3 b^2 a \cdot b \cdot a$, $a^4 b = a^3 b^2 a \cdot a^3$.

Ex. 10. If f is an element of G not in H, the order of f relative to H is 3. Hence G contains an element g of order 3. Take as the partitions of § 3 the partitions of G with respect to $\{g\}$.

Ex. 11. Take the conjugate set of subgroups as $H_1, H_2, \dots$ of the Corollary.

§ 4. Ex. 4. 2, 3, 4.
Ex. 5. 4, 2, 2.
Ex. 6. (i) A red-sided decagon. (ii) Place inside a red-sided pentagon a parallel red-sided pentagon. Draw arrows round the pentagons in the same directions. Join adjacent vertices by black lines (cf. Fig. 9). (iii) As in (ii) but with the arrows in opposite directions round the two pentagons. (iv) A decagon with sides alternately red and black.

Ex. 7. Draw four parallel concentric red-sided squares. Put clockwise arrows round the two inner squares and counter-clockwise arrows round the two outer. Join adjacent vertices of the two inner and two outer squares by blue lines, and join adjacent vertices of innermost and outermost squares and of the other two squares by black lines.

Ex. 8. (i) Draw β parallel regular concentric λ-sided red polygons. Join adjacent vertices of consecutive polygons (and of the innermost and outermost polygons) by black lines. Put clockwise arrows round each polygon. (ii) Consider the common vertices of one red-sided and one black-sided polygon.

Ex. 9. (i) Draw four parallel regular concentric red-sided octagons. Put clockwise arrows round the first and third and counter-clockwise arrows round the second and fourth. Join the first, third, fifth, and seventh vertices of the first and second octagon and of the third and fourth by black lines. Join similarly the second, fourth, sixth, and eighth vertices of the second and third octagon and of the first and fourth. (ii) As in (i) but with all arrows clockwise.

Ex. 11. $a^2 = b^3 = (ab)^3 = 1$.
Ex. 12. $a^3 = b^3 = (ab)^2 = 1$.

SOLUTIONS. CH. VI   207

Ex. 13. (i) $a^m = b^2 = 1$, $ab = ba$. (ii) $a^m = b^2 = 1$, $ab = ba^{\frac{1}{2}(m+2)}$.
Ex. 14. (i) $a^m = b^2 = (ab)^2 = 1$. (ii) $a^m = b^2 = 1$, $ab = ba^{\frac{1}{2}(m-2)}$.
(iii) $a^m = b^2 = 1$, $a^{\frac{m}{2}} = (ab)^2 = b^2$.
Ex. 15. See *American Journal Math.*, xviii. p. 159.

§ 5. Ex. 2. Prove as in VI 1_{24}.
Ex. 3. By Ex. 2 the permutations of such a normal subgroup would not displace any symbol.
Ex. 4. Use Ex. 3.
Ex. 5. (i) $\{c\}$ is normal in G. Now use Ex. 3. (ii) If one cycle of c is of degree r, c^r displaces no symbol of that cycle and $\therefore c^r = 1$. See also the solution of VI 9_5.
Ex. 6, 7. Use Ex. 5.
Ex. 8. S is normal in $\{S, G\}$. Now use Ex. 5.
Ex. 9. No two normal elements c, c_1 replace x_1 by the same symbol; for otherwise $c_1 c^{-1}$ would be a normal element not displacing x_1 (Ex. 5). Hence the m symbols are permuted by the elements of the central in $m \div \mu$ sets of μ each (VI 1_6).
Ex. 10. (i) Prove as in Ex. 9 using Ex. 8 instead of Ex. 5. (ii) The group P' of VI 2_1.
Ex. 11. The group formed by permutations of the type
$$\begin{pmatrix} g_1 & g_2 & \cdots & g_n \\ g_i^{-1} g_1 g_i & g_i^{-1} g_2 g_i & \cdots & g_i^{-1} g_n g_i \end{pmatrix};$$
for these permutations do not displace the symbol corresponding to identity.

§ 6. Ex. 1. Prove as in VI 1_{24}.
Ex. 3. See § 2.
Ex. 4. The subgroup H not displacing one symbol (VI 5_3).
Ex. 5. Use VI 5_4.
Ex. 6. (i) The m subgroups of order $n \div m$ whose elements do not displace one of the symbols have identity in common and therefore contain at most $m\left(\dfrac{n}{m} - 1\right) + 1 = n - m + 1$ distinct elements between them. There remain at least $n - (n - m + 1) = m - 1$ elements of G displacing every symbol. (ii) Any transform of a permutation displacing m symbols displaces m symbols.
Ex. 7. If in one of the subgroups not displacing one symbol there are μ_r permutations not displacing r symbols, $n \div m = \Sigma \mu_r$. But each of the μ_r permutations belongs to r of the subgroups not displacing one symbol. $\therefore r\nu_r = m\mu_r$.

Ex. 8. Suppose $k \geq 2$. Then there are $\dfrac{n}{m}$ elements replacing x_1 by x_r and $\dfrac{n}{m(m-1)}$ replacing x_1, x_s by x_r, x_s. Hence there are at least $\dfrac{n}{m} - \dfrac{n(m-2)}{m(m-1)} = \dfrac{n}{m(m-1)} \geq q$ elements replacing x_1 by x_r and displacing every symbol. If g, h are two of these, gh^{-1} does not displace x_1.

Ex. 9. Since $ab = ba^2$, every element of $\{a, b\}$ is of the form $b^y a^x$; hence the order of $\{a, b\}$ is 20. $\{a, b\}$ is doubly transitive, since $b^u a^t$ replaces 1 by s and 5 by t when u is suitably chosen.

§ 7. Ex. 2. Every permutation of G is included in the direct product.
Ex. 3. Use Ex. 2.
Ex. 4. See § 8.
Ex. 5. Let A be the subgroup and let $g_1, g_2, \ldots, g_r$ replace x_1 by $x_1, x_2, \ldots, x_r$. Then $G \equiv Ag_1 + Ag_2 + \ldots + Ag_r$.
Ex. 6. $x_1, x_2, \ldots, x_r$ are a transitive set.
Ex. 7. Use V 4_6.
Ex. 8. $[1, 2, 3, 4], [5, 6, 7, 8], [9, 10] \cdot [1, 2, 3, 4], [5, 6]$.

§ 8. Ex. 1. $H/K = G/\{K, K'\} = H'/K'$.
Ex. 2. The permutations formed by multiplying each element of H by the corresponding elements of the isomorphic group H' are all distinct, are all in G, and their number = the order of G.
Ex. 3. (i) $H = K$ cyclic of order 4, $H' = K'$ cyclic of order 2. (ii) $\sigma \equiv [9, 10]$; H of order 2, $H' = G$, $K \equiv 1$, K' non-cyclic of order 4. $\sigma \equiv [5, 6, 7, 8, 9, 10]$; $H = H' = G$, $K = K' \equiv 1$.

§ 9. Ex. 4. See § 10.
Ex. 5. Let c be a normal element of a transitive group G. Every element of G transforms c into itself and hence permutes the cycles of c. Hence these cycles are imprimitive systems of G.
Ex. 6, 7. Use Ex. 1, 5.
Ex. 8. S_i replaces each symbol of Hg_x by a symbol of $Hg_x g_i$.
Ex. 10. (i) $[1, 2], [3, 4], [5, 6]$. (ii) $[1, 2, 3], [4, 5, 6]$.

§ 10. Ex. 2. G/Γ is of degree r.
Ex. 3. (i) $\Gamma \equiv \{(xyz)(abc)\}$ or 1 in the two cases respectively. (ii) $\{(1\,2)(3\,4), (3\,4)(5\,6)\}$. (iii) $\{(1\,2\,3)(4\,5\,6), (1\,2)(4\,5)\}$.

§ 11. Ex. 2. H is transitive; now use § 6.
Ex. 3. The group $\equiv \{H, K\}$, where H is a normal subgroup and K a subgroup not displacing one symbol.
Ex. 4. Use VI 7_7 or VI 9_8.

§ 12. Ex. 1. Use VI $9_{1, 2}$.
Ex. 2. Use II 6_3.
Ex. 3. (i) Let e be the first of the symbols $1, 2, \ldots, m$ which is in an imprimitive system not containing 1, 2. Considering the effect of $(1\,2\,\ldots\,m)^{e-2}$ on 1 and 2 we see that $\{(1\,2), (1\,2\,\ldots\,m)\}$ is a primitive group. (ii) Apply (i) to $(1\,2)$ and b^i.

SOLUTIONS. CH. VI   209

Ex. 4. Use III 2_{16}.

Ex. 5, 6. Suppose G contains $(1\,2\,3)$, $(1\,2\,4)$, ..., $(1\,2\,e)$ but not $(1\,2f)$. By II 7_6 G contains the alternating group on 1, 2, ..., e. If G contains $(1\,r\,s)$ where either r or s is not in σ, choose i, j in σ and distinct from r, s. Then $(1ji)(1\,r\,s)(1\,ij) = (i\,r\,s)$. Hence G contains the alternating group on 1, 2, ..., e, r, s contrary to hypothesis. Now proceed as in § 12.

§ 13. Ex. 1. Since $(1\,2\,3) = (1\,2)(4\,5).(4\,5)(1\,3)$ G contains every circular permutation of order 3.

Ex. 2. See § 14.

Ex. 3. Let H be a subgroup of index $< p$, and a any circular permutation of order p. The elements $H + Ha + Ha^2 + ...$ are more than $m!$ in number and are therefore not all distinct. Hence a^x is in $H (x < p)$ and $\therefore$ a is in H by V 1. Hence H contains every circular permutation of order p.

§ 15. Ex. 1. By VI 1_{24} the permutations form a normal subgroup of the symmetric group.

Ex. 2. Let H be a group of degree m and index $r < m$ in the symmetric group G. Let f_1 be a function of the m symbols unchanged by each element of H and changed into the distinct functions $f_1, f_2, ..., f_r$ by the permutations $g_1, g_2, ..., g_r$, where $G \equiv Hg_1 + Hg_2 + ... + Hg_r$ (VI 1_{23}). Since the $m!$ elements of G permute $f_1, f_2, ..., f_r$ and $r < m$, two elements $(g, h$ say) of G permute the f's in the same way. Hence gh^{-1} leaves each f unaltered. Now by Ex. 1 all the elements leaving each f unaltered form a normal subgroup of G and they are all contained in H.

Ex. 3. If A, B, C, D are four points on a line, the cross-ratio x of $(ABCD)$ is not altered by any permutation of the normal subgroup of order 4 in the symmetric group G on A, B, C, D. By the other permutations of G x is changed into $(1-x)^{-1}$, &c.

CHAPTER VII

§ 1. Ex. 1. See end of III 1.

Ex. 5. (i) The product of the two given substitutions of order 2 is of order r if $\sin r\phi = 0$ by III 2_{12}, and then the group is of order $2r$. (ii) Since $\cos 2\phi$ is rational, 2ϕ is a multiple of π, $\tfrac{1}{2}\pi$, or $\tfrac{1}{3}\pi$.

§ 2. Ex. The group generated by
$$x' = -\frac{x+1}{x} \text{ and } x' = -\frac{x}{x+1}.$$

§ 3. Ex. 2. Use III 3.

Ex. 5. (i) By a suitable change of variables the invariant may be put in the form $X_1^2 + X_2^2 + ... + X_m^2$. When G is expressed

210   SOLUTIONS. CH. VII

in terms of $X_1, X_2, ..., X_m$ every substitution of G is orthogonal.
(ii) Transform by $(x-y+z, y+z, z)$.

Ex. 8. We have $x_1' x_2' ... x_m' = 0$ when $x_1 x_2 ... x_m = 0$. Hence when $x_1 = 0$ one of $x_1', x_2', ..., x_m'$ is 0, and $\therefore$ one of them $= a_1 x_1$. Similarly the rest $= a_2 x_2, a_3 x_3, ..., a_m x_m$ in some order or other.

§ 4. Ex. 2. Transform the common pole into $(1, 0, 0, ..., 0)$.
Ex. 3. (i) Express G in terms of f_1 and $m-1$ other variables.
(ii) $f_1 + f_2 + ... + f_n$ is an invariant of H; now use (i).
Ex. 4. Use Ex. 3 (i) and VII 3_6.
Ex. 5. $x + y + z$ is a relative invariant of the group.

§ 5. Ex. 2. Use III 4_8.
Ex. 4. Use III $4_{10, 11}$.
Ex. 5. Use III 6_9.
Ex. 6. To the substitution $x_i' = a_{i1} x_1 + a_{i2} x_2 + ... + a_{im} x_m$ make correspond
$$\xi_i' = a_{i1} \xi_1 + a_{i2} \xi_2 + ... - \omega_{i1} \eta_1 - \omega_{i2} \eta_2 - ...$$
$$\eta_i' = \omega_{i1} \xi_1 + \omega_{i2} \xi_2 + ... + a_{i1} \eta_1 + a_{i2} \eta_2 + ... \quad (i = 1, 2, ..., m);$$
where $a_{ij} = \alpha_{ij} + \omega_{ij} \sqrt{-1}$, α_{ij} and ω_{ij} being real.
Ex. 8, 9. Use III 9_3.

§ 6. Ex. 2. (i) $2x\bar{x} + 2y\bar{y} + (\omega^2 - 1) x\bar{y} + (\omega - 1) \bar{x}y$;
(ii) $2x\bar{x} + 2y\bar{y} - (1-i) x\bar{y} - (1+i) \bar{x}y$;
(iii) $x\bar{x} + y\bar{y} + z\bar{z}$.

Ex. 3. Choose new variables such that when the positive Hermitian invariant of the group is expressed in terms of these variables it is in canonical form. Then express the group in terms of these new variables.

Ex. 4. (i) Every substitution of the group changes $x_1, x_2, ..., x_s$ into functions of $x_1, x_2, ..., x_s$. (ii) The hypohermitian invariant can be expressed in the form $X_1 \bar{X}_1 + X_2 \bar{X}_2 + ... + X_s \bar{X}_s$. Now use (i).

Ex. 5. Take real positive quantities α and β such that $\alpha + \beta = 1$. $\alpha f - \beta f'$ is always positive when $\beta \div \alpha = 0$ and is always negative when $\beta \div \alpha = \infty$. Hence we can find a value of $\beta \div \alpha$ such that $\alpha f - \beta f'$ is zero for certain values of $x_1, x_2, ..., x_m$ but is never negative. In this case $\alpha f - \beta f'$ is a hypohermitian invariant of the group. Now use Ex. 4 (ii).

§ 7. Ex. 2. Every substitution in the completely reduced form of the group is a multiplication.
Ex. 4. One of the variables is a relative linear invariant of the completely reduced form of the group.
Ex. 5. Use VII $6_{4, 5}$.

§ 8. Ex. 2. Use VII 7_5.

Ex. 3. By § 8 if every element of a group G is permutable with an element which is not a similarity, G is reducible.

Ex. 4. Transform by $(-4x+8y+5z,\ x-y-z,\ 5x-8y-6z)$ and the generators become
$$(-x,\ -y,\ z),\ (-x,\ y,\ z),\ \text{and}\ (-x,\ -y,\ z).$$

§ 9. Ex. 1. The p^{rm} expressions $a_1x_1+a_2x_2+\ldots+a_mx_m$ obtained by putting $a_i =$ any mark of the Field are permuted by every substitution of the general group.

Ex. 2. (i) Every substitution of P permutes the p^r marks of the Field, while 0 is changed into an arbitrary mark u by $x' = x+u$. (ii) Every substitution of Q permutes the p^r marks, while 0 and 1 are changed into u and v by $x' = (v-u)x+u$. (iii) Every substitution of R permutes the p^r marks together with ∞ (i. e. any mark $\div 0$), while ∞, 0, 1 are changed into u, v, w by $x = \dfrac{w-u}{w-v} \cdot \dfrac{x'-v}{x'-u}$. (iv) We can always find a mark u of the Field such that $(ad-bc)u^2 = 1$ or v, and
$$\frac{ax+b}{cx+d} \equiv \frac{aux+bu}{cux+du}.$$
(vi) $Q \equiv P+Ps+Ps^2+\ldots$ where s is $x' = ux$, u being a primitive root of the Field.

Ex. 4. We get the substitutions of H_2, K corresponding to any substitution of H_1 by changing S into $-S$, 1.

§ 10. Ex. 1. Let A be any substitution of the central. Since A is permutable with $(\lambda x_1,\ \mu x_2,\ \ldots,\ \mu x_m)$, $a_{12} = a_{13} = \ldots = a_{1m} = 0$; and similarly $a_{ij} = 0$ if $i \neq j$.

Ex. 2. $m = 2$, $p^r = 5,\ 7,\ 8,\ 11,\ 13,\ 17,\ 19,\ 16$; $m = 3$, $p^r = 3$.

Ex. 5. If $ad-bc = 1$, $x' = \dfrac{ax+b}{cx+d}$ is $S^{(1+d)\gamma}TS^cTS^{(1+a)\gamma}$ when $c \neq 0$ and is $TS^bTS^dTS^{(1+b)\delta}$ when $c = 0$; where $c\gamma \equiv d\delta \equiv 1$.

Ex. 6. Use Ex. 5 and III 2_{11}.

Ex. 8. Use $E^2 = 1$; $D^2 = E$, $DE = ED$; $C^2 = E$, $CE = EC$, $CD = EDC$; $B^3 = E$, $BE = EB$, $BD = CDB$, $BC = DB$; $A^2 = 1$, $AE = EA$, $AD = CA$, $AC = DA$, $AB = ECB^2A$.

CHAPTER VIII

§ 1. Ex. 3–7. Use IV 1 and IV 2.

§ 3. Ex. 3. (i) If a point Q approaches P indefinitely, the n points equivalent to Q coincide in sets of m. (ii) Prove as in (i) using VIII 1_2.

P 2

212   SOLUTIONS. CH. VIII

Ex. 4. If 1, g_1, g_2, ... are the movements of G bringing P to P, P_1, P_2, ..., g_x brings P_i to P_j, where $g_j = g_i g_x$.

Ex. 5. P, P_1, P_2, ... are permuted in the same way as the symbols 1, g_1, g_2, ... in VI 2.

Ex. 6–8. Use IV 9.

§ 5. Ex. 3. The order of R is n; of I is $\frac{n}{2}\{8-(-1)^n\}$.

Ex. 4. By Ex. 3 G contains an element of order n.

§ 6. Ex. Combine §§ 2, 6.

§ 7. Ex. 1. C_6, D_6, D, D, O, T, O, E, E.
Ex. 3–8. Use § 3.

§ 8. Ex. 6. $\Delta(\equiv \Delta_2)$, $\mathrm{o}(\equiv \mathrm{o}_1)$, Δ, Δ, o_2, Δ_4, Ω, Θ, Ω, H, H, C_2, D, δ_2, δ_4, δ_2, δ_2.

Ex. 10. Γ_m, Δ_m, δ_2, Θ, Ω, H, o_m (m not a power of a prime).

§ 9. Ex. 4. (i) If OA', OB' represent $t_1^{\alpha_1} t_2^{\beta_1}$, $t_1^{\alpha_2} t_2^{\beta_2}$, the net formed from OA', OB' coincides with that formed from OA_1, OB_1 if the triangles OA_1B_1, $OA'B'$ have equal area.

(ii) $\Delta \equiv \begin{vmatrix} \alpha_1 & \beta_1 & \gamma_1 \\ \alpha_2 & \beta_2 & \gamma_2 \\ \alpha_3 & \beta_3 & \gamma_3 \end{vmatrix} = 0$.

(iii) $\Delta^2 = 1$. Prove by considering the parallelepipedon whose sides represent τ_1, τ_2, τ_3.

Ex. 5. The groups generated by the movements of C_a, o_a, D_a, δ_a, Γ_a, d_a, Δ_a (including the case $a = 1$) and a translation parallel to the line OA of §§ 7, 8; by a screw about a line l; by a screw about l and a 2-al rotation or rotatory-inversion about a line meeting l at right angles; by a screw about l and an inversion about a point of l.

Ex. 6. Let P be the point whose coordinates referred to rectangular reference-axes through O are (x, y); and let Q be the point (x_1, y_1) where $x_1 + \sqrt{-1} y_1$ is a period. Then the function has the same value at all points derived from P by multiples of the translation OQ. Now proceed as in § 9.

§ 10. Ex. 1. C, o; C_2, o_2, Γ_2; D, δ_2, Δ; C_3, o_3, δ_3, D_3, Δ_3; C_4, o_4, d_4, Γ_4, δ_4, D_4, Δ_4; C_6, o_6, d_6, Γ_6, δ_6, D_6, Δ_6; T, Θ, θ, O, Ω.

Ex. 2. The corresponding nets have meshes which are parallelograms, rectangles or rhombi, squares, rhombi with angles of 60° and 120°.

Ex. 3–9. See books referred to in § 10.

§ 11. Ex. 1. Take rectangular axes through the fixed point and proceed as in § 11.

Ex. 2. (i) The determinant of an orthogonal substitution is ± 1. (ii) H can be derived as in § 11 from C_m, D_m, T, O, or E.

SOLUTIONS. CH. VIII 213

Ex. 3. The groups generated by (i) $(-x, -y, z)$, $(x, y, -z)$, and $(-x, y, z)$; (ii) $(-z, -x, -y)$ and (y, x, z); (iii) $(-y, x, z)$ and $(y, x, -z)$; (iv) (z, x, y) and $(-x, -y, z)$; (v) $(x+a, y, z)$, $(x, y+b, z)$, $(x, y, z+c)$, and $(-x, -y, -z)$; (vi) $(a-x, -y, z+c)$ and $(-a-x, -y, z+c)$.

Ex. 4. The groups generated by (i) $(-y, x)$ and $(-x, y)$; (ii) $(a-x, -y)$ and $(-a-x, -y)$; (iii) $(a-x, -y)$ and $(-x, y)$.

Ex. 5. The groups generated by (i) $x' = e^{\frac{2\pi i}{m}} x$; (ii) $x' = e^{\frac{2\pi i}{m}} x$ and $x' = \frac{1}{x}$; (iii) $x' = i\frac{1-x}{1+x}$ and $x' = \frac{1}{x}$.

Ex. 6. Use VII 5_3 and then reason as in VIII 7 using the points representing the poles of the substitutions instead of the lines OA, OB, OC, ...

Ex. 7. (i) $s' = \dfrac{\sin\frac{\alpha}{2} - \cos\frac{\alpha}{2} \cdot s}{\cos\frac{\alpha}{2} - \sin\frac{\alpha}{2} \cdot s}$, (ii) $s' = e^{-\beta i} s$.

§ 12. Ex. 1. θ is the group of movements bringing a regular tetrahedron to self-coincidence. Each movement of θ permutes the vertices of the tetrahedron, and no two movements of θ permute the vertices in the same way.

Ex. 2. Let OA, OV be lines about which take place 3-al and 5-al rotations of **E**. Let OA be brought to the positions OB, OC, OD, OE by successive rotations through $\dfrac{2\pi}{5}$ about OV. Consider the group generated by the 15 collineations of order 2 which leave unaltered the figure consisting of the regular pentagon $ABCDE$ and the line at infinity in the plane $ABCDE$ perpendicular to OV. If BC and ED meet in A', CD and the line at ∞ meet in A'', &c., these collineations have as fixed point and line A and $A'A''$, A' and $A''A$, A'' and AA', &c. They all interchange $AA'A''$ and the 4 similar triangles; the permutation being even.

Ex. 3. (i) Use IV 18_9. (ii) By IV 18_{10} the group consists of identity and 8 collineations whose fixed points and lines are the vertices of a triangle and the opposite sides.

Ex. 4. By IV 18_{10} the group consists of 4 perspective collineations whose fixed points and planes are the vertices of a tetrahedron and the opposite faces, together with identity and the 8 non-perspective collineations of order 2 whose fixed lines are a pair of opposite edges of the tetrahedron.

Ex. 5. Use IV 18_{10}.

Ex. 6. Transform the generating collineations into (i) reflexions in parallel planes; (ii) 4 inversions; (iii) 2-al rotations about 8 parallel lines.

CHAPTER IX

§ 1. Ex. 2. $\{a, b\}$ is finite.

Ex. 3. (i) See XIV 1. (ii) Every element of $\{a, b\}$ is included once and only once in $b^y a^x (x = 1, 2, \ldots, \lambda; y = 1, 2, \ldots, \beta)$.

Ex. 4. Use Ex. 3 (i).

Ex. 5. $a^{-1}b^{-1}ab = a^{k-1} = b^{l-1}$. Hence $a = b^{1-l}ab^{l-1} = a^{k^{l-1}}$, and the order of a is finite. Now use Ex. 3.

Ex. 6. Since $a^r b^s . a^u b^v = a^{r+u} . a^{-u} b^s a^u b^{-s} . b^{s+v} = a^{r+u} c^{-us} b^{s+v}$ $= a^{r+u} b^{s+v} c^{-us}$ (I 4), every element of $\{a, b\}$ is of the form $a^x b^y c^z$. Now use I 4_{10}.

Ex. 7. Every element of $\{a, b, c\}$ is of the form $a^x b^y c^z$.

Ex. 9. (i) We may arrange the work as follows. The elements in any row are the uncancelled (unbracketed) elements of the preceding row multiplied on the left by a and b. An element is cancelled if it is identical with some element already found.

$$
\begin{array}{c}
1 \\
a \quad b \\
ab \quad a^2 \quad ba \quad b^2 \\
ab^2 \ (aba = b^2) \quad a^2 b \ (a^3 = 1) \quad ba^2 \ (bab = a^2) \quad b^2 a \ (b^3 = 1) \\
ab^2 a \ (aba^2 = b^2 a) \ (a^2 b^2 = ba) \ (a^3 b = b) \ (ba^2 b = ab^2 a) \ (bab^2 = a^2 b) \\
(b^2 a^2 = ab) \ (b^3 a = a) \\
(a^2 b^2 a = ba^2) \ (bab^2 a = ab^2).
\end{array}
$$

Hence we have

$\{a, b\} \equiv 1 + a + b + a^2 + ab + ba + b^2 + a^2 b + ab^2 + ba^2 + b^2 a + ab^2 a$.

(ii) Proceed as in (i); $\{a, b\}$ is of order 24.

Ex. 10. (i) $(ba)^{-1} = (a^3 b^3)^{-1}$, $\therefore a^3 b^3 = b^2 a^2$. Hence
$$ab = a^2 . a^3 b^3 . b^2 = (a^2 b^2)^2 = (ba)^2.$$
Therefore $(ba)^6 = (ab)^3 = a(ba)^2 b = a . ab . b = ba$. (ii) Put $h = ba$, $g = b$. Since every element of $\{g, h\}$ is of the form $g^x h^y$, it is of order 20.

Ex. 11. $ab = (ba)^3$, $(ba)^{12} = a(ba)^3 b = ba$ as in Ex. 10.

Ex. 12. If
$A \equiv \{a\}$, the group $\equiv A + Ab + Aba + Abab + Ababa + \ldots$.

Ex. 13. 20, 18.

Ex. 14. 12, 24, 60, 168. (i) Put $\alpha = a^{-1}$, $\beta = ab$; then $\alpha^3 = \beta^3 = (\alpha\beta)^2 = 1$. Now use Ex. 9 (i). (ii) Put $\alpha = b$, $\beta = a^2$. Then $\alpha^3 = \beta^2 = (\alpha\beta)^3 = 1$, $a^{-1}\alpha a = \beta\alpha^2$, $a^{-1}\beta a = \beta$, $b^{-1}ab = \alpha$, $b^{-1}\beta b = \alpha^2 \beta\alpha$; $\therefore$ the group contains a normal subgroup of index 2 simply isomorphic with (i). (iii) Put $\alpha = ab$, $\beta = a^2 ba^3$. Then since $\alpha^3 = \beta^2 = (\alpha\beta)^3 = 1$, $H \equiv \{\alpha, \beta\}$ is of order 12. Now the group $\equiv H + Ha + Ha^2 + Ha^3 + Ha^4$, since $b = \alpha^2 a$, $ab = \alpha$, $a^2 b = \beta a^2$, $a^3 b = \beta\alpha a^4$, $a^4 b = \alpha^2 \beta a^3$. (iv) Put $\alpha = a^5 ba^4$, $\beta = ab$. Then since $\alpha^4 = \beta^3 = (\alpha\beta)^2 = 1$, $H \equiv \{\alpha, \beta\}$ is of order 24. Now the group $\equiv H + Ha + Ha^2 + Ha^3 + Ha^4 + Ha^5 + Ha^6$, since $b = \beta^2 a$, $ab = \beta$, $a^2 b = \beta\alpha a^2$, $a^3 b = \alpha^3 a^6$, $a^4 b = \beta\alpha^2 \beta^2 \alpha a^4$, $a^5 b = \beta\alpha^2 \beta^2 a^5$, $a^6 b = \alpha a^3$.

SOLUTIONS. CH. IX 215

§ 2. Ex. 1. (i) H is normal in G. (ii) $H \equiv \{g_a{}^\alpha g_b{}^\beta \ldots\}$ is cyclic of order ν.

Ex. 2. $a^n b^2$ is normal in the given group.

Ex. 3. (i) If $a \equiv (1\,2\,8)$ and $b \equiv (1\,2)(3\,4)$, $a^3 = b^2 = (ab)^3 = 1$. ∴ the alternating group of degree 4 generated by a and b is isomorphic with $a^3 = b^2 = (ab)^3 = 1$. Since both groups are of order 12, the isomorphism is simple. Next take a as $x' = x+1$, b as $x' = \dfrac{2}{x}$, &c. (ii) Take $a \equiv (1\,2\,3\,4)$, $b \equiv (1\,4\,3)$, &c. (iii) Take $a \equiv (1\,2\,3\,4\,5)$, $b \equiv (1\,2)(3\,4)$. Next take a as $x' = x+1$, b as $x' = \dfrac{4}{x}$; and then a as $x' = \dfrac{2x+1}{x}$, b as $x' = x+3$, &c. (iv) Take $a \equiv (1\,2\,3\,4\,5\,6\,7)$, $b \equiv (1\,2)(4\,7)$. Next take a as $x' = x+1$, b as $x' = \dfrac{6}{x}$; and then $a \equiv \left(\dfrac{x+y+1}{x}, \dfrac{x+1}{x}\right)$, $b \equiv \left(\dfrac{x}{y+1}, \dfrac{y}{y+1}\right)$.

Ex. 6. The following scheme shows the element of $\{a, b\}$ corresponding to each element of $\{a, b\}$, and suggests the equivalence of apparently distinct elements of $\{a, b\}$ (e. g. ba^2b and a^4ba) in cases where this equivalence is not immediately obvious. We must, however, verify the equivalence in each case by means of the relations $a^6 = b^2 = (ab)^3 = (a^3b)^2 = 1$; for a and b might possibly be connected by relations independent of $a^6 = b^2 = (ab)^3 = (a^3b)^2 = 1$.

1	b	ba	ba^2	$ba^3 = a^3b$
123456	126453	231564	342615	$ba^2b = a^4ba$.
a	ab	aba	aba^2	
234561	264531	315642	426153	
a^2	a^2b	a^2ba	a^2ba^2	
345612	645312	156423	261534	
a^3	a^3b	a^3ba	a^3ba^2	
456123	453126	564231	615342	
a^4	a^4b	a^4ba	a^4ba^2	
561234	531264	642315	153426	
a^5	a^5b	a^5ba	a^5ba^2	
612345	312645	423156	534261	

Ex. 7. Take $a \equiv (2x, 2x+y)$, $b \equiv (x, x+y)$.

Ex. 8. Take $a \equiv (1\,2\,3\,4\,5)$, $b \equiv (1\,2)$. $\{a, b\}$ is of order 120; for if $\alpha = a^3$ and $\beta = (ab)^2$, $\{\alpha, \beta\}$ is a normal subgroup of order 60 and index 2, since $\alpha^5 = \beta^2 = (\alpha\beta)^3 = 1$.

Ex. 9. (i) Since Θ is the direct product of T and c, Θ is simply isomorphic with $\alpha^3 = \beta^2 = (\alpha\beta)^3 = \gamma^2 = 1$, $\alpha\gamma = \gamma\alpha$, $\beta\gamma = \gamma\beta$. Now put $a = \alpha\gamma$, $b = \beta\gamma$ and we have Θ simply isomorphic with $a^6 = b^2 = (ab)^3 = (a^3b)^2 = 1$. (ii) $a^6 = b^2 = (a^3b)^2 = (a^2b)^4 = 1$. (iii) $a^{10} = b^2 = (a^5b)^2 = (a^6b)^3 = 1$.

216   SOLUTIONS. CH. IX

§ 6. Ex. 2. The orders of H and K are $\mu = n_1 n_2 n_4 n_8 \ldots$ and $\nu = n_3 n_5 n_6 n_7 n_9 \ldots$. Hence H and K have no element in common, since the order of $G \equiv \{H, K\}$ is $\mu\nu$.

Ex. 3. G is the direct product of $\{g_1\}, \{g_2\}, \ldots, \{g_x\}$.

Ex. 5. Its base is evidently $[g_1^{\frac{n_1}{n_i}}, \ldots, g_i^{\frac{n_i}{n_i}}, g_{i+1}, \ldots, g_x]$.

Ex. 6. Its base is evidently $[g_1^{n_i}, g_2^{n_i}, \ldots, g_{i-1}^{\frac{n_i}{n_{i-1}}}]$.

Ex. 8. (i) $[ab]$, (12); (ii) $[ab, b^4]$, (120, 6); (iii) $[b, ab^3]$, (36, 2); (iv) $[a^{41}b^3, a^9]$, (180, 5); (v) $[ab, bc]$, (80, 80); (vi) $[b, ab^4, a^4bc]$, (72, 8, 8).

Ex. 9. (m), $(2, 2)$, $(2, 2, 2)$, $(m, 2)$.

§ 7. Ex. 3. Every cyclic subgroup of order p^λ contains $p^{\lambda-1}(p-1)$ elements of order p^λ, and no two such subgroups have an element of this order in common.

Ex. 4. If $a, b, c, \ldots$ are elements in G of orders $p^\lambda, q^\mu, r^\nu, \ldots$, every element of order $p^\lambda q^\mu r^\nu \ldots$ in G is of the form $abc\ldots$. Similarly, in the case of subgroups (V 20_2). Hence the numbers required are $LMN\ldots, L'M'N'\ldots, LMN\ldots \div \phi(p^\lambda q^\mu r^\nu \ldots)$.

Ex. 6. If h, k are elements in G of orders α, β contained in the subgroups H, K with only identity in common, hk is in a subgroup L having only identity in common with H or K. Now $(hk)^\alpha = k^\alpha$ is in K and L, and hence β divides α. Similarly α divides β, and $\therefore \alpha = \beta$. Now use Ex. 5.

Ex. 7. Let g be an element of order p in G, and denote $a^{-i}ga^i$ by h_i. Then a is permutable with $K \equiv \{h_1, h_2, \ldots, h_{q-1}\}$ and $\therefore K \equiv G$. But the order of $K \leq p^{q-1}$ (cf. V 6_{13}).

Ex. 8. (i) See V 1_{11}. (ii) Let x be the order of a relative to G. Since a^x is in G, $(a^x)^2 = 1$ and $x = r$ or $\frac{1}{2}r$. Hence $\{G, a\} \equiv Ga + Ga^2 + \ldots + Ga^x$ is of order $2^a r$ or $2^{a-1}r$.

Ex. 9. (i) $b_{s+m} = a^{-s}b_m a^s = a^{-s}bb_1 a^s = a^{-s}ba^s \cdot a^{-s}b_1 a^s = b_s b_{s+1}$. $bb_s = bb_1 \cdot b_1 b_2 \cdot \ldots \cdot b_{s-1} b_s = b_m b_{m+1} \ldots b_{m+s-1} = a^{-m}(bb_1 b_2 \ldots b_{s-1})a^m$. (ii) Since b, b_1, bb_1 are all of order 2, $bb_1 = b_1 b$. Now assuming $b, b_1, \ldots, b_{s-1}$ all permutable prove $b, b_1, \ldots, b_s$ all permutable. Then by induction $\{b_1, b_2, \ldots, b_m\}$ is an Abelian group of order 2^k and type $(1, 1, \ldots, 1)$, $k \leq m$.

Ex. 10. (i) If the h's are not independent, it must be possible to express h_m in the form $h_1^{x_1} h_2^{x_2} \ldots h_{m-1}^{x_{m-1}}$. Equating powers of $g_1, g_2, \ldots, g_m$ and eliminating $x_1, x_2, \ldots, x_{m-1}$ we have

$$D \equiv \begin{vmatrix} a_{11} & a_{12} & \cdots & a_{1m} \\ a_{21} & a_{22} & \cdots & a_{2m} \\ \vdots & \vdots & & \vdots \\ a_{m1} & a_{m2} & \cdots & a_{mm} \end{vmatrix} = 0.$$

If the h's generate G, every element of the form $g_1^{y_1}g_2^{y_2}\ldots g_m^{y_m}$ can be expressed in the form $h_1^{x_1}h_2^{x_2}\ldots h_m^{x_m}$. $\therefore y_i = a_{1i}x_1 + a_{2i}x_2 + \ldots + a_{mi}x_m$ ($i=1, 2, \ldots, m$), and hence $Dx_i = A_{i1}y_1 + A_{i2}y_2 + \ldots + A_{im}y_m$ (A_{ij} being the cofactor of a_{ij} in D). $\therefore D$ must be a factor of A_{ij}. Let $A_{ij} = A_{ij}'D$. Then
$$D^{m-1} = |A_{ij}| = D^m |A_{ij}'| \text{ and hence } D = \pm 1.$$
(ii) The h's generate G if $D \neq 0$.

§ 8. Ex. 3. If $[g_1, g_2, \ldots, g_x]$ is a base of G, every element of order p in G and hence every subgroup of type $(1, 1, \ldots, 1)$ is contained in the group whose base is $[g_1^{p^{a_1-1}}, g_2^{p^{a_2-1}}, \ldots, g_x^{p^{a_x-1}}]$. Now use § 8.

Ex. 4. Let g_1 be any element of G. Take $[g_1, g_2, g_3, \ldots]$ as a base of G. Then g_1 is not in the subgroup $\{g_2, g_3, \ldots\}$ of index p.

Ex. 5. Prove as in V 6_{13} and IX 7_7.

Ex. 6. $\dfrac{p^y-1}{p-1}p^{y+s-1}$ cyclic subgroups and $\dfrac{(p^{y+s}-1)(p^{y+s-1}-1)}{(p^2-1)(p-1)}$ non-cyclic subgroups.

Ex. 7. $p^2(p+1)(p^2+p+1)$.

Ex. 8. $p^{16}(p^2+p+1)^2$. The group contains $(p^3-1)p^{12}$ elements of order p^3; hence the first generator h_1 of the subgroup may be chosen in $(p^3-1)p^{12}$ ways. The second generator h_2 may then be chosen in $(p^3-1)p^{13}$ ways, for it may be any one of the $(p^2-1)p^{13}$ elements of order p^3 in G whose p^2-th power is not in $\{h_1\}$. The third generator may then be chosen in $(p^3-1)p^9$ ways, for it may be any one of the $(p^3-1)p^9$ elements of order p^2 in G whose p-th power is not in $\{h_1, h_2\}$. Hence a base of the subgroup may be chosen in $X \equiv (p^3-1)(p^3-1)(p^3-1)p^{34}$ ways. Similar reasoning shows that when the subgroup is given its base may be chosen in $Y \equiv (p^2-1)(p-1)(p-1)p^{13}$ ways; and the total number of subgroups is $X \div Y$.

Ex. 9. $(p-1)^m p^{\frac{1}{4}m(m-1)(2m+5)}$.

CHAPTER X

§ 1. Ex. 5. If $g, g_1, g_2, g_3, \ldots$ are a conjugate set of elements, $g^{-1}g_1, g^{-1}g_2, g^{-1}g_3, \ldots$ are distinct commutators of G.

Ex. 6. $a \cdot g^{-1}ag = g^{-1}ag \cdot a$ since $a^{-1}g^{-1}ag$ is permutable with a.

Ex. 7. If $gag^{-1} = a^\alpha$ and $hah^{-1} = a^\beta$, $(gh)a(gh)^{-1} = a^{\alpha\beta} = (hg)a(hg)^{-1}$. $\therefore a \cdot g^{-1}h^{-1}gh = g^{-1}h^{-1}gh \cdot a$.

Ex. 8. Since $c = a^{-1}b^{-1}ab = a^{\alpha-1} = b^{1-\beta}$, c is permutable with a and b. Every element of $\{a, b\}$ is evidently of the form $b^y a^x$ and the commutator of two such elements is a power of c by I 4_{11}.

Ex. 9. $\{a^2\}$; $\{a^{k-1}\}$; use I 4_{13}.

§ 2. Ex. 4. Use VI 14.

Ex. 5. The determinant of every substitution in the commutant is 1.

§ 3. Ex. 1. If $\Delta \equiv G$, $\Delta' \equiv \Gamma$.

Ex. 2. Let H be a normal subgroup of G contained in no other normal subgroup. Then G/H is simple and is non-Abelian, since H does not contain Δ.

Ex. 3. e. g. the direct product of K and any perfect group.

Ex. 4. Let H be a normal subgroup of index p. Since G/H is Abelian, H contains Δ.

Ex. 5. If $\gamma_1, \gamma_2, \gamma_3, \ldots$ in G/H correspond to $g_1, g_2, g_3, \ldots$ in $G \equiv \{g_1, g_2, g_3, \ldots\}$, the γ's are permutable. $\therefore G/H \equiv \{\gamma_1, \gamma_2, \gamma_3, \ldots\}$ is Abelian.

Ex. 6. If a, b are two commutators of G and α, β are the corresponding elements of Γ, α, β are commutators of Γ. Since $ab = ba$, $\alpha\beta = \beta\alpha$.

Ex. 7. (i) $\{a^7, b\}$. (ii) $\{a, b\}$. (iii) If $a^{-1}b^{-1}ab = c$ and $ca = ac_1$, we can prove that $c_1 a = ac$, $cbc = b = c_1 bc_1$, $cc_1 = c_1 c$. Hence by Ex. 5 $\Delta \equiv \{c, c_1\}$. If the H. C. F. of m and r is d, the order of c is $mr \div d$ and the order of c_1 relative to $\{c\}$ is $\frac{d}{4}[3-(-1)^d]$ (cf. VI 4_9). Therefore Δ is an Abelian group of index 4 or 8. (iv) Cyclic of order r.

Ex. 8. C_m or $C_{\frac{1}{2}m}$ as m is odd or even, D, T, E.

§ 4. Ex. 1. For every element of G corresponding to such an element of A would be in C.

Ex. 2. (i) Let a, b be any elements of G. Then $ah = hac_1$, $bh = hbc_2$ where c_1, c_2 are in C. $\therefore a^{-1}b^{-1}ab \cdot h = a^{-1}b^{-1}ahbc_2$
$$= a^{-1}b^{-1}habc_1c_2 = a^{-1}hb^{-1}abc_1 = h \cdot a^{-1}b^{-1}ab.$$
(ii) The element of A corresponding to c is 1. (iii) See I 4. (iv) h^t is in C. (v) Use (iii) and (iv). (vi) If r is the maximum order of c as g runs through the elements of G, the order of c divides r whatever element h may be. $\therefore h^r$ is always in C, and hence t divides r. But $c^t = 1$ and $\therefore t = r$.

Ex. 3. Use V 15_6 and V 17_{12}.

Ex. 4. The normaliser in G of an element g corresponding to a is of index $\leq \delta$, and its central contains $\{g, C\}$ of order $\epsilon\gamma$.

Ex. 5. (i) Identity; non-cyclic of order 4; (ii) non-cyclic of order 4; (iii) $a^7 = b^7 = c^3 = 1$, $ab = ba$, $bc = cb^2$, $ac = ca$.

§ 5. Ex. 1. Let a, b be any two commutators of G and α, β the corresponding commutators of A. Then β is normal in A and $\therefore b$ is permutable with every commutator of G by X $4_{2(i)}$. Hence $ab = ba$.

Ex. 2. Use X 1_7.

SOLUTIONS. CH. X

Ex. 8. By I 4 $(ab)^t = b^t a^t c^{\frac{1}{2}t(t+1)}$, $(ba)^t = b^t a^t c^{\frac{1}{2}t(t-1)}$ since c is permutable with a and b. Hence if t is the order of ab and ba (I 8_3), $c^t = 1$. Again $a^{-1}b^{-\beta}ab^\beta = c^\beta$, and hence $c^\beta = 1$ if b^β is in $\{a\}$.

Ex. 4. (i) If t is the order of ab in Ex. 8, $b^t a^t = 1$ since t is odd and $c^t = 1$. Hence if α, β, ... are permutable elements corresponding to a, b, ... having the same orders and such that α has the same order relative to $\{\beta\}$ as a has relative to $\{b\}$, &c., $\{a, b, ...\}$ and $\{\alpha, \beta, ...\}$ are conformal. (ii) The second group of V 8_3 is metabelian but not conformal with any Abelian group.

§ 6. Ex. 3. If g', a' correspond to the elements g, a in any automorphism of G, $a'^{-1}g'a'$ corresponds to $a^{-1}ga$ in the automorphism. Hence the elements conjugate to g' correspond to the elements conjugate to g.

Ex. 4. $a^{-1}b^{-1} = (ab)^{-1}$ if $ab = ba$.

Ex. 6. The only class of outer automorphisms admitted by G is that interchanging A and B when $A = B$.

Ex. 7. No element of one of the groups can be transformed into an element of another.

Ex. 9. If g and h are two elements of G not in K, g and h are permutable with each element of K, since K is complete. Hence gh is permutable with each element of K and is not in K.

Ex. 11. If g is an element of order p^a, there is an automorphism of $\{g\}$ in which g^r corresponds to g, where r is any one of the $p^{a-1}(p-1)$ integers less than and prime to p^a. If $b^{-1}gb = g^r$, $b^{-s}gb^s = g^{r^s}$; hence when r is chosen so that $p^{a-1}(p-1)$ is the least value of s satisfying $r^s \equiv 1 \pmod{p^a}$, every automorphism of $\{g\}$ is obtained by transforming by powers of b.

Ex. 12. The generator of order 2^{a-2} corresponds to the automorphism in which g^r corresponds to g, where r is chosen so that 2^{a-2} is the least value of s satisfying $r^s \equiv 1 \pmod{2^a}$. The generator of order 2 corresponds to the automorphism in which g^{-1} corresponds to g.

Ex. 13. A cyclic group of order $2^a 3^\beta 5^\gamma \ldots$ is the direct product of cyclic groups of orders 2^a, 3^β, 5^γ, ...; now use Ex. 7.

Ex. 14. (i) If $g_i g_j = g_k$, $h_i g_i \cdot h_j g_j = h_k g_k$; and $\therefore h_i h_j = h_k$. (ii) $h_i \neq g_i^{-1}$.

Ex. 15. (i) $[a^{-1}g_1 a, a^{-1}g_2 a, ..., a^{-1}g_x a]$ is a base of $a^{-1}Ga$.

Ex. 16. (i) The elements $g_1^{x_1'} g_2^{x_2'} \ldots g_m^{x_m'}$ are all distinct when for $x_1, x_2, ..., x_m$ we put any of the integers 1, 2, ..., p, if and only if the determinant $|a| \not\equiv 0 \pmod{p}$.

Ex. 17. q divides the order of the group of automorphisms of G.

Ex. 18. By I 4_{11} the commutator of a' and b' is c^{xs-yr}, and $\therefore xs - yr \not\equiv 0 \pmod{p}$. The order of $\{a, b\}$ is p^3 and the order of the group of automorphisms = the order of the general homogeneous linear group of degree 2 in the $GF[p] = (p^2-1)(p^2-p)$.

Ex. 19. 24, 24, 120. Suppose that a' corresponds to a, b' to b

in an automorphism. Then (i) a' may be any one of the 8 elements of order 8, b' any one of the 8 elements of order 2; (ii) a' may be any one of the 6 elements of order 4 and then b' may be one of 4 elements of order 3, as is easily seen by considering the simply isomorphic group **O** and remembering that $(a'b')^2 = 1$; (iii) treat **E** similarly.

§ 7. Ex. 7. Use V 20_2.

Ex. 9. If h is any element of G not in K, there is an automorphism of G in which gh corresponds to g.

Ex. 10. (i) Use Ex. 9. (ii) There is only one invariant of maximum order.

Ex. 14. Use X 6_6.

Ex. 15. Use Ex. 14.

Ex. 16. Use X 6_{13}.

Ex. 17. Γ contains a normal subgroup H simply isomorphic with G formed by substitutions of the type $x_i' = x_i + b_i$, while Γ/H is simply isomorphic with the general homogeneous linear group of degree m in the $GF[p]$. Now use X 6_{16}.

§ 8. Ex. 1. L does not displace the symbol corresponding to identity in G. K contains a transitive subgroup P of the same degree.

Ex. 2. (i) If Γ were such a group, H would contain P' (§ 6); which is impossible. (ii) Use (i).

Ex. 3. Use § 8.

Ex. 4. (i) Use § 8 taking c as the automorphism in which a corresponds to a, ba to b and d as the automorphism in which a^k corresponds to a, b to b.

CHAPTER XI

§ 1. Ex. 4. See X 1_5.

Ex. 5. If H and K are two normal subgroups of order p, H and K both contain the commutant of G since G/H and G/K are of order p^2 and Abelian.

Ex. 6. If H is a normal subgroup of index p^2, G/H is Abelian; ∴ H contains the commutant of G.

Ex. 7. As in Ex. 6 each such normal subgroup contains the commutant.

Ex. 8. If h is an element of a normal subgroup H of G, H contains every element conjugate to h in G. Then if the G. C. S. of H and C is of order μ, the order of $H = \mu + \epsilon_r + \epsilon_s + \ldots$. Now proceed as in § 1.

Ex. 9. Use Ex. 8 and X 8.

Ex. 10. Let g be an element of G corresponding to a normal element of G/C, and let h be an element of G not permutable with g. Then the commutators of h and g, g^2, ..., g^p are in C and are all distinct.

Ex. 11. Use Ex. 10.

Ex. 12. (i) Let Γ be a normal subgroup of G contained in no other normal subgroup of G. Then G/Γ is simple and is ∴ of order p.

Ex. 13. Since in Ex. 12 G/Γ is Abelian, Γ contains the commutant of G.

Ex. 14. Let a, b be elements of G such that a is of order p and $ab = ba^t$. Then $b^{1-p}ab^{p-1} = a^{t^{p-1}} = a$ by Fermat's Theorem (I 3). Hence the index of the lowest power of b permutable with a is a factor both of $p-1$ and of the order of b (I 2_8).

Ex. 15. c is in every subgroup of index p in G (Ex. 7) and is ∴ in the normalisers of a and b. The conjugates of a in G are $b^{-t}ab^t = ac^t (t = 1, 2, ..., p)$. ∴ $c^p = 1$.

Ex. 16. By Ex. 15 $(ba)^e = b^e a^e$ when e is a multiple of p, since $c^p = 1$ (I 4). Hence the order of ba divides p^β. Also any conjugate of ba such as $g^{-1}bag = g^{-1}bg \cdot g^{-1}ag$ is of the form bac^k, and ∴ ba is an element of a conjugate set of 1 or p elements.

Ex. 17. g^p is in C; hence $\{C, g\} \equiv Cg + Cg^2 + ... + Cg^p$ and is evidently Abelian of order p^{x+1}. If k is any element of G and κ, γ are the elements of G/C corresponding to k, g in G, $\kappa^{-1}\gamma\kappa = \gamma$ and ∴ $k^{-1}gk = gc$ (c in C). Hence g has at most p^x conjugates in G; and the normaliser of g in G has a central containing $\{C, g\}$ and is of index $\leq p^x$.

Ex. 18. Use induction and Ex. 17, so long as

$$a - \tfrac{1}{2}\beta(2x + \beta - 1) \geq x + \beta.$$

Ex. 19. G contains a subgroup H of order $p^{\frac{1}{2}\epsilon(2x+\epsilon-1)+1}$. By Ex. 18 H contains a subgroup K of order

$$p^{\frac{1}{2}\epsilon(2x+\epsilon-1)+1-\frac{1}{2}(\epsilon-1)(2x+\epsilon-2)} = p^{x+\epsilon}$$

whose central is of order $p^{x+\epsilon-1}$. This is only possible if K is Abelian (X 4).

Ex. 20. Use Ex. 19.

§ 2. Ex. 1. Let G be the direct product of prime-power groups A, B, C, ... Find normal subgroups A', B', C', ... of A, B, C, ... respectively such that the product of their orders is m. Then $\{A', B', C', ...\}$ is a normal subgroup of order m in G.

Ex. 2. The subgroups required are those corresponding in G to the series of normal subgroups in G/Γ.

Ex. 3. (i) The subgroup required is one corresponding to a normal subgroup of order $p^{\beta-\gamma}$ in G/H. (ii) $\{H, K\}$ is of index $p^\lambda (\lambda \leq \gamma)$ and ∴ the G. C. S. D of H and K is of index $p^\delta (\delta \geq \beta)$ by V 18. The subgroup required is the subgroup of G corresponding to a normal subgroup of index p^β in G/D. (Cf. XI 5_2).

§ 3. Ex. 2. If H is a subgroup of index p in G containing K_1, H contains K_2, K_3, ... since H is normal.

Ex. 4. (i) H contains C since otherwise $G \equiv \{H, C\}$ and is Abelian; similarly K contains C. Again, every element of the G. C. S. of H and K is normal in H and in K and hence in $G \equiv \{H, K\}$. (ii) G/C is Abelian of type $(1, 1)$ since it is non-cyclic of order p^2. Again, if a and b are two non-permutable elements of G, $c = a^{-1}b^{-1}ab$ is permutable with a and b since the commutant Δ is in C (XI 1_7). Hence $c^p = a^{-p}b^{-1}a^p b = 1$ and every element of Δ is of order 1 or p.

Ex. 5. Using V 18_5 we see as in Ex. 4 that the central is of index p^2 and hence contains the commutant.

Ex. 6. If g is an element of G not permutable with every element of D, G contains p conjugates to g (X 1_5); ∴ the normaliser of g in G is of index p but does not contain D.

Ex. 7. If g is any element of order $< p^\alpha$ in G, $\{g\}$ is in some subgroup of index p (Ex. 1) and ∴ g is in Γ. Hence G contains elements of order p^α.

Ex. 8. As in Ex. 7 G contains an element g of order $p^r (r > s)$, $\{g^{p^{r-s}}\}$ being of order p^s is identical with K.

§ 4. Ex. 2. G/D is a subgroup of G/Δ.

Ex. 3. For the p-th power of such an element would not be in D.

Ex. 4. Since the G. C. S. of all subgroups of index p in $G/E \equiv 1$ (IX 8_4), the G. C. S. of all subgroups of index p in G containing E is E. But this G. C. S. contains D.

Ex. 5. (i) Since the p-th power of each element of G is in $\{\Delta, P\}$, each element of $G/\{\Delta, P\}$ is of order 1 or p. (ii) By Ex. 4 $\{\Delta, P\}$ contains D and by § 4 D contains $\{\Delta, P\}$.

Ex. 6. If G contains two Abelian subgroups of index p, the central C is of index p^2 and is contained in every Abelian subgroup of index p (XI 8_4). Now proceed as in § 4.

Ex. 7. Let H be a subgroup of index p not containing g_α. Choose elements $g_1, g_2, \ldots, g_{\alpha-1}$ as in § 2 for the group H. Then g_α satisfies the conditions that $g_\alpha{}^p$ and $g^{-1}g_\alpha{}^{-1}gg_\alpha$ are in H.

Ex. 8. (i), (ii) By V 13_6 the G. C. S. of the normal subgroups of index p or p^2 is of index p^λ. Now proceed as in § 4. (iii) The non-normal subgroups can be divided into conjugate sets each containing pm subgroups (m integral).

§ 5. Ex. 2. If K is a subgroup of index p in H not normal in G, H contains every subgroup conjugate to K in G. Now the number of groups conjugate to $K =$ the index of the normaliser of $K =$ a multiple of p. But H contains $lp+1$ subgroups of index p; hence at least one is normal in G.

Ex. 3. The elements of G permutable with every element of K form a subgroup Γ. The Abelian subgroups of order $p^{\beta+1}$ in G

containing H are the subgroups of Γ corresponding to the subgroups of order p in Γ/K.

Ex. 4. Let $B_1, B_2, ..., B_s$ be the normal subgroups of this index; $A_1, A_2, ..., A_r$ the normal subgroups of index p. Then the proof runs as in § 5 using XI 2_3.

§ 7. Ex. 2. Each set is of the form $b^y a^{x+lp^{a-2}}$ ($l = 1, 2, ..., p$) unless $x \equiv y \equiv 0 \pmod{p}$; see X 1_5.

Ex. 5. It is the only non-cyclic subgroup of the same order.

Ex. 6. By I 4 $(b^y a^x)^{1+mp} = b^y a^{x+xmp}$. Now if $x = p^\mu$, $\mu \leq a-3$, we have $(b^y a^x)^{1+mp} \equiv b^y a^{x+lp^{a-2}}$ on putting $m = lp^{a-\mu-2}$. Hence by Ex. 2 every subgroup of G is normal except the p subgroups conjugate to $\{b\}$.

Ex. 7. Every normal subgroup of G contains the commutant.

Ex. 9. Let $a_1 \equiv b^y a^x$ correspond to a and $b_1 \equiv b^s a^r$ to b in any automorphism of G. Then since $b_1^p = 1$, $r \equiv 0 \pmod{p^{a-2}}$; since $a_1^{p^{a-1}} = 1$, x is prime to p; since $a_1^{-1} b_1^{-1} a_1 b_1 = a_1^{p^{a-2}}$, $s = 1$ (I 4_{11}). Hence the order required is $p(p^{a-1} - p^{a-2})p = p^a(p-1)$.

Ex. 10. Let K be a normal cyclic subgroup of order p^s. By XI 2_3 we can find normal subgroups $K, K_1, K_2, ...$ each of index p in its successor. The first which is non-cyclic contains a characteristic non-cyclic subgroup of order p^2 which is the normal subgroup required.

Ex. 11. Abelian of type (3), (2, 1), or (1, 1, 1); $a^{p^2} = b^p = 1$, $ab = ba^{1+p}$; $\{a, b\}$ where a and b are each of order p and permutable with their commutator. Note that in a non-Abelian group of order p^3 the central and commutant coincide and are of order p (XI 1_{10}).

CHAPTER XII

§ 1. Ex. 1. They are Sylow subgroups of K.

Ex. 2. The Sylow subgroups are all conjugate.

Ex. 4. (i) If $\Gamma_i \equiv \Gamma_j$, Γ_i contains two normal Sylow subgroups H_i and H_j. (ii) Since Γ_1 is the normaliser of H_1 in G, the normaliser Γ_i of $h_i^{-1} H_1 h_i \equiv H_i$ in $h_i^{-1} G h_i \equiv G$ is $h_i^{-1} \Gamma_1 h_i$. (iii) Since Γ_1 is one of $kp+1$ conjugate subgroups in G, the normaliser of Γ_1 is of order $n \div (kp+1) =$ the order of Γ_1. (iv) Apply Corollary II to Γ_i.

Ex. 5. In the proof of Corollary II the number of quantities $\beta, \gamma, ... = r$ must be $\equiv 1 \pmod{p}$.

Ex. 6. The G. C. S. of H and H_i, i.e. of $h_i^{-1} H h_i$ and $h_i^{-1} H_1 h_i$ is $h_i^{-1} D h_i$ which is of order p^β. Hence G contains $p^{a-\beta}$ subgroups conjugate to H having with H a G. C. S. of order p^β, $p^{a-\gamma}$ having with H a G. C. S. of order p^γ, ...

Ex. 7. Use V 15_{13}.

Ex. 8. Use Ex. 7.

Ex. 9. Use Ex. 8 and IX 6_7, IX 8_6. The number is (i) 28, (ii) $(p^8 + 2p^7 + 3p^6 + 3p^5 + 3p^4 + 2p^3 + 2p^2 + p + 1)(q^3 + q^2 + q + 1)(r+1)$.

Ex. 10. If a, b are elements of Sylow subgroups of G whose orders are unequal, the order of $c = a^{-1}b^{-1}ab$ divides the orders of a and b (I 4_{10}), and $\therefore c = 1$.

Ex. 11. (i) The commutant of $G_i \equiv 1$, for otherwise Δ would contain an element of order p_i^x. (ii) If p_i^η is the order of G_i, the order of $\{\Delta, G_i\}$ is $p_1^\lambda p_i^\eta$, since Δ is normal in $\{\Delta, G_i\}$ while Δ and G_i have only identity in common. Hence G_i is a Sylow subgroup of $\{\Delta, G_i\}$. If there are $kp_i + 1$ Sylow subgroups of order p_i^η in $\{\Delta, G_i\}$, $kp_i + 1$ is a factor of p_1^λ. Now use Corollary IV.

Ex. 12. If g generates one of these cyclic Sylow subgroups, the permutation of P (VI 2) corresponding to g contains an odd number of cycles of even degree and is an odd permutation. Then the even permutations of P form a normal subgroup of index 2; which contains every permutation of odd order when g is of order 2.

Ex. 13. If P and Q are Sylow subgroups of order p^α and q^β, every element of G is included once among the elements PQ or QP, since P and Q have only identity in common.

Ex. 14. Take H, H_1 as subgroups of index p. If H_1 is not normal in G, $\Gamma_1 \equiv H_1$ and H_1 is not permutable with any element of G not in H_1. Then the proof of § 1 would show that there are $kp + 1$ subgroups conjugate to H_1 which is impossible.

Ex. 15. (i) Let K be the subgroup of order t formed by the permutations not displacing one symbol x (VI 5). The permutations of H not displacing x evidently form the G.C.S. of H and K, which $\equiv 1$ since t is prime to p. Hence every permutation of H displaces every symbol, and $\therefore$ the number of symbols in any transitive set of $H =$ the order of H. (ii) $G \equiv HK \equiv KH$.

Ex. 16. If p^ϵ is the highest power of p which divides e, G contains a group of order p^ϵ which lies in L. Hence λ is a multiple of p^ϵ; and so for every prime-power factor of e.

Ex. 17. Let $F \equiv g^{-1}Eg$ (g in G). Since E is normal in H, F is normal in $g^{-1}Hg$; and $\therefore H$ and $g^{-1}Hg$ are Sylow subgroups of the same order in the normaliser B of F in G and are hence conjugate in B. $\therefore$ there is an element b of B such that $H \equiv b^{-1}(g^{-1}Hg)b$. Then gb is in Γ and $(gb)^{-1}E(gb) \equiv F$.

Ex. 18. G contains $kp + 1$ subgroups of order p^α, where $kp + 1$ divides e. In this case $k = 0$.

Ex. 19. By § 1 a group G of order pq contains elements a, b of orders p, q. The Sylow subgroup $\{a\}$ is normal, since $q \not\equiv 0$ (mod $kp+1$) unless $k = 0$. Let $b^{-1}ab = a^\kappa$. If $\kappa = 1$, ab is of order pq and G is cyclic. If $\kappa \neq 1$, $b^{-q}a b^q = a^{\kappa^q}$ (I 8) and $\therefore$

SOLUTIONS. CH. XII 225

$\kappa^q \equiv 1 \pmod{p}$. $\kappa^e \not\equiv 1 \pmod{p}$ if $e < q$; for otherwise a and b^e and $\therefore a$ and b would be permutable.

Ex. 20. (i) Cyclic and dihedral; (ii) cyclic; (iii) cyclic and $a^{13} = b^3 = 1$, $ab = ba^3$; (iv) cyclic and $a^{11} = b^5 = 1$, $ab = ba^3$; (v) cyclic and $a^{19} = b^3 = 1$, $ab = ba^7$; (vi) cyclic; (vii) cyclic; (viii) cyclic and $a^{127} = b^7 = 1$, $ab = ba^2$.

Ex. 21. $825 = 11 \cdot 3 \cdot 5^2$. No factor of $825 \div 25$ is of the form $5k+1$, and no factor of $825 \div 11$ is of the form $11k+1$ unless $k = 0$; but $11 \cdot 5$ and 5^2 are of the form $8k+1$.

Ex. 22. As in Ex. 21 the group contains a normal subgroup of order 25, 17, 13, 11, 7, 13, 127, 169, 121.

Ex. 23. As in Ex. 21 prove that every Sylow subgroup is normal and use Corollary IV. (i) cyclic; (ii) cyclic or Abelian of type (665, 5); (iii) 10 types; see XI 1 and XI 7_{11}.

Ex. 24. (i) $520 = 2^3 \cdot 5 \cdot 13$. The only factors of $520 \div 13$ of the form $13k+1$ are 1 and 40. Hence a simple group G of order 520 must contain 40 subgroups of order 13, since it contains no normal subgroup of order 13. Similarly G contains 26 subgroups of order 5. Now two groups of prime orders have only identity in common. Hence G contains $26(5-1)$ distinct elements of order 5 and $40(13-1)$ distinct elements of order 13. But $26 \cdot 4 + 40 \cdot 12 > 520$. (ii) G contains 6 subgroups of order 5 and 10 of order 8; (iii) 20 subgroups of order 19 and 76 of order 5; (iv) 45 subgroups of order 11, 11 of order 5, and 55 of order 9; (v) 78 subgroups of order 7 and 14 of order 13.

Ex. 25. (i) As in Ex. 24 a simple group G of order 616 contains $56 \cdot 10$ elements of order 11 and $8 \cdot 6$ of order 7. Since $616 = 560 + 48 + 8$, G contains only a single subgroup of order 8 which is $\therefore$ normal. (ii) G contains 8 subgroups of order 7; (iii) 27 subgroups of order 13.

Ex. 26. (i) As in Ex. 23 a simple group G of order 450 contains 6 subgroups of order 25 and is $\therefore$ isomorphic with a simple transitive permutation-group G' of degree 6. The isomorphism is simple since G is simple. G' contains no odd permutation, for otherwise the even permutations of G' would form a normal subgroup of G'. $\therefore G'$ is a subgroup of the alternating group of degree 6; but 450 is not a factor of $6! \div 2$. (ii) The order of G is not a factor of $8! \div 2$, (iii) $5! \div 2$, (iv) $6! \div 2$, (v) $6! \div 2$, (vi) $11! \div 2$.

Ex. 27. (i) As in Ex. 26 a simple group G of order 90 is simply isomorphic with a transitive permutation-group G' of degree 6 containing only even permutations. By § 1 G' contains a permutation g of order 2 which (being even) is the product of two transpositions and $\therefore$ does not displace every symbol. Hence g is contained in some subgroup of index 6 consisting of the permutations of G' not displacing one symbol. But $90 \div 6$ is odd. (ii) Here G' is of degree 18 and each of the 18 subgroups of G' not displacing one symbol is of order and degree 17, while

226   SOLUTIONS. CH. XIII

there are 18 permutations of G' (not included in these 18 subgroups) which displace every symbol. One of these is of order 2 and is ∴ the product of 9 transpositions and is an odd permutation.

Ex. 29. (i) $\{a\}$; $\{b\}$, $\{ba\}$, $\{ba^2\}$. (ii) $\{a, b\}$; $\{cb^r\}$ ($r = 1, 2, \ldots, 7$). Note that every element of the group can be put in the form $c^z a^x b^y$ which transforms c into cb^{-y}.

Ex. 30. $\{(1\ 2)(3\ 4),\ (1\ 4)(2\ 3)\}$; $\{(2\ 3\ 4)\}$, $\{(3\ 4\ 1)\}$, $\{(4\ 1\ 2)\}$, $\{(1\ 2\ 3)\}$.

Ex. 31. Apply Sylow's theorem to the general homogeneous linear group. Since the period of every mark divides $p^r - 1$, no multiplication is of order divisible by p.

CHAPTER XIII

§ **3**. Ex. 1. Let A be the maximum normal subgroup of G containing H, B the maximum normal subgroup of A containing H, ... Then $G, A, B, \ldots, H, \ldots$ is a composition-series containing H if H is normal.

Ex. 2. (i) A cyclic group of order p^a contains only one normal subgroup of index p. (ii) Use XI 6.

Ex. 4. By XII 1_{10} G contains only one normal subgroup which is of order p.

Ex. 5. Use VI 14, 15.

Ex. 6. One composition-series is $G, H, 1$, and ∴ the composition-factors are $m! \div 2$ and 2. Hence if G contains a normal subgroup other than H, it is of order 2. Evidently no such normal subgroup exists.

Ex. 7. Use V 20.

Ex. 8. Use Ex. 7, noticing that a cyclic group cannot have more than one subgroup of given order.

Ex. 9. (i) The composition-factors of G are α p's, β q's, γ r's, ... which can be arranged in e different orders. Now use Ex. 8. (ii) If all the Sylow subgroups of K are cyclic the theorem is true by V $20_{2\text{(III)}}$. If the Sylow subgroup of order p^a is non-cyclic, Ex. 2 (ii) shows that there is more than one composition-series of K in which the α composition-factors p occur last.

Ex. 10. Let u_a be the number of distinct composition-series of G. Then the second group G_1 of a composition-series may by XI 7 be one of p cyclic subgroups of index p each giving rise to a single composition-series, or may be a given group of order p^{a-1} with a cyclic subgroup of index p giving rise to u_{a-1} composition-series. ∴ $u_a = p + u_{a-1}$. Now use induction.

Ex. 11. Let u_a be the number of composition-series of G. The second group G_1 in the series can be chosen in $(p^{a-1} - 1) \div (p - 1)$ ways by IX 8. ∴ $u_a = u_{a-1}(p^a - 1) \div (p - 1)$. Now use induction.

Ex. 12. Use V 14_6.

SOLUTIONS. CH. XIII 227

Ex. 13. G has a composition-series containing a Sylow subgroup of order p^a. Now use Ex. 12.

Ex. 14. (i) By Ex. 12 all the Sylow subgroups of G are normal. Now use XII 1 Corollary IV. (ii) As in XI 8 we can show that every subgroup of G is contained normally in some subgroup of higher order.

Ex. 15. The number is 1, 5, 21, 7, 3 according as the group is Abelian of the type (3), (2, 1), (1, 1, 1), dihedral, or dicyclic.

Ex. 16. (i) d_3, (D_3, δ_3, c_3), C_3, 1 and d_3, c_3, c, 1. (ii) Ω, (O, Θ, θ), T, D, (C_2, C_2, C_2), 1. (iii) H, E, 1.

§ 4. Ex. 2. If $H \equiv H_1 h_1 + H_1 h_2 + H_1 h_3 + \ldots$, $\{G_r, H\} \equiv G_r h_1 + G_r h_2 + G_r h_3 + \ldots$. (See V 13.)

Ex. 3. In Ex. 2 every subgroup of H/H_1 is simply isomorphic with a subgroup of $\{G_r, H\}/G_r$ and $\therefore$ with a subgroup of G_{r-1}/G_r, since G_{r-1} contains G_r and H. Now apply to H_1 the same reasoning as was applied to H and use Ex. 1, &c.

Ex. 4. A and cyclic groups whose orders are the prime factors of $_m N_r \div (p^r - 1) d$; except in the case $m = 2$ and $p^r = 2$ or 3 when all the composition-factor-groups are of prime order.

§ 5. Ex. 2. A soluble group has a normal subgroup of prime index, and this must contain the commutant.

Ex. 3. Use XIII 4_3.
Ex. 4. Use XIII 3_4.
Ex. 7. Use Ex. 2 and 5.
Ex. 8. Use § 4.
Ex. 9. Take $\{a\}$ as the group H of § 4; then G/H is cyclic.

§ 6. Ex. 1. G is the direct product of groups of order p and is $\therefore$ Abelian.

Ex. 2. If f is a composition-factor of G, we have $f^{t+1} = pr$; and $\therefore t = 0$.

Ex. 3. Let f be a composition-factor of the alternating group. As in Ex. 2 $f^{t+1} = 3 . 4 . 5 . \ldots m$; and $\therefore t = 0$.

Ex. 4. If K is a normal subgroup of P contained in H, its order is not a multiple of p; for otherwise K would contain one Sylow subgroup of order p in P, and $\therefore K$ would contain all the Sylow subgroups of order p, since they are all conjugate and K is normal. Hence since K is of degree pk, K is intransitive (VI 6), which is impossible (VI 11). Now use Ex. 2.

§ 8. Ex. 1. Prove as in § 4.
Ex. 2. Take the composition-series $\{a, b\}$, $\{a^2, b\}$, $\{b\}$, 1 of the group $a^4 = b^2 = (ab)^2 = 1$.
Ex. 6. By XI 2 the chief-factor-groups are of prime order.
Ex. 7. Use XI 1_3.
Ex. 8. Use § 6.

Ex. 9. (ii) Use X 1_7.
Ex. 10. Use XI 7_6 and XIII 3_{10}.
Ex. 11. (i) 1, 5, 21, 8, 3. (ii) 4, 8, 1.

§ 9. Ex. 1, 2. Use § 6.
Ex. 7. Any element permutable with a group transforms a chief-series into a chief-series.

§ 11. Ex. 1. Use XIII $5_{2,3}$.
Ex. 2. The group preceding identity in the series of derived groups.
Ex. 3. Use X 3.

§ 12. Ex. 3. See X 5_1.
Ex. 6. (i) G/C_{i-1} is Abelian, $\therefore C_{i-1}$ contains Δ_1. (ii) The commutant of G/C_{i-3} is Abelian (Ex. 8); $\therefore$ by X 3 each commutator of $\{\Delta_1, C_{i-3}\}/C_{i-3} = 1$, and hence every commutator of $\{\Delta_1, C_{i-3}\}$ is in C_{i-3}.
Ex. 7. Use XI 1_9.
Ex. 8. Prove as in XI 2.

§ 13. Ex. 1. Use XIII 5_5.
Ex. 2. By XIII 8_9 the central K of $\Delta \not\equiv 1$, since a chief-series of G can be formed containing Δ; while by X 3 the commutant of G/K is Δ/K. Now every chief-factor-group of G/K is cyclic, and $\therefore$ the central of $\Delta/K \not\equiv 1$. Continuing this reasoning we see that the class of Δ is finite.

CHAPTER XIV

§ 1. Ex. 2. (iii) Use X 5.
Ex. 3. $a^{24} = b^2 = (ab)^2 = 1$.
Ex. 4. They are permutable with a and b.
Ex. 5. Let a^l be the lowest power of a in any subgroup H, and suppose that H contains $b^y a^x$ but no element $b^\rho a^\sigma$ where $\rho < y$ or $\rho = y$, $\sigma < x$. Then I 3 shows that $yu = \beta$ where u is integral and that H contains the elements $b^{ty}a^{x(k^{yt}-1)\div(k^y-1)+il}$ ($t = 1, 2, \ldots, u$; $i = 1, 2, \ldots, l \div \lambda$). Putting $t = u$ we have l a factor of $r + x(k^\beta - 1) \div (k^y - 1)$. The groups H, $\{a^l, b^y a^x\}$ are distinct; for if H contains $b^y a^z$, it contains $(b^y a^x)^{-1}(b^y a^z) = a^{z-x}$ which is impossible when $l > z > x \geq 0$.
Ex. 7. By Ex. 4 G contains a normal subgroup of prime index.
Ex. 8. Suppose k a primitive root of $x^\epsilon \equiv 1 \pmod{\lambda}$. Then $\{a, b^\epsilon\}$ is Abelian and its Sylow subgroups are all cyclic. Hence by V $20_{2(\text{III})}$ $\{a, b^\epsilon\}$ is cyclic; and it is normal by Ex. 4. Hence $\epsilon = \beta$.

SOLUTIONS. CH. XIV

§ 2. Ex. 1. Use XIV 1_2.

Ex. 2. (ii) ba^x is of order (I) $4m \div$ (the H.C.F. of $2m$ and $x(m+1)$); (II) 2 or 4 as x is even or odd; (III) 2; (IV) 4. (iii) The conjugate sets are of the form (I) $a^x + a^{x+2m}$ and $ba^x + ba^{x+2m}$; (II) $a^x + a^{x(2m-1)}$; and ba^x (x odd), ba^x (x even) each form one or two conjugate sets as m is even or odd; (iii) $a^x + a^{-x}$; and the elements ba^x form one or two conjugate sets as m is odd or even; (IV) $a^x + a^{-x}$; and ba^x (x odd), ba^x (x even) form conjugate sets.

Ex. 3. Use XIV 1_5.

Ex. 4. $\{a^l, ba^x\}$ is Abelian or of the type I as l is even or odd.

Ex. 7. $2\phi(4m)$ or $4\phi(4m)$ as m is odd or even; $2m\phi(4m)$; $m\phi(m)$; $2m\phi(2m)$. In any automorphism let a^s correspond to a, ba^x to b; then a^s and ba^x satisfy the same relations as a and b. In group I we can have ba^s corresponding to a and ba^x to b if m is even. (See Footnote, p. 82.)

Ex. 8. The normal subgroups of III are the subgroups of $\{a\}$ and $\{a^2, b\}$, $\{a^2, ba\}$ when m is even. Now use XIII 8_2 and induction.

Ex. 9. Use § 1.

§ 3. Ex. 2. Since $\{a\}$ can have only one holomorph, the metacyclic group is abstractly the same whatever primitive root k may be.

Ex. 3. Use I 3.

Ex. 5. $\{a, b^{\frac{p-1}{2}}\}$.

Ex. 6. It is contained in $\{a\}$ or $\{b^y a^x\}$.

Ex. 7, 8. If $p-1 = qr \ldots vw$ where $q, r, \ldots, v, w$ are primes not necessarily all distinct, every composition-series is of the form $\{a, b\}$, $\{a, b^q\}$, $\{a, b^{qr}\}$, $\ldots$, $\{a, b^{qr \cdots v}\}$, $\{a\}$, 1.

Ex. 9. If in an automorphism of G a^t corresponds to a and $b^y a^x$ to b, $(b^y a^x)^{-1} a^t (b^y a^x) = a^{kt}$; which gives $y = 1$. Hence the order of the group of automorphisms $= p(p-1) =$ the order of the group of inner automorphisms $=$ the order of G.

Ex. 10. See X 8_4.

Ex. 11. Prove $S^p = T^{p-1} = 1$, $ST = TS^k$. Since $T^y S^x$ replaces 1, p by $k^y + x$, x respectively, and $k^y + x$, x may be made equivalent to any two whatever of 1, 2, ..., p; the group is doubly transitive.

§ 4. Ex. 1. If $g_1, g_2, \ldots, g_m$ are elements of orders $p_1^{a_1}, p_2^{a_2}, \ldots, p_m^{a_m}$, $g_1 g_2 \ldots g_m$ is of order n.

Ex. 2. P is the only subgroup of its kind in G.

Ex. 3. Since g_{m-1} is permutable with $\{g_m\} \equiv P_m$, $\{g_{m-1}, g_m\}$ is of order $p_{m-1}^{a_{m-1}} p_m^{a_m}$ and $\therefore \equiv P_{m-1}$. Similarly $\{g_{m-2}, g_{m-1}, g_m\} \equiv P_{m-2}$, &c.

Ex. 4. By XII 1 Corollary II every Sylow subgroup of H is contained in some Sylow subgroup of G.

230   SOLUTIONS. CH. XV

Ex. 8. As in § 4 (4) prove the existence of P_r and then use V 14.
Ex. 9. G contains elements whose orders divide
$$p_r{}^{s+1} p_{r+1}^{a_{r+1}} \dots p_m{}^{a_m} \text{ but not } p_r{}^s p_{r+1}^{a_{r+1}} \dots p_m{}^{a_m}.$$
Hence G contains an element of order $p_r{}^{s+1}$. Now proceed as in § 4 (1).

§ 5. Ex. 1. By § 5 Γ is of the type $a^\lambda = 1$, $b^\beta = a^r$, $ab = ba^k$. Putting $b^\lambda = b'$, we have Γ generated by a and b' which satisfy relations of the given form since λ is prime to β.

Ex. 2. (i) $\sigma \equiv 0$, $y \equiv 1 \pmod{\beta}$, ρ is prime to λ, $x(k^\beta - 1) \div (k-1) \equiv (\rho-1)r \pmod{\lambda}$.

(ii) $\phi(\lambda) \times \left(\text{the H. C. F. of } \lambda \text{ and } \dfrac{k^\mu - 1}{k - 1} \right)$.   (See Footnote, p. 82.)

§ 6. Ex. 4. Use Corollary IV of XII 1.
Ex. 6. Since $(ab)^2 = a^2$, $a^{-1}ba = b^{-1}$ and $a^{-1}b^2a = b^{-2} = a^{-2}$.
$\therefore b^2 = a^{-2} = a^2$ and $a^4 = 1$.
Ex. 7. $ba^3 = ab = bab^2$; $\therefore a^2 = b^2$. Now use Ex. 6.
Ex. 9 (ii). If c, d are the elements of the group of automorphisms corresponding to those automorphisms in which b^3 corresponds to a and ba to b, a to a and ba to b, then $c^3 = d^4 = (cd)^2 = 1$. Now use VI 3_8.
Ex. 10. Use X 4_1.

§ 8. Ex. 2. (i) Generated by the elements of H excluding identity; (ii) generated by the elements aB, bB, abB. (iii) and (iv) The G.C.S. of all subgroups of index 2 or 4 is $\{a^2\}$. Now consider the number of subgroups of index 2 or 4 in $G/\{a^2\}$ which is Abelian of order 2^{a-1} and type $(1, 1, \dots, 1)$. (v) The first generator of such a subgroup may be chosen in $2^a - 2^{a-2}$ ways and then the second in 2^{a-1} ways. Hence the generators may be chosen in $2^{a-1}(2^a - 2^{a-2})$ ways. Putting $a = 3$ we have 24 ways of choosing the generators of a quaternion group. Hence the number of quaternion subgroups is $2^{a-1}(2^a - 2^{a-2}) \div 24$.

Ex. 3. If E is a normal subgroup of order p, K/E has every subgroup normal and is therefore Abelian. Hence E is the commutant of K.

CHAPTER XV

§ 1. Ex. 2. The distinct representations of the cyclic group $\{a\}$ of order 3 are obtained by making 1, a, a^2 correspond respectively to (1) $x' = x, x, x$; (2) $x' = x, \omega x, \omega^2 x$; (3) $x' = x, \omega^2 x, \omega x$, where $\omega^3 = 1$. Representations (2) and (3) give the same substitution-group.

Ex. 3. Each of $\omega_1, \omega_2, \omega_3, \dots$ is ± 1.

Ex. 4. With G/H, where H is the normal subgroup formed

by the elements corresponding to $(x_1, x_2, x_3, \ldots)$ in the representation.

Ex. 7. Use VII 8.

Ex. 8. e.g. $a^2 = b^2 = (ab)^2 = 1$.

§ 2. Ex. 2. $\chi_k{}^i$ is the sum of $\chi_1{}^i$ quantities whose modulus is 1. Now use the theorem 'the sum of the moduli of two or more complex quantities is $\leq$ the modulus of their sum'.

Ex. 3. By Ex. 2 every element of H must correspond to $(x_1, x_2, x_3, \ldots)$ in S_j.

Ex. 5. Every conjugate set is self-inverse.

§ 3. Ex. 1. Let $g = g_1{}^{\beta_1} g_2{}^{\beta_2} \ldots g_t{}^{\beta_t}$. Put $i_1 = 1$, $i_2 = a_2$, $i_3 = a_3$, $\ldots, i_t = a_t$. Then $\beta_1 = a_1$ or $\tfrac{1}{2} a_1$. Similarly $\beta_2 = a_2$ or $\tfrac{1}{2} a_2$, ...

Ex. 2. Each such representation is Abelian and is therefore a representation of G/Δ by X 3 and XV 1_4. But the number of representations of $G/\Delta = $ its order.

Ex. 3. Use § 3.

Ex. 4. Multiply each row by the characteristic of the element heading the row and do the same for the columns. If we then add each row to the first, every term in the first row is the same, and is therefore a linear factor of the determinant. Do this for each of the n characteristics.

Ex. 5. (i) Apply the method of Ex. 4 to the characteristics in the q representations of the first degree (Ex. 2).
(ii) $1 + a + b + c + d + e$, $1 + a + b - c - d - e$.

Ex. 6. $\chi_k(\chi_1 + \chi_2 + \ldots + \chi_n) = \chi_1 \chi_k + \chi_2 \chi_k + \ldots + \chi_n \chi_k = \chi_1 + \chi_2 + \ldots + \chi_n$. Now choose $\chi_k \neq 1$.

Ex. 7. As in Ex. 6.

§ 4. Ex. 4. If H, K are a pair of reciprocal groups, K and G/H have the same invariants.

Ex. 5. Use Ex. 4 and IX 8_3.

Ex. 6. Use Ex. 4 and IX 8_6.

Ex. 7. (i) Use Ex. 6 and proceed as in XI 4. (ii) $y = s = 1$.

§ 5. Ex. 3. Put $j = 1$ in (ii).

Ex. 4. Put $\chi_s{}'^i$ for $\chi_s{}^i$ in (ii).

Ex. 6. Use XV 3_6.

Ex. 7. (i) Two Abelian representations and $\tfrac{1}{2}(p-1)$ generated by substitutions of the form
$$\left(\cos \frac{2t\pi}{p} x - \sin \frac{2t\pi}{p} y, \ \sin \frac{2t\pi}{p} x + \cos \frac{2t\pi}{p} y \right), \ (-x, y).$$
(ii) Four Abelian representations and that generated by $(-y, x)$, $(-x, y)$. (iii) Four Abelian representations and those generated by
$$\left(\cos \frac{2\pi}{8} x - \sin \frac{2\pi}{8} y, \ \sin \frac{2\pi}{8} x + \cos \frac{2\pi}{8} y \right), \ (-x, y) \text{ and }$$
$$\left(\cos \frac{\pi}{8} x - \sin \frac{\pi}{8} y, \ \sin \frac{\pi}{8} x + \cos \frac{\pi}{8} y \right), \ (-x, y).$$

232   SOLUTIONS. CH. XV

Ex. 8. Taking in (i) $C_1 \equiv 1$, $C_2 \equiv a^3$, $C_3 = a+a^5$, $C_4 = a^2+a^4$; $C_5 \equiv b+ba^2+ba^4$; $C_6 \equiv ba+ba^3+ba^5$ and in (ii) $C_1 \equiv 1$, $C_2 \equiv a^2$, $C_3 \equiv a+a^3$, $C_4 \equiv b+ba^2$, $C_5 \equiv ba+ba^3$ we have as sets of characteristics respectively

1	1	1	1	1	1		1	1	1	1	1
1	1	1	1	-1	-1		1	1	1	-1	-1
1	-1	-1	1	i	$-i$	and	1	1	-1	1	-1
1	-1	-1	1	$-i$	i		1	1	-1	-1	1
2	2	-1	-1	0	0		2	-2	0	0	0
2	-2	1	-1	0	0						

Ex. 9. Taking $C_1 \equiv 1$, $C_2 \equiv a+a^2+a^4$, $C_3 \equiv a^3+a^6+a^5$; $C_4 \equiv b+ba+ba^2+ba^3+ba^4+ba^5+ba^6$; $C_5 \equiv b^2a+b^2a^2+b^2a^3+b^2a^4+b^2a^5+b^2a^6$, we have as sets of characteristics

1	1	1	1	1
1	1	1	ω	ω^2
1	1	1	ω^2	ω
3	α_1	α_2	0	0
3	α_2	α_1	0	0

where $\omega^3 = 1$, $\alpha_1\alpha_2 = 2$, $\alpha_1+\alpha_2+1 = 0$.

Ex. 10. Taking $C_1 \equiv 1$, $C_2 \equiv$ the permutations of order 3, $C_3 \equiv$ the permutations of order 4, $C_4 \equiv$ the even and $C_5 \equiv$ the odd permutations of order 2, we have as sets of characteristics

1	1	1	1	1
1	1	-1	1	-1
2	-1	0	2	0
3	0	-1	-1	1
3	0	1	-1	-1

Ex. 11. Taking $C_1 \equiv 1$, C_2, C_3, $C_4 \equiv$ the permutations of orders 3, 4, 5 respectively, $C_5 \equiv$ the even and C_6 the odd permutations of order 2, C_7 the permutations of order 6, we have as sets of characteristics.

(i)
1	1	1	1	1
3	0	$\tfrac{1}{2}(1-\sqrt{5})$	$\tfrac{1}{2}(1+\sqrt{5})$	-1
3	0	$\tfrac{1}{2}(1+\sqrt{5})$	$\tfrac{1}{2}(1-\sqrt{5})$	-1
4	1	-1	-1	0
5	-1	0	0	1

(ii)
1	1	1	1	1	1	1
1	1	-1	1	1	-1	-1
4	1	0	-1	0	2	-1
4	1	0	-1	0	-2	1
5	-1	-1	0	1	1	1
5	-1	1	0	1	-1	-1
6	0	0	1	-2	0	0

§ 6. Ex. (i) The number of elements conjugate to a normal element of a Sylow subgroup of order q^β is a power of p. **(ii)** No factor-group of G is simple unless it is of prime order.

APPENDIX

In the hope that some of my readers will wish to add to existing knowledge of group-theory, I give a few interesting questions still awaiting solution.*

1. Can a group of odd order be both non-cyclic and simple?

2. Discuss every type of group with an Abelian commutant (See X 5_1).

3. Can a perfect group contain elements which are not commutators of the group?

4. The greatest common subgroup of the normalisers of no two elements of a group G is identity. Can G be simple?

5. Can a group be simple if it cannot be generated by less than three independent generators?

6. A group G has a finite number of generators, and the order of every element $\leq$ a finite number r. Is G necessarily finite?

7. Can a non-Abelian group have an Abelian group of automorphisms?

8. Can a group of order p^a have a group of automorphisms whose order is also a power of p?

9. Can an outer automorphism permute among themselves the elements of each conjugate set of elements of a group, or does it necessarily permute some of the conjugate sets?†

10. Find the group of automorphisms of the group in XIV 1.§ Find also its group-characteristics.

11. Find a proof of the theorem of XV 6 which does not involve the properties of irreducible groups of linear substitutions.

12. Is it always possible to transform a finite homogeneous linear substitution-group into a group in which the coefficients of every substitution are rational functions of roots of unity?

---

* I am indebted for the majority of these questions to the kindness of Prof. W. Burnside, who is one of the greatest authorities on the subject.
† See X 6_3.
§ For the special case of the group in XI 7, see *Amer. Journ. Math.* xxv, p. 206.

INDEX

Abelian group, 51.
Absolute invariant, 99.
Abstract group, 55.
Adjoined groups, 167.
Alternating group, 79.
Appendix, 233.
Automorphism, 136.
Automorphisms, group of, 137.

Bauer's theorem, 145.
Bilinear form, 16.
Birational substitution, 12.
Burnside's theorem, 186.

C_m, c, c_m (point-groups), 113, 114, 212.
Canonical Hermitian form, 20.
Cayley's colour-groups, 86.
Central, 63, 167.
Centre of symmetry, 42.
Characteristic equation, 21.
 of a conjugate set, 179.
 series, 165.
 subgroup, 139.
Chief-composition-series, 164.
Chief-factor-groups, 164.
Chief-factors, 164.
Chief-series, 164.
Circular permutation, 7.
Class of a group, 167.
 of integral functions, 28.
 of outer automorphisms, 137.
Cogredient automorphism, 136.
 groups, 167.
Collinear transformation, 44.
Collineation, 45.
Colour-groups, 86.
Commutant, 133.
Commutative elements, 1.
 group, 51.
Commutator, 4.
 of a group, 133.
 subgroup, 133.
Complete group, 137.
Completely reducible group, 100.
Component groups, 69.
Composite group, 63.

Composition-factor-groups, 158.
Composition-factors, 158.
Composition-series, 158.
Conformal groups, 55.
Congruent figures, 39.
Conjugate complex quantities of a Field, 32.
 elements and subgroups, 61.
 substitution, 16.
Contragredient automorphism, 136.
Cycle, 8.
Cyclic or cyclical group, 60.

D, D_m, d_m, δ_m, Δ, Δ_m (point-groups), 113, 114, 115.
Decomposable groups, 67.
Definite Hermitian form, 20.
Degree of a cycle, 8,
 of a permutation, 6.
 of a permutation-group, 79.
 of a substitution, 12.
 of a substitution-group, 98.
Derived groups, 166.
Determinant of a substitution, 16.
Dicyclic group, 150, 170.
Dihedral group, 113, 170.
Direct product, 69.
Distinct representations, 179.

E, H (point-groups), 113, 115.
Element, 1.
Elliptic substitution, 27.
Enantiomorphous figures, 39.
Equivalent representations, 179.
 system of points, lines, &c., 109.
Euler's construction, 36.
Even permutation, 11.
Extended point-groups, 114.

Factor-group, 72.
Finite group, 51.
First adjoined group, 135.
 central, 167.
 cogredient, 135.
 derived group, 133.
Fractional linear substitution, 26.

INDEX

Fractional linear substitution-group, 98, 107.
Frobenius' theorem, 75, 156.

Γ_m (point-group), 114.
Galois Field, 29.
Gauss' theorem, 187.
Geometrical movement, 33.
    representation of a movement, 40.
General homogeneous linear substitution-group, 105.
Generator, 55.
Generators of an Abelian group, 126.
Gliding-reflexion, 38.
Gnomonic projection, 47.
Greatest common subgroup (G.C.S.), 66.
Group, 51.
    of automorphisms, 187.
    of cogredient isomorphisms, 135.
    of inner automorphisms, 135.
    of isomorphisms, 137.
    of movements, 108.

Hamiltonian group, 175.
Hermitian form, 18.
    group, 104.
    invariant, 102.
    substitution, 16.
Hints for solution of the examples, 189.
Holoaxial point-group, 111.
Holohedral isomorphism, 71.
Holomorph, 139.
Homogeneous linear substitution, 12, 15.
    linear substitution-group, 98.
Hyperbolic substitution, 27.
Hypohermitian form, 20.

Icosahedral group, $\mathbf{E}$, 113.
Identical element, 1.
    group, 57.
Imprimitive group, 93.
    systems, 93.
Independent elements, 55.
Index of a subgroup, 58.
Infinite group, 51.
Inner automorphism, 136.
Integral mark, 29.
Intransitive group, 79.
Invariant element, 62.
    of an Abelian group, 127, 130.
    of a substitution-group, 99.
    subgroup, 63.

Inverse conjugate sets, 61.
    element, 1.
    representations, 179.
Inversion about a point, 33.
Irreducible group, 100.
Isomorphism, 70.
Isomorphisms, group of, 137.

Latin square, 82.
Lattice, 117.
Loxodromic substitution, 27.

Marks of a Galois Field, 29.
Maximum normal subgroup, 158.
Merohedral isomorphism, 71.
Metabelian group, 135.
Metacyclic group, 171.
Minimum normal subgroup, 162.
Modular group, 102.
Monomial substitution, 23.
Movement, geometrical, 33.
    of the first or second sort, 39.
Multiple isomorphism, 71.
Multiplication, 23.
    table of a group, 51.
Multiply transitive group, 79.

n-al rotation or rotatory-inversion, 110.
Negative permutation, 11.
Net, 115.
Non-perspective collineation of order two, 47.
Normal element, 62.
    form of a substitution, 26.
    subgroup, 63.
Normaliser of an element, 64.
    of a subgroup, 65.
Not-square of a Field, 32.

$\mathbf{O}$, $\mathbf{\Omega}$ (point-groups), 113, 115.
Octahedral group, $\mathbf{O}$, 113.
Odd permutation, 11.
Operation, 1.
Order of a group, 51.
    of an element, 2.
    of an element relative to a group, 51.
Orthogonal substitution, 16.
Outer automorphism, 136.

Parabolic substitution, 27.
Partition, 58.

Perfect group, 183.
Period of a mark, 31.
Permutable elements, 1.
　element and group, 61.
　groups, 67.
　movements, 33.
Permutation, 6.
Permutation-group, 79,
Perspective collineation, 47.
Point-group, 108.
Pole of a fractional linear substitution, 27.
　of a homogeneous linear substitution, 20.
Positive Hermitian form, 20.
　permutation, 11.
Prime-power Abelian group, 130.
　group, 142.
Primitive group, 98.
　root of congruence, 156, 169.
　root of equation in a Field, 31.
　root of Field, 32.
Product of elements, 1.
　of movements, 39.
　of permutations, 6.
　of substitutions, 12, 13.
Projective transformation, 44.
Pseudo-substitution, 121.

Quadratic group, 113.
Quaternion group, 175.
Quotient-group, 72.

Rank of hypohermitian form, 20.
Real substitution, 16.
Reciprocal subgroups, 183.
Reducible group, 100.
Reflexions, product of two, 33.
Regular permutation, 8.
　permutation-group, 79.
Relative invariant, 99.
　order, 51.
Representations, 179.
Residue of a function, 28.
Resultant of elements, 1.
　of two reflexions, 33.
Rodrigue's construction, 36.
Rotation-axis, 42.
Rotatory-inversion, 37, 41.
Rotatory-reflexion, 37.

Screw, 38.
Self-conjugate element, 62.
　subgroup, 63.
Self-inverse conjugate sets, 61.
　representation, 179.
Semi-group, 51.
Series of adjoined groups, 167.
　of derived groups, 166.
Set of characteristics, 181.
Similar movements, 41.
　permutations, 8.
Similarity-substitution, 23.
Simple group, 63, 107.
　isomorphism, 71.
Simply transitive group, 79.
Soluble group, 161.
Solutions of examples, 189.
Speciality of a group, 167.
Square of a Field, 32.
Stereographic projection, 43.
Subgroup, 57.
Substitution, 6, 12.
Substitution-group, 98.
Sylow subgroup, 153.
Sylow's theorem, 152.
Symmetric group, 79.
　substitution, 16.
Symmetry, 42.
Symmetry-axis, 42.
Symmetry-plane, 42.

T, Θ, θ (point-groups), 113, 114.
Tetrahedral group, T, 113.
Transform of an element, 3.
　of a group, 61.
　of a movement, 41.
　of a permutation, 9.
　of a substitution, 14.
Transitive permutation-group, 79.
　sets, 91.
Translation, 33.
Translation-group, 110.
Transposed substitution, 16.
Transposition, 7.
Type of an Abelian group, 127, 130.
　of any group, 167.

Unitary substitution, 16.

Vierergruppe, 118.

Printed in the United States
124528LV00005B/153/A